INTERNATIONAL LAW AND THE REVOLUTIONARY STATE

A Case Study of the Soviet Union
and Customary International Law

by
RICHARD J. ERICKSON

OCEANA PUBLICATIONS, INC. — DOBBS FERRY, N.Y.
A.W. SIJTHOFF — LEIDEN
1972

Library of Congress Cataloging in Publication Data

Erickson, Richard J
  International law and the revolutionary state.

  Bibliography: p.
  1. International law. 2. Law and socialism.
3. Russia — Foreign relations. I. Title.
JX3110.E7I5   341'.04   72-8649
ISBN 0-379-00169-1   (Oceana)
ISBN 90-286-0342-5   (Sijthoff)

Manufactured in the United States of America

to
"J. K."
for reasons she
only knows.

ACKNOWLEDGMENT

The author of this work wishes to express his sincere appreciation and gratitude to Professor Paul Shoup for his advice which has been of immeasurable assistance; to Professor Mason Willrich for offering thought provoking comments and queries which frequently stimulated previously unthought thoughts; to his former teachers of international and comparative law, Professor R. R. Oglesby of Florida State, Professor M. Khadduri of Johns Hopkins and Professors W. W. Bishop Jr. and Whitmore Gray of the University of Michigan Law School for their long hours of patiently striving to educate this student of the law thus placing him greatly in their debt; to Professor Elke Frank of Mary Baldwin College and Professor Marian D. Irish of American University for years of continuing encouragement and friendship; to Mr. Charles Bevans of the United States Department of State for assisting in obtaining research materials; to Mr. Philip C. Dean and many other friends for counsel and advice freely given; to his parents for inculcating in him an early love of learning; and, above all, to his wife.

TABLE OF CONTENTS

ACKNOWLEDGMENT iv

INTRODUCTION ix

Chapter I
SOVIET IDEOLOGY AND CUSTOMARY INTERNATIONAL
LAW 1
  1. Pavel Ivanovich Stuchka 2
  2. Evgenii Aleksandrovich Korovin 3
  3. Andrei Sabinin 6
  4. Korovin and Sabinin Discredited 7
  5. A New View Emerges: Evgenii Bronislavovich Pashukanis 7
  6. Pashukanis Is A Traitor: A Crisis Materializes 8
  7. The Post-War Call For A Renewed Effort: Two Schools Evolve 10
  8. De-Emphasizing Ideological Considerations 12
  9. Sergei Borisovich Krylov 14
  10. Korovin-Tunkin Debate 14
  11. The Present-Day Soviet View: Grigorii Ivanovich Tunkin 15
  12. Korovin As An Alternative 16
  13. Summary 17
  Notes 19

Chapter II
SOVIET THEORY OF THE LEGAL NATURE OF CUSTOMARY
INTERNATIONAL LAW 27
  1. The Importance of Custom 28
  2. Practice As An Indication of Custom 29
  3. Time, Repetition And Continuity As Factors 30
  4. Agreement As The Decisive Factor 32
  5. "New" States And "Old" Norms 35
  6. The United Nations Charter As A Source of Customary
    Norms 36
  7. Summary 38
  Notes 40

Chapter III
SUBJECTS OF INTERNATIONAL LAW 46
  1. The Principle of Peaceful Coexistence
    (a) Meaning 46
    (b) Source 49
  2. The Principle of Sovereign Equality of States
    (a) Meaning 50
    (b) Source 54

3. The Principle of National Self-Determination
    (a) Meaning 55
    (b) Source 56
4. The Principle of Non-Intervention
    (a) Meaning 57
    (b) Source 58
5. Some Principles of Recognition
    (a) Meaning 59
    (b) Source 61
6. Summary 61
Notes 63

Chapter IV
INTERNATIONAL TREATIES 73
1. The Principle of *Pacta Sunt Servanda*
    (a) Meaning 73
    (b) Source 75
2. The "Principle" of *Clausula Rebus Sic Stantibus* 75
3. The Principle of Unequal Treaties
    (a) Meaning 77
    (b) Source 79
4. The Principle of *Res Inter Alios Gesta* (State Succession)
    (a) Meaning 80
    (b) Source 83
5. The "All States" Principle
    (a) Meaning 83
    (b) Source 85
6. The Principle of *Jus Cogens*
    (a) Meaning 85
    (b) Source 86
7. Summary 87
Notes 89

Chapter V
DIPLOMATIC AND CONSULAR INTERCOURSE: PRIVILEGES
AND IMMUNITIES 96
1. The Principle of Diplomatic Immunity 97
2. The Principle of Consular Immunity 99
3. The Principle of *Persona Non Grata* 101
4. The Principle of Inviolability of Diplomatic And Consular
    Premises 101
5. The Principle of Free Communication 104
6. Summary 105
Notes 108

Chapter VI
TERRITORY AND POPULATION 113
1. The Principle of *"Usque Ad Coelum"*
   (a) Meaning 114
   (b) Source 116
2. The Principle of Outer Space As *"Res Communis?"*
   (a) Meaning 117
   (b) Source 120
3. The Principle of The High Seas As *"Res Communis"*
   (a) Meaning 120
   (b) Source 122
4. The Principle of Territorial Waters As Part Of The Littoral State
   (a) Meaning 122
   (b) Source 125
5. The Principle of Discovery And Occupation As A Basis For
   Land Acquisition
   (a) Meaning 127
   (b) Source 128
6. The Principle Of The Status Of Populations As Within The
   Jurisdiction Of Municipal Law
   (a) Meaning 128
   (b) Source 130
7. Summary 131
Notes 132

Chapter VII
PEACEFUL SETTLEMENT OF DISPUTES AND THE LAWS
OF WAR 140
1. The "Principle" Of *Nemo Debet Esse Judex In Propria Causa*
   (Third Party Judgment) 140
2. The Principle Of Peaceful Settlement Of Disputes By Voluntary
   Negotiations, Arbitration And/Or Adjudication
   (a) Meaning 141
   (b) Source 144
3. The Principle Of Self-Help
   (a) Meaning 145
   (b) Source 145
4. The Principle Of Non-Aggression
   (a) Meaning 146
   (b) Source 147
5. The Principle Of The Inviolability Of Civilian Populations
   In Time Of War
   (a) Meaning 148
   (b) Source 149
7. Summary 149
Notes 151

Chapter VIII
NEW MYTHS AND NEW REALITIES 156
Impact On Soviet Ideology 156
Soviet Conception of the Legal Nature of Customary
International Law 157
Impact on Soviet Foreign Policy 159
Impact on Customary International Law 163
Notes 166

APPENDICES
Appendix A   SOVIET REPRESENTATION IN PUBLIC AND
PRIVATE INTERNATIONAL ORGANIZATIONS 169

Appendix B   OFFICERS AND MEMBERS: SOVIET DOMESTIC
ASSOCIATIONS AND EDITORIAL BOARDS OF PRINCIPAL
PUBLICATIONS CONCERNED WITH INTERNATIONAL
LAW 177

Appendix C   WHO'S WHO: SOVIET SCHOLARS OF INTER-
NATIONAL LAW 181

BIBLIOGRAPHY 197

INDEX 247

INTRODUCTION

Dealing with the process of change has always been a problem confronting law and society. In the international context revolutionary change, a dramatic alteration of the *status quo*, sparked by a "revolutionary state" creates serious challenges to the "law of nations". Revolutionary change is not simply a replacement of the leadership of a state by force of arms. The appearance of a new idea-orientation, belief-system or ideological motivation is additionally required. Guided by this new light and vision, the revolutionary state poses a threat to the existing system, including the fundamental rules of law established to govern that system.

These are revolutionary times. The traditional "law of nations" is western in origin, and consequently, has been challenged in rising crescendo since World War I by the growth of communism and by the multiplication of newly independent states. Old principles have been questioned while new principles have been asserted. Under such pressure from the "socialist camp" and the Third World, how is international law to remain universal in application in a world ideologically severed between East and West and economically divided between rich and poor? It must be admitted that contemporary international law is unsettled and is undergoing adjustment in light of these challenges, challenges unparalleled since the days of Grotius. The present is a period of transition from a system of international law of the Western European and North American family of Christian nations to a universal law of the world community.

The historic record contains many accounts of revolutionary states and their impact upon the world. How does the revolutionary state adjust to international society and, conversely, how does international society adjust to the revolutionary state? Life cannot subsist without reciprocal concessions and the assumption is made in favor of adjustment.

With the intention of providing greater insight into the broad question of the accommodation of the revolutionary state and international law, each to the other, a case study of the Soviet Union and customary international law is undertaken. The reasons for focusing on the USSR are clear. As the archtype revolutionary state, at least in the Twentieth Century, an analysis of Soviet policy will provide superlative evidence of the participation of a revolutionary state in international affairs. This is especially so since more than five decades of Soviet experience may be drawn upon.

Moreover, this study is not concerned with the entirety of international law. The focus is narrowed to customary international law (*mezhdunarodnoe obychnoe pravo*). There are several reasons for concentrating on customary law of which the reader should be aware. First, the nature of custom, its coming into and passing out of being, presents complex problems for the best trained legal minds of the Soviet Union.

Second, custom is mainly the product of long established practices of western states and offers the greatest challenge to Soviet ideology and policy. Customary law requires not only a re-examination of the traditional revolutionary Marxist view of law but it also requires a rationalization or redefinition of the legal norms of western origin. Third, custom reflects the practice of states, practice having reciprocal advantage, and its commands cannot be easily denied. The Soviet Union must cope with custom as it copes with reality. Finally, the Soviet view of customary international law is a fertile field, yet unstudied to any significant degree by western scholars, which potentially can reveal much to us about the "revolutionary state and international law."[1]

How do Soviet scholars define "customary international law"? Turning to Article 38 of the Statutes of the International Court of Justice (ICJ), as a Soviet scholar would, there is to be found the following list of sources of international law:

(a) international conventions, whether general or particular, establishing rules expressly recognized by the contesting countries;
(b) international custom, as evidence of general practice accepted as law;
(c) the general principles of law recognized by civilized nations;
(d) subject to the provisions of Article 59, judicial decisions and teachings of the most qualified publicists of the various nations, as subsidary means for the determination of the rules of law.

International rules or principles created through international convention or treaty (Article 38a), will not be considered in this study. Soviet international legal scholars define "customary international law" in terms of Article 38b as ". . . rules which have acquired legal significance as a result of their application by states over a prolonged period and their recognition as legal rules."[2]

A distinction should be made between "treaty law" and "laws of treaty-making". "Treaty law" is law created through treaty (Article 38a) in contrast to custom (Article 38b). "Laws of treaty-making" are those principles which govern the methods by which treaties are made.[3] Some of these have themselves been created through treaty and some through custom. The "laws of treaty-making" whose source is custom shall be given attention.[4]

Another source of international law is "general principles" (Article 38c). "General principles" is a hodgepodge source of international law and has been regarded at various times by western scholars as including legal analogy, natural law, general principles of positive national law and general principles of international law in contrast to specific rules of international law.[5] Soviet writers do not, however, recognize "general principles" as a separate source of international law inasmuch as they believe that "they, [general principles] are realized either through the appropriate international treaty or through international custom and are in fact their generalizations."[6] Those "general principles" whose source is custom, in the Soviet view, shall be considered in this study.

Soviet scholars consider "judicial decisions and teachings of most highly qualified publicists" (Article 38d) as a potential source of international law. "Judicial decisions and teachings of most highly qualified publicists" may become a binding source of international law either through treaty or custom. The role of custom in the area of Article 38d will also be noted.

The primary sources of international law, in the Soviet view, may be stated: "treaty, then custom."[7] Soviet stress upon treaty law combined with the efforts of the U. N. International Law Commission (ILC) to convert customary law into treaty law through codification draws attention to Professor Evgenii A. Korovin's thesis that custom is typical for the bourgeois period of international law but that treaty law is characteristic of the "two camp" period.

The purpose of this study is not to condemn or defend, but to analyze the Soviet view of customary law and, secondarily, to shed light on the general relation and interaction between ideology, power, policy and law. Organization follows purpose. Chapter I presents the ideological problem, "Soviet Ideology and Customary International Law." Nothing in the background of the leaders of the Bolshevik Revolution predisposed them favorably toward customary law, except perhaps a streak of pragmatism. Why and how traditional Marxism was "squared" with a law binding diverse social systems gives insight into the broader question of the revolutionary state and international law.

Chapter II, "Soviet Theory of the Legal Nature of Customary International Law" is a comparison of Soviet and western views on the conditions necessary for the creation and termination of a binding customary norm. As Rosalyn Higgins so aptly put it, "unless there is agreement on this subject [how binding custom develops] there can be no real harmony on whether particular rules continue to be binding or on whether certain other new binding rules have evolved."[8] The juridical nature of customary international law, as is true of custom generally, includes consideration of some of the oldest and most difficult problems of law. Difficulty arises from the intangibles of custom, in the numerous factors that come into play, in the great many views spread over centuries and in the resulting ambiguity of terms. The great task is to define what custom is.

Chapters III through VII deal with principles of customary international law which the Soviets have accepted, rejected, advocated or modified. A complete review of the entire body of customary international law as accepted by the Soviet Union would be an arduous and lengthy task for a group of highly qualified scholars representing the principal fields of international law. This study must be restricted to considering, in a most meaningful way, a select number of customary principles which will be illustrative of the whole field. Twenty-seven principles have been selected and organized into five major sub-divisions of international law.

Each of the five sub-divisions has been organized into a chapter: Chapter III, "Subjects of International Law;" Chapter IV, "International Treaties;" Chapter V, "Diplomatic and Consular Intercourse: Privileges and Immunities;" Chapter VI, "Territory and Population;" and Chapter VII, "Peaceful Settlement of Disputes and the Laws of War."

The sources of research include materials in English, Russian and French. In addition to numerous articles in the *American Journal of International Law* (AJIL), *British Yearbook of International Law* (BYIL), *Annuaire Français* (French Annual), *Recueil des Cours* (Collection of Lectures), *Current Digest of the Soviet Press* and *International Affairs* (Moscow), there are many other journal articles and monographs set forth in the bibliography. Among the Russian sources are a myriad of Soviet texts. For articles in Russian special attention is drawn to *Sovetskoe ezhegodnik mezhdunarodnogo prava* (Soviet Yearbook of International Law) and *Sovetskoe gosudarstvo i pravo* (Soviet State and Law). In terms of the reports of public and private international organizations the following were primarily relied upon: International Court of Justice; International Law Commisson; Sixth (Legal) Committee of the U. N. General Assembly; U. N. Conferences on the Law of the Sea, Consular Relations, Diplomatic Relations and the Laws of Treaties; International Law Association (Brussels); and the Congress of the International Association of Democratic Lawyers.[9] Other sources of pronouncements, records and reported actions of the Soviet Foreign Ministry were relied upon where appropriate such as *Sobraine deistvuiushchikh dogovorov SSSR* (Collection of Treaties of the USSR) and the *United Nations Treaty Series* (UNTS).

[1]Professor John N. Hazard observed, "It remains only for someone to treat as thoroughly Soviet practice of customary law." Remark made in his review of the Triska-Slusser study, *American Journal of International Law*, vol. 57 (1963), pp. 448-449.

[2]Akademii nauk SSSR, Institut gosudarstva i prava, *International Law: Textbook for Use in Law School*, translated by Dennis Ogden (Moscow: Foreign Languages Publishing House, n.d.), p. 12.

[3]Such principles of "treaty-making" include: *pacta sunt servanda,* unequal treaties, the effect of duress on treaties, the ratification process, conflict of treaty and municipal law.

[4]See Chapter IV, "International Treaties," *infra.*

[5]See Harold Briggs, *The Law of Nations*, second edition, (New York: Appleton-Century-Crofts, 1952), p. 48.

[6]Akademii nauk SSSR, Institut gosudarstva i prava, *International Law: Textbook for Use in Law School, op. cit.,* p. 12.

[7]See Fedor I. Kozhevnikov, U.N. *Yearbook of the International Law Commission*, A/CN.4/SR237 (August 11, 1953)/43/p. 367; Sergei B. Krylov, U.N. *Yearbook of the International Law Commission,* A/CN.4/SR378 (June 29, 1956)/189/p. 278; Akademii nauk SSSR, Institut gosudarstva i prave, *International Law: Textbook for Use in Law Schools, op.|cit.,* p. 12.

[8]Rosalyn Higgins, *Conflict and Interests: International Law in a Divided World*, (Chester Springs: Dufour Press, 1965), p. 140.

[9]The International Association of Democratic Lawyers is an organization of lawyers from the various communist countries.

CHAPTER I.
SOVIET IDEOLOGY AND CUSTOMARY INTERNATIONAL LAW

In 1917, caught up in the spirit of a spreading world revolution, the new Soviet régime denounced the then existing system of international law. Among the 21 conditions for admission to the Communist International as approved by the Second Comintern Congress on August 6, 1920, was Article 3,

The class struggle in almost every country of Europe and America is entering the phase of civil war. Under such conditions the Communists can have no confidence in bourgeois laws. They would create everywhere a parallel illegal apparatus, which at the decisive moment would do its duty to the party . . . [1].

From the outset, however, the Soviet State had to accept, out of urgent necessity, principles of established treaty and customary international law. From Brest-Litovsk on, treaties were negotiated, peace arranged, boundaries settled, recognition granted and diplomats exchanged. The RSFSR[2] could not avoid the language and methods of international relations developed over the centuries. Not all of the traditional principles of international law were accepted by the Soviet leadership. But many principles were accepted, a few were rejected while some new ones were proposed. Increasingly the Bolshevik Government sought to bind others "by the rules of the game" and in turn bound itself.

As the revolutionary response to smashing everything associated with the old order was tempered by logic, reason and necessity, Soviet scholars could begin the task of squaring Marxism with customary international law. The ideological question presented by the acceptance of custom was: how can a single body of customary law bind diverse social systems, socialist and capitalist, when Marx proclaimed that "all law is class law" and that "law is an instrument of the ruling class?" Efforts to answer this question may roughly be divided into three periods. The first, from 1917 to 1937, may appropriately be called, "the period in search of a theory of reconciliation." During this initial period the major contributions were those of Evgenii Korovin and Evgenii Pashukanis. Korovin suggested conceptualizing international law (treaty and custom) as "compromise law" of the transitional period. He was eclipsed by Pashukanis whose "form-content" formula made treaty and customary law "a weapon in the international class struggle."

In the second period, from 1937 to 1953, a "crisis in theory" arose. Soviet theoreticians were unable to offer a viable theory reconciling ideology and customary international law because both Korovin and Pashukanis had been denounced and their writings together represented the full spectrum of thought on the subject. Criticism was too complete. Andrei Ia. Vyshinskii's thesis, "international law as a means of struggle and cooperation among states," held sway during this period but was unsatisfactory as a theory of reconciliation because it failed to come to grips with the ideological question.

The third and present period, beginning with the death of Stalin in 1953, is characterized by the abandonment of the "search for a theory of reconciliation." Culminating in pragmatic Khrushchevian| peaceful coesistence, no real effort to reconcile ideology with customary international law is discernible. Soviet theoreticians turned their attention to dealing with the legal issues. "How is custom created?" is the question asked rather than, "How can diverse social systems be bound by the same law?"

1. *Pavel Ivanovich Stuchka*

Lenin was faced with the task of introducing a new order based upon the teachings of Marx. Neither Marx nor Engels gave consideration to the nature of law during the transitional period (generally referred to as "socialism"). Perhaps Marx and Engels could avoid the question because there was no pressing need to answer it, or then again, perhaps they simply overlooked it. Lenin could neither avoid nor overlook it for he found himself in the midst of that period.

Although a lawyer, having passed the state bar examination with honors in 1891, Lenin rarely theorized on the subject of the law.[3] Instead he left such matters to his Commissar of Justice, Pavel I. Stuchka.[4] In his work, *Revolutsionaya rol prava i gosudarstva* (The Role of Law and the Revolutionary State) published in 1921, Stuchka concentrated on the general question of "law in the transitional period." "Law," he wrote, "is a system (or order) of social relationships which corresponds to the interests of the dominant class and is safeguarded by the organized force of that class."[5] Stuchka avoided labeling the law of the transitional period as "bourgeois" as Pashukanis would later do. He simply referred to it as "bourgeois law without a bourgeoisie."[6]

How did Stuchka reconcile his concept of law as a system of social relationships representing the interests of the dominant class and safeguarded by the state with a concept of international treaty and customary law? "Taking our definition of law as a starting point," he wrote, "we assign a relatively unimportant sphere to international law."[7] There is no solution offered to the theoretical problem. Hans Kelsen went to the heart of the matter, "The sphere assigned to international law may be 'unimportant', but if it is law at all and a law the subjects of which are states, it must be a system of relationships corresponding to the interests of a dominant class formed by some of these states, dominating over another class formed by other states."[8] Stuchka avoided the thorny issue and it may fairly be said that he did not deal with the matter of international law, treaty or custom, to any significant extent.

2. *Evgenii Aleksandrovich Korovin*

On October 31, 1922, Lenin announced the New Economic Policy (NEP) to the All-Union Central Executive Committee.[9] The NEP called for a "temporary retreat" allowing for increased private ownership in the economic field and the strengthening of law in the judicial sphere.

Internally from 1917 to 1922 there were no codes of law, civil or otherwise in Soviet Russia. "Justice" was administered by "judges" using their "revolutionary legal conscience" and by the few decrees issued on various subjects from time to time. The NEP was a period of intense domestic codification. "In 1922 and 1923 there appeared a judicial act, a civil code, a code of civil procedure, a code of criminal procedure, a criminal code, a land code and a new labor code."[10]

However, as late as 1924, Stuchka's nihilistic characterization of international law as "unimportant" continued to be the dominant view. The compelling reason for internal law reform, the NEP, was not an immediate catalyst for reconsideration of the "law among nations." The Communist (Sverdlov) University at Moscow excluded international law from the program of study and called for the "need to destroy pitilessly the theory of state and national sovereignty, in all its historical configurations, from Bodin to Hobbes through Rousseau and Montesquieu, to Jellinek, the mensheviks and social revolutionaries."[11]

But E.A. Korovin[12] could not accept this nihilism. "One cannot," he wrote in his treatise, *Mezhdunarodnoe pravo perekhodnogo vremeni* (International Law During the Transitional Period), the first Soviet work on international law, "brush away [international treaty and customary law] by simple negation, by relegating, with one sweep of the pen, the whole complex system of norms of contemporary international law into the archives of bourgeois anachronism."[13] On the contrary, he asserted, international treaty and customary law was revitalized by the appearance of the Soviet State because international law (treaty and custom) "has developed and continues to develop only when there is struggle and competition between international forces . . ."[14]

He envisaged the nature of treaty and customary international law during the transitional period, therefore, as the resultant of the struggle and competition of bourgeois and socialist states. Korovin did not view the law between nations of the transitional period as a "temporary retreat," as an acceptance of bourgeois treaty and customary law pressed by political necessity, but as "a new system of legal relationships,"[15] as the construction of a "bridge between the bourgeois and socialist halves of humanity."[16] The bridge would be constructed by the acceptance of both systems of new norms of international treaty and customary law, which as he saw it, would through time evolve into socialist international law. The "return to legality" of the NEP period gave Korovin the opportunity to set forth his theory. But by conceptualizing international law (treaty and custom), not in NEP terms of a "temporary retreat" but rather in the more far-sighted terms of "co-existence," Korovin was far in advance of his contemporaries.[17]

There was, he argued, no universal international law valid for all states. Rather there were several operative systems of international law: the European system (chiefly among the great powers); the American system; the colonial system (between the imperialist state and its colony or semi-colony); and the transitional socialist-capitalist system (between bourgeois and proletarian states).[18] Each of the traditional systems (European, American and colonial) possessed a solidarity of interests and ideas. The states of these legal systems all represented the bourgeoisie, the dominant class. Consequently, when a new state representing another class appeared, new norms of international treaty and customary law became absolutely necessary. It was not possible for a proletarian state to accept and be bound by bourgeois international law. "The deeply rooted fundamental differences of the legal and social order of capitalist society on the one hand and socialist order on the other entails a manifold and substantial alternative of legal norms governing mutual relations between the bourgeois countries and the socialist ones."[19]

Hence the central question became, what is the content of the law which is applicable to both social systems and how is that content determined? Korovin considered this central issue under the rubric of "sources" of international law, which he envisaged as divided into two orders: a broad and a narrow one. The broad order equated "source" with some theory as to the basis of obligation of international law. The narrow order equated "source" with the methods or procedure by which international law is created.[20]

With respect to the broad order of the term "source," Korovin denied the validity of the natural law theory and the theory of the idealistic school as unsuitable for the transitional period.[21] The theory of the historical school was more acceptable but not wholly adequate. Common interest determines the content of the law binding between bourgeois and socialist countries but not common interest based upon ideological solidarity. ". . . An intercourse on the basis of intellectual unity (ideological solidarity) between countries of the bourgeois and socialist cultures, cannot exist as a rule and hence the rule of international law covering this intercourse becomes pointless."[22]

On the other hand, with respect to economic interests, he was more optimistic. He saw two types of economic interests, the "technical type" (postal, rail, telegraphic, river and so forth), and the "material type" (trade, customs, currency, protection of industrial property and so on). The first, the "technical type," lent itself readily to "more or less wide compromise," while the second, the "material type" would be "entirely determined by political requirements of a given moment."[23] Thus, Korovin saw possibilities for the development of a partial legal community based upon common economic interests.

With respect to the narrow order of the term "source," Korovin discerned a fundamental difference between traditional or "bourgeois" international law and the international law of the transitional period. In the traditional law of nations custom rather than treaties was the principal source of law and "the role of the treaty is often confined to the registration of a customary practice which has come into being (see for example, the law of diplomacy or the laws of war)."[24] During the transitional period, however, the "treaty dominates unchallenged and custom is reduced to an auxiliary (subsidiary) source."[25]

The actual treaty relations of the Soviet State, he asserted, demonstrated the "unbroken sway of treaties" during the transitional period.[26] Korovin was thus led to say, "the conclusion is that the presumption of *custom* is typical for contemporary bourgeois international law and the presumption of *treaty* is equally characteristic for the law of the transitional period."[27]

In minimizing the importance of custom as a source of international law, Korovin offered no analysis of the nature and function of custom as a basis for creating international legal norms with the exception of equating custom with bourgeois international law. Korovin reached this conclusion because, as he saw it, customary norms of international law were formulated, accepted and established prior to the existence of the Soviet State by "ideologically hostile" forces. Unlike treaties, custom lacked the explicitly expressed common consent of states. Customary norms of international law were not necessarily created by the habitual practice of *all* states. This was contrary to the concept of state sovereignty (which, ironically, was a customary principle that the Soviet Government had come to accept), inasmuch as a state became bound by principles it had not participated in formulating.

In an article written in 1928, Korovin went so far as to ignore facts concerning Soviet reliance on custom.[28] He claimed that the Soviet Union negotiated treaties only with respect to substantive matters and *only rarely* mentioned principles of customary international law: "Watching each other closely, the two participants, the USSR and the 'capitalist states,' met on the strictly limited ground of mutual agreement of a conventional character, only to return at once each to his own principles. The sacred formula so dear to every adherent of international law, namely, that of the 'common principles of international law,' has only rarely been made in Soviet treaties, most frequently in those with Germany, and has been of inconsiderable practical importance."[29]

There is no denying that custom was greatly de-emphasized by Korovin as a source of international law. There is also no denying that in practice the Soviet State acknowledged the binding character of many customary norms. The basis upon which customary principles were to be accepted or rejected, as Korovin envisaged it, was summarized by Professor John Hazard as follows, "It [the Soviet State] should not in any case reject the principles of international law unless they were manifestly harmful to it or out of keeping with its foreign policy."[30] National interest was the standard to be applied, and an important element of national interest was the realities of the contemporary international community. Customary norms, as standards of international conduct, were a part of that political reality.

3. Andrei Sabinin

Korovin's theory was not accepted at face value by all Soviet scholars. On the contrary, it evoked considerable discussion. One critic was Andrei Sabinin, Professor of Law at the University of Moscow and later Chief of the Legal Department of Narkomindel.[31]

Sabinin felt that Korovin had gravely underestimated the importance of custom as a source of international law. To his way of thinking, Korovin's theory of "international law during the transitional period," was practically unrealistic and legally impossible. At first glance, Korovin's analysis that treaties far overshadowed custom might seem correct, he conceded, but upon closer and more careful scrutiny,

if one thinks about the problem more deeply, this assertion contains a clear misunderstanding. Treaty prevails over custom as a source, to take the area of embassy law alone, only in the first, most elementary phase of the transitional period when relations do not exist between two states . . . Was not the author [Korovin] led to his conclusion by the circumstances that of the seventeen Soviet treaties concerning the establishment of diplomatic relations, seven are so-called de facto treaties which cannot fail to contain provisions on rights and privileges of mutual official representatives who are not diplomatic agents stricto jure? After all, the rights of these agents are protected by custom. For comparison, let us cite the treaties with Germany of May 6, 1921 and of April 6, 1922; we would search in vain in the second treaty (de jure) for those articles on the mutual position of representatives which appear abundantly in the first (de facto).[32]

Sabinin's purpose was not to denigrate treaties to a secondary or auxiliary source of international law. Treaties were a primary source. Rather, he sought to elevate custom to its appropriate position, to right the balance between treaty and custom as sources of law which he believed Korovin had distorted. Custom was also an important source of law, at times a primary source. In proposing a re-evaluation of the significance of custom, Sabinin brought the theory of international law more closely into line with the practice of Soviet foreign policy, most especially in the area of diplomatic law, whose source was chiefly custom.[33]

There were other aspects of Korovin's theory with which Sabinin took issue. For example, he did not adhere to the belief that a proletarian state should seek to create a new and different system of international law. It should, he contended, seek to improve to the fullest the existing system.[34] Where Korovin's writings were descriptive of a period of coexistence, Sabinin's view of living with the present system was more consonant with NEP policy.

4. *Korovin and Sabinin Discredited*

There began in the early 1930's a heated discussion over the state of the "most backward sector" of the law, that of international law. Verbal and paper volleys were exchanged in the Institute of Soviet Construction and Law (until 1936 separate from the USSR Academy of Sciences), the International Law Section of the University of Moscow and in academic journals, chief among them *Sovetskoe gosudarstvo i revolutsiya prava* (Soviet State and Revolutionary Law). Korovin and Sabinin were time and again challenged to defend their previous writings. Largely with the support of Evgenii B. Pashukanis,[35] Fedor I. Kozhevnikov[36] became the principal critic. In his article, "Concerning the Most Backward Sector of Soviet Law,"[37] Kozhevnikov bitterly attacked Korovin, Sabinin and others for their responsibility for the shabby and destitute state of Soviet international legal theory. His attack was given authoritative approval in a resolution of the 1931 Congress of Marxist Theoreticians of Law which condemned the theories of Korovin as "pseudo-Marxist" and those of Sabinin as "bourgeois."

5. *A New View Emerges: Evgenii Bronislavovich Pashukanis*

Professor E.B. Pashukanis was destined, even before the death of the Commissar of Justice, Pavel I. Stuchka, to become his principal successor. He was to outshine his predecessor by becoming the most prominent representative of the entire period from 1917 to 1937.

Pashukanis in *Ocherki po mezhdunarodnomu pravu* (Essays on International Law) published in 1935, attempted to resolve the question of the binding force of international law — custom and treaty — on diverse social systems by drawing a distinction between *form* and *content*. Although the form of international law might be alike for all states, opposing social systems could use these legal forms to their own ends.

Contrary to Korovin's analysis, international treaty and customary law was and remained the same old bourgeois international law. Pashukanis categorically denied the possibility of the evolution of international law,

If it happens that the Soviet Union insists on recognition of certain new provisions in international law which it puts forward, this does not mean that an evolution of international law is taking place by which it is transformed from bourgeois into socialist law, passing through some transitional stage.[38]

Whereas Korovin saw treaty and customary international law as

7

evolving through a "transitional period," Pashukanis viewed international law (treaty and custom) as the same traditional universal system it had always been with the same identical form into which each social system poured a different class content.[39] The fact that treaty and customary international law was bourgeois did not prohibit Soviet policy-makers from using it as an instrument of class conflict or as a defense of Soviet interests. He recognized all law, international or otherwise, as bourgeois and anticipated that all law would eventually "wither away." Until that time, he expected that it would be used by the Soviet State. International treaty and customary law provided the framework of relentless struggle. This was a case of old form and new content and nothing more. There exists no international "community of values."[40]

Pashukanis dealt with the sources of international law. Repudiating as "absolutely wrong" those scholars (namely Korovin), who suggested that "the Soviet Government should recognize only treaties [as a source of] international law and should reject custom," he wrote,

An attempt to impose upon the Soviet Government a doctrine it has nowhere expressed is dictated by the patent desire to deprive the Soviet Government of those rights which require no treaty formulation and derive from the fact that normal diplomatic relations exist.[41]

Pashukanis accepted customary international law because of its importance to the Soviet Union. Not only was such an assertion that the Soviet Government rejected custom inconvenient and dangerous for Soviet diplomacy but, according to Pashukanis, it was "unfounded."[42] "Treaty along with custom represent sources of international law."[43] But treaty and custom were accepted as sources of international law "between the two systems (only) until the socialist system should establish its superiority beyond the borders of the USSR." Moreover, Pashukanis limited all treaties to "those . . . in which we have taken part or to which we have adhered later," and suggested that custom be recognized "only within those limitations in which it does not contradict the dictatorship of the proletariat and the principles of our foreign policy."[44]

The writings of Pashukanis were an accurate accessment of the role of legal institutions in Soviet foreign policy. He was an advocate of a policy-oriented international law.[45] Yet, on the theoretical level his analysis was incomplete. In many instances he pointed to theoretical problems (such as the class nature of international law), without offering any solution. The ideological reconciliation of Marxism and international law, treaty and custom, was blurred by Pashukanis, whereas a few years earlier it was beginning to take shape. He acknowledged custom as a source of law but he did not discuss its nature and function.[46]

6. *Pashukanis Is A Traitor: A Crisis Materializes*

In the mid-1930's a new legal philosophy emerged, expounded by Andrei

Ia. Vyshinskii,[47] that of "socialist legality" (sotsialisticheskaya zakonnost'). As chief legal spokesman Vyshinskii violently criticized Pashukanis and his followers for having deliberately attempted to undermine the Soviet State and its law by "spar[ing] no effort to litter our judicial literature with pseudo-scientific research."[48] Vyshinskii considered as "pseudo-scientific" two principal teachings of the Pashukanite school: first, that the law of the transitional period was bourgeois law, and second, that this law must begin to gradually "wither away" immediately.[49]

Vyshinskii, however, made too thorough a job of cleansing the Soviet science of international law.[50] Not content with damning Pashukanis and his followers, Vyshinskii ironically reiterated the harsh words of Pashukanis and condemned Korovin's theory of "international law of the transitional period" as heretical. By denouncing both Pashukanis and Korovin, Vyshinskii created a "crisis in theory." What explanation could Soviet theoreticians offer for customary international law? Whereas Pashukanis viewed all law as bourgeois, reaching its highest stage under capitalism, Korovin saw international law (treaty and custom) of the transitional period as neither bourgeois nor socialist. While Pashukanis viewed the Soviet Union as bound by bourgeois principles of customary international law, although the Soviet State read new content into the old law, Korovin rejected the possibility of a proletarian state being bound by bourgeois principles. While Pashukanis viewed customary law as "withering away" to the extent that market and exchange of commodities disappeared, Korovin saw the interrelation between capitalist countries and Soviet Russia as the point of departure for the evolution of a new legal system, ultimately in time becoming socialist. Although Pashukanis viewed international law (treaty and custom) in NEP terms as a "temporary retreat," Korovin saw international law (treaty and custom) as the law of coexistence, the law of competition and cooperation among states of diverse social systems.[51]

The crisis in theory was highlighted by an article which appeared in Sovetskoe gosudarstvo (Soviet State), in 1938. Entitled, "Theses of International Law," the article was authoritative in its anonymity and may be taken to reflect the views, if not the exact works, of the editor of the journal, Andrei Vyshinskii.

In discussing the sources of international law, the "Theses" was more than vague. The article recognized custom to the extent that it recognized a number of principles in international law which, although not formed in treaties, nonetheless were generally accepted, such as diplomatic and consular privileges, questions of national maritime law and so forth. It was admitted that the Soviet Union uses those "bourgeois" institutions of international law which it finds acceptable, such as embassy law, but with a "deepening of their democratic aspects."[52]

No effort was made in the "Theses" to explain customary law in terms of Marxism. The noticeable reluctance of the author to discuss such theoretical problems set the tone for others. Not only were so many theories discredited that presentation of an ideological explanation became very difficult, if not impossible, but the "Theses" seemed to encourage Soviet theoreticians not to make the effort.

Vyshinskii did not offer an explanation in any of his writings, in Marxist terms, of the nature of a single body of customary international law binding both capitalist and socialist states. He did, however, comment on the sources of international law. He suggested why it was that the Soviet Union preferred treaty to customary law. "It must be clear to everyone," he wrote matter of factly,". . . that solid international law and order can be assured only on the basis of understanding and the recognition of the mutual needs, interests and rights of sovereign states. That is why the Soviet theory of international law regards the treaty, resting on the principle of sovereign equality of peoples and the respect for mutual interests and rights as the basic source of international law. This secures for international law and its institutions full moral as well as juridical force, since at their base will lie the obligations agreed to and voluntarily assumed by nations."[53]

The point of departure for all binding law upon both social systems was agreement between the socialist and nonsocialist worlds. Because one could more assuredly guarantee this necessary requirement of "agreement" through treaties in contrast to custom, the Soviet Union's most prominent spokesman elevated treaties to a position of primacy. In writings custom was nearly eclipsed as a source of international law and Vyshinskii did not discuss it at any length.

7. The Post-War Call For A Renewed Effort: Two Schools Evolve

By the end of World War II the crisis in theory was nearly ten years old. Soviet international lawyers gave no indication that they were willing to raise, let alone answer, the fundamental theoretical question, as succinctly put by Korovin much later, "How is it possible, in the light of Marxist-Leninist teachings concerning the basis and the superstructure, and those concerning state and law, that there exists norms of international law which are equally binding for socialist and bourgeois states?"[54]

On October 5, 1946, the Central Committee of the Communist Party of the Soviet Union (CPSU) issued a directive concerning the plight of legal education in the USSR and cited specifically the defects in international law. The directive ordered the Institute of Law of the USSR Academy of Sciences to prepare and publish during 1947 a textbook on international law. No textbook had been published since 1926.[55]

Beginning in 1946, a steady stream of books and articles and other printed matter on international law poured off Soviet presses.[56] In specific response to the 1946 Central Committee directive, two Soviet scholars, Korovin and Kozhevnikov, undertook the task. Although each approached the "theoretical problem" within the bounds of Soviet diplomatic practice and the broad framework provided by Vyshinskii, telling differences developed in emphasis and in general direction between them.

Both Korovin and Kozhevnikov accepted as a basis for international law the "struggle and cooperation" of states. Korovin defined international law as "one of the branches of law, regulating legal relations between states which are established as a result of their struggle and cooperation in the world arena."[57] Kozhevnikov defined international law as "the sum total of rules of conduct arising and changing in the course of history (conventional and customary norms) which regulate, in the interest of the governing classes, the political, economic and other relations of struggle and cooperation between states in conditions of war and peace."[58]

The order and content in which the words "struggle" and "cooperation" appear in Soviet definitions of international law offers a clue to the approach.[59] In both definitions "struggle" appears first and is stressed over "cooperation."[60] Within the framework of "struggle and cooperation" Korovin and Kozhevnikov both saw international law (treaty and custom) in terms of what they called the "two line formula" which was, in fact, a direct rewording of the "form-content" theory of Pashukanis.[61]

Briefly the "two line formula" may be defined in Korovin's words,

Like any other law, international law reflects the will of the ruling classes. The reality of international law, however, is not precluded by the fact that for the time being there are on the international stage bourgeois states as well as feudal and socialist ones. Each of them, carrying out its own line and directed by its own motives, might be interested in supporting and preserving a certain amount of generally binding legal norms in international relations.[62]

The "two line formula" takes account of ideological diversity by conceiving of present-day treaty and customary international law as resting upon a dual superstructure (bourgeois and socialist). Socialist and bourgeois states, each with their own distinct line, however, interpret principles differently because of different class backgrounds. But adds Korovin, this ideological diversity does not destroy the possibility of a certain body of international legal principles (treaty and custom) from developing and becoming binding on both social systems.

For whatever reason Kozhevnikov began to shift his position away from the "two line formula" approach. By mid-1951, he had become an exponent of a modified "oneness" theory. Writing in *Sovetskoe gosudarstvo i pravo* (Soviet State and Law), he bluntly declared, "At the foundation of contemporary international law there are not two bases existing in separation from each other but the objective factor of the coexistence of these two bases."[63] These words of Kozhevnikov were the genesis of a second school of thought which matured under the guidance of Grigorii I. Tunkin. The Kozhevnikov-Tunkin approach, in years following, prevailed over the Korovin approach (the "two line formula").[64] The Kozhevnikov-Tunkin approach was an admission, by implication, that the Soviet State would opt for pragmatism in world politics over revolutionary ideology. Customary international law would be accepted with a minimization of ideological issues.

8. *De-Emphasizing Ideological Considerations*

The debate continued into the post-war period as to the importance and status of custom as a source of international law. Korovin, for example, placed strong emphasis on treaties, "The new international law and order that is being born after the Second World War presupposes maximum strengthening of the force and significance of international treaties, as the chief foundation for the entire postwar system of international law."[65] Nonetheless, although he believed that treaties had become the "chief foundation of international law," he was not prepared to reduce custom from a basic to a subsidiary source of international law.[66]

Vladimir M. Koretskii[67] was willing to argue for such a reduction in status. As the Soviet Representative to the United Nations International Law Commission (ILC), he was somewhat at a loss to understand the interest in the agenda item, "Ways and Means of Making the Evidence of Customary International Law More Readily Available." Praising international conventions as "progressive"[68] and citing the United Nations Charter[69] and the Charter of the Nuremberg Tribunal as the source of the new post-war principles, he felt that those (and he was addressing himself specifically to the remarks of the French Representative, Mr. Scelle), who held that custom was a basic source of international law were absolutely wrong.[70] In the discussion that followed, he offered two major reasons as to why custom had lost its importance: first, "Customary law . . . was backward and belonged to the period of the 'whiteman's burden,' the period of the domination by a few powerful states who had disregarded the national sovereignty of weaker states."[71] Secondly, ". . . customary international law was too vague to be important and might moreover be fashioned into a tool to serve certain deplorable tendencies."[72]

For a short period, from 1950 to 1951, certain Soviet scholars, among them Korovin, adopted a unique analysis of the sources of international law that went beyond the issue of whether custom was a basic or subsidiary source of international law. In an article on international law which appeared in *Diplomaticheskii slovar* (Diplomatic Dictionary),[73] in 1950, treaties were cited as the basic source of international law; custom and domestic legislation as subsidiary sources; and the writings of "distinguished" jurists and scholars as merely "argumentation in favor of the existence or non-existence of this or that norm of international law." What was unique about this analysis was that the author, for the first time, treated "general principles" as a basic source of international law, considering them as "binding on all governments, regardless of whether they were applied through custom or through international conventions." Among these principles which the "Soviet juridical doctrine not only recognizes but stresses" were sovereignty, non-interference, equality of states and the fulfillment of international obligations.

Similarly N.N. Polianskii in his monograph on the International Court of Justice (ICJ)[74] treated "general principles" as a basic source of international law. He likewise regarded treaties, "resting on the principle of the sovereign equality of peoples and the respect for mutual interests and rights,"[75] and custom "only insofar as it reflected the agreement of governments,"[76] as basic sources. Polianskii's work was pioneering, moreover, for the hierarchy it recognized among the basic sources. He rejected the view of a "few members" (sic) that "general principles" were merely common principles underlying the codes of individual nations. He also rejected the "dominant view" that "general principles" were secondary in importance to treaties. He asserted that when "general principles" are in conflict with treaty provisions the latter must yield.

Thus, certain Soviet scholars were seeking to move Soviet international law toward the position that "general principles" could be cited as a basis for voiding specific treaty provisions.[77] The majority of Soviet scholars, nonetheless, continued to advocate the traditional Soviet view of sources.[78]

The movement for elevating "general principles" was brought to an abrupt end in 1951. In that year an international law text appeared which de-emphasized "general principles." "General principles" could not become a source of international law unless they were specifically embodied in treaty or custom.[79] It was not so much what the textbook said about "general principles", although that was important, as who said it. Korovin was the author of the work and he had been one of the prime-movers for elevating "general principles." His reversal of position in this work signaled an end to that effort.

Why did Korovin shift position? It was probably the realization that such a conceptualization of "general principles" cuts two ways, that other nations could cite them to invalidate specific treaty provisions which the Soviet Union found favorable. Pragmatism laid that view of sources to rest. By the end of 1951, Soviet scholars were again in general agreement that treaty and custom were the only basic sources of international law; treaty, however, was emphasized over custom as the more important source.[80]

It was from 1946 to 1952 that the first significant writings on the "legal nature of custom" appeared. Discussions concentrated on questions of formation of custom, defining custom and the like, rather than on the issue of bringing the Soviet concept of customary international law into line with Marxist ideology (or vice versa).[81] Increasingly ideological consider-

13

ations were down-played, if not ignored, by theoreticians. This shifting focus from the ideological to pragmatic legal problems began in this period and continues to the present day.[82]

9. Sergei Borisovich Krylov

As a leading theoretician S.B. Krylov was also a practitioner of international law as the first Soviet judge on the International Court of Justice, 1946-1952.[83] He was the first Soviet citizen invited to lecture to the Hague Academie de Droit International.[84] In these lectures Krylov spoke of international law (treaty and custom), not in terms of law representing a class but rather in terms of law representing "agreement" between classes. By stressing "agreement" instead of attempting to resolve the "class nature of customary international law," Krylov was in accord with the vast majority of Soviet scholars who had shifted their attention from ideological issues to legal questions. The concept of "agreement" is the basis for custom-formation, in the Soviet view, but it is largely an irrelevant concept in determining the class nature of customary law. In short, Krylov was avoiding questions of Marxist theory. He was making a legal analysis.

Like his colleagues, Krylov considered custom as a source of international law. Treaties ranked first and custom second as basic sources.[85] Treaties, bilateral and multilateral, were preferred to custom because the latter lacked the "necessary precision" and contained "many vague points."[86] All of these shortcomings notwithstanding, Krylov adopted the Pashukanite position that custom eases and expedites international relations and he pointed to Sabinin's example of the law of diplomacy. He stressed the "considerable significance" of international custom, resting as it does "upon a practice which extended over centuries." In the absence of "an international code" and since "the content of numerous international treaties does not cover all the problems of law which arises in international intercourse," custom plays an important role in international affairs.[87]

10. Korovin-Tunkin Debate

The "two line formula" advocated by Evgenii A. Korovin served as the point of departure for the debate.[88] Challenging his analysis, Grigorii I. Tunkin[89] suggested the "oneness" theory. The debate was carried on in Sovetskoe gosudarstvo i pravo (Soviet State and Law), from July 1952 until 1956, the watershed year.[90] In that year Tunkin, named to the Editorial Board of Sovetskoe gosudarstvo i pravo (Soviet State and Law) and as Soviet Representative to the U. N. International Law Commission, emerged triumphant over Korovin and established the theoretical position presently held by Soviet academicians.

14

The reason for Tunkin's victory can be seen from the nature of the two views at issue. The "two line formula" served best a "hard line" isolationistic policy. It emphasized "struggle" over "cooperation". It accented differences rather than likenesses between diverse social systems. It dismissed as unacceptable the idea of a single base for customary international law and envisaged custom as submerged in the class struggle. It recognized implicitly, if not in fact explicitly, two customary international subsystems (each social system projects its own content into the law as reflected by its class bias) loosely joined together, in form, as a "universal" system of customary law. If a socialist system of international law (treaty and custom) were ever to develop, it would be created through conflict and clash between the legal subsystems until the socialist one was victorious.

The "oneness" theory, on the other hand, was responsive to relations with the world at large. It stressed "cooperation" over "struggle" and emphasized likenesses rather than differences. It accepted a single base for customary international law and saw one system of customary law, the traditional system, as evolving under the influence of socialist diplomatic practice in a spirit of compromise and cooperation toward a socialist international law (treaty and custom).

The "oneness" theory advocated by Tunkin was practically wise but ideologically weak. The position did support a foreign policy of rapprochement with the West at a time when the Soviet Union was seeking to strengthen its relations with that quarter. So theoretically weak, however, was the position that Vladim I. Lissovskii, author of the first book on international law after Stalin's death, sidestepped the entire philosophical question.[91]

11. The Present-Day Soviet View: Grigorii Ivanovich Tunkin

By 1956, Tunkin was the acknowledged chief spokesman of the Soviet science of international law. His "oneness" theory which stood for a single-base customary international law was the official view. Since customary principles were the result of agreement, Tunkin concluded that customary law was an amalgam, neither socialist nor bourgeois in character. Stress was placed upon a unitary system of binding norms. This position raised a number of ideological questions,

(1) How is it possible that general customary international law which encompasses capitalist and socialist states has only one superstructural base?

(2) How is it possible that general customary international law which is a form of law can represent neither the bourgeois nor socialist states but rather agreement between them?

(3) How is it possible that socialist international law which is a unique system of law is compatible with general customary international law?

Tunkin gave no ideological answers to these questions. Alternatively he advised his colleagues to free themselves "from dogmatism, from the use of citations [of Marx] instead of creative thought, from crying hallelujah and from the isolation from actual reality which interferes with the development of the Soviet science of international law."[92] Tunkin advanced his conceptualization of customary law in terms of legal problems rather than in terms of the requirements of Marx. Others were encouraged to do likewise.

In discussing the sources of international law, Tunkin asserted that international treaties and custom together exhausted the primary sources.[93] Citing several Soviet authorities, Tunkin reiterated, however, that treaty now plays the "predominant role in developing, creating and amending the rules of general international law."[94] Nonetheless he added that customary international law was important and that there could "hardly be any doubt that the problem of customary international law . . . is one of the most difficult of all the problems of international law."[95]

The "problem" to which Tunkin was referring concerned the legal analysis of factors necessary for the creation of customary law. As for "general principles" enumerated in Article 38c of the Statute of the International Court of Justice, "they became international law either through international agreements or by way of custom and for this reason cannot be regarded as an independent source of international law."[96] "Norms of general international law come into being solely as a result of the completion of the international norm-making process, which takes place either in the form of a treaty or in the form of international custom."[97]

12. *Korovin As An Alternative*

Notwithstanding Korovin's acknowledgment of defeat in the 1952-1956 debates with Tunkin, he did not thereafter significantly alter his position. Although becoming less vocal, Korovin adhered to his former views and stands as an alternative to Tunkin. What is the nature of the Korovin alternative?

Korovin and Tunkin do not stand as "either-or" alternatives. Korovin's does not compose an antipodal body of doctrine. Although Korovin's writings are heavy-laden with "two line formula" phraseology and are more "hard line" than Tunkin's, it would be erroneous to summarize the differences in theoretical positions between them in terms of advocating divergent jurisprudential premises instead of in terms of stress or emphasis of some premises over others.

It is one thing to say that Korovin recognizes the validity of a particular premise and Tunkin does not, and quite another to say that Korovin places more weight on a particular premise than does Tunkin. These are fine lines not broad canyons. Although Korovin tends to view international law in terms of "form-content," he would admit the binding charac-

16

ter of customary international law. Tunkin, on the other hand, stresses "oneness" of customary law, yet he would not deny the unique content that socialist states project into the legal form.[98] It is this desire of Soviet scholars to have the "best of all possible worlds" — a universal customary legal system and a universal ideology — which is the crux of the entire history of the theoretical struggle. The differences in "schools," "approaches," or "positions" are differences in degree, differences in emphasis of one "world" over the other.

With the death of Korovin in the autumn of 1965, the "Korovin alternative" did not become academic, for it applies to all Korovins and to all Tunkins. Tunkin's "oneness" theory is in accord with the Soviet foreign policy of peaceful coexistence stressing "cooperation over struggle" as the basis for a single system of customary law. Should peaceful coexistence as a foreign policy fail, should international or domestic conditions supporting that policy alter, should Soviet policy return to an emphasize of "struggle over cooperation" then the "Korovin alternative" will again become relevant. Korovin's "two line formula" represents a continuing potential alternative to Tunkin's approach.

13. Summary

In 1917 a revolutionary state emerged on the world scene. It possessed an ideology which its leaders held with fervor and which they believed to have universal application in all aspects of man's existence. In dealing with nonsocialist states, the Soviet Government, out of urgent necessity, accepted customary international law. Customary law, created over centuries by the practice of capitalist states, was acknowledged by the Soviet leadership as binding. "But how was this acceptance to be explained in terms of the universal ideology?" *That* was the fundamental theoretical question facing the Soviet Marxist.

From Pavel I. Stuchka to Grigorii I. Tunkin, no Soviet academician has been able to "square" ideology with customary international law. The question posed remains unanswered. Customary law which binds diverse social systems, socialist and capitalist, is irreconcilable with the Marxist concept of class law. In response to the ideological impasse, G.I. Tunkin advised Soviet colleagues to de-emphasize or avoid, if possible, considerations of this perplexing question. Homage is paid to Marx and Lenin but no penetrating analysis of an ideological nature is presently underway in the USSR.

Ideological debate concerning custom germinated many ideas which Soviet lawyers have applied to the legal nature of customary law, that is, to the question of how custom is created and terminated. The "consensus doctrine" rooted in "agreement", for example, was put forward as an explanation of how customary law could rest on a single superstructure while at the same time binding diverse social systems (an ideological

17

[14]*Ibid.*, p. 9.

[15]*Ibid.*, p. 95.

[16]*Ibid.*, p. 136.

[17]As G.M. Mason noted, "This goes a long way toward explaining both the difficulties Korovin experienced in the 1930's and the fact that he survived the sharpest criticism without 'organizational consequences' and reappeared in a position of scientific authority exactly at a time when the Soviet Union reached the state of development which his theory so pointedly — although perhaps unconsciously — anticipated." "Toward Indivisible International Law?" *Social Research,* Vol. 23 (Spring 1956), p. 65.

[18]At this time no claim was made for a socialist system of international law, the Soviet State being the only socialist state.

[19]Evgenii A. Korovin, *Sovremennoe mezhdunarodnoe publichnoe pravo* (Present-Day Public International Law), (Moscow: 1926), p. 8.

[20]See Harold W. Briggs, *The Law of Nations,* second edition, (New York: Appleton-Century-Crofts, 1952), p. 44 for "meanings and confusions over the term 'source'."

[21]Korovin wrote, "The *theory of natural law* merits rejection not only for reasons associated with its origin but chiefly because from a Marxist standpoint it is inconceivable to speak of the existence of any ideal law common to all mankind which stands above classes. If it is quite legitimate to contrast law which exists with law which one would like to see exist (since from this antithesis a revolution in law emerges which smashes the petrified forms of the old law forms of the old law for the sake of establishing new and more equitable forms), one ought not to forget nevertheless that the very content of the concept 'socially just' is not given to mankind in ready-made form, equally binding upon all, but is developed through prolonged struggle as a result of class or group (national for instance — given the absence of sufficient class differentiations) collective self-consciousness.

"For similar reasons we must equally reject the arguments of *the idealistic school.* Neither the moral nature of man as an individual (an ethical variant) nor his intuitive-legal experiences (the psychological variant) can be considered a source of any law whatsoever and much less a source of international law; international law is the product of later stages of social development and an expression of a complex historical process in human society, organized on a collective basis." Evgenii A. Korovin, *Mezhdunarodnoe pravo perekhodnogo vremeni* (International Law During the Transitional Period), (Moscow: 1924), pp. 25-26.

[22]Evgenii A. Korovin, *Sovremennoe mezhdunarodnoe publichnoe pravo* (Present-Day Public International Law), (Moscow: 1926), pp. 12-13.

[23]Evgenii A. Korovin, *Mezhdunardnoe pravo perekhodnogo vremeni* (International Law During the Transitional Period), (Moscow: 1924), pp. 16-17.

[24]*Ibid.*, pp. 8-9.

[25]*Ibid.* For a slightly different emphasis see Evgenii A. Korovin, *Sovremennoe mezhdunarodnoe publichoe pravo* (Present-Day Public International Law), (Moscow: 1926), pp. 8-9. In this work Korovin added that "decisions of the highest organ of the League of Nations constitute a source of international law for member states."

[26]When Korovin makes reference to treaties, he makes reference to bilateral not multilateral treaties. *Ibid.*, p. 27. See also, Evgenii A. Korovin, *Mezhdunarodnya dogovory i akty novogo vremeni* (International Treaties and Acts of the Modern World), (Moscow-Leningrad: 1925), p. 225.

[27]Evgenii A. Korovin, *Sovremennoe mezhdunarodnoe publichoe pravo* (Present-Day Public International Law), (Moscow: 1926), p. 26.

²⁸See Evgenii A. Korovin, "Soviet Treaties and International Law," *American Journal of International Law*, Vol. 22 (1928), p. 753.

²⁹*Ibid*. Between 1920 and 1927 Triska and Slusser found 29 references to common principles in treaties other than those with Germany. See treaties with Estonia of Feb. 2, 1920, Art. 7, para. 4b; Georgia, May 7, 1920, Art. 5, para. 8; Latvia, Aug. 11, 1920, Art. 4 para. 4; Persia, Feb. 26, 1921. Art. 22; Afghanistan, Feb. 28, 1921, Art. 3; Latvia-Ukraine, Aug. 3, 1921, Preamble and Art. 2; Estonia-Ukraine, Nov. 25, 1921, Preamble, Art. 3, para. 4 and Art. 14; Austria, Dec. 7, 1921, Art. 6, para. 1, Art. 8, para. 1, and Art. 12; Finland, June 1, 1922, Art. 6; Italy, Dec. 26, 1921, Art. 24; Turkey-Ukraine, Jan. 2, 1922, Art. 11; Czechoslovakia, June 4, 1922, Arts. 2 and 16; Czechoslovakia-Ukraine, June 6, 1922, Arts. 2 and 16; Denmark, April 23, 1923, Art. 1, para. 4, and Art. 3; Norway, Dec. 15, 1925, Art. 1; Turkey, March 11, 1927, Art. 13; and Sweden, Oct. 8, 1927, Art. 6. Jan F. Triska, "Treaties and Sources of Order in International Relations: The Soviet View," *American Journal of International Law*, Vol. 52 (October 1958), pp. 703-704.

³⁰John N. Hazard paraphrasing Evgenii A. Korovin, "The Soviet Union and International Law," *Soviet Studies* (University of Glasgow), Vol. 1, no. 3 (January 1950), p. 190.

³¹"Narkomindel" is an abbreviation for "Narodny Komissariat Inostrannych Del," People's Commissariat of Foreign Affairs.

³²Andrei Sabinin, "Pervyi Sovetskii kurs mezhdunarodnogo prava" (The First Soviet Course on International Law), *Mezhdunarodnaia zhizn* (International Affairs), no. 2 (1925), pp. 119-120.

³³See *Ibid.*, pp. 116-120.

³⁴See Andrei Sabinin, "Sovetskaya drzhava i mezhdunarodnoe pravo," (Soviet Power and International Law), *Mezhdunarodnaia zhizn* (International Affairs), p. 15 as quoted by Hrabar, "Das heritige Völkerrech von Standpunkt eines Sowjetjuriston," *Zeitschift fur Völkerrecht* (Journal of International Law), 1928, p. 191.

³⁵Evgenii B. Pashukanis became editor of *Sovetskoe gosudarstvo i revolutsiya prava* (Soviet State and Revolutionary Law) in 1930. The post was previously held by Pavel I. Stuchka. See Appendix C, biographical sketch of Evgenii B. Pashukanis.

³⁶See Appendix C, biographical sketch of Fedor I. Kozhevnikov.

³⁷Fedor I. Kozhevnikov, "Concerning the Most Backward Sector of Soviet Law," *Sovetskoe gosudarstvo i revolutsiya prava* (Soviet State and Revolutionary Law), 1930, no. 3, pp. 147ff.

³⁸Evgenii B. Pashukanis, *Ocherki po mezhdunarodnomu pravu* (Essays on International Law), (Moscow: 1935), p. 15.

³⁹*Ibid*.

⁴⁰See Evgenii B. Pashukanis, *Ocherki po mezhdunarodnomu pravu* (Essays on International Law), (Moscow: 1935), p. 16. "Pashukanis," writes John Hazard, "saw no reason to suppose that in utilizing principles of international law for its own purposes the USSR was thereby compromising its principles in an effort to live in a world which held states defending the conflicting interests of different classes." "Pashukanis Is No Traitor," *American Journal of International Law*, Vol. 51 (1957), p. 387.

⁴¹Evgenii B. Pashukanis, *Ocherki po mezhdunarodnomu pravu* (Essays on International Law), (Moscow: 1935), Chapter 2.

[42]For example Pashukanis could have made reference to Art. 3 of the Treaty between the RSFSR and Afghanistan of Feb. 28, 1924, which stipulated that "the embassies and consulates of each contracting party shall enjoy all diplomatic privileges in conformity with the customs of international law." *Sbon. Deistv. Dogo.*, Vol. 1 (1924), p. 40. See also Art. 4 of the Treaty of Commerce between the USSR and Estonia of May 17, 1929, *Sobr. Zak. i. Rasp. SSSR*, Vol. 2 (1929), p. 917 or *League of Nations Treaty Series* (LNTS), Vol. 94, p. 323.

[43]Evgenii B. Pashukanis, *Ocherki po mezhdunarodnomu pravu* (Essays on International Law), (Moscow: 1935), p. 20.
When Pashukanis speaks of "treaty" as a source of law he means multilateral as well as bilateral treaties. As a member of the League of Nations, the USSR no longer de-emphasized multilateral treaties. See Jan F. Triska and Robert M. Slusser, *loc. cit.*, p. 706.

[44]Evgenii B. Pashukanis as quoted by Jan F. Triska and Robert M. Slusser, *loc. cit.*, p. 706.

[45]There have been advocates of a policy-oriented international law in the West. Among them, most notably today, is Professor Myres S. McDougal of Yale University. See Myres S. McDougal and Harold D. Lasswell, *Studies in Public Order* (New Haven: Yale University Press, 1960), p. 1007.

[46]For further discussion of Pashukanis' view on international law see: Hans Kelsen, *op. cit.*, pp. 152-155; Ivo Lapenna, *Conceptions Soviétique de Droit International Public* (Soviet Conceptions of Public International Law), (Paris: A. Pedone, 1954), pp. 166ff; and Edward McWhinney, *"Peaceful Coexistence" and Soviet-Western International Law*, (Leyden: A.W. Sythoff, 1964), pp. 46-47.

[47] see Appendix C, biographical sketch of Andrei Ia. Vyshinskii.

[48]Andrei Ia. Vyshinskii, *The Law of the Soviet State*, (New York: MacMillan Company, 1948), p. 38.

[49]As Vyshinskii saw it, it was from these two core misconceptions that all of the other "errors" of Pashukanis germinated. For Vyshinskii's entire analysis of the Pashukanite school see, Andrei Ia. Vyshinskii, *op. cit.*, pp. 52-61.

[50]See G. M. Mason, *loc. cit.*, p. 72.

[51]*Ibid.*, p. 64.

[52]"Tezisy po mezhdunarodnomu pravu," (Theses on International Law), *Sovetskoe gosudarstvo* (Soviet State), no. 5 (1938), p. 119.

[53]Andrei Ia. Vyshinskii, "Mezhdunarodnoe pravo i mezhdunarodnaia organizatsiia," (International Law and International Organization), *Sovetskoe gosudarstvo i pravo* (Soviet State and Law), no. 1 (1948), p. 22.
The reader's attention is called to Chapter II dealing with "agreement as the decisive factor." It is interesting to note that Soviet scholars have taken the treaty-formation characteristic of "agreement" and read it into custom-formation.

[54]Evgenii A. Korovin, *Sovetskoe gosudarstvo i pravo* (Soviet State and Law), no. 9 (1951), p. 14.

[55]For a discussion of the directive see, Evgenii A. Korovin, "Book Review and Notes," *American Journal of International Law*, Vol. 43 (April 1947), p. 387.

[56]See Grigorii I. Tunkin, "XXII S'ezd i zadachi Sovetskii naukii mezhdunarodnogo prava," (22nd Party Congress and the Task of the Soviet Science of International Law), *Sovetskoe gosudarstvo i pravo* (Soviet State and Law), no. 5 (1962), p. 4.

Tunkin also noted in this article that after the 20th Party Congress (1956) and the denunciation of the "cult of the personality," that there was a flood of material. Between 1956 and 1962 more works on international law appeared than in the previous forty years.

[57]Evgenii A. Korovin, *Mezhdunarodnoe pravo na sovremennom etape* (International Law During the Present Stage), (Moscow: 1946), p. 11.

[58]Fedor I. Kozhevnikov, *Sovetskoe gosudarstvo i mezhdunarodnoe pravo 1917-1947* (The Soviet State and International Law, 1917-1947), (Moscow: 1948), p. 5. The work was written in 1947.

[59]For a further discussion of the order and content of the words "struggle" and "cooperation" in Soviet definitions see: Oliver J. Lissitzyn, "The Soviet Union and International Law," *International Conciliation*, 542 (March), p. 16.

[60]Compare Korovin's definition given in 1954, "International law is the sum total of norms regulating relations among states and protected by them which are formed in the process of their international *cooperation* and *struggle* and are directed toward the satisfaction of their mutual material and spiritual needs, in the interest of the classes which govern these states." Evgenii A. Korovin, *Sovetskoe gosudarstvo i pravo* (Soviet State and Law), no. 6 (1954), p. 42. Emphasis supplied.

[61]The past experiences of Korovin and Kozhevnikov in dealing with "theoretical questions" ought to be briefly reviewed: Korovin, who Professor Percy Corbett in his *Law and Diplomacy* (Princeton: Princeton University Press, 1959), at page 91, calls "the dean of the corp of tormented theorists," had a "tireless capacity for solution and recantation." In 1924, he expounded his "oneness theory" of international law (treaty and custom), so-called because he envisaged the "international law of the transitional period" as resting upon a single bourgeois superstructure. This theory was denounced by E.B. Pashukanis in the mid-1930's and again by A. Ia. Vyshinskii in the late 1930's. For these "errors" Korovin recanted. Caution and silence were his watchwords for several years. In 1944, he reappeared as the author of the Red Army Manual on International Law (see: Evgenii A. Korovin, *Kratkiy kurs mezhdunarodnogo prava*, Short Course on International Law, Part II, Moscow: 1944. part I was never published). In 1945, he was the Soviet international legal expert to the U. N. Preparatory Commission in London. By the end of World War II, as a Correspondent Member of the USSR Academy of Sciences, Korovin was once more a prominent Soviet authority, but this time he was, ironically, advocating a "two line formula" which was remarkably similar to Pashukanis' "form-content" theory.

Kozhevnikov, on the other hand, did not have to go through the mental gymnastics that Korovin did. Having given expression to the "two line formula" in trial-balloon fashion prior to World War II, he had only to reiterate and develop this position. Like Korovin, Kozhevnikov approached the issue with prudence realizing the uncertainty of expounding a rewording of the discredited Pashukanite theory.

[62]Evgenii A. Korovin, *Bolshevik*, October 1946, p. 25.

[63]Fedor I. Kozhevnikov, "Some Problems of International Law in the Light of J.V. Stalin's Work 'Marxism and Linguistics'," *Sovetskoe gosudarstvo i pravo* (Soviet State and Law), no. 6. (June 1951), p. 35.
Stress on "oneness" and coexistence in international law (treaty and custom) is reminiscent of Korovin's theory of the 1920's.

[64]The successful emergence of the Kozhevnikov-Tunkin approach is discussed in section 10, "The Korovin-Tunkin Debate", of this chapter.

[65]Evgenii A. Korovin, "The Second World War and International Law," *American Journal of International Law*, Vol. 40 (1946), p. 751.

[66]See Evgenii A. Korovin, *Mezhdunarodnoe pravo na sovremennom etape* (International Law During the Present Stage), (Moscow: 1946), p. 1.

[67]See Appendix C, biographical sketch of Vladimir M. Koretskii.

[68]See Evgenii A. Korovin, *Sovremennoe mezhdunarodnoe publichnoe pravo* (Present-Day Public International Law), (Moscow: 1926), p. 26, for comparison. Korovin wrote in 1926, "the conclusion is that the presumption of *custom* is typical for contemporary bourgeois international law and the presumption of *treaty* is equally characteristic for the law of the transitional period [socialism]."

[69]In speaking of the United Nations Charter, V.M. Koretskii was recorded as having said, ". . . The Charter of the United Nations, for instance, which laid down new principles of international law, was *essentially* a treaty which had been signed by all peace-loving nations in San Francisco." V.M. Koretskii, U.N. *Yearbook of the International Law Commission.* A/CN.4/SR32/13 (June 2, 1949), p. 232. Emphasis supplied.

Professor Grigorii I. Tunkin, a later Soviet Representative to the Commission (ILC) stated that, "the principles of the United Nations Charter were binding on non-members as an expression of *customary* international law." Grigorii I. Tunkin, U.N. *Yearbook of the International Law Commission*, A/CN.4/SR621/46 (June 26, 1961), p. 258. Emphasis supplied.

[70]Vladimir M. Koretskii, U.N. *Yearbook of the International Law Commission*, A/CN.4/SR32/13 (June 2, 1949), p. 232.

[71]*Ibid.*, A/CN.4/SR32/14 (June 2, 1949), p. 232.

[72]*Ibid.*, A/CN.4/SR31/99 (June 2, 1949), p. 230.

[73]"Mezhdunarodnoe pravo," (International Law), *Diplomaticheskii slovar* (Diplomatic Dictionary), Andrei Ia. Vyshinskii (ed), Vol. 2, cols. 123-131 (Moscow: 1950). It is believed that Evgenii A. Korovin, a member of the Editorial Board, was the author of the article.

[74]N.N. Polianskii, *Mezhdunarodnoe sud* (The International Court of Justice), (Moscow: 1951). Edited by Evgenii A. Korovin.

[75]N.N. Polianskii quoted Andrei Ia. Vyshinskii's "Mezhdunarodnoe pravo i mezhdunarodnaia organizatsiia" (International Law and International Organizations), *loc. cit.*, p. 22.

[76]N.N. Polianskii, *Mezhdunarodnoe sud* (The International Court of Justice), *op. cit.*

[77]See Chapter IV for a discussion of the principle of *jus cogens.*

[78]Some writers such as Denisov and Kiritchenko did not even mention "general principles" in their discussion of sources, either as a basic or a subsidiary source. See A.I. Denisov and M.G. Kiritchenko, *Osnovi Sovetskogo gosudarstva i prava* (Foundations of Soviet State and Law), (Moscow: 1951), p. 33.

[79]See Evgenii A. Korovin, *Mezhdunarodnoe pravo* (International Law), (Moscow: 1951), pp. 16-19.

[80]See *Ibid.*, p. 16. See also, David B. Levin, "Falsification of the Concept of International Law by Bourgeois Pseudo-Scholarship," *Sovetskoe gosudarstvo i pravo* (Soviet State and Law), no. 4 (April 1952), pp. 55-63.

[81]For example, Evgenii A. Korovin in his 1946 work considered the question of the sources of international law and the question of the creation of custom. He believed that custom was established in international law through "state recognition." Evgenii A. Korovin, *Mezhdunarodnoe pravo na sovremennom etape* (International Law During the Present Stage), *op. cit.*, p. 1. Fedor I. Kozhevnikov followed suit discussing the same two questions. On the issue of custom-creation, he wrote, "In the case of customary law, this consent is tacit or implied, and becomes concretized through widespread international practice." Fedor I. Kozhevnikov, *Russkoe gosudarstvo i mezhdunarodnoe pravo* (The Russian State and

International Law), (Moscow: 1947), p. 165. N.N. Polianskii in his book on the International Court of Justice also considered these legal questions. He concluded that custom is a valid source of international law "only insofar as it reflected the agreement of governments." N.N. Polianskii, *Mezhdunarodnoe sud* (The International Court of Justice), *op. cit.*, p. 123. E.A. Korovin writing again in 1951 discussed the legal issues (avoiding the ideological questions). He wrote of custom as "the norms of behavior of governments," including only those "norms which are not in contradiction with the socialist legal conscience and which are generally accepted, *i.e.*, accepted as such by the Soviet Government as well." Evgenii A. Korovin (ed.), *Mezhdunarodnoe pravo* (International Law), (Moscow: 1951), p. 16.

[82]The reason for the shift was, of course, the continuing inability (and the entire history of Soviet theoretical writings on customary international law illustrates this) of Soviet scholars to fit customary international law within a Marxist framework without sacrificing either custom or ideology.

[83]See Appendix C, biographical sketch of Sergei B. Krylov.

[84]Sergei B. Krylov, "Les Notions Principales du Droit des Gens: La Doctrine Soviétique du Droit International," (The Principal Notions of the Law of Nations: The Soviet Doctrine of International Law), *Recueil des Cours* (Collection of Lectures), Vol. 70 (1947-I), pp. 407-476.

[85]*Ibid.*, pp. 441-444.

[86]*Ibid.*, p. 437.

[87]Sergei B. Krylov and V.N. Durdenevskii, *Mezhdunarodnoe pravo* (International Law), (Moscow: 1947), p. 23.

[88]See discussion of the "two line formula", section 7, "The Post-War Call For a Renewed Effort: Two Schools Evolve."

[89]See Appendix C, biographical sketch of Grigorii I. Tunkin.

[90]See the following articles: Grigorii I. Tunkin, *Sovetskoe gosudarstvo i pravo* (Soviet State and Law), no. 7 (July 1952), p. 69; Evgenii A. Korovin, "Nedotorye osnovnye voprosy sovremennoi teorii mezhdunarodnogo prava," (Some Fundamental Questions of Contemporary Theory of International Law), *Sovetskoe gosudarstvo i pravo* (Soviet State and Law), no. 6 (October 1954), pp. 34-44; V.M. Shurshalov, "Some Questions of the Theory of International Law," *Sovetskoe gosudarstvo i pravo* (Soviet State and Law), no. 8 (December 1954), pp. 91-92; "On the Results of the Discussion of Certain Questions of Contemporary Theory of International Law," *Sovetskoe gosudarstvo i pravo* (Soviet State and Law), no. 5 (May 1955), pp. 45-50; and Grigorii I. Tunkin, "Mirnoe sosuschestvovanie i mezhdunarodnoe pravo," (Peaceful Coexistence and International Law), *Sovetskoe gosudarstvo i pravo* (Soviet State and Law), no. 7 (1956), pp. 5-6.

[91]See Vladim I. Lissovskii, *Mezhdunarodnoe pravo* (International Law), (Kiev: 1955). Edited by A.M. Ladyzhenskii.

[92]Grigorii I. Tunkin, "XXII S'ezd KPSS i zadachi Sovetskoi nauk mezhdunarodnogo prava," (The 22nd Congress of the CPSU and the Tasks of the Soviet Science of International Law), *loc. cit.*, p. 3.

[93]Grigorii I. Tunkin. "Forty Years of Coexistence and International Law," *1958 Sovetskii ezhegodnik mezhdunarodnogo prava* (1958 Soviet Yearbook of International Law), p. 15.

[94]Grigorii I. Tunkin, U.N. *Yearbook of the International Law Commission*, A/CN.4/SR795 (June 2, 1965), p. 134.

[95]Grigorii I. Tunkin, "Coexistence and International Law," *Recueil des Cours* (Collection of Lectures), Vol. 95 (1958-III), p. 419.

[96]*Ibid., p. 26.*

[97]*Ibid.,* p. 31.

[98]The prime example is the "principle" of peaceful coexistence. See Chapter III.

[99]The reverse is equally true.

CHAPTER II.
SOVIET THEORY OF THE LEGAL NATURE
OF CUSTOMARY INTERNATIONAL LAW

In municipal law[1] custom is an important source of law for the Soviet State but this fact has not disposed the USSR to enthusiastically embrace it.

Customary law was applied under the Imperial regime to relations among the peasants. As has been indicated earlier, more than three quarters of the nation had no occasion, except in the event of serious crime, to appeal to the Codes of the Empire. Some of this heritage remains. Division of property belonging to a peasant household communally and inheritance of such property still is governed by peasant custom. A village "comradely" court of peasants settles such matters, and cases have been reported in which the question in issue was whether a family was a peasant family or a worker's family living in a village. The latter would be subject to the Civil Code's provisions concerning the ownership of property and not to peasant custom. In spite of this situation, Soviet text writers are very cautious in viewing custom as a source of law.[2]

Soviet writers approach customary international law with equal caution. Although traces of customary law were implicit in the actions of the Soviet State from the very beginning, Soviet spokesmen at first refused to recognize custom as a primary source of law, placing reliance solely upon treaty law.[3] But ever since Evgenii B. Pashukanis' penetrating question in 1935, "why should the Soviet Government be deprived of those rights which require no treaty formation and derive from the very fact that normal diplomatic relations exist?" the Soviet Union has openly accepted custom as a primary source of international law.[4]

Today, Soviet scholars are in general accord that treaty and custom are the only primary sources of international law, although treaty is emphasized as the more important source.[5] "Nobody has ever contested," Tunkin conceded, "that there are customary norms of international law."[6] "It is also indisputable," he added, "that many of the rules of international law are rules of custom."[7] More revealing yet is the statement, "Daily observation manifests the considerable role in international law of customary norms, states constantly refer to them in their inter-state relations."[8]

Notwithstanding the acceptance of custom in the 1930's, a clear statement of the legal (in contrast to the ideological) nature of customary international law was not forthcoming until the post-Stalin period.[9] It was at that time that Grigorii I. Tunkin, Chief Legal Advisor to the Soviet Foreign Ministry, called for less dogmatism and more pragmatism, for a concentrated effort to deal with real world problems rather than "great ideological generalities." Soviet writers responded in the mid-1950's by shifting their focus from an ideological consideration of the class nature of customary law to a legal analysis of the nature of international custom itself. Among the legal questions posed were: What is customary international law? How is customary law created? When does a customary norm cease to be binding?

Prior to 1953, books and articles devoted to a legal analysis of custom were virtually unknown. After 1953, such writings began to appear with increasing regularity.[10] The importance of this shift cannot be overstressed. It meant that ideological considerations were to be de-emphasized and that the Soviet Union would begin to contribute to the body of legal knowlege about international custom.

1. *The Importance of Custom*

The Soviet Union recognizes custom along with treaty as the only primary sources of international law. But why does Moscow carefully and consistently stress that treaty-law is the more important source?[11] Several explanations underlie Soviet valuation of custom. These reasons suggest a strong influence of ideology as well as pragmatic foreign policy considerations.

The first of these reasons is the "bourgeois character" attributed to customary law. Evolving from the practice of capitalist states ancient custom is suspect as serving primarily capitalist interests. A Soviet law text recites, "exaggeration of the importance of international custom . . . is in line with the policy of certain imperialist circles, a policy of violating treaty obligations and giving legal form to illegal international practices under the label of 'international custom'."[12] As long as the Soviet State continues to view custom as composed primarily of norms created prior to the Great October Revolution a certain aloofness from customary international law is to be expected.

Another reason is that law regulates the actions of states. Customary norms delineate what is proper and what is improper. There must be a certain uneasiness among Soviet practitioners at having their actions circumscribed by a law they had no part in making. This is not a unique feeling. The new nations of the "Third World" have expressed similar dissatisfactions.

On the other hand, Soviet scholars have come to argue that a series of new and progressive customary norms such as peaceful coexistence, national self-determination and unequal treaties, have been introduced into international law at their insistence.[13] As a result, in Soviet eyes, the "bourgeois character" of custom may be lessening somewhat and the USSR may presently feel that customary law bears a recognizable Russian imprimatur.

A final reason for Soviet dislike of custom is the very nature of customary law as unwritten law. Unwritten law is uncertain law as to principles and as to the meaning of those principles, they reason. These qualities run counter to the concept of developing relations strictly on the basis of negotiation and agreement, which is the preferred modality of the Soviet

28

Union for establishing relations with opposing social systems.[14] As the USSR grows in strength and acquires a greater sense of security in dealing with non-communist states, it is possible that the Soviet State may be willing to accept more uncertainty and make greater use of custom.

For the present, Moscow has tended to rely on custom only if a treaty source cannot be located and only if there is a "felt need" to cite an authoritative source of law. Treaties are relied upon in preference to custom but in the absence of a treaty, custom serves a valuable function. Occasionally Soviet practitioners will not discuss the source of a principle at all or they will conceal its source in ambiguous language. In using ambiguous language two techniques are discernible. One technique is to claim that a norm has acquired binding force because it is a "general principle" of law. Since Soviet lawyers refuse to admit to "general principles" as an independent source of international law and since they hold that only if incorporated through treaty or custom can "general principles" have the force of law, failure to indicate whether the source of a "general principle" is treaty or custom is not very helpful. The other method is to assert that the source of a principle is the United Nations Charter. As Soviet scholars admit the U.N. Charter may give rise to treaty as well as customary law. Without further clarification the source remains clouded.[15]

Generally speaking the task is to clarify exactly and to state specifically how customary norms are created and in what manner they cease to be binding. By asserting guidelines Soviet attorneys set forth the standard by which they will judge the process of customary law-making. No doubt the interplay of international politics will hold Soviet interpretation of this process within tolerable limits. Nonetheless the Soviet lawyer may claim some latitude for his Foreign Ministry deciding on the crucial factors necessary for the creation (or termination) of a customary norm of international law. Grigorii I. Tunkin realized the great importance of this task, while not overlooking the difficulties, when he said,

There may hardly be any doubt that the problem of customary international law is one of the most difficult of all the problems of international law. It is also one of the most important. Upon the solution of this problem [how custom is created and terminated] depends to a very great extent the whole concept of international law.[16]

2. Practice As An Indication Of Custom

"Customary norms of international law," Tunkin told those assembled for his Hague Academy lecture in 1958, "grow out of international practice."[17] The practice of states may consist in their taking action in a certain situation or in abstaining from action. "As a rule," Tunkin noted, "it is much easier, of course, to establish the existence of a customary norm of international law in the presence of positive action by states, but there is no reason to deny the possiblity of a customary norm of international law being established by the practice of abstinence from action."[18]

Chief among the positive acts of states which have resulted in customary norms of international law are diplomatic practices. Certain prescribed actions are expected to be performed by states with respect to diplomatic officers as a matter of law.[19] The abstinence from action, or rather, the "negative actions" of states, may undoubtedly lead to the creation of a rule of conduct that may become a judicial norm.[20] "It should be pointed out," writes Tunkin,

> that many principles and norms of international law involve, in one measure or another, commitments on the part of states to refrain from certain actions in their relations with other states. Thus, the respect-of-sovereignty principle commits states to refrain from any action constituting a violation of the sovereignty of another state. In accordance with the principle of non-intervention in the internal affairs of another member of the international community, every state is obligated to abstain from any action constituting interference in the internal affairs of another state. Even the open seas principle, for instance, involves an obligation of a negative character, which is that states must abstain from any action likely to injure "the interests of other states in their exercise of the freedom of the high seas." (Convention of the High Seas, Article 2, A/CONF.13/L. 35/1958, A/CONF. 13/38, Vol. II). Could these customary norms of international law appear if we were to deny that the practice of abstinence can also lead to the creation of a customary norm of international law.[21]

Western scholars are in general agreement with their Soviet counterparts. Wheaton, Brierly, Rousseau, Kunz unanimously agree that "customary international law is the generalization of the practice of states."[22] Several western writers have, however, called attention to an ambiguity of terms and a confusion of logic. Hans Kelsen has forthrightly declared the term "custom" as equivocal since it denotes at one and the same time the factual situation creating a rule and the rule created by the factual situation, hence "customary rule."[23] This confusion notwithstanding, Soviet and western scholars are agreed that practice is an indication of custom.

3. Time, Repetition And Continuity As Factors

According to the Soviet view, duration or in other words the element that time plays is important in the process of converting positive or negative actions of states into customary law. "However, the element of time does not *in itself* create a presumption in favour of the existence of a customary norm of international law."[24] A norm can be created almost instantaneously as in the practice of sending satellites into cosmic space over the territories of other states. "The fact that the Soviet Union and the United States," writes Carol Wolfke expressing the Soviet viewpoint, "mutually tolerate such practice and do not raise objections against such flights for peaceful purposes over their territories, and that other states, who do not, as yet, participate in this practice, have not protested, justifies the conclusion that [a customary principle has evolved because] states do not consider such flights as infringing their sovereignty, and even that sovereignty does not extend into outer space."[25]

Moreover, notes Tunkin, "there is even less ground to think that juridically it is necessary for a customary rule to be 'old' or of long standing."[26] The description that a rule is "old" may mean one of two things. Either that the given rule, having been observed for a long time in international practice has passed the test of time, or that "this very characteristic may give rise to some doubts as to whether the rule of such an ancient origin corresponds to the present circumstances."[27]

The element of repetition constitutes for the Soviet scholar another factor in the formation of custom. It is the reiterated actions of states with the passage of time. "In the majority of cases it is precisely the repetition of certain actions in analogous situations that leads to such practices becoming a rule of conduct."[28] But not every repetition of one and the same action creates a customary norm of international law. The "habit of doing certain actions may not result in forming a norm of conduct, and if a norm of conduct has been formed this norm may not necessarily be a legal norm. This may be a norm of international morality or a norm of *comitas gentium* [international comity or courtesy]."[29] In ambassadorial law there are many practices of long standing, repeated daily, which are not norms of international law, for example, the exemption of baggage from customs. It is also conceivable, but such instances are rare, for the element of repetition not to occur and for a rule of conduct to result from a single precedent.[30]

A third element is continuity. Soviet writers reject the opinion that 'international practice leading to the formation of a customary rule must have been continued and repeated without *interruption* of continuity."[31] This view is untenable for "no rule of international law has ever been created by practice," writes Tunkin, "without interruption of continuity."[32] This does not mean that an interruption in international practice does not effect the formation of a customary rule of conduct. "Discontinuity," adds Tunkin, "may destroy a customary norm which is still in the process of formation, it all depends on what character the discontinuity assumes."[33]

Each of these factors inquires into a different aspect of the nature of practice. The element of time asks, "how long?"; the element of repetition asks, "how often?"; and the element of continuity asks, "how constant?" is the practice. None of these factors or elements alone nor all of them together "plays a decisive role in the formation of a norm of international law" from the Soviet viewpoint.[34] Each may be necessary for the creation of a customary norm but none of them are sufficient.

It is not possible to speak of agreement between western and Soviet writers as to the importance of time, repetition and continuity because western scholars do not agree among themselves.[35] Western thinking is in a transitional state. The traditional view seems to have been that the development of customary international law was a very slow process. However, the rapidity with which event follows event in contemporary international relations has led to a re-evaluation. For western scholars there is some confusion over the nature of custom.

4. *Agreement As The Decisive Factor*

"Practices, even if long standing," states a Soviet law review article, "are not in themselves norms of international law. They may merely mark some particular state in the process of formation of such a norm."[36] Practice constitutes what may be described as the "raw material" of custom, but it is the element of acceptance which gives it the mark of law. The essence in the process "consists in agreement among states."[37] "It is precisely in this sense, in our opinion," writes Tunkin, "that one must understand subsection 'b' of section 1, Article 38 of the Statute of the World Court, under which one of the sources of international law is 'international custom, as evidence of a general practice accepted as law'."[38] Without agreement there can be no norms of international law. Carol Wolfke, a Polish Professor of international law, summarized the Soviet position in this way,

One may risk saying, that in present international law there are no precise pre-established conditions for custom-creating practices, except the one general condition that it must give sufficient foundation for presumption that the state concerned accepted it as binding.[39]

How is "agreement" reached among states? To Tunkin, "agreement, as to the means of creating norms of contemporary international law, is the result of the co-ordination of wills of different states, which in fact are the wills of their ruling classes."[40] The process of reaching agreement he described as follows,

First, the process of concluding international treaties. In the modern conditions of the co-existence of states belonging to two different social systems the process of conclusion of general international treaties shows that we there have a collision of different positions on problems of international law, a collision of wills of states. Then we witness the process of co-ordinating those wills by negotiation. The result of this process, fixed by treaty, is usually more or less different from what each particular state has originally suggested. In the process of creating customary norms of international law there are no negotiations as such, but as we have shown previously, the essence of this process consists also in framing an agreement between states on the question of recognizing or accepting this or that norm of international law. This agreement is reached, not by the way of formal negotiations, but by, figuratively speaking, negotiations conducted in the language of fact and actions.[41]

"Coordination of wills" of states does not signify their merging into some kind of "common weal," "general will," or "single will" in the process of creating a customary norm. These "wills" cannot fuse because the aims and tasks of states belonging to diverse socio-economic systems, a reflection of their class interests, are different and even antagonistic. The "wills" of socialist and capitalist states can be "coordinated" so as to establish a definite rule of conduct. "A norm of general international law is an expression not of a 'single will' but of 'coordinated wills,' *i.e.*, wills equally directed toward a definite aim — recognition of a given rule as a norm of international law."[42]

How is this "coordination" of wills to be achieved? "Agreement between states includes a mutual conditioning of wills, the substance of which is that the assent of one state to recognize a particular rule as a norm of international law is conditional on analogous assent by the other state. This 'inter-conditionality' is the thread which links the wills of different states in the process of shaping (developing or annulling) or extending the sphere of operation of a norm of international law. This 'inter-conditionality' is characteristic of an agreement as the mode of creating norms of international law."[43] This sounds like mutuality of consideration in American contract law.

The nature of the *process* of coordinating wills to reach agreement on the formation of customary norms is only one aspect of the element of agreement. Another is the *content*, what must be agreed to in order to create a customary norm. States of diverse socio-economic systems recognize that a norm which regulates their actions, is binding upon them not because of morality, not because of comity or courtesy but because it is a rule of law. Norms have the force of law because states accept them "with the intention of being bound by norms of law."[44] This means that either implicitly or explicitly a state must agree to the adoption of a customary norm as law. A state may agree through the medium of words, as for example, a declaration expressing its intention to be bound. Professor Tunkin cites as instances of this, Soviet declarations on prohibition of aggressive wars, the recognition of the criminality of aggressive wars, self-determination of nations and peaceful coexistence.[45] A state may also agree to a norm as law through its actions. One is warned, however, that actions do not always "speak for themselves" and are subject to misinterpretation and that great care must be exercised in this respect.[46]

Since customary norms result from agreement among states, Soviet writers conclude that the sphere of validity of a norm is limited to those states which recognize it as a norm of law. Consequently customary norms of international law may exist between as few as two states or between all states of the international community. In the latter instance the norm is said to be "universal." It is conceivable therefore, that a norm of law may appear first as a norm of legal conduct between a few states and gradually expand through acceptance on the part of other states until it finally becomes a universal principle of international law.[47] In this respect, Tunkin writes,

The Soviet State has advanced the principle of banning aggressive wars and treating such wars as crimes, the principle of self-determination of nations, the principle of peaceful coexistence, and a number of other principles of international law. In all these cases, the principles originally proclaimed by a single state were gradually recognized by other states and

33

have become, partly by custom and partly by treaty, generally recognized principles of modern international law.[48]

Tunkin continued by reiterating, "Only a customary rule which is recognized by the states of both systems can now be regarded as customary norms of international law."[49]

Does this mean that only the "great powers" in each camp must recognize a particular norm for it to become universally binding or does this mean that all states must consent, great and small alike? Tunkin suggests, in what he terms the "all states doctrine," that for a given norm to become a universal norm of international law it must be recognized by all states.[50] Over this view, Tunkin has exchanged strong words with Professor Hans Kelsen, a noted western international lawyer. Customary norms, according to Kelsen, are not created by "the common consent of the members of the international community" but by "a long established practice of a great number of states, including the states which, with respect to their power, their culture and so on, are of certain importance."[51] Tunkin disputes this view,

It does not follow from the concept of agreement that all states should participate in creating every specific customary norm of international law. It is not necessary at all that "practice" should be universal. A customary norm of international law may be created by the practice of a limited number of states and in fact it may become first a customary norm with a limited sphere of application. But to become a norm of international law of universal application it should be recognized by all the states.[52]

Continuing his argument on the basis of the principle of the sovereign equality of all states, Tunkin added,

This concept [of Kelsen] is in complete contradiction with the fundamental universally recognized principles of international law, and especially with the principle of equality of states. There is no doubt that the attitude of the majority of states, including states of both social systems, and especially the position of great powers, is of primary importance in the process of creation of universally recognized norms of international law. It is a factual situation. Judicially wills of different states in the process of creating norms of international law are equal. In international relations the majority of states cannot create norms binding upon other states; this is an immediate consequence of the principle of sovereign equality of states.[53]

Tunkin's approach is legalistic — before the law all nations, great and small, are equal. How does this compare with the facts of international life? Is it possible for the great powers or a majority of the world community to wield such influence as to force a nation to yield its will, unwillingly, to their will? Would Tunkin recognize such political influence, in fact, as creating a legally binding obligation upon the yielding state? Or would he find coercion or duress? Or would his finding depend upon the ultimate political question of who was doing the influencing? If Tunkin is not willing to admit some politics into the legal arena, how can he justify Soviet influence, or does he? If Tunkin's analysis does admit some politics into the legal arena, how different is his position from Kelsen's?[54]

34

Many western scholars believe that in addition to practice (the material element) there is a second condition for the creation of custom, the psychological element of *opinio juris sive necessitatis*. *Opinio juris* may be defined as "a certain conviction of the judicial necessity of the act in question."[55] Brierly speaks of recognition by states of "a certain practice as obligatory"[56] Hudson requires a conception that in each case the "action was enjoined by law."[57] For Schwarzenberger, "it is necessary to prove that they act in such a way because they admit a legal oblibation to act or to refrain from acting in a certain manner."[58] Oppenheim, Wheaton, Higgins and Kunz, among others, adhere to the view that it is the psychological element of *opinio juris* which differentiates usage from custom.[59]

Opinio juris differs from the Soviet "agreement" requirement. The element of *opinio juris* is required during the formation process *before* custom can evolve. In the Soviet view, it is not until *after* "agreement" is reached that custom emerges and a conviction of judicial necessity to act arises. Soviet scholars reject *opinio juris*.[60]

5. *"New" States And "Old" Norms*

Western scholars are in general agreement that the need to maintain an on-going world public order system demands that states be bound by rules of international law formed prior to their statehood.[61] In the Soviet view, the issue of "new" states and "old" norms is directly related to "the question of the sphere of action of customary norms." Noting the reservation made by Professor Vendross that "although the formation of a general customary norm does not infer its application by all states, no general customary norm can appear that contradicts the legal views of any civilized nation."[62] Professor Tunkin extrapolates,

But if recognition of a new customary norm of international law as such is required from an existing state, why must a newly emerging state find itself in an inferior position? Why cannot the new state object to any customary norm of international law if it disagrees with it?

The concept that customary norms of international law accepted as such by a large number of states must be binding upon all other states is actually based upon the presumption that the majority of states is [sic] able in international relations to dictate norms of international law to all other states.[63]

From the Soviet viewpoint the process of creating a universal norm of international law is never permanently accomplished.[64] All states of the international community may consent to a norm as binding law and at that moment that norm becomes a universal norm of international law. But as soon as a "new" state is born, that state acquires the same rights as the original states possessed when they created the binding universal norm in the first place. Namely, the "new" state may review the "old" universal norm and decide whether it wishes to be bound by it or not. To refuse to permit "new" states the right of review would contradict "the basic generally recognized principles of modern international law, the principle of equality of states in particular."[65]

Soviet lawyers have not, however, espoused an unqualified "right of review." Perhaps realizing the inherent dangers in an unlimited right, Soviet spokesmen have circumscribed the "right of review" by specifying the procedure to be followed in its exercise,

As for the newly emerging states, they have the judicial right not to recognize this or that customary norm of international law. However, if a new state enters without reservation into official relations with other states, this means that it recognizes a certain body of principles and norms of existing international law, which constitutes the basic principles of international relations.[66]

If a "new" state enters into relations with the international community "without reservation" it is to be assumed that that state has accepted the existing international legal system — at least its fundamental principles. A "new" state's ability to "review" is limited to the early period of its existence. What substantive law gives, procedure takes away.

6. The United Nations Charter As A Source Of Customary Norms

In the Soviet view, for the signatories of the Charter, the principles and norms eminating therefrom have their source in treaty, the Charter. The question arises as to what "bindingness" these principles and norms have on non-signatories such as Switzerland, the People's Republic of China, North and South Korea, North and South Viet-Nam, and East and West Germany. In the case of the *Free Zones of Upper Savoy and the District of Gex*, the Permanent Court of International Justice (PCIJ) stated clearly the long established principle that treaties cannot bind third parties without their consent.[67] Article 2, paragraph 6 of the United Nations Charter reads, "The Organization shall ensure that states which are not members of the United Nations act in accordance with these Principles so far as may be necessary to the maintenance of international peace and security." This provision of the Charter may express the will of the Organization or the desires of its members, but could such a provision create legal obligations for non-signatories? If such a provision could create a binding legal obligation for third parties what effect would this have on the concept of consent and the principle of state sovereignty?

Soviet scholars take the position that such a provision, as Article 2, paragraph 6 of the Charter, can never create binding obligations on third parties. However, Soviet scholars believe that the principles and norms expressed in the U.N. Charter are so basic to inter-state relations that the Charter is special and that the principles and norms contained therein do bind non-signatories. "The U.N. Charter is not the usual treaty. In the first place, it is the legal basis for the formation of a world wide international organization for peace and security. In the second place, states have given it pre-eminence over all their other treaties."[68] These special traits give the United Nations Charter a special character. As Vladimir M. Koretskii told the 1949 Session of the International Law Commission (ILC), ". . . the Charter of the United Nations, for instance, which laid down new principles of international law, was *essentially* a treaty which has been signed by all peace-loving nations in San Francisco."[69] But it was also something more than a treaty. In the words of Grigorii Tunkin, a later Soviet Representative to the Commission, it was a source of customary norms as "the new principles of the United Nations Charter were binding on non-members as an expression of customary international law."[70] The unique character of the Charter itself and not the wording of any particular provision in the Charter (for example, Article 2, paragraph 6), gave the principles and norms of that document their binding effect upon signatories and non-signatories alike.

Does this mean that principles and norms of the U.N. Charter, binding on the Soviet Union, have their source in custom? On the contrary, "the same norm of general international law could often be conventional for some states and customary for others."[71] Principles and norms of the Charter are binding on the USSR as a signatory of the treaty. The same principles and norms are binding upon non-signatories as custom.

This analysis is indicative of the Soviet view of the hierarchial importance of the sources of international law. In the Soviet conception, if custom had ranked higher than treaty as a source of law, then Soviet writers would have concluded that for all states (including the Soviet State) the principles and norms expressed in the Charter were rooted in custom. Instead Soviet scholars consider the principles and norms of the Charter as treaty-law for the Soviet Union.

The foregoing should not be construed as implying that custom is of no consequence to the Soviet Government if a principle is "codified" in the Charter. On the contrary, custom serves to fill the gap and explain how non-signatories to a treaty can be bound. This is not an inconsequential function. Moreover, treaties have frequently been an important factor in the evolution of custom *in the future*. As Pavel I. Lunkin noted, "many international customary norms have resulted from international treaties."[72] Treaties constitute a precedent, an element of practice, an expression of "coordinated wills."

The daily acts of international organizations and of member-states may contribute to customary norm-creation. As Tunkin noted, "It is obvious that change in the Charter of an international organization by custom, *i.e.*, by practice gaining recognition as a legal norm, is possible only with the general agreement of member-states of the international organization."[73]

Prior to 1945, the Soviet Union had accepted many of the principles and norms presently found in the Charter as binding custom. Among those principles were sovereign equality of states, non-intervention and national self-determination. The subsequent "codification" of these customary norms into the Charter does not arrest future evolution by accumulated practice of additional custom.[74] The process is continuous. Moreover, it is important to recognize that from 1917 to 1945, custom was the source of law of these principles for the Soviet Union. This was a crucial period in that country's relations with the international community and custom played a prominent role.[75]

7. Summary

"There is a fairly close similarity," writes Triska and Slusser, "between Soviet and western views on sources of order in international relations . . ."[76] Treaties rank first and custom second as the only primary sources of international law. Custom is recognized by Soviet lawyers as an important source of legal norms. The principles of international law which are custom-based are fundamental to the international system. With the exception of the stress which Soviet writers place on the element of "agreement", Soviet and western views are remarkably in accord as to the legal nature of customary-norm creation process. Recognizing, of course, that there is wide disagreement among western scholars themselves over some aspects of custom.

The Soviet view of the legal nature of customary law may graphically be summarized,

Soviet View of the Legal Nature of Customary Law: Summarized

Element	Necessary	/	Sufficient
Practice (a) positive (or) (b) negative	*yes		no
Time	*yes		no
Repetition	*yes		no
Continuity	*yes		no
Agreement	yes		yes
Opinio juris	no		no
	*Necessary in the usual case		

"Agreement" is the essential element, in Soviet eyes, for the creation (and termination) of customary law. First, Soviet lawyers view the element of "agreement" as adding a measure of certainty to traditional western notions of customary law. A nation which "accepts" as binding a customary norm has some notice of the nature and scope of its obligations. Uncertainty has always been a character trait of custom which Soviet spokesmen have found distasteful. Second, Soviet diplomats view the element of "agreement" as containing political advantages for the Soviet Union. Soviet policymakers may now choose which norms will bind them and which will not.

It is fair to ask at this point whether the element of "agreement," in fact, has contributed to the lessening of uncertainty or provided the Soviet Foreign Ministry with political advantages. Is custom more certain today because of the Soviet position? Do the Soviets obtain political advantages in the contemporary world by agreeing or not agreeing to a customary norm? In the last analysis, in practice, Soviet and western disagreement over whether "agreement" is the essential element for the creation (or termination) of customary law has had little impact. Uncertainty remains a character trait of custom. The Soviet Union has "accepted" the great majority of traditional customary norms. The remaining chapters of this study are devoted to an examination of the Soviet attitude toward specific principles of customary international law in an effort to delineate the scope of that "acceptance".

NOTES

[1]The term "municipal law" refers to the domestic or internal law of a nation-state.

[2]John N. Hazard, "The Future Codification in the USSR," *Tulane Law Review*, Vol. 29 (February 1955). pp. 243-244.

[3]See generally Jan F. Triska and Robert M. Slusser, *The Theory, Law and Policy of Soviet Treaties*, (Stanford: Stanford University Press, 1962). See also Chapter I of this work, especially section 1 "Pavel Ivanovich Stuchka" and section 2 "Evgenii Aleksandrovich Korovin."

[4]Evgenii B. Pashukanis, *Ocherki po mezhdunarodnomu pravu* (Essays on International Law), (Moscow: 1935), Chapter 2.

[5] see Fedor I. Kozhevnikov, U.N. *Yearbook of the International Law Commission*, A/CN.4/ SR237/46/p. 367; Sergei B. Krylov, U.N. *Yearbook of the International Law Commission*, A/CN.4/SR378/189/p. 278; and Akademii nauk SSSR, Institut prava, *International Law*, (Moscow: n.d.), p. 12. See western writers on the Soviet position: Charles de Visscher, *Theory and Reality in Public International Law*, translated by Percy E. Corbett, (Princeton: Princeton University Press, 1957), p. 163; and Jan F. Triska and Robert M. Slusser, *op. cit.*, pp. 9-31.

[6]Grigorii I. Tunkin, "Coexistence and International Law," *Recueil des Cours* (Collection of Lectures), Vol. 95 (1958-III), p. 9.

[7]Grigorii I. Tunkin, "Forty Years of Coexistence and International Law," *1958 Sovetskii ezhegodnik mezhdunarodnogo prava* (1958 Soviet Yearbook of International Law), p. 42.

[8]Grigorii I. Tunkin, *Droit International Public* (International Law), translation of *Voprosy teorii mezhdunarodnoe prava* (Theoretical Problems of International Law), (Paris: A. Pedone, 1965), p. 76. It is doubtful that Tunkin would go so far as to agree with his Polish colleague, Carol Wolfke, "Premature it seems is the recently expressed opinion that, as a result of the accelerated tempo and growing complexity of international law, customary law is rapidly losing its importance. Customary law being more elastic and best adaptable to new conditions and needs is evolving with the evolution of all international life." *Custom in Present International Law*, (Mroclaw: Zaklad Norodowy im Ossolwskich, 1964), pp. 9-10.

[9]A discussion of the post-Stalin shift in interest from ideological questions of reconciling Marxism and customary law to the pragmatic questions of the legal nature of custom is considered in Chapter I of this work.

[10] see especially: Petr Ivanovich Lunkin, *Istochniki mezhdunarodnogo prava* (Sources of International Law), (Moscow: Academy of Sciences of the USSR, 1960); N.M. Minasian, *Istochniki sovremennogo mezhdunarodnogo prava* (Sources of Present-Day International Law), (Rostov-on-Don: Rostov State University Press, 1960); N.M. Minasian, *Pravo mirnogo sosushchestvovaniia* (The Law of Peaceful Coexistence), (Rostov-on-Don: Rostov State University Press, 1966); Grigorii I. Tunkin, *Voprosy teorii mezhdunarodnogo prava* (Theoretical Questions of International Law), (Moscow: 1962); Grigorii I. Tunkin, "Coexistence and International Law," *loc. cit.*; and Grigorii I. Tunkin, "Remarks on the Judicial Nature of Customary International Law," *California Law Review*, Vol. 49 (August 1961), pp. 419-430.

[11]For a depreciation of custom by Soviet writers see: Grigorii I. Tunkin, "Forty Years of Coexistence and International Law," *loc. cit.*, pp. 15-29; Grigorii I. Tunkin "Remarks on the Judicial Nature of Customary Norms of International Law," *loc. cit.*, pp. 428-429; A.N. Talalayev and V.G. Boyarshinov, "Unequal Treaties as a Form of Subjugation to Colonial Dependency of the New States of Asia," *1961 Sovetskii ezhegodnik mezhdunarodnogo prava* (1961 Soviet Yearbook of International Law), p. 156; N.N. Ulanova, "State and Government Recognition and Participation in Multilateral Treaties," *1961 Sovetskii ezhegodnik*

mezhdunarodnogo prava (1961 Soviet Yearbook of International Law); and N.V. Zakharova, "Bilateral Treaties of Friendship, Collaboration and Co-operation Among Socialist States," *Sovetskoe gosudarstvo i pravo* (Soviet State and Law), 1962, no. 2, p. 80.

[12]Academy of Sciences of the USSR, Institute of Law, *International Law*, (Moscow: n.d.), p. 12. The normal predilection of lawyers for precedent becomes a "bourgeois deviation" if it involves reference to bourgeois writers, bourgeois legislation or bourgeois norms in such a way as to point up their superiority to that of socialist writers, socialist legislation or socialist norms (an ideological problem).

[13]See for example, David B. Levin, *Osnovnye problemy sovremennogo mezhdunarodnogo prava* (Basic Problems of Contemporary International Law), (Moscow: 1958), p. 11; and Grigorii I. Tunkin, "Forty Years of Coexistence and International Law," *loc. cit.*, p. 35.

[14]See Charles de Visscher, *op. cit.*, p. 163.

[15]The question of the United Nations Charter as a source of customary law could easily be the subject of a separate work. To the extent relevant it is discussed in this chapter, section 6, "The United Nations Charter As A Source of Customary Norms."

[16]Grigorii I. Tunkin, "Coexistence and International Law," *loc. cit.*, p. 9.

[17]Grigorii I. Tunkin, "Coexistence and International Law," *loc. cit.*, p. 9. See also, Grigorii I. Tunkin, "Remarks on the Judicial Nature of Customary Norms of International Law." *loc. cit.*, p. 419.

[18]Grigorii I. Tunkin, "Remarks on the Judicial Nature of Customary Norms of International Law," *loc. cit.*, p. 421.

[19]It is recognized that the United Nations Convention on Diplomatic Intercourse and Immunities has weakened this example.

[20]Grigorii I. Tunkin, "Remarks on the Judicial Nature of Customary Norms of International Law," *loc. cit.*, p. 421. See also, Grigorii I. Tunkin, "Coexistence and International Law," *loc. cit.*, pp. 11-12.

[21]Grigorii I. Tunkin, "Coexistence and International Law," *loc. cit.*, p. 422. Implicit in these words of Tunkin is that sovereignty, non-intervention in the domestic affairs of states and freedom of the high seas are, in whole or in part, customary norms.

[22]Judge Read, Fisheries Case, *ICJ Reports 1951*, p. 191. See also, *Wheaton's Elements of International Law*, edited by A. Berriedale Kieth, 6th edition, (London: Stevens and Sons Ltd., 1929), Vol. II, p. 10; James L. Brierly, *The Law of Nations*, 6th edition, (Oxford: Oxford University Press, 1964), pp. 59-60; Charles Rousseau, *Droit International Public*, (Paris: Recueil Sirey, 1953), p. 64; and Josef Kunz, "The Nature of Customary International Law," *American Journal of International Law*, Vol. 47 (1953), p. 666.

[23]Hans Kelsen, "Théorie du Droit International Coutumier," (The Theory of Customary International Law), *Revue Internationale de la Théorie du Droit* (International Review of Legal Theory), Vol. I (1939), p. 262.

[24]Grigorii I. Tunkin, "Remarks on the Judicial Nature of Customary Norms of International Law," *loc. cit.*, pp. 419-420. Emphasis supplied.

[25]Carol Wolfke, *op. cit.*, p. 64. It is recognized that the Outer Space Treaty has weakened this example.

[26]Grigorii I. Tunkin, "Remarks on the Judicial Nature of Customary Norms of International Law," *loc. cit.*, p. 420. It is interesting to note that on this point Tunkin cites in his article, "Coexistence and International Law," *loc. cit.*, at pp. 9-10, two western authorities for his

position: Jules Basadevant, "Règles générales du droit de la paix," (The General Rules of the Law of Peace), *Recueil des Cours* (Collection of Lectures), Vol. 58 (1936-IV), p. 518 and Josef Kunz, *loc. cit.*, p. 666.

[27]Grigorii I. Tunkin, "Coexistence and International Law," *loc. cit.*, p. 10.

[28]Grigorii I. Tunkin, "Remarks on the Judicial Nature of Customary Norms of International Law," *loc. cit.*, p. 419.

[29]Grigorii I. Tunkin, "Coexistence and International Law," *loc. cit.*, p. 10. Tunkin makes the same distinction between "custom" and "usage" as does his western colleagues. He writes, "but it is generally accepted and with good practice that 'custom in its legal sense means something more than mere habit or usage' (James Brierly, *The Law of Nations*, 1955, p. 60)." *Ibid.*, p. 12. Other western writers cited to support his view were: A. Vendross, *Völkerrecht* (International Law), (Wien, 1955), p. 119 and Josef Kunz, *loc. cit.*, p. 667.

[30]This writer was unable to find an example given by a Soviet writer of a customary norm created by a single precedent. It may be presumed that the launching of Sputniki I created a customary norm concerning the passage of satellites over the territory of foreign states in a single act.

[31]Grigorii I. Tunkin, "Coexistence and International Law," *loc. cit.*, p. 10. Among the western scholars who hold this view as cited by Tunkin are: Cavaglieri, "Règles générales du droit de paix," (General Rules of the Law of Peace), *Recueil des Cours* (Collection of Lectures), Vol. 26 (1929), pp. 336-337; and Morelli, *Nozionii di diritto internazionale* (Elements of International Law), para. 18, 3rd edition, (1951).

[32]*Ibid.*

[33]Grigorii I. Tunkin, "Remarks on the Judicial Nature of Customary Norms of International Law," *loc. cit.*, p. 420.

[34]*Ibid.*, p. 421. See also, Grigorii I. Tunkin, "Coexistence and International Law," *loc. cit.*, p. 11.

[35]See: James L. Brierly, *op. cit.*, pp. 62-63; Charles de Visscher, *op. cit.*, p. 149; Green H. Hackworth, *Digest of International Law*, 1940, Vol. 1, p. 1; Max Sørensen, *Les Sources du droit International* (The Sources of International Law), (Copenhagen: 1946), p. 98; Josef Kunz, *loc. cit.*, p. 666; Sir Hersch Lauterpacht, "Sovereignty Over Submarine Areas," *British Yearbook of International Law*, Vol. 27 (1950), p. 393; and I.C. MacGibbon, "Customary International Law and Acquiencence," *British Yearbook of International Law*, Vol. 33 (1957), pp. 120-121.

[36]Grigorii I. Tunkin, "The United Nations 1945-1955 (Problems of International Law)," *Soviet Law and Government*, Vol. 4 (Spring 1966), p. 7. A reprint from *Sovetskoe gosudarstvo i pravo* (Soviet State and Law), 1965, no. 10.

[37]Grigorii I. Tunkin, "Remarks on the Judicial Nature of Customary Norms of International Law," *loc. cit.*, p. 423. See also, N.M. Minasian, *Istochniki sovremennogo mezhdunarodnogo prava* (Sources of Present-Day International Law), (Rostov-on-Don: Rostov State University Press, 1960), p. 1ff.

[38]Grigorii I. Tunkin, "The United Nations 1945-1955 (Problems of International Law)," *loc. cit.*, p. 7. For a full discussion see: Grigorii I. Tunkin, *Voprosy teorii mezhdunarodnogo prava* (Theoretical Questions of International Law), *op. cit.*, pp. 84-104.

[39]Carol Wolfke, *op. cit.*, p. 51.

[40]See Grigorii I. Tunkin, *Osnovy sovremennogo mezhdunarodnogo prava* (Principles of Present-Day International Law), (Moscow: 1956), p. 4.

⁴¹Grigorii I. Tunkin, "Coexistence and International Law," *loc. cit.*, pp. 34-35.

⁴²Grigorii I. Tunkin, "Forty Years of Coexistence and International Law," *loc. cit.*, p. 44. The reader's attention is called to the influence of ideology in Tunkin's legal analysis.

⁴³Grigorii I. Tunkin, "Coexistence and International Law," *loc. cit.*, pp. 35-36. Professor Tunkin is concerned at this point with both the creation and termination of customary norms.

⁴⁴See Grigorii I. Tunkin, *Droit International Public* (International Public Law), *op. cit.*, p. 76. See additionally, Grigorii I. Tunkin, "Coexistence and International Law," *loc. cit.*, p. 13. To support his position Tunkin cites, K. Strupp, "Règles générales du droit de la paix," (General Rules of the Law of Peace), *Recueil des Cours* (Collection of Lectures), Vol. 47 (1934-I), p. 306.

⁴⁵See Grigorii I. Tunkin, *Droit International Public* (International Public Law), *op. cit.*, pp. 76ff.

⁴⁶See Grigorii I. Tunkin, "Coexistence and International Law," *loc. cit.*, pp. 12-13; and Grigorii I. Tunkin, "Forty Years of Coexistence and International Law," *loc. cit.*, p. 42.

⁴⁷See Grigorii I. Tunkin, "Coexistence and International Law," *loc. cit.*, p. 14; and Grigorii I. Tunkin, "Remarks on the Judicial Nature of Customary Norms of International Law," *loc. cit.*, p. 428.

⁴⁸Grigorii I. Tunkin, "Remarks on the Judicial Nature of Customary Norms of International Law," *loc. cit.*, p. 428. This view of the evolution of universal norms of international law lends itself well to Soviet claims of direct responsibility for positive developments in international law.

⁴⁹*Ibid.*

⁵⁰See Grigorii I. Tunkin, "Coexistence and International Law," *loc. cit.*, pp. 19-20; and Grigorii I. Tunkin, "Forty Years of Coexistence and International Law," *loc. cit.*, p. 15.

⁵¹Hans Kelsen, *Principles of International Law*, (New York: 1952), p. 313.

⁵²Grigorii I. Tunkin, "Coexistence and International Law," *loc. cit.*, pp. 17-18.

⁵³*Ibid.*, p. 19.

⁵⁴See Section 5, "'New' States and 'Old' Norms," of this Chapter which sheds additional light on these questions.

⁵⁵Max Sørensen, *op. cit.*, p. 85.

⁵⁶James L. Brierly, *op. cit.*, p. 61. Earlier in the same work Brierly said, "Customary rule is observed not because it has been consented to but because it is believed to be binding." *op. cit.*, p. 52. This runs counter to the belief expressed by Green H. Hackworth that "Customary . . . international law is based upon the common consent of nations." *op. cit.*, Vol. 1, p. 1.

⁵⁷Manley O. Hudson as quoted by Harold W. Briggs, *The Law of Nations*, 2nd edition, (New York: Appleton-Century-Crofts, 1952), p. 47.

⁵⁸Georg Schwarzenberger, *A Manual of International Law*, (London: Stevens and Sons, 1950), p. 11.

⁵⁹L. Oppenheim: "International jurists speak of custom when a clear and continuous habit of doing certain actions has grown up under the aegis of the conviction that these actions

are, according to international law, obligatory or right." *International Law: A Treatise*, edited by Hersch Lauterpacht, 7th edition (London: Longmans Green and Company, 1948), Vol. 1, p. 25; Wheaton: ". . . it is usage developed into a rule which is adhered to in the belief that an obligation so to act exists." *op. cit.*, Vol. 1, p. 10; Higgins: "Custom is more than a mere international usage; it is a widespread practice which states engage in because they believe that the law requires it of them." *op. cit.*, p. 141; and Kunz: "These conditions are two: usage and *opinio juris*; they have equal importance." *loc. cit.*, p. 665.

[60]Not all western scholars accept *opinio juris* either. See Lazare Kopelmanas, "Custom as a Means of Creation of International Law," *British Yearbook of International Law*, 1937, pp. 127-151; Hans Kelsen, *op. cit.*, pp. 262-266; and Paul Guggenheim, "Les Deux Elements de la Coutume en Droit International," (Two Elements of Customary International Law), *La Technique et les Principles du Droit Public, Etudes en l'Honneur de George Scelle* (Technique and Principles of Public Law, Studies in Honor of George Scelle), (Paris: 1950), Vol. 1, pp. 275-284.

[61]See Basdevant: "All agree that a new state is bound by international law formed prior to the emergence of this state." Jules Basdevant, *loc. cit.*, p. 515; Kelsen: "The states are bound by general international law without and even against their will . . . It may be assumed that international law becomes applicable to a newly established community when the latter is recognized as a state by other states." Hans Kelsen, *op. cit.*, p. 154; and Vendross, "International customary law is also binding upon these states which did not exist at the time of its inception." A. Vendross, *op. cit.*, p. 85.

[62]A. Vendross, *op. cit.*, p. 85.

[63]Grigorii I. Tunkin, "Remarks on the Judicial Nature of Customary Norms of International Law," *loc. cit.*, p. 427.

[64]This should not be confused with the fact that a particular state's acceptance of a principle is permanent in the sense that unilateral withdrawal of consent is not permissible.

[65]Grigorii I. Tunkin, "Remarks on the Judicial Nature of Customary Norms of International Law," *loc. cit.*, p. 427.

[66]*Ibid.*, p. 428-429.

[67]*Free Zones of Upper Savoy and the District of Gex*, Permanent Court of International Justice (PCIJ), June 7, 1932, P.C.I.J. Ser. A/B, no. 46, p. 96.

[68]Grigorii I. Tunkin, "The United Nations 1945-1955 (Problems of International Law)," *loc. cit.*, p. 8. See also, Grigorii I. Tunkin, "Coexistence and International Law," *loc. cit.*, p. 22.

[69]Vladimir M. Koretskii, U.N. *Yearbook of the International Law Commission*, A/CN.4/SR 32/13 (June 2, 1949)/ p. 232. Emphasis supplied.

[70]Grigorii I. Tunkin, U.N. *Yearbook of the International Law Commission*, A/CN.4/SR621 /46 (June 29, 1961)/ p. 258.

[71]Grigorii I. Tunkin, U.N. *Yearbook of the International Law Commission*, A/CN.4/SR794 /47 (June 2, 1965)/ p. 134.

[72]Pavel I. Lunkin, *op. cit.*, p. 87.

[73]Grigorii I. Tunkin, "The United Nations 1945-1955 (Problems of International Law)," *loc. cit.*, p. 9.

[74]These words apply equally to Draft Conventions of the International Law Commission (ILC).

[75]It has been the opinion of western writers that treaties and international conventions may become the basis of a rule of customary law. In 1844, Reddie, whose treatment of the subject was astute, explained that a treaty stipulation may "by subsequent imitation and adoption, without special stipulation . . . have become a rule of common and conseutudinary international law." Reddie, *Researches in Maritime International Law*, (Edinburgh: 1844), Vol. 1, p. 8. In 1913, Alvarez wrote of rules expressed in treaties that were later acknowledged by third states as having "changed their nature, one can no longer consider them as conventional but as customary." A. Alvarez, *La Codification du Droit International* (Codification of International Law), (Paris: 1913), p. 148. In that same year Oppenheim wrote of looking forward to the time when the Panama Canal shall have been in use for such a length of time "as to call into existence — under the influence and working of the Hay-Pauncefote Treaty — a customary rule of international law according to which the Canal is permanently neutralized and open to vessels of all nations." L. Oppenheim, *Panama Canal Conflict*, 2nd edition, (Cambridge: 1913), p. 46. In 1917, Roxburgh noted, "In practice, this process of extension of a conventional into a customary rule is not only possible but of very constant occurrence." Ronald F. Roxburgh, *International Conventions and Third States*, (New York: Longmans, Green and Company, 1917), p. 75. In 1925, Kosters likewise noted, "Already in the conception of past centuries, the conclusion of a treaty is an act which . . . can contribute to the formation of customary international law." J. Kosters, "Les fondements du droit des gens," (Foundations of International Law), *Bibliotheca Visseriana*, Vol. IV (1925), p. 221. In 1932, Derying wrote, "Every treaty to some extent . . . contributes to the formation and specification of rules of particular or common law." Antoni Derying, *The Principal Trends of Development of the Law of Nations in the Light of Decisions of the Permanent Court of International Justice*, (Lwow: 1932), p. 39. In 1957, Schwarzenberger described the "widespread process of transforming of treaty law into international customary law." Georg Schwarzenberger, *International Law*, 3rd edition, (London: 1957), Vol. I, p. 563. In 1966, Professor Quincy Wright speaking about the U.N. Charter wrote, "The Charter is more than a treaty . . . it gives the United Nations a universal competence to maintain peace, thus going far toward making the principle of Article 2 universal international law." Quincy Wright, "Custom as a Basis for International Law in the Post War Period," *Texas International Law Forum*, Vol. 2 (Summer 1966), p. 149.

The question of the binding effect of resolutions of the United Nations General Assembly is recognized but not considered in depth in this study.

[76]Jan F. Triska and Robert M. Slusser, "Treaties and Other Sources of Order in International Relations: The Soviet View," *American Journal of International Law*, Vol. 52 (1958), p. 726.

CHAPTER III.
SUBJECTS OF INTERNATIONAL LAW

To what extent has the Soviet Union accepted customary principles of international law? How has the USSR interpreted these customary norms? Have they given them the same "meaning" as have their western counterparts or have they, in fact, practiced Korovin's "form-content" theory? Have Soviet practitioners accepted the old form of custom but read into the old law a unique socialist meaning? How has revolutionary Russia decided to deal with the international legal system? These are questions which the present and following chapters seek to deal with.

This chapter is concerned with the "meaning" and "source" of principles of international law which relate directly to what Soviet scholars term, "subjects of international law." The phrase "subjects of international law" is defined and used throughout this chapter as a Soviet scholar would define and use it. "By the term, a 'subject of international law'," records a Soviet text on international law, "we mean a bearer of sovereign rights and equally [sic] of rights and obligations flowing from international treaties and custom."[1] Sovereignty is the central trait of a "subject of international law." Emanating from the concept of sovereignty are rights and obligations. Legal rights attach themselves to "subjects of international law" because they are sovereign and these rights include such principles as equality of states and the right of national self-determination. Legal obligations, restrictions or limitations on the unbridled exercise of sovereign rights include such principles as peaceful coexistence and non-intervention.

Many of these principles are essential, or believed to be essential, to the continued functioning of the contemporary inter-state system.[2] This chapter, organized along the same lines that a Soviet scholar would follow, will consider under the rubric "subjects of international law," the principles of peaceful coexistence, sovereign equality of states, national self-determination, non-intervention and recognition. Frequently the principle of legal responsibility of state succession is also discussed under the heading of "subjects of international law." But because that principle deals largely with the continuity of treaty obligations, for purposes of this study, it shall be considered in Chapter IV, "International Treaties."

1. The Principle of Peaceful Coexistence

(a) Meaning
In one sense the principle of peaceful coexistence may be a poor principle with which to begin. It is at one and the same time an announced goal of Soviet foreign policy, an ideological description of the present epoch

of historical development and a juridical principle of international law. Nonetheless, if we are to begin at the beginning, peaceful coexistence must be the first consideration. At least within the last decade, for the Soviet Union, peaceful coexistence has become "the criteria of the legality of all other norms formulated by states in international relations."[3]

To fully understand the Soviet interpretation of the juridical principle of peaceful coexistence it is necessary to keep in mind the meaning of peaceful coexistence in Soviet foreign policy. As Nikita S. Khrushchev told the 20th Party Congress (1956), peaceful coexistence is "not a tactical move, but a fundamental principle of Soviet foreign policy."[4] It is a strategy, valid for "a historical epoch" more or less prolonged.

Peaceful coexistence became the main theme of Soviet foreign policy during the Khrushchev Era. Recognizing the mutually suicidal character of a general war,[5] peaceful coexistence represented the intention of the Soviet State to contain the East-West conflict.[6] By its very nature, as a foreign policy objective, peaceful coexistence was inapplicable to relations among socialist states. Peaceful coexistence was not universally applicable but applied only to relations between socialist and capitalist states.[7] Peaceful coexistence does not mean, noted Nikita Khrushchev in 1959, "friendship and cooperation" between East and West but rather peaceful competition, continued intensification of the "economic, political and ideological struggle."[8]

Peaceful competition, an element of peaceful coexistence, makes relations between diverse social systems dynamic rather than static in the Nuclear Age. Conditions between socialist and capitalist camps are not frozen. The official history of the CPSU summarizes peaceful coexistence as a foreign policy goal in this way.

Peaceful coexistence means competition in the economic and cultural spheres between countries of different social systems. This policy cannot lead to renunciation of the class struggle, to reconciliation of the socialist and bourgeois ideologies. It implies the development of the working class struggle for the triumph of socialist ideas. But ideological and political disputes between states should not be settled through war.[9]

Moving from foreign policy to law, Soviet publicists feel that "principles of law should correspond to the spirit of the times" and that the present epoch is the era of peaceful coexistence.[10] International law, including customary law, "is called upon to make its contribution," wrote Grigorii Tunkin, "to the realization of the magnificent prospects for assuring peaceful coexistence."[11] It therefore follows that peaceful coexistence should also be a fundamental principle of international law. The *Report* of the Soviet Branch to the International Law Association in 1960 declared peaceful coexistence to be a principle of international law.[12]

What does the legal principle of peaceful coexistence mean? Western scholars criticize it for its vagueness, "no one knows what peaceful coexistence means," "it is formulated at a very high level of generality and abstraction," and there are "no annotations telling us what the language means."[13]

Soviet scholars reply that, "some say that general principles are useless and even harmful because they may be interpreted in different ways. If they are harmful, then all international law is harmful because these principles constitute the very core of contemporary international law."[14] What is denied is that such principles are harmful, not that they may not "be interpreted in different ways."

At the 50th biennial reunion of the International Law Association (1962) the Soviet Branch submitted a Draft Declaration in which they attempted for the first time to clarify the legal principle of peaceful coexistence. The full text is short and is worth quoting in its entirety,

The principle of peaceful coexistence is a fundamental principle of modern international law. No distinctions in the social and state structures shall hinder the exercise and development of relations and cooperation between states, since every nation has the right to establish such a social system, and to choose such a form of government as it considers expedient and necessary for the purposes of insuring the economic and cultural prosperity of its country.[15]

Could one then sum up the principle of peaceful coexistence as "you live there, we live here; what's yours is yours, and what's our is ours; we will not interfere in your affairs, and you will not interfere in ours; our affairs involving you will be conducted on the principle of equality, honesty and candor, and your affairs involving us will be likewise governed; and on this basis we will progress, each in his own way, toward the goals we each have set for ourselves"?[16] If so, the principle of peaceful coexistence "means nothing more or less than the continuation of the classical system of international law as it has developed since the days of Grotius."[17] For it is a fact of international life that states coexist and live together with one another and that international law plays a part in that coexistence.

Many western scholars believe that the Soviet concept of the principle of peaceful coexistence has a different quality, that it may mean more than simply "live and let live." Former Senator Albert Gore (Tennessee), former U.S. Representative to the International Law Commission (ILC), summarized his doubts briefly as (1) peaceful coexistence is a Cold War slogan, (2) peaceful coexistence as a descriptive phrase is associated with Soviet foreign policy, and (3) therefore, as a politically value - laden term it should not be used as "every consideration of reason and comity suggests that unnecessary political controversy should be avoided.[18]

Professor Edward McWhinney of the University of Toronto Faculty of Law focused on the claim made by Soviet scholars that peaceful coexistence is a *new* principle of international law which *they* were the first to propose. By making such a claim, he noted, Soviet jurists hope to reserve "to themselves at any time the right to inject their own special content" into the principle, the logic being that he who suggests a principle has the right to define it.[19] Historically there may be grounds for this concern as Secretary of State Charles Evans Hughes, in 1923, claimed that "as the policy embodied in the Monroe Doctrine is distinctively the policy of the United States, the Government of the United States reserves to itself its defintion, interpretation and application."[20]

(b) Source

The Committee on Peaceful Coexistence of the Soviet Association of International Law declared in 1962, "the principle of peaceful coexistence is a universally recognized principle of modern international law . . ."[21] From what source, treaty or custom (for the Soviet view admits only these two sources of international law), does peaceful coexistence acquire its legitimacy as an international legal norm?

The first explicit mention of peaceful coexistence in treaty form was in the Sino-Indian Treaty concerning Tibet of April 29, 1954. Peaceful coexistence was reiterated, according to Soviet scholars, in the Declaration of Bandung (1955) and reaffirmed by the two conferences of African States at Accra (1958) and Addis Ababa (1960).[22] Giving expression to the principle, Lasar Foscanéanu found between 1954 and 1956, four treaties, 40 bilateral or multilateral declarations and 30 unilateral declarations, reports or interviews.[23]

Yet in all the *explicit* actions of states to date, there does not exist sufficient authority for claiming that peaceful coexistence is a *universal* principle of international law. There exists no universal treaty or combination of treaties global in nature expressing that principle. As for custom, Soviet practitioners place decisive importance on "agreement" for norm-creation. "Only a customary rule which is recognized by the states of both systems can now be regarded as a customary norm of international law."[24] The United States, among other western states, is conspicuously absent as an advocate of peaceful coexistence. Bernard Ramundo concludes that "peaceful coexistence, however, is generally not considered a legal principle in the West."[25] Where is the "agreement"?

From the Soviet viewpoint, peaceful coexistence was an *implied* principle upon which the United Nations was founded, and, therefore, the West was bound to adhere to it. "It suffices to refer to the United Nations Charter which expresses the goal of 'practice tolerance and live together in peace with one another as good neighbors' to join forces 'to maintain international peace and security' and to secure that 'armed force shall not be used, save in the common interest'."[26] It follows that peaceful coexistence must be a principle of the Charter and that "the principles of the Charter should, in our opinion," wrote Tunkin, "be regarded as universally recognized principles of international law."[27] Peaceful coexistence is a principle whose source of law is the U.N. Charter, a multilateral treaty, for the Soviet Union and all other signatories. It is custom for all non-signatories of the Charter. The writings of Soviet academicians shed no further light on how non-signatories have come to "accept" this customary norm.

The Soviet Union has exerted considerable effort to have the principle of peaceful coexistence codified. Many reasons may be suggested for this. Through codification the status of peaceful coexistence as a principle would be settled. Mrs. Zgurskaya, Ukrainian SSR delegate to the Sixth (Legal) Committee of the U.N. General Assembly, suggested another reason for codification,

The Charter contained the essence of the principles of international law, but a declaration of the principles of peaceful coexistence was necessary for account must be taken of the march of events since the adoption of the Charter.[28]

The practice of states having progressed beyond the Charter, a more ditailed wording of the principle of peaceful coexistence was necessary in order to incorporate those additional practices. The implications of Mrs. Zgurskaya's statement is, of course, that there may be some aspects of peaceful coexistence which were created by the practice of states since the signing of the U.N. Charter and which have their source in custom, at present, for the Soviet Union as well as for other states. Mrs. Zgurskaya gave no hint as to what those additional practices might be.

2. The Principle of Sovereign Equality of States

(a) *Meaning*
In addition to peaceful coexistence the concept of sovereign equality of states is central to the Soviet view of "subjects of international law".[29] It was Professor S.B. Krylov's belief that "truly all the material of international law is divisible into two parts, the question of the sovereignty of a state and the question of peaceful coexistence."[30] To understand the legal principle of sovereign equality of states it is necessary to consider: (1) what is sovereignty? (2) who may claim sovereignty? (3) what is the relationship between sovereignty and equality?

The first question is: what is sovereignty? To Soviet scholars, sovereignty is "the independence of the state of any other state, this independence amounts to the right to decide freely and according to its own judgment all its domestic and foreign affairs without interference on the part of other states."[31] "Sovereignty" is the possession of supreme power *(summa potestas)* unlimited by any other state resulting in autonomy within a state and independence in relation to other states.[32] A state of dependency is created when sovereignty is limited; the way in which sovereignty is limited determines the kind of dependency created. The sovereignty of states is to be absolutely respected.[33]

Although claiming absolute respect for sovereignty, the Soviet Union does not advocate a 19th Century classical concept of sovereignty.[34] At the 1964 Mexico City Meeting of the U.N. Special Committee on Principles of International Law Concerning Friendly Relations and Cooperation Among States, the Soviet Representative Mr. Khlestov, went on record as saying,

Some countries even considered that international law, too, was an invasion of state sovereignty. His own delegation, however, did not share that view; it held that rules of international law restricted the freedom of states with a view to safeguarding international peace and security, without infringing the sovereignty of states concerned. His country's policies and Soviet legal doctrine were consistent with that view.[35]

"In the interest of international cooperation states voluntarily and reciprocally restrict their sovereignty" and having assumed an international responsibility "a sovereign state must not in its international relations behave in an arbitrary fashion."[36] "The violation of the rules of international law, of the rights and interests of other states, cannot be justified by reference to sovereignty, insofar as such acts are not an expression of sovereignty but an abuse of it."[37]

This should not be interpreted, Soviet scholars add, as meaning that international law has "primacy" over municipal law. Instead both legal systems are seen as equal. "Primacy" as a descriptive term is ruled out because each is viewed as an independent legal system having its own special tasks and spheres of operation. "There can be no talk of the primacy of international law or the primacy of internal state law."[38] This does not mean that international law and municipal law are of equal influence in the dialectical process. All know that the "progressive" ingredients are to be found in the municipal socialist legal system. In spite of the fact that municipal socialist law possesses a certain degree of precedent in the synthesis framework, it does not, as might be otherwise expected, possess primacy over international law.[39]

With respect to the issue of the relationship between international and municipal law, it is evident that the Soviet Union has attempted to develop an analysis which will on the one hand maintain the validity of the concept of sovereignty as a means of defense against encroachment in its internal affairs while at the same time verbally avoiding the classical 19th Century postion. A defect in the Soviet analysis is their failure to suggest "choice of law" rules in case of international and municipal law conflict.[40]

In the interest of Soviet foreign policy, the USSR has been ready to rationalize a limitation of the sovereignty of other states. Writing at the end of World War II, E.A. Korovin suggested that it was necessary "to limit to a considerable degree the sovereignty" of Germany and Japan because, for those states, sovereignty was "turned into a privilege for a group of the choosen and an iron heel for all the rest."[41] At the London Conference for the negotiation of the Charter of the International Military Tribunal (Nuremberg), the Soviet Representative accepted "crimes against humanity" as a violation of international law and as a basis in law for "count four", the actions of Germany in mistreating and killing their own citizens in concentration camps.[42] Vladimir Koretskii later sought to "clarify" the Soviet postion: "the Charter affirmed the sovereign legislative rights of the states to which the German State had surrendered, thereby losing its own sovereignty, *i.e.*, the law of the Great Powers and not international law."[43] The Soviet Union was willing to admit to a limitation of German sovereignty not because of the primacy of international law over German municipal law but because each of the victorious powers, able to prosecute war crimes within its own territory, could prosecute such crimes within the zone of its occupation.

As for recognizing limitations on Soviet sovereignty in international interest, the Soviet Foreign Ministry has been most reluctant to do so. "The fact remains," writes Judge Charles de Visscher (Belgium) of the action of all states, "that over against the law the state holds in reserve the plea of sovereignty."[44] The USSR has pleaded sovereignty in numerous instances, among these are: to challenge the jurisdiction of the Permanent Court of International Justice (PCIJ) and the International Court of Justice (ICJ) when the interest of policy requires it,[45] to prevent the establishment of an international criminal code with self-enforcing international criminal court,[46] in submitting reservations to international multilateral conventions such as the Genocide Convention and the Convention on Privileges and Immunities of the United Nations,[47] in condemning the creation of military bases and the stationing of troops abroad by capitalist states,[48] and in asserting the immunities of state owned instrumentalities, *i.e.*, state shipping, state news agencies and the like.[49]

The second question for consideration is: who may claim sovereignty? "Being a subject of international law is a form of expression of the sovereignty of a state in international relations and like sovereignty itself, it is inherent in a state as such."[50] Only the state possesses the characteristic of "sovereignty."[51] Unanimously recognized by Soviet scholars as included within the term "state" are the Republics of the USSR.[52] Also included, *via* the principle of self-determination, are nations struggling for freedom.[53]

Although states may possess sovereignty they may not be able to exercise the independence of sovereignty. Injury to the socialist movement has been used by Soviet scholars to explain why the sovereignty of Soviet Republics or of national minorities within the USSR must be restricted.[54] With the Czech Crisis of 1968 this reasoning was elevated officially to the international plane in what has become known as the "Brezhnev Doctrine".[55] The Soviet Union made it clear that Czechoslovakia could maintain its independence (sovereignty) only as a socialist country. "The sovereignty of individual countries," wrote S. Kovalyov explaining the Brezhnev Doctrine, "cannot be used in opposition to the interests of world socialism and the revolutionary world movement."[56] Czechoslovakian sovereignty had to be subordinated to the extent that it ran counter to the laws of the class struggle and of social development.[57]

Concern has been expressed by some western scholars as to whether the Soviet Union intends to extend this analysis beyond the "Socialist Commonwealth" to all states so as to qualify the general principle of sovereign equality of states.[58] Recent Soviet writings seem to indicate a willingness to distinguish between the sovereignty of socialist and of capitalist states. Writes N.A. Ushakov in 1969, "The sovereignty of states with differing socio-economic systems has a different social basis. In this sense, the sovereignty of socialist states differs fundamentally from that of bourgeois states."[59] Soviet intentions are not clear at present, however.

The USSR has unequivocally refused to affirm the individual as a "subject of international law" because the individual cannot possess sovereignty. A number of western scholars, among them the late Sir Hersch Lauterpacht and Judge Philip C. Jessup, have stressed the need to include the individual as a subject.[60] But the Soviet Union has staunchly refused to recognize individuals as "subjects of international law" because it would restrict the sovereignty of states over their own citizens and nationals and foster the development of world government. Individuals are not "subjects of international law."[61] Similarly, the USSR has refused to recognize international organizations as "subjects".

The third and final question for discussion is: what is the relationship between sovereignty and equality? "For states, in order to be equal, must be sovereign, and in order to be sovereign, they must be equal."[62] Equality like sovereignty is an inherent characteristic of a state, a "subject of international law". What then is meant by "sovereign equality of states"?

In the first place, although states differed from each other in size, population, volume of industrial and agricultural production, economic and military power, level of living, and most important, socio-economic structure, the differences between them by no means meant that the stronger states were entitled to dictate to or dominate the weaker ones. . .

Secondly, sovereign equality meant that every nation had the right to choose its social system and to dispose freely of its national wealth and resources, and that no one was entitled to restrict or infringe that right. No provision of international law, or of treaties which might no longer correspond to current requirements, could be invoked to justify interference with a nation's right to dispose of its resources. The use of treaties to that end was at variance with the principle of sovereign equality . .

Thirdly, a state independence in international relations meant that the states had the right to participate in international agreements of concern to them and to join international organizations dealing with matters affecting their interests.[63]

Soviet publicists include within their concept of equality both equal protection of the law (*e.g.*, "stronger states are not entitled to dominate the weaker ones") and equality of rights and functions (*e.g.*, "all states have a right to participate in international agreements of concern to them"). Western scholars generally hold that equality means equal protection of the laws but does not include equality of rights and functions. As James L. Brierly noted, "all states do not have equal rights no more than all Englishmen have equal rights but it is true that all states are equally entitled to have those rights which they have protected. In both the Charter and the Covenant the great powers exercised primacy among states."[64]

Soviet spokesmen do not deny the role played by the great powers. Special rights such as the veto in the U.N. Security Council were justified on several grounds: that all members of the U.N. had voluntarily accepted the Charter and its Articles so that there could be no involuntary limitation on sovereignty,[65] that by granting to the great powers such rights "a stable legal foundation" would be established,[66] or simply "international law recognizes a series of derogations from the principle of equality of states, as for example, concerning the role reserved to the great powers in international organizations."[67] These explanations would have greater force if the Soviet Union had adopted the western position, equality defined only in terms of "equality before the law". By also viewing equality as "equality of rights and functions", contradiction emerges. Such a stand, however, permits the Soviet Union to simultaneously defend special rights of the great powers while claiming that "all states should have an opportunity of participating in discussions of questions of world-wide interest and in the formation of the rule of law affecting them." The latter argument has served, for years, as the basis for the assertion that the People's Republic of China has a legal right to sit in the world councils.[68] In recent days, as a result of cooling Sino-Soviet relations, the USSR has not as vigorously voiced this right.

(b) Source

The principle of sovereign equality of states is a universally recognized principle of international law.[69] Soviet publicists and practitioners of international law consider the source of legitimacy of the principle of sovereign equality of states to be the same as the juridical principle of peaceful coexistence. Like the principle of peaceful coexistence, Soviet spokesmen agree that the principle of sovereign equality of states is fundamental to international relations and is "the very keystone of the United Nations, for Article 2 (1) of the Charter expressly stated that the Organization was based on the principles of the sovereign equality of all its members."[70] The U.N. Charter makes the principle of sovereign equality binding law for all signatories of that multilateral convention. As for non-signatories, they are bound by the principle as a result of the accepted practice of states, that is to say, by custom. Treaty *and* custom explain how the principle of sovereign equality of states attained the status of a universal principle of contemporary international law.

Unlike the principle of peaceful coexistence, the principle of sovereign equality of states is not a relatively new principle of international law. It is quite ancient. It regulated relations among states prior to its "codification" in the United Nations Charter. Before 1945, even for the Soviet Union, the principle of sovereign equality was a "customary norm of international law".[71]

Moreover, there are derivative principles of international law emanating from the principle of sovereign equality of states, which may be termed "concrete principles," which have their source in custom. One such derivative principle is the principle of immunity of state owned vessels. Nowhere does the Soviet Union make the claim that this principle requires the obedience of all states because of the United Nations Charter. Rather the Soviet case for the principle of immunity of state owned vessels is made in terms of custom. At the 1958 U.N. Conference on the Law of the Sea, Mr. Keilin (USSR), said,

the immunity of government ships, including those operated for commercial purposes, was one of the oldest-established principles of international law. It was based on the generally accepted respect for the sovereignty of foreign states, in virtue of which no state was entitled to exercise jurisdiction over another state; the time-honored principle was expressed in the maxim: *par in parem non habet imperium.*[72]

Having made an appeal to the customary practice of states, Keilin continued by citing specific acts of the courts of the United States, Great Britain and France, maritime powers over the last 150 years to demonstrate his point. He called attention to the cases of the *Schooner Exchange, Parlement Belge, Jassy, Esposende, Quilmark, Gagara, Porto Alexandre, Christina, Maipo, Pesaro* and the *Navemar*, discussing each and drawing the conclusion that the principle of immunity of state owned vessels was a principle of international law.[73]

3. *The Principle Of National Self-Determination*

(a) *Meaning*
"The principle of self-determination presupposes the recognition of the right of every nation freely to determine its political, economic and cultural status, that is, to decide all questions of its existence right up to and including secession and formation of an independent state."[74] In the United Nations on the question of non-self-governing and trust territories, the Soviet Union has taken the position that if the local population demand independence from the governing authority the governing authority must immediately grant it. Moreover, and related to this, the governing authority has the legal responsibility of bringing these territories to self-government.[75]

Upon closer examination of this principle, a dual right emerges of "not only the right to decide the question of its state affiliation, but also the right freely to choose the form of state system."[76] Professor Gleb B. Starushenko, a leading Soviet authority on self-determination, describes this dual right in terms of an international aspect and an internal aspect of the principle,

The international aspect of the principle of self-determination presupposes the right of a people (or nation) to (a) secede and form an independent state; (b) secede and join another state; and (c) remain in a state as a federal, autonomous, etc., member.[77]

The internal aspect of the principle of self-determination, that is, the people's right to manage its domestic affairs without interferences from without, presupposes recognition of the right of a people (or nation) to (a) decide what its political and social system will be like; (b) freely dispose of its natural resources and manage its economy; and (c) decide all other domestic issues concerning culture, religion, etc.[78]

In summary, "the principle of self-determination of peoples and nations means the right of every people and every nation to decide all questions concerning its relations with other peoples and nations up to and including secession and formation of independent states, as well as all questions concerning the internal system without interference from other states."[79]

Professor David B. Levin would introduce limitations upon the applicability of this principle, perhaps for the self-protection of the Soviet Union as a federal multi-national state. He would terminate the right of peoples (or a nation) to secede when they had voluntarily exercised their own free will and opted to join a multi-national state. Only if the "contract" of union was violated could that people (or nation) again re-acquire the right of self-determination. Levin would not grant the right of self-determination to minorities scattered throughout the territory of a state. Minorities must live together. To move against a group exercising its right of self-determination is to commit aggression under international law.[80]

(b) *Source*
"The right of self-determination enunciated, notably, in General Assembly resolution 1514(XV), was not universally recognized, and recognition must also be conceded to the right of colonial peoples to fight to assert it."[81] Moscow's analysis of the source of the principle of self-determination is similar to that of the juridical principle of peaceful coexistence. The West has shunned peaceful coexistence as a binding legal principle and has, in like manner, preferred to consider self-determination as "a pragmatic policy statement", "a political formula", "a meta-legal norm", anything but a juridical precept.[82]

Under such circumstances illustrating "universality" becomes difficult for Soviet scholars. G.B. Starushenko offered an explanation. Previously self-determination had been a "political principle", but, he added, it has evolved into a principle which has "gradually assumed a legal character. In other words, there appeared a new principle in international law and it was later formulated as a principle of national self-determination."[83] The end product of a long process was the "codification" of the principle of self-determination in the United Nations Charter, making self-determination a universal principle recognized in international law.

The U.N. Charter, it is universally recognized, is a "law-making" and "universal" treaty. (See L. Oppenheim, *International Law*, Vol. 1, sec. 1, p. 47). It is an important source of modern international law. The principles and statutes it contains are the conventional principles of international law. Consequently, the principle of national self-determination is a conventional principle too.[84]

The Soviet Union, therefore, is bound by the principle of national self-determination as a signatory of the U.N. Charter, a treaty. As for non-signatories, as Starushenko noted, "the conventional character of the principle of self-determination is also confirmed by its proclaimation in the final comminuqué of the Bandung Conference in which 29 states took part, and in numerous bilateral governmental declarations."[85] Thus, "the principle of national self-determination is both conventional and an ordinary principle of international law" and non-signatories are bound by law to order their international relations according to this norm whose source of law for them is custom.

4. *The Principle of Non-Intervention*

(a) *Meaning*
The principle of non-intervention in the internal affairs of foreign states is a fundamental principle of contemporary international law. While a prime element of sovereignty, it is at the same time an independent legal precept.[86] The principle prohibits "not only armed intervention, but all direct or indirect intervention of a political or economic nature and political or economic pressure aimed at preventing peoples from choosing their social system or from taking economic measures to further interests in their own country."[87]

This principle, like the principle of peaceful coexistence, sovereign equality of states and national self-determination, is general and abstract and opened to varied interpretations. The following illustrative passage sheds some light upon its elasticity. Discussing western activity in the Middle East, we find,

The imperialists, contrary to the United Nations Charter, openly interfere in the domestic affairs of independent states. The attempt to dispute the right of Egypt to nationalize the Suez Canal Company, and to establish international control over the Canal was an obvious example. An act of outright aggression was committed against Egypt in October-November 1956, by Israel, Britain and France with the aim of compelling the Egyptian people to renounce their independent policy both at home and abroad. British military intervention in Oman in 1957, the American intervention in Lebanon and that of the British in Jordan in 1958 were also examples of gross intervention by the imperialist powers in affairs of other countries.[88]

The text continues,

The imperialists do not hesitate to use the United Nations Charter as a cover for interven-tion in the internal affairs of other states. Thus, contrary to Article 2 (7) of the Charter, and despite the protests of the legitimate Government of Hungary, a discussion of the "Hungarian Question" was imposed on the United Nations.[89]

On the one hand the West's activities in the Middle East were a violation of the principle of non-intervention while, on the other hand, Soviet ac-tion in Hungary in 1956 did not alter the essentially domestic character of the Hungarian situation and that it was, on the contrary, the United Nations which had violated international law by submitting to western demands for consideration of the "Hungarian Question".

(b) *Source*
The principle of non-intervention is a fundamental norm of international law, in Soviet eyes, and as such is a "universally recognized principle of modern international law."[90] The origins of the principle date back some 180 years to the French Revolution. At that time, "its essence was restricted to the impermissibility of armed intervention, and its sphere of operation was confined if not exclusively to revolutionary France, then at least to Europe."[91] Later at the insistence of other states the principle was extended. The Monroe Doctrine extended the principle to the Amer-icas. The Drago-Porter Convention of 1907, signed by 39 states, confir-med the principle for most of the countries of the world. The Soviet State, noted Platon D. Morozov, "from the earliest days of the revolu-tion of October 1917 had advocated the principle of non-intervention and as early as 1921 had included the principle in treaties."[92] Regional international agreements such as the Declaration of Lima, 1938, adop-ted at the Eighth International Conference of American States recon-firmed it. The agreed practice of states had transformed non-intervention into a binding principle of customary international law. As G.I. Tunkin wrote in one of his works under the heading of "International Custom,"

little by little the principle of non-intervention was transformed into a principle of general international law.[93]

The practice of states concerning non-intervention was reflected in the United Nations Charter. "The principle of non-intervention derived from the principles of equal rights and self-determination of peoples set forth in Article 1(2) of the Charter, and was based on Article 2(7) of the Charter."[94] Article 2(7) was an explicit prohibition against inter-ferences in the domestic affairs of any state by any other state or by the United Nations.[95] A principle whose source was custom became a treaty-norm for the Soviet Union.

Soviet spokesmen, nonetheless, continued to discuss the principle of non-intervention as a principle of customary international law as well as a treaty-norm. Speaking in terms of state practice, Mr. Kazantsev (USSR), said at the 1964 Mexico City Meeting of the U.N. Special Committee on Principles of International Law Concerning Friendly Relations and Cooperation Among States that,

The many bilateral and multilateral agreements showed that the principle of non-intervention was a principle of international law recognized by all states which served as a basis for good-neighborly relations and peaceful coexistence between states.[96]

Among the bilateral and multilateral agreements mentioned were, "the Soviet-Malian Communiqué of 1 June 1962; Soviet-Ghanian Communiqué of 21 February 1961; Warsaw Treaty of 1955; Vienna Convention on Consular Relations, 1963; Vienna Convention on Diplomatic Relations, 1961; 1945 Pact of the League of Arab States; 1955 Bandung Declaration on World Peace and Cooperation; Belgrade Declaration of the Non-Aligned Countries, 1961; Charter of the Organization of African Unity (OAU), 1963; and contributions of Latin American states."[97]

In the Soviet mind, the principle of non-intervention is conceptualized in the same manner as the principles of peaceful coexistence, sovereign equality of states and national self-determination. For the USSR, the principle has its source in treaty law. For all signatories of the U.N. Charter the principle is a treaty principle. For all non-signatories, the principle is one of customary international law.

5. *Some Principles Of Recognition*

(a) *Meaning*
"By recognition in international law we mean a legal act by which one state or group of states declare the character and scope of their relations with the government of a new state as an international person."[98] Not wholly accurate, this statement misrepresents contemporary Soviet doctrine because recognition is not limited to declaring the character and scope of one's relations with the government of a new state. Recognition can also be accorded to states (in contrast to governments), insurgents and belligerents as well as nations.[99]

The process of recognition is governed by several norms of international law. They are basically two kinds: First, there are principles describing what must or must not be done. *e.g.*, that non-recognition of a new state is a violation of international law (in the Soviet view). A new state emerging as a result of the national-liberation struggle has a legal right to final and complete (*de jure*) recognition. Selective recognition is unacceptable.[100] It is a principle of law that "a new state regardless of its location, size of territory and population, nature of social system, form of government and state structure, has a right to complete and final recognition."[101] "Non-recognition is one form of indicating hostility to it, and contradicts the generally recognized principles of international law," most notably the principle of self-determination.[102]

As a safeguard against failure to secure general consent to the existence of a legal obligation to recognize new states Soviet publicists repudiated the constitutive theory which holds that "through recognition only and exclusively [could] a state become an international person and a subject of international law."[103] The constitutive theory was to the advantage of colonial powers assisting them in maintaining dependency relations. The progressive development of international law in the era of peaceful coexistence has changed all that. In present-day international law "recognition does not create a new state. The latter emerges and exists irrespective of recognition."[104] Rather than constitutive, recognition is declarative in nature merely normalizing relations between the state recognized and the state recognizing.

A second kind of principle of recognition describes the legal rights and duties which emanate from certain actions, *e.g.*, the different rights and duties flowing from *de facto* and *de jure* recognition. This distinction is mainly one of scope of legal obligations,

In the case of *de facto* recognition, the relations between the recognizing state and the state recognized are such that they are not wholly stable in character and are somewhat provisional. Recognition *de facto* is incomplete; it is a transitional stage leading to *de jure* recognition although this may follow only much later.

Recognition *de jure* is full recognition, leading to the establishment of extensive relations of many kinds, more stable in character than is so in the case of *de facto* recognition.[105]

In modern international law there is, however, a legal limitation on the use of *de facto* recognition since its use is "incompatible with the principle of sovereign equality of states" and the principle of self-determination.[106] The limitation on the use of *de facto* recognition is a logical result of the legal obligation to recognize new states fully and completely.

Recognition of insurgents, according to Soviet writers, differs in legal consequences from recognition of belligerents. Recognition of insurgency guarantees, between the recognizing state and the insurgent party, observation of a "certain legal minimum". In the locality in which the civil strife is in progress such recognition protects the interests of the recognizing state. Recognition of belligerency carries with it greater legal consequences.

Following recognition as a belligerent party, a situation is created akin to that existing when two independent governments are at war. The party struggling for power, as a result of its recognition as a belligerent party, acquires the rights and obligations of a belligerent state.

From the point of view of international law, recognition legalizes the military action of the belligerent party, which henceforward cannot be considered as crimes, provided, of course, they are not aggressive in character. Recognition also implies the obligation of the belligerent party to observe the laws and customs of war.

In recognizing insurgents or belligerents third states are obliged to observe neutrality.[107]

The scope of obligations arising from the principles of recognition are an integral part of international law.

(b) *Source*

Why is it a violation of the law of nations for a state to refuse to recognize a new state? How were the rights and duties of states appertaining to *de facto* and *de jure* recognition or to insurgent and belligerent recognition made legally binding? How were these principles of law formed? What is the source of their authority?

Frequently Soviet academicians relate the principle of the legal right of a new state to recognition to more fundamental principles. Failure to extend recognition to a new state would contradict the principle of national self-determination and would be incompatible with the principle of sovereign equality of states.[108] This answer does not suffice. It only avoids the central issue of how was it decided that failure to conform to the principle of new state recognition would violate international law. In addition, states are permitted discretion in recognition. They may within certain limits determine whether recognition will be *de facto* or *de jure*, or whether it will be recognition of insurgency or belligerency. How was it "agreed" that the legal rights and duties which do follow in each case would indeed follow?

Soviet writers admit that, "there are no international treaty rules of international law regarding this matter [*de facto* and *de jure* recognition]"[109] or again that "there are no treaty rules defining the concrete content of these two conceptions [insurgency and belligerency]."[110] If treaty law is not the source of recognition principles; custom must be. The Soviet Foreign Ministry acknowledges only two primary sources of international law, treaty and custom. "Accepted international practice of states" or some similar phrase is used by Soviet writers to describe the binding character of principles of recognition.[111] A certain pattern of action has evolved with respect to recognition and states are expected to adhere to that pattern, to that custom.

6. *Summary*

The ancient concept of sovereignty which underlies many principles of the law, while under increasing attack today from several quarters, has received sustaining support from the USSR. The impact of international law on the Soviet Union is illustrated by Soviet support of sovereignty. While most western and non-aligned nations could be expected to take a rather strong position in favor of state sovereignty, no such expectation could have been initially made about revolutionary Russia. Its leaders had assumed power expounding traditional Marxism which stood for the proposition that the state (and its sovereignty) were "withering away". Today, however, the USSR, ironically enough, has become the strongest advocate of state sovereignty, of protecting the state from foreign intrusions.

Also by suggesting new principles of international law such as peaceful coexistence and national self-determination, which the United States for example has refused to accept, the Soviet Union has placed its imprimatur on international law. These Soviet efforts are having their effect as Soviet proposals are widely discussed and are receiving increasing support. The meaning which the Soviet Union attributes to these new principles, as is true of the meaning which the Soviet Union attributes to principles of international law in general, are bound to have an effect on the legal system. As a great power, the actions of the USSR are bound to stir reactions.

In considering the source of law of the five principles discussed in this chapter, it is evident that the Soviet Union admits three instances in which custom plays an important role:

(1) To explain the source of a principle which the Soviet Union accepts as universally binding and for which there is no treaty authority.

(2) To explain the source of a principle which the Soviet Union accepts as universally binding and for which there is treaty authority but the treaty authority is inadequate because a non-signatory is involved.

(3) To explain the source of a principle which the Soviet Union accepts as universally binding and for which there is treaty authority but the treaty authority is inadequate because the principle involved has evolved since the time of the making of the treaty and there has been no recent restatement of the principle in treaty form to include subsequent developments.

The Soviet Union seeks to replace custom with treaty-law whenever possible. The United Nations Charter has been the chief vehicle for accomplishing this end. In recent years the codification work of the International Law Commission (ILC) has become increasingly important. Yet it must be admitted that treaty-law does not suffice to explain the "bindingness" of every principle of international law. Several universal principles of a fundamental character, as for example those relating to recognition, have their source solely in custom. Other fundamental principles, such as peaceful coexistence, sovereign equality of states, national self-determination and non-intervention, at least in part, have their source in custom. Where treaty-law leaves a gap; custom steps in. The chapters which follow develop this theme.

NOTES

[1]Akademiia nauk SSSR, Institut gosudarstva i prava, *International Law: A Textbook For Use in Law Schools*, translated by Dennis Ogden, (Moscow: Foreign Languages Publishing House, n.d.), p. 89.

[2]N.M. Minasian reported the following twelve basic principles of international law to the Second Annual Meeting of the Soviet Association of International Law: (1) The principle of peaceful coexistence and cooperation of states of two opposing systems to achieve universal peace and to secure the progress of countries and peoples; (2) sovereignty and territorial integrity; (3) non-interference in the internal affairs of other states; (4) the right of nations to self-determination; (5) non-aggression; (6) prohibition of aggressive wars; (7) the principle of just and democratic peace; (8) equality of states and nations, large and small; (9) inviolability of diplomatic representation; (10) *pacta sunt servanda;* (11) the principle of freedom of the high seas; and (12) peaceful settlement of international disputes. "Proceedings of the Second Annual Meeting of the Soviet Association of International Law," *1959 Sovetskii ezhegodnik mezhdunarodnogo prava* (1959 Soviet Yearbook of International Law), p. 416.

[3]P.Y. Nedbailo, (Ukrainian SSR), Sixth (Legal) Committee of the U.N. General Assembly, A/C.6/SR757/13 (November 12, 1962), p. 117.

[4]Nikita S. Khrushchev, "Speech to the 20th Party Congress," in G.F. Hudson *et al, The Sino-Soviet Dispute* (New York: Praeger, 1961), p. 42. See also, *Program of the CPSU,* 1961, part 1, chapter 8.

[5]See Nikita S. Khrushchev, *Pravda,* February 1956. See also, *The History of the Communist Party of the Soviet Union* (Moscow: Foreign Languages Publishing House, 1964?), p. 97.

[6]See D. Shepilov, *Pravda,* February 13, 1957.

[7]Nikita S. Khrushchev, *Pravda,* June 30, 1957. See also, N.V. Zakharova, "Bilateral Treaties of Friendship, Cooperation and Mutual Aid Among Socialist States," *Sovetskoe gosudarstvo i pravo* (Soviet State and Law), no. 2 (February 1962), p. 83.

[8]Nikita S. Khrushchev as quoted by R.R. Baxter (USA), *Report of the 49th Conference, Hamburg, 1960*, International Law Association, p. 268. See also, Nikita S. Khrushchev, "On Peaceful Coexistence," *Foreign Affairs*, Vol. 38 (October 1959), p. 86; Sh. Sanakoyev, "The Socialist Community and Mankind's Progress," *Mezhdunarodnoe zhizn* (International Affairs), no. 3 (March 1962), p. 12; Grigorii I. Tunkin, "The 22nd Congress of the CPSU and the Tasks of the Soviet Science of International Law," *Sovetskoe gosudarstvo i pravo* (Soviet State and Law), no. 5 (1962), p. 12; and Grigorii I. Tunkin, "Success of the Policy of Peaceful Coexistence," *1962 Sovetskii ezhegodnik mezhdunarodnogo prava* (1962 Soviet Yearbook of International Law), pp. 15-24.

[9]*The History of the Communist Party of the Soviet Union, op. cit.*, p. 644.

[10]Mrs. Zgurskaya (Ukrainian SSR), Sixth (Legal) Committee of the U.N. General Assembly, A/C.6/SR809/21 (November 12, 1963), p. 154.

[11]Grigorii I. Tunkin, "The 22nd Congress of the CPSU and the Tasks of the Soviet Science of International Law," *loc. cit.*, pp. 18-19.

[12]"Soviet Branch Report: Report and Declaration," *Report of the 49th Conference, Hamburg, 1960*, International Law Association, pp. 362-363. See also, Sergei B. Krylov, U.N. *Yearbook of the International Law Commission*, A/CN.4/SR331/1 (April 23, 1956), p. i; Platon D. Morozov (USSR), Sixth (Legal) Committee of the U.N. General Assembly, A/C. 6/SR802/18-38 (October 24, 1963), pp. 109-112; and the entire issue of the *1958 Sovetskii ezhegodnik mezhdunarodnogo prava* (1958 Soviet Yearbook of International Law).

[13]See for discussion: John N. Hazard, "Coexistence Codification Reconsidered," *American Journal of International Law*, Vol. 57 (1963), p. 91; John N. Hazard, "A Pragmatic View of New International Law," *Proceedings of the American Society of International Law*, 57th Year (1963), pp. 80-81; Leon Lipson, "Soviet Impact on International Law," U.S. Department of State, External Research Paper number 156, May 1964, p. 2; Leon Lipson, "Peaceful Coexistence," *Soviet Impact on International Law*, edited by Hans Baade, (New York: Oceana Publications, 1965), p. 36; Oliver Lissitzyn, "Soviet Union and International Law," *International Conciliation*, 542 (March), pp. 18-19; Oliver Lissitzyn, "Book Reviews and Notes," *American Journal of International Law*, Vol. 59 (1965), p. 957; and Edward Mc-Whinney, "Soviet and Western Internal Law and the Cold War in the Era of Bipolarity," *Strategy of World Order*, Vol 2 of *International Law*, edited by Richard A. Falk and Saul H. Mendlovitz, (New York: World Law Fund, 1966), pp. 193-194.

[14]Grigorii I. Tunkin, *Report of the 49th Conference, Hamburg, 1960*, International Law Association, p. 263.

[15]Soviet Branch, "Draft Declaration of Principles of Peaceful Coexistence," *Report of the 50th Conference, Brussels, 1962*, International Law Association.

[16]Richard V. Allen, "Peace and Peaceful Coexistence," *Detente: Cold War Strategies in Transition*, edited by Eleanor Lansing Dulles and Robert D. Crane, (New York: Praeger, 1965), p. 24.

[17]Wolfgang Friedmann, *Changing Structure of International Law*, (New York: Columbia University Press, 1964), p. 16. See also Harold D. Lasswell, "The 'right to coexist' cannot qualify as a novel doctrine in international law; it rephrases a long recognized norm, which is the right of a nation-state, once accepted by the world community, to be protected in continued existence and to enjoy formal equality." "A Brief Discourse About Method in Current Madness," *Proceedings of the American Society of International Law*, 57th Year (1963), p. 73.

[18]Albert Gore, "Principles of International Law Concerning Friendly Relations Among States," *Department of State Bulletin*, Vol. 47 (1962), p. 973.
The following is a summarization of the USSR attempt to have "peaceful coexistence" accepted as a legal norm of international law:
(a) It all began at a series of UNESCO sponsored conferences: The 8th session of the General Conference of UNESCO, Montevideo, 1954, (See, *Records of the General Conference*, pp. 423-431; 482-483; and 507-509); the Stockholm round table conference organized by the International Political Science Association and sponsored by UNESCO, August 20-30, 1955; and the meeting at UNESCO House, Paris, February 17-21, 1956. For an account of UNESCO debates see: John N. Hazard, "Legal Research on Peaceful Coexistence," *American Journal of International Law*, Vol. 51 (1957), p. 63; and "Peaceful Coexistence: A New Challenge to the United Nations," Twelfth Report, Commission to Study the Organization of Peace, Arthur N. Holcombe, Chairman, June 1960.

(b) The Soviet Union and Eastern European jurists in the mid 1950's carried the discussion to private non-governmental international law associations: the 6th Congress of the International Association of Democratic Lawyers, May 22-25, 1956 (See: *Proceedings of the Commission on the Legal Principles of Peaceful Coexistence*). Socialist lawyers first appeared at the 1956 Dubrovnik Meeting of the International Law Association and at that meeting the Committee on "Judicial Aspects of Peaceful Coexistence" was first established. At the 1964 Tokyo Meeting of the International Law Association, the Association changed the name of the Committee on "Judicial Aspects of Peaceful Coexistence" to the Committee on "Principles of International Security and Cooperation" reflecting the change of sentiment concerning further study of "peaceful coexistence." (See: *Report of the 47th Conference, Dubrovnik, 1956*, International Law Association, pp. 17-63; *Report of the 48th Conference, New York, 1958*, International Law Association, pp. 417-505; *Report of the 49th Conference, Hamburg, 1960*, International Law Association, pp. 332-384; *Report of the 50th Conference, Brussels, 1962*, International Law Association, pp. 260-374; and *Report of the 51st Conference, Tokyo, 1964*, International Law Association).

(c) The matter has been raised from time to time in the Sixth (Legal) Committee of the U.N. General Assembly and the U.N. International Law Commission (ILC). See especially the *Summary Records* and *Reports* of the U.N. Committee on Principles of International Law Concerning Friendly Relations and Cooperation Among States, Mexico City Meeting (August 27-October 2, 1964), and the New York Meeting (March 8-April 25, 1966).

[19]Edward McWhinney, *"Peaceful Coexistence" and Soviet-Western International Law.* (Leyden: A.W. Sythoff, 1964), p. 36.

[20]Charles Evans Hughes, "Observations on the Monroe Doctrine," *American Journal of International Law,* Vol. 17 (1923), p. 616.

[21]Quoted by Leon Lipson, "Peaceful Coexistence," *loc. cit.,* p. 871.

[22]See Russel H. Fifield, "The Five Principles of Coexistence," *American Journal of International Law,* Vol. 52 (July 1958), pp. 504-510; and Eugeniusz Wyzner, "Selected Problems of the United Nations Program for Codification and Progressive Development of International Law," *Proceedings of the American Society of International Law,* 56th Year (1962), p. 98.

[23]Lazar Foscanéanu, "Les 'cinq principles' de Coexistence et le Droit International," (The 'Five Principles' of Coexistence of International Law), *Annuaire Français de Droit International* (French Annual of International Law), 1956, pp. 153-156. The four treaties involved India, People's Republic of China; Albania, Bulgaria, Hungary, East Germany, Poland, Rumania, USSR and Czechoslovakia. The 40 bilateral or multilateral declarations involved India, People's Republic of China, Burma, USSR, Yugoslavia, Cambodia, North Viet-Nam, Laos, Indonesia, Poland, Finland, East Germany, Saudi Arabia, Afghanistan, Ethiopia, Egypt, Liberia, Denmark, Sweden, France, Rumania, Belgium, and Syria. The 30 unilateral declarations involved India, People's Republic of China, Burma, Yugoslavia, USSR, Cambodia, Laos, Nepal, Pakistan, Thailand, Turkey and North Viet-Nam.

[24]Grigorii I. Tunkin, "Remarks on the Judicial Nature of Customary Norms of International Law," *California Law Review,* Vol. 49 (August 1961), p. 428.

[25]Bernard Ramundo, *The (Soviet) Socialist Theory of International Law,* (Washington: George Washington University Press, 1964), p. 29. See also, Ivo Lapenna, "Legal Aspects and Political Significance of the Soviet Concept of Peaceful Coexistence," *International and Comparative Law Quarterly,* Vol. 12 (1963), pp. 766-767; and Oliver Lissitzyn, *loc. cit.,* pp. 18-20.

[26]Soviet Union Branch, "Report and Declaration," *Report of the 49th Conference, Hamburg, 1960,* International Law Association, p. 354. See also, Grigorii I. Tunkin, *Osnovy sovremennego mezhdunarodnogo prava* (Fundamental Principles of Contemporary International Law), (Moscow: 1956), p. 17.

[27]Grigorii I. Tunkin, "Coexistence and International Law," *Recueil des Cours* (Collection of Lectures), Vol. 95 (1958-III), p. 65. See also Chapter II, section 6 of this study, "The United Nations Charter as a source of Customary Norms."

[28]Mrs. Zgurskaya (Ukrainian SSR), Sixth (Legal) Committee of the U.N. General Assembly, A/C.6/SR809/21 (November 12, 1963), p. 154. See additionally, Soviet Union Branch, "Report and Declaration," *Report of the 49th Conference, Hamburg, 1960.* International Law Association, pp. 362-363; V.M. Chikvadze, "Problems of International Law at the 20th Sessions of the General Assembly of the UNO," *Sovetskoe gosudarstvo i pravo* (Soviet State and Law), no. 3 (May 1966), pp. 67-78; A.P. Movchan, "Codification of the International Legal Principles of Peaceful Coexistence," *1963 Sovetskii ezhegodnik mezhdunarodnogo prava* (1963 Soviet Yearbook of International Law), pp. 15-30.
Another reason why Soviet scholars feel uncomfortable with their present position concerning the "source" of the juridical principle of peaceful coexistence is that it requires

them to undertake a liberal construction of the United Nations Charter — to read a principle into it. This contradicts the general Soviet position of strict interpretation.

[29]See Vladimir M. Koretskii, U.N. *Yearbook of the International Law Commission*, A/CN.4 /SR21/ (May 16, 1949), p. 155; and Soviet Union Branch, "Report and Declaration," *Report of the 49th Conference, Hamburg, 1960*, International Law Association, p. 357.

[30]Sergei B. Krylov, *Report of the 47th Conference, Dubrovnik, 1956*, International Law Association, p. 42.

[31]V.V. Evgenyev, "Subjects of Law, Sovereignty and Non-Intervention in International Law," *Sovetskoe gosudarstvo i pravo* (Soviet State and Law), no. 2 (March 1955), p. 77.

[32]See N.N. Polyanskii, "The Principle of Sovereignty in the Security Council," *Sovetskoe gosudarstvo i pravo*, no. 3 (1946), p. 30ff.

[33]Of necessity the actions of the Soviet State toward Finland (1939), Poland (1939), Hungary (1956) and Czechoslovakia (1968) have demanded a certain rationalization. See, concerning Finland (1939), Fedor I. Kozhevnikov, "Creative Role of the USSR in the Just Solution of Territorial Problems," *Panstwo i prawo* (State and Law), no. 12 (1950), p. 4; concerning Poland (1939), V.M. Molotov's broadcast to the Soviet People of September 17, 1939, *Pravda* reprint, October 31, 1939; V.M. Molotov, "On the Foreign Policy of the Soviet Union," before the 5th Extraordinary Session of the Supreme Soviet, October 31, 1939; and Georg Ginsburg, "Case Study in the Soviet Use of International Law: Eastern Poland 1939," *American Journal of International Law*, Vol. 52 (January 1958), pp. 69-84; concerning Hungary (1956), Grigorii I. Tunkin, "On Some Problems of International Treaties . . ." *Sovetskoe gosudarstvo i pravo* (Soviet State and Law), no. 1 (1956), p. 103; and concerning Czechoslovakia (1968), S. Kovalyov, "Sovereignty and International Obligations of Socialist States," *Pravda*, September 26, 1968; and Helmut Schmidt, "The Consequences of the Brezhnev Doctrine," *Atlantic Community Quarterly*, no. 7 (Summer 1969), pp. 184-195.

[34]See Vladimir M. Koretskii, U.N. Sixth (Legal) Committee of the U.N. General Assembly, A/C.6/SR183/63 (November 3, 1949), p. 278; and A/C.6/SR176/76 (October 28, 1949), p. 229.

[35]Mr. Khlestov (USSR), 1964 Mexico City Meeting of the U.N. Special Committee on Principles of International Law Concerning Friendly Relations and Cooperation Among States, A/AC.119/SR22/ (September 14, 1964), p. 28.

[36]Akademii nauk SSSR, Institut gosudarstva i prava, *International Law, op. cit.*, pp. 96-97.

[37]*Ibid.*, p. 130.

[38]David B. Levin, *Osnovnye problemy sovremennogo mezhdunarodnogo prava* (Fundamental Problems of Contemporary International Law), (Moscow: 1958), pp. 114-115. See also, David B. Levin, "What Hides Behind the Theory of the 'Primacy' of International Law Over State Law," *Sovetskoe gosudarstvo i pravo* (Soviet State and Law), no. 7 (1955), p. 116; and I.P. Blishchenko, "The Theory of the Primacy of International Law in the Practice of the USA," *Voprosy mezhdunarodnogo prava v teorii i praktiki SShA* (Questions of International Law in the Theory and Practice of the USA), edited by Evgenii A. Korovin, (Moscow: 1957), pp. 173-175.

[39]See Andrei Ia. Vyshinskii, *Voprosy mezhdunarodnogo prava i mezhdunarodnoi politiki* (Questions of International Law and International Politics), (Moscow: 1948), pp. 476-481; I.P. Blishchenko, *Mezhdunarodnoi i vnutrigosudarstvennoe pravo* (International and Internal Law), (Moscow: 1960), pp. 198-199; and David B. Levin, "The Problem of the Correlation of International Law and Internal State Law," in *Sbornik statei po filosofii, istorii, pravu* (Collection of Articles on Philosophy, History and Law), (Moscow: 1957), pp. 87-91.

[40]Soviet jurists envisage no difficulty of conflict between the two systems. See, Vladimir M.

Koretskii, *Ocshchie printsipy prava v. mezhdunarodnom prave* (General Principle of Law in International Law), (Moscow: 1957), p. 8; David B. Levin, "The Problem of the Correlation of International and Internal State Law," *loc. cit.*, p. 95; and N.V. Moronov, "On the Relationship of International Treaty and Municipal Law," *1963 Sovetskii ezhegodnik mezhdunarodnogo prava* (1963 Soviet Yearbook of International Law), pp. 15-170.

[41]Evgenii A. Korovin, "The Second World War and International Law," *American Journal of International Law*, Vol. 40 (1946), pp. 743-747. See also: Sergei B. Krylov, "Les Notions Principales du Droit des Gens (La Doctrine Soviétique du Droit International)," (The Principal Notion of the Law of Nations: The Soviet Doctrine of International Law), *Recueil des Cours* (Collection of Lectures), Vol. 70 (1947-I), pp. 466-467.

[42]For the Nuremberg history see: *The Charter and Judgment of the Nuremberg Tribunal. History and Analysis*, U.N. Document A/CN.4/5 (March 3, 1949).

[43]Vladimir M. Koretskii, U.N. *Yearbook of the International Law Commission*, A/CN.4/SR29 (May 27, 1949), p. 213.

[44]Charles de Visscher, *Theory and Reality in Public International Law*, translated by Percy E. Corbett, (Princeton: Princeton University Press, 1957), p. 101.

[45]See the following cases for Soviet criticism of the International Court's jurisdiction: "Separate Opinion of Judges Basadevant, Alvarez, Winarski, Zoričič, de Visscher, Badawi Pasha, and Krylov," *Corfu Channel Case: Judgment on Preliminary Objections*, ICJ Reports 1948, pp. 31-32; "Dissenting Opinion of Judge Krylov," *Admission of a State to the United Nations (Charter, Article 4)*, ICJ Reports 1948, pp. 108-109; Sergei B. Krylov's comments on *Anglo-Iranian Oil Company Case, Interim Protection and Preliminary Objections, Sovetskoe gosudarstvo i pravo* (Soviet State and Law), no. 1 (1952), p. 73; "Declaration of Judge Kozhevnikov," *Concerning Right of Passage Over Indian Territory, Preliminary Objections,* ICJ Reports 1957, p. 153 and *Merits*, ICJ Reports 1960, p. 52; and "Declaration of Judge Koretskii," *Case Concerning the Northern Cameroons (Cameroons v. United Kingdom)*, ICJ Reports 1963, pp. 39-40. See the following cases for Soviet approval of the International Court's assumption of jurisdiction: *Status of Eastern Carelia Case*, PCIJ Publication C, no. 3, Vol. 1 (1923). p. 70; comments of Judge Krylov concerning the *Case of the Monetary Gold Removed From Rome in 1943, Preliminary Objections* and the *Case of the Treatment in Hungary of Aircraft of the United States of America* in article by Zigurds L. Zile, "Soviet Contribution to International Adjudication: Professor Krylov's Jurisprudential Legacy," *American Journal of International Law*, Vol. 58 (April 1964), p. 369. See also, Sergei B. Krylov, *Mezhdunarodnyi sud* (The International Court of Justice), (Moscow: 1958), p. 10; and Ivo Lapenna, *Conceptions Sovietique de Droit International Public* (Soviet Conceptions of Public International Law), (Paris: A. Pedone, 1954), p. 299.

[46]See remarks of Vladimir M. Koretskii (USSR), Sixth (legal) Committee of the U.N. General Assembly, A/C.6/SR164/15 (October 15, 1949), p. 140; and Mr. Baranovskii (Ukrainian SSR), A/C.6/SR324/1 (November 11, 1952), p. 111.

[47]See concerning the Genocide Convention, U.N. Document A/CN.4/SR10 (April 27, 1949); for discussion as well see remarks of Platon D. Morozov (USSR), Sixth (Legal) Committee of the U.N. General Assembly, A/C.6/SR243/1 (November 23, 1950), p. 223. See concerning Convention on Privileges and Immunities of United Nations, *Sobranie deistvuiushchikh dogovorov SSSR* (Collection of Treaties of the USSR in Force), Vol. 15, p. 40; or the *United Nations Treaty Series* (UNTS), Vol. 15, p. 1.

[48]See D.V. Bykov, "Agreements on the Legal Status of Soviet Troops Temporarily Quartered Abroad," *1958 Sovetskii ezhegodnik mezhdunarodnogo prava* (1958 Soviet Yearbook of International Law), pp. 381-387; M.I. Lazarev, "Groundlessness of the Conception of the Immunity of the U.S. Armed Forces Abroad," *1959 Sovetskii ezhegodnik mezhdunarodnogo prava* (1959 Soviet Yearbook of International Law), pp. 283-299. In this article Lazarev denies the existence of a customary principle of international law granting to the forces of one state while on the territory of another immunity from the laws of the host country.

See also, S.V. Molodstov, "Some Problems of Territory in International Law," *Sovetskoe gosudarstvo i pravo* (Soviet State and Law), no. 8 (1955), pp. 63-73, especially p. 69.

[49]Soviet spokesmen have acknowledged custom as a source of the principle of immunity of state shipping vessels. See Platon D. Morozov (USSR), Sixth (Legal) Committee of the U.N. General Assembly, A/C.6/SR488/20-21 (December 3, 1956); Mr. Keilin (USSR), 1958 U.N. Conference on the Law of the Sea, A/CONF. 13/SR25/18-29 (April 3, 1958).

For western writings see: Harold J. Berman, "Force Majeure and the Denial of an Export License Under Soviet Law," *Harvard Law Review*, Vol. 73 (April 1960), pp. 1128-1146; and Martin Domke, "The Israeli-Soviet Oil Arbitration," *American Journal of International Law*, Vol. 53 (1959), pp. 787-796.

For claims of immunity of state news agencies see: *Krajena v. Tass Agency*, 1949, 2 All England Law Reports, p. 274 or *Journal du Droit International* (Journal of International Law), Vol. 77 (1950), p. 872.

[50]P.Y. Nedbailo and V.A. Vassilenko, "Soviet Union Republics as Subjects of International Law," *1963 Sovetskii ezhegodnik mezhdunarodnogo prava* 1963 Soviet Yearbook of International Law), p. 105.

[51]See Vladimir M. Koretskii, Sixth (Legal) Committee of the U.N. General Assembly, A/C.6 /SR160/93 (October 13, 1949), p. 111; Grigorii I. Tunkin, U.N. *Yearbook of the International Law Commission*, A/CN.4/SR669/3 (June 27, 1962), p. 267; David B. Levin, "Falsification of the Concept of International Law by Bourgeois Pseudo-Scholarship," *Sovetskoe gosudarstvo i pravo* (Soviet State and Law), no. 4 (April 1952), pp. 55-63; and V.V. Evgenev, "Subjects of Law, Sovereignty and Non-Intervention in International Law," *Sovetskoe gosudarstvo i pravo* (Soviet State and Law), no. 2 (March 1955), pp. 75-84.

[52]In the 1930's E.A. Korovin, for example, listed other subjects of international law: worker's and other proletarian organizations, the Vatican, the League of Nations, international unions and commissions, the Red Cross and primitive peoples. See Hans Kelsen, *Communist Theory of Law* (New York: Praeger, 1955), p. 164. The only "subject" listed by Korovin which is recognized today is the Holy See, which is recognized as a "state." See Grigorii I. Tunkin, U.N. *Yearbook of the International Law Commission*, A/CN.4/SR669/3 (June 27, 1962), p. 267.

[53]See Fedor I. Kozhevnikov (ed.), *Mezhdunarodnoe pravo* (International Law), (Moscow: 1957), p. 87; David B. Levin, *Osnovnye problemy sovremennogo mezhdunarodnogo prava* (Basic Problems of Contemporary International Law), (Moscow: 1958), p. 79; Lidija A. Modzhorian, *Subekty mezhdunarodnogo prava* (Subjects of International Law), (Moscow: 1958), p. 8; G.B. Starushenko, *Printsip samo-opredeleniya narodnov i natsii vo vneshnei politike sovetskogo* (The Principle of National Self-Determination in Soviet Foreign Policy), (Moscow: 1960), pp. 143-145; Evgenii A. Korovin, "Sovereignty and Peace," *Mezhdunarodnaia zhizn* (International Affairs), Vol. 9 (1960), pp. 9-18; and Sergei B. Krylov, "A Contribution to the Discussion of Questions of Theory of International Law," *Sovetskoe gosudarstvo i pravo* (Soviet State and Law), no. 7 (November 1954), p. 76.

[54]See Josef V. Stalin, "The Policy of the Soviet Government on the National Question in Russia," *Pravda*, October 10, 1920 as quoted in *Works of J.V. Stalin, Vol. 4, pp. 363-364.*

[55]The origin of the "Brezhnev Doctrine" is in dispute. It has alternatively been attributed to (1) an article by S. Kovalyov, "Sovereignty and International Obligations of Socialist Countries," *Pravda*, September 16, 1968: (2) a speech by Andrei Gromyko (USSR Foreign Minister) to the U.N. General Assembly, October 3, 1968; or (3) a speech of Leonid Brezhnev (First Secretary of the CPSU), at Warsaw on November 12, 1968. See: Helmut Schmidt, *loc. cit.*, pp. 184-185.

Brezhnev clearly stated the Doctrine on November 12, 1968, in his Warsaw speech, "If the internal and external enemies of socialism think they can attempt to direct the development of any single socialist country to a restoration of the capitalist system, if there then arises a threat to socialism in this country which is a threat to the security of the entire socialist community of states, then this is not merely a problem for the country concerned, but a general problem that must engage the attention of all socialist states." See: Helmut Schmidt, *loc. cit.*, p. 185.

[56]S. Kovalyov, *loc. cit.*, *Pravda*, September 26, 1968.

[57]See, Helmut Schmidt, *loc. cit.*, pp. 184-185. Several other socialist states have expressed concern over the implications of the "Brezhnev Doctrine" for them. See, L. Radovanovic, *Review of International Affairs* (Yugoslavia), October 5, 1968. Rumanian Communist Party Leader Nicolae Ceauseau rejected the Doctrine on November 29, 1968. See, Helmut Schmidt, *loc. cit.*, p. 189.

[58]See Helmut Schmidt, *loc. cit.*, pp. 184-185.

[59]N.A. Ushakov, "International Law and Sovereignty," *Contemporary International Law*, edited by Grigorii I. Tunkin, (Moscow: Progress Publishers, 1969), p. 98.

[60]See Wolfgang Friedmann, *op. cit.*, p. 67.

[61]Individuals are not subjects of international law. See: Vladimir M. Koretskii, U.N. *Yearbook of the International Law Commission*, A/CN.4/SR29/25 (May 27, 1949), p. 210; Fedor I. Kozhevnikov, U.N. *Yearbook of the International Law Commission*, A/CN.4/SR 211/28 (July 8, 1953), pp. 172-173; A/CN.4/SR219/52 (July 20, 1953), p. 233; A/CN.4/SR220/4 (July 21, 1953), p. 235; and A/CN.4/SR223, 14-16 (July 24, 1953), pp. 259-260; Platon D. Morozov (USSR), Sixth (Legal) Committe of the U.N. General Assembly, A/C.6/SR401/52 (October 12, 1954), p. 25; Akademii nauk SSSR, Institut gosudarstva i prava, *International Law, op. cit.*, pp. 131-135; V.V. Evgenev, *loc. cit.*, pp. 75-76; Evgenii A. Korovin, "New Textbooks on International Law," *Sovetskoe gosudarstvo i pravo* (Soviet State and Law), no. 8 (1948), p. 72; Sergei B. Krylov, "A Contribution to the Discussion of Questions of the Theory of International Law," *loc. cit.*, p. 77; and David B Levin, "Falsification of the Concept of International Law by Bourgeois Pseudo-Scholarship," *loc. cit.*, pp. 55-63.

[62]Vladimir M. Koretskii, U.N. *Yearbook of the International Law Commission*, A/CN.4/SR19 (April 25, 1949), p. 71.

[63]Mr. Khlestov (USSR), 1964 Mexico City Meeting of the U.N. Special Committee on Principles of International Law Concerning Friendly Relations and Cooperation Among States, A/AC.119/SR35/ (September 24, 1964), pp. 17-18. See also, Platon D. Morozov (USSR), Sixth (Legal) Committee of the U.N. General Assembly, A/C.6/SR802/33-35 (October 29, 1963), p. 112; and G.A. Osnitskaya, "Colonialist Concepts of Equal and Unequal Subjects of International Law in the Theory and Practice of Imperialist States," *1962 Sovetskii ezhegodnik mezhdunarodnogo prava* (1962 Soviet Yearbook of International Law), pp. 49-63.

[64]James L. Brierly, *The Law of Nations* (Oxford: Oxford University Press, 1958), 6th edition, Chapter 4, para. 3, "The Doctrine of Equality of States." See also, H. Weinschel, "The Doctrine of the Equality of States and Its Recent Modification," *American Journal of International Law*, Vol. 45 (1951), pp. 417-442.

[65]See S.V. Molodstov, "The Rule of Unanimity of the Permanent Members of the Security Council — The Immovable Foundation of the United Nations," *Sovetskoe gosudarstvo i pravo* (Soviet State and Law), pp. 44-57; and N.A. Ushakov, "The Right of Veto in the United Nations," *1959 Sovetskii ezhegodnik mezhdunarodnogo prava* (1959 Soviet Yearbook of International Law), pp. 221-228.

[66]Evgenii A. Korovin, "The Second World War and International Law," *loc. cit.*, p. 747.

[67]Sergei B. Krylov, "Les Notions Principales du Droit des Gens (La Doctrine Soviétique du Droit International)," (Principal Notions of the Law of Nations: The Soviet Doctrine of International Law), *loc. cit.*, p. 453.

⁶⁸See for example, Grigorii I. Tunkin (USSR), Second Plenary Meeting, 1958 U.N. Conference on the Law of the Sea, A/CONF.13/SR2/19-20 (February 25, 1958), p. 5.

⁶⁹See Grigorii I. Tunkin, "Coexistence and International Law," *loc. cit.,* p. 14.

⁷⁰Mr. Khlestov (USSR), 1964 Mexico City Meeting of the U.N. Special Committee on Principles of International Law Concerning Friendly Relations and Cooperation Among States, A/AC.119/SR35/ (September 24, 1964), pp. 16-17.

⁷¹See Grigorii I. Tunkin, "Remarks on the Judicial Nature of Customary Norms of International Law," *loc. cit.,* p. 422.

⁷²Mr. Keilin (USSR), 1958 U.N. Conference on the Law of the Sea, A/CONF.13/C.2/SR 25/16 (April 3, 1958), p. 69. The maxim, *par in parem non habet imperium,* translates "An equal has no dominion over an equal." It is to be noted that all Soviet vessels are government ships.

⁷³*Ibid.,* A/CONF.13/C.2/SR25/18-25 (April 3, 1958), pp. 69-70. See also, Platon D. Morozov (USSR), Sixth (Legal) Committee of the U.N. General Assembly, A/C.6/SR488/20 (December 3, 1956), p. 37. It is interesting to note that several of the "concrete principles" which the USSR recognizes (such as immunity of state owned vessels) have their source in custom, whereas the more abstract principles such as peaceful coexistence and sovereign equality of states are grounded in the United Nations Charter.

⁷⁴G.B. Starushenko, *The Principle of National Self-Determination in Soviet Foreign Policy,* (Moscow: Foreign Languages Publishing House, 1963?), p. 6. See also, the statement of G. B. Starushenko (USSR), *Report of the 51st Conference, Tokyo, 1964,* International Law Association, pp. 789-792 and at the 1966 New York Meeting of the U.N. Special Committee on Principles of International Law Concerning Friendly Relations and Cooperation Among States, A/AC125/.

⁷⁵For a brief examination of the Soviet position on non-self-governing and trust territories see: Georg Ginsburg, "Wars of National Liberation and the Modern Law of Nations — The Soviet Thesis," *Soviet Impact on International Law,* edited by Hans Baade, *op. cit.,* p. 81.

⁷⁶David B. Levin, "The Principle of Self-Determination of Nations in International Law," *1962 Sovetskii ezhegodnik mezhdunarodnogo prava* (1962 Soviet Yearbook of International Law), p. 47.

⁷⁷G.B. Starushenko, *op. cit.,* p. 173.

⁷⁸*Ibid.,* p. 180.

⁷⁹*Ibid.,* p. 169.

⁸⁰David B. Levin, "The Principle of Self-Determination of Nations in International Law," *loc. cit.,* pp. 25-48.

⁸¹Mr. Khlestov (USSR), 1964 Mexico City Meeting of the U.N. Special Committee on Principles of International Law Concerning Friendly Relations and Cooperation Among States, A/AC.119/SR14/ (September 8, 1964), p. 11. General Assembly Resolution 1514(XV) is the "Declaration on Granting of Independence to Colonial Countries and Peoples," adopted December 14, 1960.

⁸²For western commentary on the "principle" of national self-determination see, Harold Briggs, *International Law,* 2nd edition, (New York: Appleton-Century Crofts, 1952), p. 65; Clyde Eagleton, "Self Determination in the United Nations," *American Journal of International Law,* Vol. 47 (1953), p. 88; Leland Goodrich and E. Hambro, *Charter of the United Nations* (1946), p. 235; and Hans Kelsen, *The Law of the United Nations: A Critical Analysis of Its Fundamental Problems* (1950), pp. 50-51.

[83]G.B. Starushenko, *op. cit.*, p. 160.

[84]*Ibid.*, p. 162. See for similar view, Grigorii I. Tunkin, "Coexistence and International Law," *loc. cit.*, p. 67; and Tuzmukhamedov, "Peaceful Coexistence and Wars of National Liberation," *Sovetskoe gosudarstvo i pravo* (Soviet State and Law), no. 3 (1963), pp. 92-93.

[85]*Ibid.*, p. 163. See also Lazar Foscaneánu, *loc. cit.*, pp. 153-156.

[86]For discussion see: Mr. Kazantsev (USSR), 1964 Mexico City Meeting of the U.N. Special Committee on Principles of International Law Concerning Friendly Relations and Cooperation Among States, A/AC.119/SR28 (September 21, 1964), pp. 12-13; and Soviet Union Branch, "Report and Declaration," *Report of the 51st Conference, Tokyo, 1964*, International Law Association, p. 357.

[87]Mr. Kazantsev (USSR), 1964 Mexico City Meeting of the U.N. Special Committee on Principles of International Law Concerning Friendly Relations and Cooperation Among States, A/AC.119/SR28/ (September 21, 1964), pp. 15-16. For a similar view see, Evgenii A. Korovin, (ed.), *Mezhdunarodnoe pravo* (International Law), (Moscow: 1951), pp. 195-196.

[88]Akademii nauk SSSR, Institut gosudarstva i prava, *International Law, op. cit.*, p. 115.

[89]*Ibid.*

[90]Soviet Union Branch, "Report and Declaration," *Report of the 51st Conference, Tokyo, 1964*, International Law Association, p. 357. For similar statement see, Mr. Kazantsev (USSR), 1964 Mexico City Meeting of the U.N. Special Committee on Principles of International Law Concerning Friendly Relations and Cooperation Among States, A/AC.119/SR28 (September 21, 1964), pp. 12-13; Grigorii I. Tunkin, *Droit International Public* (Public International Law), translation of *Voprosy teorii mezhdunarodnoe prava* (Theoretical Questions of International Law), (Paris: A. Pedone, 1965), p. 37; and Lidija A. Modzhorian, "The Restoration of China's Legitimate Rights in the U.N.", *1959 Sovetskii ezhegodnik mezhdunarodnogo prava* (1959 Soviet Yearbook of International Law), p. 209.

[91]A.S. Piradov and G.B. Starushenko, "Non-Intervention and Contemporary International Law," *1958 Sovetskii ezhegodnik mezhdunarodnogo prava* (1958 Soviet Yearbook of International Law), p. 251.

[92]Platon D. Morozov (USSR), Sixth (Legal) Committee of the U.N. General Assembly, A/C.6/SR802/30 (October 29, 1963), p. 111. For further discussion see, Mr. Kazantsev (USSR), 1964 Mexico City Meeting of the U.N. Special Committee on Principles of International Law Concerning Friendly Relations and Cooperation Among States, A/AC.119/SR28 (September 21, 1964), p. 11.

[93]Grigorii I. Tunkin, *Droit International Public* (Public International Law), *op. cit.*, p. 77.

[94]Mr. Kazantsev (USSR), 1964 Mexico City Meeting of the U.N. Special Committee on Principles of International Law Concerning Friendly Relations and Cooperation Among States, A/AC.119/SR28 (September 21, 1964), p. 11.

[95]See, Article 2(7) of the U.N. Charter, "Nothing contained in the present Charter shall authorize the United Nations to interfere in matters which are essentially within the domestic jurisdiction of any state or shall require the Member to submit such matters to settlement under the present Charter; but this principle shall not prejudice the application of enforcement measures under Chapter VII."

[96]Mr. Kazantsev (USSR), 1964 Mexico City Meeting of the U.N. Special Committee on Principles of International Law Concerning Friendly Relations and Cooperation Among States, A/AC.119/SR28 (September 21, 1964), p. 15.

[97]*Ibid.* See for further discussion, Platon D. Morozov (USSR), Sixth (Legal) Committee of the U.N. General Assembly, A/C.6/SR802/32 (October 29, 1963), p. 111; and Lazar Foscancánu, *loc. cit.*, pp. 153-156.

[98]Akademii nauk SSSR, Institut gosudarstva i prava, *International Law, op. cit.*, p. 117. See also, M.I. Lazarev, "International Law of Recognition of States and Governments," in *Mehdunarodnoe pravo* (International Law), edited by Evgenii A. Korovin, (Moscow: 1951), p. 175.

[99]See T.B. Tcherepakhina, *Prizananiye v mezhdunarodnom publichnom prava* (Recognition in Public International Law), published in *Uceniye zapiski* (Scientific Reports), Institute of Sverdlovsk, 1947.

[100]Selective recognition has been practiced by the Soviet Union. See for example, USSR recognition of the Union of Zanzibar and Tanganyika. See Bernard A. Ramundo, *Peaceful Coexistence: International Law and the Building of Communism*, (Baltimore: Johns Hopkins University Press, 1967), p. 100.

[101]D.I. Feldman, "Some Forms and Methods of International Recognition of New States," *1963 Sovetskii ezhegodnik mezhdunarodnogo prava* (1963 Soviet Yearbook of International Law), p. 129. For a similar view see, D.I. Feldman, *Priznanie pravielstv v mezhdunarodnum prave* (Recognition of Governments in International Law), (Kazan: University of Kazan, 1961); and V.K. Sobakin, *Sovremennoe mezhdunarodnoe pravo* (Present-Day International Law), "Resolution of the 40th Session of the Institute of International Law of New States and Governments," 13 March 1963, (Moscow: 1964), pp. 88-92.

[102]Akademii nauk SSSR, Institut gosudarstva i prava, *International Law, op. cit.*, p. 117.

[103]Constitutive theory as described by L. Oppenheim, *International Law*, 6th edition, (London: 1947), Vol. 1, pp. 122-123.

[104]Akademii nauk SSSR, Institut gosudarstva i prava, *International Law, op. cit.*, p. 118. See for a similar view, Vladimir M. Koretskii, U.N. *Yearbook of the International Law Commission*, A/CN.4/SR11/22 (April 27, 1949), p. 85; Lidija A. Modzhorian, *Osnovnye prava in obiazannosti gosudarstv* (Fundamental Rights and Duties of States), (Moscow: 1965); and D.I. Feldman, *loc. cit.*, p. 149.

[105]*Ibid.*

[106]D.I. Feldman, *loc. cit.*, p. 147.

[107]Akademii nauk SSSR, Institut gosudarstva i prava, *International Law, op. cit.*, pp. 120-121.

[108]See for example, Vladimir M. Koretskii, U.N. *Yearbook of the International Law Commission*, A/CN.4/SR11 (April 27, 1949), p. 85; Akademii nauk SSSR, Institut gosudarstva i prava, *International Law, op. cit.*, pp. 117-118; D.I. Feldman, *op. cit.*, pp. 225 and 241-242; and D.I. Feldman, *loc. cit.*, p. 149.

[109]Akademii nauk SSR, Institut gosudarstva i prava, *International Law, op. cit.*, p. 118.

[110]*Ibid.*, pp. 120-121.

[111]See for discussion, D.I. Feldman, *op. cit.*, pp. 241-242; D.I. Feldman, *Sovremennye teorii mezhdunarodno-pravovogo priznaniya* (Present-Day Theory of International Legal Recognition), (Kazan: University of Kazan, 1963); Lidija A. Modzhorian, *op. cit.*; and D.I. Feldman, *loc. cit.*

CHAPTER IV.
INTERNATIONAL TREATIES

An international treaty is defined by Soviet scholars as "a formally expressed agreement between two or more states regarding the establishment, amendment and termination of their reciprocal rights and obligations."[1] There are exceptions to this definition such as the oral Treaty of Alliance between Peter I and Augustus II in 1698 and the so-called "Gentlemen's Agreement" between the Soviet Union and the Mongolian People's Republic of November 27, 1934,[2] but the written form is considered typical. The International Law Commission (ILC) reiterated the traditional view of "treaty" in Article 1 of the Draft Convention on the Law of Treaties,

(a) treaty means an international agreement concluded between states in written form and governed by international law, whether embodied in a single instrument or in two or more instruments and whatever its particular designation.[3]

A distinction must be drawn between "treaty law" and the "laws of treaty-making." "Treaty law" is law created through treaty (Article 38a of the Statute of the International Court of Justice) in contrast to custom (Article 38b of the Statute). "Laws of treaty-making" are those principles which govern the methods by which treaties are made and fulfilled. Some of these principles have themselves been created through treaty, but in contemporary international law the great majority of them have their source in custom.[4] Among the principles of "treaty-making" considered in this chapter are those of *pacta sunt servanda* (treaties are to be obeyed), *clausula rebus sic stantibus* (if conditions fundamentally change, a treaty obligation may be ignored through invalidation), unequal treaties, *res inter alios gesta* (state succession), and *jus cogens* (there are some principles of customary international law which are so fundamental that no treaty can contravene them).

1. The Principle of Pacta Sunt Servanda

(a) Meaning
"Without the recognition of the principle that international treaties must be observed there could be no intercourse between peoples and no international law,"[5] notes a Soviet law text. Through the concept of *pacta sunt servanda* states agree to be law-abiding. The principle is a recognition of the need for rules of the game *vis-à-vis* nation-to-nation dealings, an expression of the desire for certainty and foreseeability. Nothing could be more basic for orderly international relations.

Today the Soviet Union is firmly committed to this principle, although this has not always been the case. In the early years of Bolshevik rule, at a time when Leon Trotskii was proclaiming the uselessness of the Foreign

Ministry, Soviet legal scholars in unison were denouncing the principle of *pacta sunt servanda* and justifying Soviet violation of Tsarist treaty commitments.[6] As the revolution yielded to reason and political pressures, the Soviet State came to accept the validity of the principle that "treaties must be obeyed." Judge Sergei Krylov, writing in 1957, said of this principle, that it was "something taken for granted." He added,

Among international lawyers of various countries and differing political views there is not the slightest difference of opinion concerning the fact that this principle is the basis of all international relations and derives from the very nature of intercourse among states. As a matter of fact, when this principle lapses, international law is replaced by the law of force.[7]

This principle serves the USSR in two ways: First, there is the ordering aspect. *Pacta sunt servanda* provides a basis for arguing that treaty arrangements entered into by the Soviet Union with the West, the Third World or other socialist states will be fully observed. In terms of foreign policy objectives it is desirable to be able to hold treaty partners to favorable treaty provisions. The Soviet Union is well-known as a firm advocate of the strict interpretation of treaty instruments. The United Nations Charter is an example.

Second, there is a provocative aspect. The principle of *pacta sunt servanda* can serve the narrow-national interests of the Soviet Union by providing the basis for a legal argument for condemning as "improper" the actions of other states in an effort to discredit them. Attention is drawn to the dissenting opinion of Judge Kozhevnikov, Soviet Judge on the International Court of Justice, in the *Case of the Application of the Convention of 1902 Governing the Guardianship of Infants (Netherlands v. Sweden),* as an example.[8] In that opinion, based exclusively on the principle of *pacta sunt servanda,* Kozhevnikov castigated the Swedish Government for failing to live up to its obligations under the 1902 Convention.

From the viewpoint of the Soviet policy-maker, however, exacting application of this principle to every treaty would have its disadvantages. *Pacta sunt servanda* can be a two-edged sword. If the Soviet Union can wield it, others can too. If the Soviet Union can use it to impress upon others the need to observe treaty obligations, others may impress the same fact upon the Soviet Foreign Ministry. Likewise, if the Soviet Union can use it to criticize the "improper activities" of other states, so too, others may criticize the policies of the Soviet Union. Russian foreign policy demands a selective application of this principle.[9]

There is an axiom in the law — no principle without exceptions. It is through the device of exceptions that selectivity is achieved. The exceptions themselves are treated as "principles" of international law and may include, for example, *clausula rebus sic stantibus,* unequal treaties, and *res inter alios gesta* (state succession). It is important to recognize that the Soviet Union recognizes *pacta sunt servanda* but, like all states, not too much *servanda.*

(b) Source

In the Soviet view, contemporary international law is chiefly the law of international treaties. Yet, paradoxically, the principle of *pacta sunt servanda*, the fundamental principle of "treaty-making," is a customary norm of international law.[10] When the question is hypothetically posed, "From whence does the principle of peaceful coexistence derive its legitimacy?" The Soviet scholar would answer, "Between the Soviet Union and another member of the U.N. it derives its source of legality from the Charter, a treaty." The question may then be asked, "Why obey, from a legal point of view, the Charter of the United Nations?" The Soviet response given is, "*Pacta sunt servanda,* a customary norm requires it." In the last analysis, even in Soviet eyes, does not international law rest on custom?

It would be possible, no doubt, for Soviet academicians to imply a good faith notion into the United Nations Charter and convert *pacta sunt servanda* into a treaty norm. They have not sought to do so. Perhaps because it would run counter to their announced position of strict construction of the U.N. Charter. Whatever the reason, Soviet scholars and practitioners have striven instead for the codification of this customary principle into treaty law. The work of the International Law Commission (ILC) on the "Draft Convention on the Law of Treaties" has been the vehicle in this regard.[11]

2. The "Principle" Of Clausula Rebus Sic Stantibus

Clausula rebus sic stantibus, meaning that "upon a change in that state of facts whose continued existence was envisaged when the treaty was concluded" the treaty may be annulled, is one way around the rigors of *pacta sunt servanda.*[12] The source of such a "principle"[13] would have to be custom as there is no treaty-law to that effect. In the Soviet view custom requires "agreement". Whether the Soviet Union would be willing to "accept" *rebus sic stantibus*, which it has criticized in the past as arbitrary, extremely broad and as granting to states too much latitude as to whether they will adhere to their treaty obligations or not,[14] remains uncertain. To date Soviet jurists have found western proposals of a *rebus sic stantibus* principle as too revolutionary and they have resisted any such liberalizing trend. However, beginning in 1963, there have been some signs of Soviet willingness to accept a limited version of *rebus sic stantibus.*[15]

The reason for the Soviet shift in policy concerning *rebus sic stantibus* may be gleaned from her past experience and from present world conditions. Initially the Soviet Union required a rationalization for abrogating the binding effect of Tsarist treaties (including those treaties dealing with the Tsarist debt) as well as the Treaty of Brest-Litovsk. Without resorting to the "principle" of *rebus sic stantibus*, but by developing and shap-

75

ing unique narrowly defined alternative principles, the Soviet Union sought to provide such a rationalization.[16] These exceptions to the principles of *pacta sunt servanda* were basically the principles of unequal treaties and *res inter alios gesta* (state succession).[17] These were the only particular kinds of conditions which in the Soviet view justified nullification of a treaty obligation.[18]

In one sense the international community is indebted to the Soviet Union. To the extent that *rebus sic stantibus* is accepted as a principle, *pacta sunt servanda* is threatened. The Soviet position, in these early years, served to preserve order in international relations because it permitted nullification of a treaty obligation only on narrow grounds. Judiciously the USSR was able to carve out "exceptions" to the principle of *pacta sunt servanda* which were believed necessary to its foreign policy needs. This was an abuse of international law but a restrained abuse.

Over the years, however, the changing world has greatly circumscribed the usefulness to Soviet foreign policy of the specific exceptions which they carved out. These "specific" kinds of conditions described in the principles of unequal treaties and *res inter alios gesta* (state succession) do not serve the Soviet Union as they once did. As one of the most powerful nations in the world, the USSR can hardly assert that it was coerced into an unequal treaty. It is more likely than not that a lesser power will claim that the Soviet Union forced an unequal treaty relationship upon it.[19] As for *res inter alios gesta* (state succession), the Soviet Union has long since passed through the stage of historical transformation from one social system to another which would permit the invocation of this principle. These principles continue, nonetheless, to have some limited usefulness to the Kremlin. The USSR has increasingly relied upon them to support the demands of the Third World for alteration of treaty arrangements.

Additionally the Soviet Union is confronted with a changing Eastern Europe. Neither the principle of unequal treaties nor the principle of *res inter alios gesta* (state succession) is formulated to meet the growing needs of Soviet policy in dealing with these communist states. Treaties are becoming increasingly important as a mode of regulating relations between the Soviet Union and Eastern Europe as other less formal means are becoming increasingly less effective. These principles which provide a weak nation with an excuse for nullifying a treaty obligation can only be counterproductive to Soviet policy. How are treaties among communist states abrogated? The mere fact that such a question must be asked and answered is indicative in itself of the great upheavals in the socialist world.

All of these developments tend to support the view that the Soviet Union may be more receptive today than in yesteryear to the "principle" of *rebus sic stantibus,* narrowly defined of course. This is not to say that the principles of unequal treaties and of *res inter alios gesta* (state succession) will cease to be operative principles of law, from the Soviet viewpoint, or that they will be swallowed up by the "principle" of *rebus sic stantibus*. On the contrary, the principles of unequal treaties and *res inter alios gesta* (state succession) have their advantage in "specificity", a "specificity clearly understood by Moscow, and also they have a firm basis in doctrine — the rights of social systems in transition. What is likely is that these principles will be given a more circumscribed application to conform to changing foreign policy needs.

The "principle" of *rebus sic stantibus* is likewise likely to be employed with caution by Soviet practitioners and its use by others severely criticized at times, as the Soviet Union may wish to restrict what it considers to be a dangerously broad "principle". Early evidence of this trend was visible at the 1968 U.N. Vienna Conference on the Draft Convention on the Law of Treaties. At that time the Soviet delegate, Mr. Kovalev, spoke favorably of Article 59, "Fundamental Change in Circumstances", which is the *rebus sic stantibus* provision of the Draft Convention.[20] A few years before the Soviet Representative to the International Law Commission (ILC), Grigorii I. Tunkin warned, however, that "fundamental change of circumstances" was not to be considered as "on an equal footing" with *pacta sunt servanda*. He added that "fundamental change of circumstances" could not be regarded as having a wide application.[21] Mr. Kovalev gave no indication of deviating from that position.

3. *The Principle Of Unequal Treaties*

(a) *Meaning*

Treaties which are unequal are not protected by the principle of *pacta sunt servanda*. Agreement not force is the logical basis of international law. Such treaties, in the Soviet view, are contrary to international law and hence need not be obeyed.[22] In this respect the principle of unequal treaties is unique compared to *rebus sic stantibus*. Unequal treaties are void *ab initio*. In contrast to the "principle" of *rebus sic stanibus* which bases treaty invalidity on subsequent change in circumstances, that is, treaties become voidable but they are not initially void. "Unequal treaties are legally worthless" at all times.[23] Repudiation of an unequal treaty cannot be considered a violation of international law.

I.I. Lukashuk defined unequal treaties as "treaties which do not correspond to the real will of the signatories."[24] A.N. Talalayev cites as illegal international treaties which are "aggressive, colonialist, coercive, unequal."[25] The concept of unequal treaties is an extreme form of the western notion of duress. To the West, a treaty is void if the envoy sent to negotiate it is himself coerced into making the agreement. But when the exercise of force is properly directed against a state — according to the provisions of the U.N. Charter — then a treaty resulting from such application of force will be legally binding.[26] The principle of unequal treaties transcends this view. Mrs. Zgurskava, Ukrainian Representative to the Sixth (Legal) Committee of the U.N. General Assembly, offered insight into the scope of the principle of unequal treaties when she said,

The existence of unjust, one-sided treaties presented a more serious and more complicated problem than at first glance. Flagrantly unjust treaties, in which one party manifestly received all the benefits while the other party received none at all, were a rarity nowadays; however, there was a danger that newly independent countries might be induced to enter into treaties which, while ostensibly fair and acceptable, were really instruments of exploitation and economic subjugation. In codifying the laws of treaties, the Committee and the [International Law] Commission must make it possible to root out existing unjust treaties and to prevent the adoption of new ones.[27]

Duress may be accomplished through one of several means — economic, military or political. A typology of unequal treaties may be suggested.[28] The first type is the unequal treaty of economic assistance designated either to secure colonial privileges or to create economic dependency out of economic vulnerability. According to V.M. Shurshalov, all aid treaties of the United States are expressions of inequality whereas "every international treaty of the Soviet Union with any state may serve as a clear illustration of Lenin's teachings on the equality of states."[29] Soviet critique of the Marshall Plan is a prime example of the application of the unequal treaty doctrine to an American assistance program. Soviet jurists attack the Marshall Plan as a violation of international law because the preamble of the Economic Co-operation Act described its purpose as contributing to the general welfare and national interest of the United States — a clear expression of the desire to subordinate the sovereignty of other states. Other arguments were based upon the operative provisions of the Act. No agreement on the part of the receiving state was provided for concerning the naming of economic ministers which the United States was to send to Europe. Moreover, the fact that these economic ministers were to be liaison with the economic agencies of the recipient government rather than with their heads of state violated fundamental precepts of diplomatic intercourse.[30] The reply of the United States, namely that international law permits states voluntarily to negotiate privileges for certain obligations was dismissed as unimpressive.

A second type of unequal treaty is that of military assistance and granting of military bases.[31] The inequality of such treaties arises when, "military personnel stationed in a foreign country . . . enjoy virtually unlimited privileges and immunities, while the host country virtually surrenders all sovereignty over the bases. The more powerful party could violate the terms of the treaty as it saw fit; the weaker party had no redress. The bases existed, not for legitimate purposes of defense against aggression but to maintain [narrow-national] . . . interests in the areas concerned."[32]

A third type is the unequal treaty forced upon a newly independent nation as the price of freedom or as the price for continued freedom. One such treaty, in the Soviet view, was the 1936 Anglo-Egyptian treaty permitting English troops to be stationed in the Suez Canal Zone.[33] Another typical example was the Evian Agreement of March 18, 1962, between France and Algeria. The United States-Moroccan consular treaty adjudicated by the International Court of Justice (ICJ) was yet another instance. According to Judge Krylov (USSR) who dissented in the case, "Legitimizing the consular jurisdiction of Americans and thus elevating the latter to a position of 'masters' over the local population of Morocco, is one of the most reactionary decisions in the practice of the International Court."[34] In brief, it violated the progessive principle of unequal treaties.

Not only has the principle of unequal treaties been fashioned as an instrument of critique but it has also served to justify Soviet abrogation of Tsarist treaty obligations. In the words of Professor Grigorii Tunkin, "the Soviet Government had abrogated all the unequal treaties imposed by Czarist Russia on the Governments of Eastern countries, and the *secret treaties* concluded by the Czars with Western countries concerning their respective spheres of influence in certain Eastern countries. Examples were the treaty of 1916 between Russia and Japan concerning the colonialist activity of these two countries in China, the treaty of 1915 between Russia [and] Great Britain concerning their spheres of influence in Persia. The Soviet Union has also repudiated the system of capitulations and consular jurisdictions in the countries of the Orient, and that initiative had led to the disappearance of consular jurisdiction and capitulations in general."[35]

(b) *Source*

The principle of unequal treaties is a universal principle of international law. A requirement of a universal principle is universal acceptance in the Soviet view. Western scholars do not accept "this alleged norm of international law."[36] Yet Soviet scholars are not deterred from their insistence upon universality. They interject the notion that the West cannot spurn this principle because it embodies the development of history.

As for the source of this universal principle, Soviet academicians themselves are confused. At times, the principle of unequal treaties is viewed as an expression of the spirit of the United Nations Charter, the Preamble calling for "equal rights of nations large and small, and with the Purpose, defined in Article 1, paragraph 2, of developing friendly relations among nations based on respect for the principle of equal rights and of self-determination of peoples."[37] The implication is that the U.N. Charter, a treaty, is the source. In such a case, "unequal treaties" would be a treaty-source principle for the USSR and all members of the United Nations and a customary norm for all non-members.

On other occasions, however, Soviet scholars have discussed the principle of unequal treaties as one developing historically.[38] The United Nations Charter, although it contains evidence of this principle, has not codified it. To read this principle into the Charter would do violence to that instrument *via* liberal interpretation. Following this view, unequal treaties is a customary principle of international law. A reason for uncertainty in Soviet thinking in this area may be attributed to the fact that consideration of the question of the source of the principle of unequal treaties is of the "first impression". Only recently have Soviet writers shifted their attention from ideological questions to legal issues.

4. *The Principle Of Res Inter Alios Gesta* (State Succession)

(a) *Meaning*
The replacement of one government by another is not sufficient as "the question of succession arises only when the government is part of a change of state from one historical form to another."[39] A new historical type must emerge. At that moment, the new state acquires the right to determine its attitude toward the treaties concluded by its predecessor. If there is not explicit announcement by the new state, treaties continue as binding obligations (tacit affirmation).[40]

The key is fundamental change.[41] When change goes to the very heart of a social system revision of external obligations are made necessary. The principle of *pacta sunt servanda* cannot operate, in the Soviet view, to prevent re-evaluation because the very being of a new social structure "calls into question the validity of every legal undertaking."[42] In these circumstances "governments and systems are not bound to respect the obligations of fallen governments."[43]

The Moscow Government argued, for example, that the principle of *res inter alios gesta* (state succession) was properly applied in nullifying the treaties relating to the Tsarist debt.[44] By a decree of January 28 (February 10), 1918, the Soviet Government repudiated as of December 1, 1917, the foreign debts incurred by the previous Russian Governments.[45] On March 28, 1918, the French and British Governments issured a Communiqué asserting in part, "the Imperial Russian Government, when it contracted, incontestably represented Russia and obligated it definitely . . . No principle is better established than that according to which a nation is responsible for acts of its governments, no change of authority affecting obligations incurred."[46]

The Soviet response was interwoven with the principle of state succession. The memorandum asserted in part,

If the Soviet authority has refused to take over the obligations of former governments, or to satisfy the claims of persons who have suffered losses caused by measures of domestic policy, such as nationalizations of enterprises, the municipalization of dwellings, the requisition of confiscation of property, it is not because it was unable or uninclined to fulfill the obligations, but because of matters of principles and political necessity.

The Revolution of 1917 completely destroyed all old economic, social and political relations, and by substituting a new society for the old one with the strength of the sovereignty of a revolting people, has transferred the state authority of Russia to a new social class. By so doing it has severed the continuity of all civil obligations which were essential to the economic life of the social class and which have fallen with it.[47]

Finally on May 11, 1922, the Soviet Government issued its official reply to the proposals of the European Powers, "The Russian delegation," the communiqué began, "feels obliged to recall the principle of law according to which revolutions which are a violent rupture with the past carry with them new judicial relations in the foreign and domestic affairs of states. Governments and systems that spring from revolutions are not bound to respect the obligations of fallen governments." The communiqué continued, "revolution, assimilated like all great popular movements, being akin to *force majeure*, does not confer any title to indemnity upon those who have suffered from it . . . Russia is in no wise obliged to pay the debts of the past, to restore property, or to compensate their former owners, nor is she obligated to pay indemnities for other damages suffered by foreign nationals, whether as a result of legislation adopted by Russia in the exercise of her sovereignty, or as a result of revolutionary events." In concluding, the communiqué rejected the possibility of arbitration of these debts because "in the trial of disputes of this kind, the specific disagreements will inevitably end in opposing to one another two forms of property, whose antagonism assumes today for the time in history, a real and practical character. In such circumstances there can be no question of an impartial super-arbiter."[48]

Several years later, Professor Evgenii A. Korovin, then one of the foremost Soviet international law scholars, sought to explain in greater detail the Soviet Government postion on state succession and social revolution as it related to the Tsarist debt. He wrote,

Every international agreement is the expression of an established social order, with a certain balance of collective balance. So long as this social order endures, such treaties as remain in force, following the principle of *pacta sunt servanda* must be scrupulously observed. But if in the storm of a social cataclysm one class replaces the other at the helm of the state, for the purpose of reorganization not only of economic ties but the governing principles of internal and external politics, the old agreements, in so far as they reflect the pre-existing order of things, destroyed by the revolution, became null and void. To demand of a people at last freed of the yoke of centuries the payment of debts contracted by their oppressors for the purpose of holding them in slavery would be contrary to those elementary principles of equity which are due all nations in their relations with each other. Thus in this sense the Soviet Doctrine appears to be an extension of the principle of *rebus sic stantibus*, while at the same time limiting the field of its application by a single circumstance — the social revolution.[49]

Korovin's words illustrate that the principle of *res inter alios gesta*

81

(state succession) makes treaties voidable as contrasted with the principle of unequal treaties which makes treaties void. In this respect, *res inter alios gesta* (state succession) is akin to the "principle" of *rebus sic stantibus*. Korovin, however, strenuously endeavored to justify the policies of the nascent Soviet régime without a reliance upon the *clausula* principle. He asserted the narrowly defined principle of *res inter alios gesta* (state succession) grounded in the special circumstances of social revolutionary change.[50]

The advantages of this principle is that by focusing on the continuity of the state personality before and after revolutionary change, it is simple to declare, for example, that Tsarist debts are outside the ambit of responsibility of the Soviet Government. But what effect does this rupture in continuity of the state personality have on the rights of the Soviet Government? Are the rights of former Russian Governments lost along with obligations? According to a communiqué of April 2, 1924, of the Soviet Government, "A general abrogation of all treaties concluded by Russia under the former régime and under the Provisional Government never took place."[51] That is to say, a social revolution does not nullify all pre-existing treaties but only those which the new government views as incompatible with its principles. The Soviet Government continued to claim "the historical right of priority in the discovery of the Antarctic continent" as belonging "to the Soviet Union by succession from Russia."[52]

In the contemporary world the principle of state succession has lost its original significance for the Kremlin. The Soviet Union has long since passed through the period of revolutionary change which would permit it to appeal to this principle for purposes of abrogating treaty obligations. Today, however, the Moscow Government is breathing new life into this principle as they seek to broaden its application to the emerging new nations of the Third World. It is no secret that the new nations find many of the treaty obligations saddled on them by their former colonial rulers as burdensome, especially in the economic sphere. Phrases such as "national liberation struggle" appear in Soviet discussions of the principle of *res inter alios gesta* (state succession). V.M. Shurshalov, writing in 1957, said treaty obligations may be repudiated "when a revolution or a national liberation struggle gives rise to a new social struggle and a new state authority, which is entitled to denounce the humiliating and unacceptable treaties of the deposed governments."[53] The full scope of the "new principle" was made clear at the 1966 Helsinki Meeting of the International Law Association by Professor I. I. Lukashuk (USSR),

Today there exists cases where universal succession is out of the question: first, when a new state appears as the result of a separation from another, second, when a state emerges from the status of dependency by succession from a metropolitan country in assertion of the right of self-determination, and third, when a new type of state emerges as a result of social revolution. I mean, of course, not a political coup, but such a deep revolution as changes the very foundation of the state — its social, economic and political foundations.[54]

Earlier Soviet conceptions of the application of this principle was limited to point three in Professor Lukashuk's statement. In recent years the principle has been expanded to include the unique situation of the newly emerging nations.

(b) *Source*

One may wish to take issue whith the principle of *res inter alios gesta* (state succession) as conceived by Soviet scholars as did Professor Brierly when he protested that "succession" is a private law principle, a notion taken from property law. States do not die in the same sense as do people, their populations and so forth live on."[55] Although western scholarship for the most part does not accept this principle,[56] Soviet scholars assert that the principle of *res inter alios gesta* (state succession) is a universal principle of international law — a principle whose operation the states of Europe had to accept in their relations, post 1917, with the Soviet Government.

As a universal principle of international law, its legitimacy is derived from custom. Although Soviet scholars have not discussed this matter at great length, their limited discussions acknowledge custom as its source. A Soviet textbook in general use records, "The new state itself determines its attitude to the treaties concluded by its predecessor, customarily making the appropriate declarations to this effect."[57]

Soviet jurists argue for *res inter alios gesta* (state succession) as a means of avoiding undesirable treaty obligations. It is ironic that the Soviet Foreign Ministry should appeal to a customary norm in order to annul treaty law especially in light of the fact that treaty law is considered a more progressive form of law than custom. This irony disappears, however, when the focus is allowed to shift from a consistency in legal reasoning to a consistency in foreign policy objectives supported by law.

5. *The "All States" Principle*

(a) *Meaning*

A corollary of the principle of equality of states is the "all states" principle, that "no state can be prevented from participating in the settlement of questions affecting its interests."[58] In the case of a bilateral treaty limited by its subject-matter to particular states, the right to participate is absent. The establishment of diplomatic relations is a matter between two states alone.[59] By contrast, a multilateral treaty not limited by its subject-matter to the particular states involved, creates in those states which also have an interest, the right to participate. When a group of states draft a convention to regulate the navigation of a stream common to all of them, any state, invited or not, which has a legitimate interest in the subject-matter of that convention has a right to participate. "In the case of multilateral treaties," observed Professor G.I. Tunkin, "it was questionable whether any state or group of states had the right to settle by treaty, problems which were of interest to certain other states and to exclude them from participation or negotiation."[60]

In the case of universal multilateral treaties, such as those drafted by the International Law Commission (ILC), all states have an absolute right of participation. As Soviet jurists themselves assert, "all states had equal rights to participate in settling problems which were of general interest,"[61] because "treaties dealing with matters of legitimate interests to all states should be open to participation by all states."[62] "All states had a right to participate in multilateral international treaties that were not limited by the subject-matter to particular states."[63] Professor Tunkin offered the following illustration, "if a group of states called a conference to draft a treaty concerning the regime of the high seas, other states could hardly be debarred from participating, for the high seas were *res communis omnium*."[64] Since the high seas were *res communis omnium*, a thing common to all, all states had a legitimate interest.

The reasoning underlying the application of the "all states" principle to universal multilateral treaties may be summarized: a treaty is "universal in character either because its object was one of universal interest or because it creates rules intended to be universally accepted."[65] Contemporary international society is composed of sovereign states and agreement" is the only possible way of creating binding obligations upon all states. In times past a minority or even a majority of states may have been able to create binding obligations upon all states irregardless of their consent but this is not possible today reason Soviet jurists. Treaties create rights and duties only for parties thereto (*pacta tertiis nec nocere nec prodesse*). It is logical therefore that if a universal treaty is the end objective then all states ought to be invited to participate.[66] To exclude any state is to strike the\death-knell for a general treaty.[67] Soviet representatives have warned time and again at international conferences that the absence of the Government of the People's Republic of China "would be harmful" because unanimity of all states was absolutely necessary for a universal treaty.[68]

According to Grigorii I. Tunkin, the "all states" principle secures that "no state or group of states would be able to exclude any other state or group of states from negotiating or participating in treaty dealings with matters of common concern."[69] It is illegal, assert Soviet delegates to U.N. organs, to deny the representatives of the People's Republic of China their right to participate in the dealings of universal treaties. Two objectives are advanced. First, Communist China's "right to participate" is elevated from the political to the legal sphere;[70] and second, the West is implicitly criticized for acting contrary to international law.

Western scholars have refused to accept the "all states" principle as representing the contemporary state of international affairs. At the 1963 Session of the Sixth (Legal) Committee of the U.N. General Assembly, the decision was made not to include the "all states" principle into the Draft Convention on the Law of Treaties.[71]

(b) *Source*

Although western jurists have from the outset expressed serious doubts as to whether the "all states" principle corresponds to existing realities (citing the United Nations Charter, the most universal of contemporary agreements, as an example),[72] Soviet diplomats doggedly insist that it is a universal principle of international law. In reference to the "all states" principle Soviet representatives have employed such phraseology as, "the modern rule,"[73] "illegal to exclude any state,"[74] "failure to invite the states in question was contrary to basic principles of modern international law,"[75] "has been a grave violation of international law,"[76] and "in accordance with accepted principles of international law."[77]

It is difficult to determine the source of this universal norm. A discussion of why this is so, is in itself illuminating. Frequently the "all states" principle is regarded as if it were a part of the principle of sovereign equality of states.[78] At other times the "all states" principle has been viewed as likened to the principle of unequal treaties, that is, emanating from the notion of equality but standing as an independent principle of law not rooted in the U.N. Charter. If the latter be the case, the "all states" principle, from the Soviet viewpoint, would have its source of legitimacy in custom. Moscow's unwillingness to give a liberal interpretation to the Charter is support for this analysis.

Soviet scholars have not discussed the issue at any length. What is somewhat disconcerting is that western diplomats have not pressed them for an answer to the question. Admittedly, western scholars reject the "all states" principle because they do not accept it as a customary norm or as any other kind of international legal principle. But one wonders why western spokesmen have not posed that legal question to their Soviet counterparts.

6. *The Principle Of Jus Cogens*

(a) *Meaning*
Jus cogens is a pre-emptory rule of law which states that a treaty or treaty provision which conflicts with certain basic principles of international law is void *ab initio*. The basic principles of international law which governments cannot derogate from, not even by mutual consent, are called

"pre-emptory principles of international law." When a treaty or treaty provision is not in full conformity with a pre-emptory principle it is void (not voidable) and not within the scope of protection of *pacta sunt servanda*. An essential requirement of an enforceable treaty is that it be valid. A treaty contrary to pre-emptory principles is invalid.[79]

Not all of the customary principles of international law are *jus cogens*. States may by mutual agreement detract from many of the principles of customary law. Professor Tunkin suggested some examples, on the other hand, of principles which were pre-emptory. They included *pacta sunt servanda,* unequal treaties and sovereign equality of states. Agreements to commit aggression or agreements to annex portions of the high seas also violated pre-emptory principles.[80] In an article entitled, "International Law is on the Side of Panama," Professor O. Khlestov (USSR) applied the principle of *jus cogens* to the United States — Panamanian Treaty of 1903.[81] He found that the 1903 treaty violated the principle of sovereign equality of states and was therefore void because "it is now generally recognized that an international treaty which runs counter to the basic principles of international law is invalid."

Jus cogens stands as another instrument in the arsenal of the Soviet Foreign Ministry. But as an instrument it is both limited and limiting because it confines Soviet diplomats to a framework of judicial analysis. Realizing this Soviet jurists have become increasingly concerned over the scope of its application. Shurshalov was severely criticized by G.I. Tunkin for holding that the "laws of social development" were a criteria of *jus cogens* in the determination of treaty validity. Shurshalov was charged with confusing the "laws of social development" with judicial laws. Tunkin made it very clear that the only standard by which the validity of treaties was to be adjudged was that of pre-emptory legal norms.[82] By narrowing the methods of challenging the validity of treaty obligations to the judicial sphere, Tunkin took a most "unrevolutionary" position.

(b) *Source*

There is disagreement among western scholars as to the principle of *jus cogens,* some acknowledging it and others not.[83] Tunkin rebuked "bourgeois scholars," notably Hans Kelsen and Alfred Vendross (for his earlier writings), for allegedly refusing to admit to pre-emptory principles.[84] Notwithstanding the confusion in western scholarship, Soviet academicians assert that *jus cogens* is a universal principle. Such a concept as *jus cogens* must be binding on all states by its very nature. Pre-emptory principles encompass basic principles of international law relating to the maintenance of international peace and security. These principles must be steadfastly adhered to — no state may enter into treaty arrangements to the contrary.[85]

The principle of *jus cogens* like the principle of *pacta sunt servanda* has its source in custom. The United Nations Charter gives no more of an expression to the notion of pre-emptory principles than it does to the notion that treaties must be obeyed. Soviet academicians appear unwilling to read either principle into the Charter. This is consistent with their position of strict construction of that instrument.

Consistent with their position on the desirability of moving from custom-based to a treaty-based international law, Soviet diplomats have supported the incorporation of Article 50, "Treaties Conflicting With a Pre-emptory Norm of General International Law *(jus cogens),*"[86] into the Draft Convention on the Law of Treaties. Upon ratification of the Draft Convention, the principle of *jus cogens* would become a treaty-based principle for the Soviet Union. At present, however, its source is custom and for states which do not ratify the Draft Convention (Article 50), it will remain a customary norm.

The principle of *jus cogens* like the principle of *res inter alios gesta* (state succession) is a customary norm which stands as a check on the treaty-making power of a state. Treaties contrary to pre-emptory principles are unenforceable. Soviet diplomats, although believing that treaties are more important than custom in modern international law, have realized, it may be speculated, that on occassion "unfortunate" treaties may be entered into and that it may become necessary to nullify burdensome obligations. In such case (assuming that the parties to the treaties are unwilling to renegotiate), the Soviet Union may be expected to appeal to one of these treaty voiding principles: unequal treaties, *res inter alios gesta* (state succession), or *jus cogens.* Custom plays a useful role.

7. Summary

A review of the law of "treaty-making" indicates that for the Soviet Union as for the West, custom is a source of fundamental principles. The fact that *pacta sunt servanda* is a custom-based norm is enough to make custom a very important source of international law. Add to this the principle of *jus cogens*, functioning as a limitation on treaty-making power, and it becomes increasingly understandable why Moscow could not reject custom. Because of the "bourgeois character" of custom or because of its "uncertainty",[87] the Kremlin might reduce its *stature* recognizing custom as less "progressive" than treaty law, even second to it. But they cannot reject the *status* of custom. Rather they admit custom, like treaty law, as a primary source of international law. In fact, custom and treaty are the only two primary sources of international law recognized by the USSR. Properly it may be said of Soviet diplomats that they too stand in the sunlight of custom even if their backs are to the sun.

Soviet representatives have joined with others in the International Law Commission (ILC) in drafting a convention on the "Law of Treaties". The aim was to replace customary norms with treaty law. A Draft Convention, completed in 1969, containing a codification of *pacta sunt servanda* (Article 26), *jus cogens* (Article 53), and *rebus sic stantibus* (Article 62), awaits ratification. The impact of this Convention on customary law, even if ratified by all states tomorrow, will not be significant for some time to come. Article 4 of the Draft Convention, added at the last moment, provides that the Convention "applies only to treaties which are concluded by States after the entry into force of the present Convention with regard to such States." The non-retroactivity of the Convention means that all treaties, prior in time to the coming into force of the Draft Convention, will continue to be governed by customary law. As Ambassador Richard Kearney, U.S. Representative to the International Law Commission noted, "This turning of the Convention toward the future may delay its effectiveness in the short run."[88] In thinking of treaties negotiated prior to the Convention's coming into force, treaties relating to the United Nations, NATO, Warsaw Pact, Antarctica, Air Space and the like, it is clear that custom will play an important role for a fairly long "short run."

NOTES

[1] Akademii nauk SSSR, Institut gosudarstva i prava, *International Law,* translated by Dennis Ogden, (Moscow: Foreign Languages Publishing House, n.d.), p. 247.

[2] See U.N. International Law Commission Document A/CN.4/37.

[3] Draft Convention on the Law of Treaties, Article 1(1) a, A/CN.4/SER.A/1966/Add 1/ p. 114.

[4] For further discussion see: Mr. Khomusho (Ukrainian SSR), U.N. General Assembly, Sixth (Legal) Committee, A/C.6/SR223 (October 16, 1960)/35/p. 70; the discussions of the International Law Commission on the "Draft Convention of the Law of Treaties," A/ CN.4/SR653/18-20, 25(May 29, 1962)/pp. 155-156; A/CN.4/SR664/23(June 19, 1962)/p. 231; A/CN.4/SR784/53-56 (May 14, 1965)/p. 61; A/CN.4/SR799/35 (June 10, 1965)/p. 167; and U.N. International Law Commission Document, "Reservations to Multilateral Conventions, 'Opinion of Writers'," A/CN.4/41, Vol. 2 (1951), pp. 10-11.

Books and articles concerned with "treaty-making" principles include: S.V. Filippov, *Ogovorki v teorii i praktike mezhdunarodnogo dogovora* (Reservations in the Theory and Practice of International Treaties), (Moscow: 1958); S. Borisov (pseud. Sergei B. Krylov), "Sovereign Rights of Governments Participating in Multilateral Pacts to Claim Reservations," *Sovetskoe gosudarstvo i pravo* (Soviet State and Law), no. 4 (April 1952), pp. 64-69; V.F. Gubin, "The Soviet Union and Reservations to Multilateral Treaties," *1959 Sovetskii ezhegodnik mezhdunarodnogo prava* (1959 Soviet Yearbook of International Law), pp. 126-143; and Grigorii I. Tunkin and B.N. Nechaev, "The Law of Treaties Discussed at the 15th Session of the United Nations International Law Commission," *Sovetskoe gosudarstvo i pravo* (Soviet State and Law), Vol. 34, no. 2 (February 1964), pp. 84-92.

Note: Upon ratification of the "Draft Convention on the Law of Treaties" the role of custom will be altered somewhat. The implications of this Draft Convention will be discussed later in this chapter.

[5] Akademii nauk SSSR, Institut gosudarstva i prava, *International Law, op. cit.,* p. 248. See also, V.M. Shurshalov, "Judicial Content of the Principle of *Pacta Sunt Servanda* and Its Realization in International Relations," *1958 Sovetskii ezhegodnik mezhdunarodnogo prava* (1958 Soviet Yearbook of International Law), p. 166.

[6] See Evgenii A. Korovin, "The Principle of *rebus sic stantibus* in the International Practice of the RSFSR," *Sovetskoe pravo* (Soviet Law), no. 3 (1923), pp. 53-56. The statement has been attributed to Lenin, unconfirmed by this writer, that "Treaties are like pie crusts; they are meant to be broken."

[7] Sergei Krylov, "Shifting the Blame," *Izvestiia,* May 26, 1957, p. 5. See also, Andrei Ia. Vyshinskii, "The Danube Conference and Some Questions of International Law," *Sovetskoe gosudarstvo i pravo* (Soviet State and Law), no. 10 (1948), p. 21.

[8] Dissenting Opinion of Judge Kozhevnikov (USSR), *Case Concerning the Application of the Convention of 1902 Governing the Guardianship of Infants (Netherlands v. Sweden),* Judgment of November 28, 1958, at 1958 ICJ Reports, p. 72. See also, Hans Wehberg, "Pacta Sunt Servanda," *American Journal of International Law,* Vol. 53 (1955), p. 785.

[9] This is another way of saying that in order for Soviet foreign policy to achieve its maximum, a proper balance must be obtained between the ordering and provocative functions of international law.

[10] See Grigorii I. Tunkin, "Coexistence and International Law, *Recueil des Cours* (Collection of Lectures), Vol. 95 (1958-III), p. 39.

[11] See A.N. Talalayev, "Codification of the International Law of Treaties," *1962 Sovetskii ezhegodnik mezhdunarodnogo prava* (1962 Soviet Yearbook of International Law), p.

147. See also, *Official Reports* and *Records*, of the 1968 U.N. Vienna Conference on the Draft Convention on the Law of Treaties, A/CONF.39/C.1/ (May 1968).

[12]Akademii nauk SSSR, Institut gosudarstva i prava, *International Law, op. cit.*, p. 107. See also, p. 281.

[13]The word "principle" appears in quotation marks to denote the fact that Soviet scholars have not as yet accepted *rebus sic stantibus* as a principle of law.

[14]See S.V. Filippov, *op. cit.*, pp. 61-101; Fedor I. Kozhevnikov (ed.), *Mezhdunarodnoe pravo* (International Law), (Moscow: 1957), p. 281; V.M. Shurshalov, *Osnovnye voprosy terorii mezhdunarodnogo dogovora* (Essays on the Theoretical Questions of International Treaties), (Moscow: 1959), pp. 193-208; V.F. Gubin, *loc. cit.*, pp. 155-157; and Evgenii A. Korovin, *American Journal of International Law*, Vol. 22 (1928), p. 762.

[15]See Grigorii I. Tunkin, U.N. *Yearbook of the International Law Commission*, A/CN.4/SR710/83 (1963), p. 253; and discussion of Article 59, "Fundamental Change of Circumstances," of the Draft Convention on the Law of Treaties, by the USSR delegates to the 1968 U.N. Vienna Conference on the Law of Treaties, A/CONF.39/C.1/SR63-65 and 81.

[16]In a book review Professor Oliver J. Lissitzyn wrote, it is "an unexcuseable error in flatly maintaining that Soviet jurists invariably reject the doctrine of *rebus sic stantibus*." *American Journal of International Law*, Vol. 59 (1958), p. 958. If by this statement Professor Lissitzyn meant that Moscow accepts the "notion" of *rebus sic stantibus* he is undoubtedly correct in his admonishment. The principle of *res inter alios gesta* (state succession), a classic example of the application of *rebus sic stantibus* notion, is accepted by the USSR. If on the other hand, Professor Lissitzyn meant that the Soviet Union accepts the "principle" of *rebus sic stantibus*, his admonishment is doubtful.

[17]The principles of unequal treaties and *res inter alios gesta* are discussed in sections 3 and 4 of this chapter respectively.

[18]See Edward McWhinney, *"Peaceful Coexistence" and Soviet-Western International Law* (Leyden: A.W. Sythoff, 1964). p. 66.

[19]Communist China now alleges that the 19th Century treaties by which Russia obtained vast lands from China (*e.g.*, Southern Siberia) are "unequal." See *Economist*, March 16, 1963. See also, Wolfgang Friedmann, *The Changing Structure of International Law*, (New York: Columbia University Press, 1964), p. 380.

[20]Mr. Kovalev (USSR), U.N. Vienna Conference on the Draft Convention on the Law of Treaties, A/CONF.39/C.1/SR64 (May 10, 1968). Article 59, "Fundamental Change of Circumstances," reads:
"1. A fundamental change of circumstances which has occurred with regard to those existing at the time of the conclusion of a treaty, and which was not foreseen by the parties, may not be invoked as a ground for terminating or withdrawing from a treaty unless:
"(a) The existence of those circumstances constituted an essential basis of the consent of the parties to be bound by the treaty; and
"(b) The effect of the change is radically to transform the scope of obligations still to be performed under the treaty.
"2. A fundamental change of circumstances may not be invoked:
"(a) As a ground for terminating or withdrawing from a treaty establishing a boundary;
"(b) If the fundamental change is the result of a breach by the party invoking it either of the treaty or of a different international obligation owed to the other parties to the treaty."

[21]Grigorii I. Tunkin, U.N. *Yearbook of the International Law Commission*, A/CN.4/SR710/83 (1963), p. 253. Mr. Lachs (Poland) speaking to the Commission in 1963, no doubt voicing Soviet feelings as well, said that he was reluctant to accept *rebus sic stantibus* having in

mind Hitler's abuse of that "principle" and the horrors which befell them as a result. U.N. *Yearbook of the International Law Commission*, A/CN.4/SR710/73 (1963), p. 252.

²²See Sergei B. Krylov, "Les Notions Principales du Droit des Gens 'La Doctrine Soviétique du Droit International)," (The Principal Notions of the Law of Nations: The Soviet Doctrine of International Law), *Recueil des Cours* (Collection of Lectures), Vol. 70 (1947-I), pp. 433-434. In addition see: V.I. Lissovskii, *Mezhdunarodnoe pravo* (International Law), (Kiev?: 1955), *passim;* and Akademii nauk SSSR, Institut gosudarstva i prava, *International Law, op. cit.*, p. 248.

²³Akademii nauk SSSR, Institut gosudarstva i prava, *International Law, op. cit.*, p. 83.

²⁴I.I. Lukashuk, "The Soviet Union and International Treaties," *1959 Sovetskii ezhegodnik nezhdunarodnogo prava* (1959 Soviet Yearbook of International Law), p. 16.

²⁵A. N. Talalayev, *loc. cit.*, p. 144.

²⁶See Wolfgang Friedmann, *op. cit.*, p. 380.

²⁷Mrs. Zgurskaya (Ukrainian SSR), Sixth (Legal) Committee of the U.N. General Assembly, A/C.6/SR784/9 (October 4, 1963), p. 18.

²⁸This typology was suggested by Mrs. Zgurskaya (Ukrainian SSR), Sixth (Legal) Committee of the U.N. General Assembly, A/C.6/SR784/10-12 (October 4, 1964), p. 18.

²⁹V.M. Shurshalov, *Osnovaniia deistvietelnosti mezhdunarodnykh dogovorov* (Essays on Existing International Treaties), (Moscow: 1957), pp. 52-58.

³⁰See V.M. Shurshalov, *ibid.*, pp. 152-153. See also, V.I. Lissovskii, "The American 'Law of 1948 Economic Cooperation' and International Law," *Sovetskoe gosudarstvo i pravo* (Soviet State and Law), no. 8 (1948), p. 28.

³¹See M.I. Lazarev, *Imperialisticheshie voennye bazy na chuzikh territororliakh i nezhdunardnoe pravo* (Imperialist Military Bases in Foreign Countries and International Law), (Moscow: 1963): M.I. Lazarev, "Guantanamo Military Base of the USA and Present International Law," *Voprosy mezhdunarodnogo prava* (Problems of International Law), no. 4 (1962), pp. 117-147; and A. Piradov, "Military Bases and International Law," *Mezhdunarnodaia zhizn* (International Affairs), Vol. 11, no. 5 (May 1964), pp. 140-142.

³²Mrs. Zgurskaya (Ukrainian SSR), Sixth (Legal) Committee of the U.N. General Assembly, A/C.6/SR784/11 (October 4, 1963), p. 18.

³³See Fedor I. Kozhevnikov, *op. cit.*, pp. 280-281; and Akademii nauk SSSR, Institut gosudarstva i prava, *International Law, op. cit.*, p. 200.

³⁴Dissenting Opinion of Judge Krylov (USSR), *Case Concerning Rights of Nationals of the USA in Morocco*, 1952 ICJ Reports, p. 176.

³⁵Grigorii I. Tunkin (USSR), Sixth (Legal) Committee of the U.N. General Assembly, A/C.6/SR717/15 (November 21, 1961), p. 137. Emphasis supplied. It may be observed that the principle of *res inter alios gesta* (state succession) may give an equally plausible justification for abrogation of these treaties in the Soviet mind.

³⁶Oliver J. Lissitzyn, "Soviet Union and International Law," *International Conciliation*, 542 (March), pp. 19-20.

³⁷Mrs. Zgurskaya (Ukrainian SSR), Sixth (Legal) Committee of the U.N. General Assembly, A/C.6/SR784/13 (October 4, 1963), p. 18.

[38]I. I. Lukashuk, *op. cit.*, p. 45.

[39]Akademii nauk SSSR, Institut gosudarstva i prava, *International Law, op. cit.*, p. 129. See also, Peter A. Toma, "Soviet Attitude Toward the Acquisition of Territorial Sovereignty in the Antarctic," *American Journal of International Law*, Vol. 50 (1956), p. 615. Ivo Lapenna wrote, "Korovin estimates that only such an interpretation of the class structure of the state makes possible a correct comprehension of the [Soviet Union] on international relations. This theory serves not only to justify the refusal to pay the foreign debts, but also to justify the conduct of the Soviet Government in the first years following the revolution, as for example, the annulment of the Treaty of Brest-Litovsk on February 21, 1921 on the protection of foreign communists." *Conceptions Soviétique de Droit International Public* (Soviet Conceptions of Public International Law), (Paris: A. Pedone, 1954), p. 175.

[40]Akademii nauk SSSR, Institut gosudarstva i prava, *International Law, op. cit.*, pp. 125-126.

[41]See Percy E. Corbett, *Law in Diplomacy* (Princeton: Princeton University Press, 1959), p. 89.

[42]See Charles de Visscher, *Theory and Reality in Public International Law*, translated by Percy E. Corbett, (Princeton: Princeton University Press, 1957), p. 163.

[43]Timothy A. Taracouzio, *The Soviet Union and International Law: A Study Based on the Legislation, Treaties, and Foreign Relations of the Union of Soviet Socialist Republics*, (New York: Macmillian, 1935), p. 21.

[44]"Tsarist debt" is used rather than the term "Soviet debt". In strict terminology the Soviet Government does not and has not recognized the obligation as outstanding against it.

[45]January 28 (February 10), 1918, *Collection of Laws of the RSFSR, 1917-1918*, no. 27, Article 353. See also, International Law Commission Document, A/CN.4/37, "Memorandum of the Soviet Doctrine and Practice With Respect to the Law of Treaties," November 21, 1950, p. 29; Akademii nauk SSSR, Institut gosudarstva i prava, *International Law, op. cit.*, pp. 125-126; and James L. Brierly, *The Law of Nations* (New York: Oxford University Press), 6th edition, pp. 212-213.

[46]45 I. D. I. 1918, p. 861.

[47]Y.V. Klyuchnikov and A.V. Sabanin, *Mezhdunarodnaya politika noveishego vremni v dogovorakh, notakh i deklareteiyakh* (International Politics of Modern Times in Treaties, Notes and Declarations), (Moscow: 1928), Part 3, Vol. 1, p. 179. See also, "Memorandum of the Soviet Doctrine and Practice With Respect to the Law of Treaties," U.N. International Law Commission Document, A/CN.4/37, p. 28.

[48]Soviet reply on May 11, 1922, *Papers Relating to the International Economic Conference, Genoa*, April-May 1922, cmd 1667, pp. 38-47; Great Britain, *Accounts and Papers*, Vol. 23 (1922); *State Papers*, Vol. 13 (1922).

[49]Evgenii A. Korovin, "Soviet Treaties and International Law," *American Journal of International Law*, Vol. 22 (1928), p. 763. See also, "Memorandum of the Soviet Doctrine and Practice With Respect to the Law of Treaties," U.N. International Law Commission Document, A/CN.4/37, p. 28; and Peter A. Toma, *loc. cit.*, pp. 614-615.

[50]See Hans Kelsen, *The Communist Theory of Law*, (New York: Praeger, 1955), p. 166. With respect to Korovin's statement concerning the Tsarist debt, Kelsen concluded, "That means the *clausula rebus sic stantibus* is part of socialist international law. . ."

[51]*Bulletin de L'Institut Intermédiare International*, Vol. 11 (1925), pp. 154-155. See also, Evgenii A. Korovin, "Soviet Treaties and International Law," *loc. cit.*, p. 763; Michael T. Florinsky, "Soviet Union and International Agreements," *Political Science Quarterly*, 1946,

pp. 61-89; John N. Hazard, "Cleansing Soviet International Law of Anti-Marxist Theories," *American Journal of International Law*, Vol. 32 (1938), pp. 244-252; and Peter A. Toma, *loc. cit.*, p. 615.

⁵²B.V. Kostritsin, "On the Question of the Régime of Antarctic," *Sovetskoe gosudarstvo i pravo* (Soviet State and Law), no. 3 (March 1951), p. 38. It should be noted that not all Soviet writers agree on the issue of the Soviet Union as successor to the legal relations of the Russian Empire. See Fedor I. Kozhevnikov, *Sovetskoe gosudarstvo i mezhdunarodnoe pravo* (The Soviet State and International Law), (Moscow: 1948), pp. 32-50; and Sergei B. Krylov, *Mezhdunarodnoe pravo* (International Law), (Moscow: 1947), pp. 153-156. It should additionally be noted that the Antarctic Treaty is a new factor.

⁵³V.M. Shurshalov, *loc. cit.*, p. 150.

⁵⁴I.I. Lukashuk (USSR), *Report of the 52nd Conference, Helsinki, 1966*, International Law Association, p. 562.

⁵⁵See James L. Brierly, *op. cit.*, pp. 151-152.

⁵⁶See C. Wilfred Jenks, *The Common Law of Mankind*, (New York: Praeger, 1958), pp. 93-94; and Timothy A. Taracouzio, *op. cit.*, p. 21.

⁵⁷Akademii nauk SSR, Institut gosudarstva i prava, *International Law, op. cit.*, p. 125.

⁵⁸Soviet Union Branch, "Report and Declaration," *Report of the 50th Conference, Brussels, 1962*, International Law Association, p. 357.

⁵⁹See Grigorii I. Tunkin, U.N. *Yearbook of the International Law Commission*, A/CN.4/ SR502/61 (May 27, 1959), pp. 104-105; and A/CN.4/SR504/18 (May 29, 1959), p. 113.

⁶⁰Grigorii I. Tunkin, U.N. *Yearbook of the International Law Commission*, A/CN.4/SR502 (May 27, 1959)/61/pp. 104-105. On another occasion Tunkin said, "The freedom to choose partners in the conclusion of treaties like any other liberty, could not be absolute. That remark applies not only to general multilateral treaties, but also to other treaties; even three states could not settle a matter which also concerned a fourth state without allowing that state to participate in the settlement." U.N. *Yearbook of the International Law Commission*, A/CN.4/SR794/53 (June 2, 1965, p. 134.

⁶¹Grigorii I. Tunkin, U.N. *Yearbook of the International Law Commission*, A/CN.4/SR502 /19 (May 27, 1959), p. 102.

⁶²Grigorii I. Tunkin, U.N. *Yearbook of the International Law Commission*, A/CN.4/SR666 /107 (June 22, 1962), p. 246.

⁶³Platon D. Morozov (USSR), Sixth (Legal) Committee of the U.N. General Assembly, A/ C.6/SR797/31 (October 21, 1963), p. 83.

⁶⁴Grigorii I. Tunkin, U.N. *Yearbook of the International Law Commission*, A/CN.4/SR504 /18 (May 29, 1959), p. 113.

⁶⁵Grigorii I. Tunkin, U.N. *Yearbook of the International Law Commission*, A/CN.4/SR503 /56 (May 28, 1959), p. 111.

⁶⁶Grigorii I. Tunkin, U.N. *Yearbook of the International Law Commission*, A/CN.4/SR503 /20 (May 28, 1959), p. 108; and A/CN.4/SR794/49 (June 2, 1965), p. 134.

⁶⁷With the *caveat*, of course, that the excluded state may ratify the treaty or convention notwithstanding the fact that it had been excluded from participating in deliberations concerning the drafting.

[68]See for example, statements of Soviet Representatives, Grigorii I. Tunkin, U.N. *Yearbook of the International Law Commission*, A/CN.4/SR484/35 (April 27, 1959), p. 25, and A/CN.4/SR794/50 (June 2, 1965), p. 134; Grigorii I. Tunkin, 1958 U.N. Conference on the Law of the Sea, A/CONF.13/SR1/14-15 (February 28, 1958), p. 2; and M. Avilov, 1963 U.N. Conference on Consular Relations, A/CONF.25/SR1/19 (March 4, 1963), p. 3.

[69]Grigorii I. Tunkin, U.N. *Yearbook of the International Law Commission*, A/CN.4/SR 666/107 (June 22, 1962), pp. 246-247.

[70]The right to participate has been urged by Soviet representatives for the German Democratic Republic (GDR), the Democratic Republic of Korea, and the Democratic Republic of Viet-Nam as well.

[71]Sixth (Legal) Committee of the U.N. General Assembly, A/C.6/SR801 (October 1963).

[72]See comments of Mr. Ago (Italy), U.N. *Yearbook of the International Law Commission*, A/CN.4/SR504/21-22 (May 29, 1959), pp. 113-114.

[73]Grigorii I. Tunkin, U.N. *Yearbook of the International Law Commission*, A/CN.4/SR503 /20 (May 28, 1959), p. 108.

[74]Grigorii I. Tunkin, U.N. *Yearbook of the International Law Commission*, A/CN.4SR503/ 56 (May 28, 1959), p. 111.

[75]Grigorii I. Tunkin, 1958 U.N. Conference on the Law of the Sea, A/CONF.13/SR1/15 (February 24, 1958), p. 2.

[76]Grigorii I. Tunkin, 1961 U.N. Conference on Diplomatic Intercourse and Immunities, A/CONF.20/SR1/22 (March 2, 1961), pp. 2-3.

[77]Grigorii I. Tunkin, 1961 U.N. Conference on Diplomatic Intercourse and Immunities, A/CONF.20/SR41/27 (April 5, 1961), p. 238.

[78]Grigorii I. Tunkin, U.N. *Yearbook of the International Law Commission*, A/CN.4/SR666 /124 (June 22, 1962), pp. 246-247. See discussion of the Principle of Sovereign Equality of States, Chapter III, section 2, this study.

[79]See Mrs. Zgurskaya (Ukrainian SSR), Sixth (Legal) Committee of the U.N. General Assembly, A/C.6/SR784/7 (October 4, 1963), p. 17; Mr. Sapozhnikov (Ukrainian SSR), Sixth (Legal) Committee of the U.N. General Assembly, A/C.6/SR843/45 (October 7, 1965), p. 26; Mr. G.I. Tunkin, U.N. *Yearbook of the International Law Commission*, A/CN.4/SR809 /87 (June 23, 1965), p. 242; and Mr. Yakimenko (Ukrainian SSR), Sixth (Legal) Committee of the U.N. General Assembly, A/C.6/SR910/21 (October 14, 1966), p. 51.

[80]See Grigorii I. Tunkin, *Voprosy teorii mezhdunarodnoe prava* (Theoretical Questions of International Law), (Moscow: 1962); Mr. Sapozhnikov (Ukrainian SSR), Sixth (Legal) Committee of the U.N. General Assembly, A/C.6/SR843/44 (October 7, 1965), p. 26; and Mr. Yakimenko, (Ukrainian SSR), Sixth (Legal) Committee of the U.N. General Assembly, A/C.6/SR905/4 (October 7, 1966), p. 23.

[81]O.N. Khlestov, "International Law Is On The Side of Panama (in its Dispute with the United States), *International Affairs* (Moscow), April 1964, pp. 92-93.

[82]Grigorii I. Tunkin, *op. cit., passim.*

[83]See Paul Guggenheim, *Traité de Droit International Public* (Treatise on Public International Law), (Paris: 1958), Vol 1, pp. 57-58; Myres McDougal, Harold D. Lasswell and Ivan A. Vlassic, *Law and Public Order in Space* (New Haven: Yale University Press, 1963), pp. 153-154; Stello Séférladès, "L'echange des populations," (Exchange of Populations), *Recueil des Cours* (Collection of Lectures), Vol. 24 (1928-IV), p. 311; Alfred Vendross,

"Forbidden Treaties of International Law," *American Journal of International Law*, Vol. 31 (1937), p. 571; and Alfred Vendross, *"Jus Dispositivum and Jus Cogens* in International Law," *American Journal of International Law*, Vol. 60 (1966), pp. 56-57.

[84]Grigorii I. Tunkin, *op. cit., passim.*

[85]See Grigorii I. Tunkin, U.N. *Yearbook of the International Law Commission*, A/CN.4/ SR609/9-10 (June 13, 1961), p. 170.

[86]Article 50, "Treaties Conflicting With a Preemptory Norm of General International Law *(jus cogens)*" of the 1968 Draft Convention of the Law of Treaties reads,
"A treaty is void if it conflicts with a preemptory norm of general international law from which no derogation is permitted and which can be modified only by a subsequent norm of general international law having the same character."

[87]See Chapter II, section 1, "The Importance of Custom," of this study.

[88]Richard D. Kearney, "The Future Law of Treaties," *International Lawyers*, Vol. 4, no. 5 (October 1970), p. 826.

CHAPTER V.
DIPLOMATIC AND CONSULAR INTERCOURSE: PRIVILEGES AND IMMUNITIES

From very ancient times states have acknowledged the special rights of foreign representatives. However, not since the Vienna Convention of 1815 have these special rights been formally embodied in written form. Over the last 155 years practice has modified that Convention until, at present, custom is regarded as the source of law on the subject. The Soviet Union joins in recognizing that universal principles of diplomatic and consular law have their source in custom and that this area of international law is an important one.[1]

The Soviet Union has not always accepted diplomatic and consular law. Soviet Russia of 1917, under the leadership of men possessing revolutionary spirit, looked upon foreign relations with disdain. Peace with the Central Powers was not to be negotiated, ambassadors were not to be named. However, when the Kaiser's Germany insisted upon a peace treaty with Russia in order to terminate hostilities between them, the weaker Soviet State yielded. Representatives were chosen to negotiate a peace with Germany at Brest-Litovsk. This was one of the first instances of the Moscow Government conforming to the expectations of the international system. Today, the USSR is one of the strongest advocates of privileges and immunities of diplomats and consuls.

Soviet scholars define diplomatic and consular law as, "the sum total of principles and rules established as a result of agreement and backed up by the subject of international law, expressing the will of the people and the ruling classes, of those subjects of international law which share in the intercourse of nations and regulating the status and functions of those subjects' foreign relations bodies in order to maintain and strengthen peace and peaceful coexistence."[2] Professor David B. Levin of the USSR suggests that the subject might best be divided into "three principle groups: inviolability, immunity of jurisdiction and franchises and special privileges."[3] "Inviolability" applies to persons (diplomats and consuls) and places (embassies and consulates). "Immunity of jurisdiction" encompasses the penal, civil and administrative jurisdiction of the host state. "Franchises and special privileges" includes privileges of communication and, less importantly, of ceremony.

Following the organization suggested by Professor Levin, the principles reviewed in this chapter are: the principle of diplomatic immunity, the principle of consular immunity, the principle of *persona non grata*, the principle of the inviolability of diplomatic and consular premises, and the principle of free communication (including the right of consuls to contact nationals of the state they represent and the privileged status of diplomatic mail).[4]

1. The Principle Of Diplomatic Immunity

Count Mirbach-Garff, the German Ambassador in Moscow, was assassinated on July 6, 1918. The Soviet Government promptly expressed regrets. The German Government responded in a sharp note demanding that the Soviet Government permit the stationing of German troops at the German mission for future protection. The Soviet Government refused this request but pledged itself to guarantee the safety of the mission.[5] The German Government agreed. The Soviet Government by 1918 had not only agreed to receive foreign ambassadors but to guarantee their protection.

Contemporary disputes between the USSR and other states have arisen not over whether diplomatic immunity exists, the Soviet Union agrees that it does,[6] but over who possesses diplomatic status and under what conditions. The Soviet Union recognizes that the Heads of State and of Government have immunity.[7] Also, ambassadors and ministers have immunity.[8] But when does immunity attach to an ambassador or minister? The Gubitchev espionage case involving a Russian national employed in the service of the United Nations in New York City demonstrates that although "the consent or acquiescence of the 'receiving' state is a necessary condition precedent to immunity, the attitude of the 'sending' state cannot always be ignored . . . "[9] In that case the dispute arose as to whether Gubitchev had been received by the United States as a public minister since he was an employee of the United Nations. The USSR argued that Gubitchev had been received by the United States on a diplomatic visa which had not been revoked and that he was entitled to diplomatic immunity and that to deny him that immunity was a violation of customary international law.[10] A U.S. court held otherwise, declaring that Gubitchev had not acquired diplomatic immunity merely because he entered the United States on a diplomatic visa.[11] The State Department, fearing reprisals against Americans in Eastern Europe, recommended to the court, a suspended sentence, if Gubitchev would leave the country immediately.

Families of envoys have immunity. As simple and as straight-forward as that statement may sound, it contains the perplexing problem of defining the word "family". Soviet jurists suggest that customary practice recognizes only the categories of "spouses" and "minor children" and that if an expanded concept of "family" is held and additional categories such as "grandparents", "uncle and aunt", and "cousins" are requested, extensions of immunity to them is a matter of *comitas gentium*.[12]

The unfortunate incident of Mr. Alvaro Cruz, son of the Chilean Ambassador to the USSR, illustrates another difficulty. According to the Chilean Government, in December 1946, Miss Liessina, a national of the

Soviet Union, married Mr. Alvaro Cruz and had thus become a member of the family of the Chilean Ambassador and as such had acquired the right of diplomatic immunity. When the Ambassador and his family prepared to leave Moscow at the end of his tour of duty, Mrs. Alvaro Cruz (the former Miss Liessina) requested and was denied permission to leave the Soviet Union.[13] The Chilean Government sought to exert political pressure on the Soviet Government but to no avail. The Soviet Government claimed "no violation of diplomatic immunity" asserting,

Diplomatic immunity did not extent to all the members of a diplomat's family. Moreover, the Institute of International Law, after long deliberations, had recognized that nationals of the country to which they were accredited could not claim diplomatic privileges. Thus Mrs. Alvaro Cruz, who had not even been personally accredited to the Government of the USSR, could not invoke the principle of diplomatic immunity.[14]

The Soviet Government sought to analogize Mrs. Cruz's position to that of an employee of a mission who was a national of the host country. To the Soviet Union, diplomatic immunity obviously did not extend to a person merely because he (or she) was a member of the immediate family of a foreign diplomat.

According to the Soviet interpretation of customary practice of states there is no established rule of international law requiring the granting of diplomatic immunity to administrative, technical and service staff.[15] Diplomatic immunity should be granted only to the "diplomatic staff", in the strict sense of the term. As a matter of comity, of course, diplomatic immunity may be extended to other staff personnel.

Considerations of reciprocity, more than comity, have at times induced the Soviet Government to broaden the application of diplomatic immunity to "non-diplomatic staff".[16] For example by decree of 1927, the Soviet Government announced that diplomatic immunity would be granted only to persons who held the rank of diplomatic officers.[17] The laws of France and Switzerland contained similar provisions. But Great Britain, the United States and a large portion of the world community had laws extending diplomatic immunity to administrative, technical and service personnel (with certain exceptions). According to American Professor Oliver Lissitzyn "to rectify this imbalance, the British Diplomatic Immunities Act (1955) empowered the British Government to withdraw certain immunities from personnel of the diplomatic mission of a state to the extent that the personnel of the British diplomatic mission in that state were denied similar immunities."[18] The immunity of the Soviet "non-diplomatic staff" in London was threatened and the Soviet Government responded by modifying the 1927 Decree. Under the Act of 27 March 1956, the Government of the Soviet Union was empowered to grant diplomatic immunity to administrative, technical and service staff (with the exception of Soviet nationals) on the basis of strict reciprocity.[19] As a result of political pressures the USSR was persuaded to re-evaluate its position that diplomatic immunity ought to be narrowly applied and to bring its practices more into conformity with the world community.

Diplomats have immunity not only *in situ* (the place of the embassy or mission), but also *in transitu* (while travelling to and from their diplomatic post). The Soviet Union applies the "concept of functional necessity." A diplomat travelling through a third state to his post does not have the same degree of immunity in the third state as he would possess in the host state where his post is located. His immunity in the third state is to facilitate traversal. "What, after all," asked Grigorii Tunkin, "was the foundation for according immunities to diplomatic agents in third states?" They perform no function in third states and need only the protection of passage.[20]

Waiver of immunity (civil or criminal), according to customary practice was the prerogative of a government. An individual could not waive his diplomatic immunity. When the French Delegate to the 1961 U.N. Conference on Diplomatic Intercourse and Immunities proposed as an amendment to the Draft Convention that "the sending state may permit a diplomatic agent to waive immunity from jurisdiction," Mr. G. Tunkin (USSR) responded that such a proposal "was contrary to international law."[21] In the Soviet view, diplomatic immunity was necessary so that diplomats could discharge their duties. That being so noted Tunkin, "his immunities were not his to dispose of."[22]

2. The Principle Of Consular Immunity

The rights and privileges of consuls are derived from customary international law and exist irrespective of treaty.[23] As with diplomatic immunity, consular immunity also thrives on reciprocity and as a result, Soviet consular regulations (in large part) reflect the generally recognized rules of international law.[24]

Governments cannot establish consulates on the territory of another state without expressed consent.[25] Immunity attaches to a consul when the host state is notified and acknowledges the appointment. Mr. Tunkin (USSR), speaking for his Government at the International Law Commission (ILC), emphasized that what is important is not the form of the communication (whether there is an official document of consular commission or an *exequatur*) but notification and acknowledgement. As an example of what he meant, Tunkin described Soviet-Turkish relations,

. . . the Soviet Ministry at Ankara simply notified the Turkish Ministry of Foreign Affairs that a certain person had been appointed as USSR consul-general at Istanbul, with the request that the necessary instructions should be given local authorities to recognize him in that capacity. Inversely, the same procedure had been followed in the case of a Turkish consul stationed at Batum.[26]

Consuls have rights and privileges in accordance with their functions. Their persons,[27] offices, archives and dwellings enjoy immunity from search and seizure and they are not subject to taxes or customs duties.[28]

Regarding acts not performed in the exercise of consular duties, Moscow agrees that consuls do not possess immunity. Unless otherwise provided by treaty, consuls are subject to the civil and criminal jurisdiction of the receiving state, unlike diplomats.[29] A duty is placed upon the host government to notify the diplomatic envoy of the state employing the consul "without delay" of the arrest or intended arrest of their consul.[30] Failure to do so would be to act contrary to the universally accepted practice of states.

There is an aspect of consular relations which has been characterized as "uncertain" by the Soviets.[31] The disputation with the West concerns the "obsolete view that economic relations were conducted independently of the state as a subject of international law." The Soviet Government could not accept the thesis that "consular officers acted only incidentally in defense of the rights and interests of the state as such . . ."[32] Such a thesis would be contrary to the socialist state system of economic monopoly — Soviet consuls are not representatives, nor could they be, of private economic interests. Such a position would be untenable.

Unable to reach an understanding with the West over this matter, the Soviet Government has divested its consular officers of all responsibility to promote economic relations. Instead trade missions which are exclusively composed of governmental agents are given the task.[33] According to the Soviet Union these "trade missions are an integral part of the diplomatic mission of the USSR abroad" and enjoy diplomatic immunity (not consular immunity) even in the absence of a treaty to that effect.[34] The Soviet Union conceives of its commercial agents as ranking with diplomats. Although asserting that such was the practice of states, the Soviet Representative to the International Law Commission (ILC) sought to avoid mention of trade missions in the commentary to the Draft Convention on Consular Relations because the "question relating to trade missions were being settled in practice quite satisfactorily by means of bilateral agreements. . ." implying that there was a disagreement among states concerning the status of trade missions and implicitly indicating that he did not wish to have the matter decided by the Commission at this time.[35]

The Soviet Foreign Ministry claims that "the exercise of consular functions by a diplomatic mission has been regarded as a matter regulated by customary law and no one had denied that it was a general practice."[36] Every diplomatic mission might perform consular duties. Since diplomatic relations were comprehensive, they could include consular functions as well. To require the permission of the receiving state for a diplomatic mission to exercise consular functions would be unduly burdensome, especially since, in Professor Tunkin's (USSR) words, "he knew of no case where objections had been raised to consular functions being carried out by diplomatic missions. . ."[37] In point of fact, until the 1968 US-USSR Consular Treaty was concluded (the first bilateral treaty on any subject between the two great powers), the Soviet diplomatic mission carried on all Soviet consular-like relations with the United States.

The only occasion which would present difficulty would be the desire to establish consular relations where no diplomatic relations existed between the two states concerned. Soviet authorities fall back upon a broader concept to sustain their position, "All states were free to determine through what organs their intercourse with other states should be conducted."[38] The question arises, however, may this determination be made by the receiving as well as the sending state?

3. *The Principle Of Persona Non Grata*

The principle of *persona non grata* is a way of ameliorating the harshness of diplomatic immunities. When a state declares a diplomat *persona non grata* he is designated as "undesirable" and loses his diplomatic status. Among the reasons that the receiving state may demand recall of a diplomat are: hostile activity, interference in the internal affairs of the receiving state, infringement of local laws, espionage, the commission of unfriendly acts and the like.[39]

If a state should abuse this principle the state which has suffered the abuse has the right of retaliation in kind — the law of retribution. Once a person ceases to be a member of the diplomatic corps, he becomes an ordinary alien and it is not necessary for the receiving state to invite him to leave its territory because under the "general rules of international law" the receiving state may treat him as an alien and order him out of the country.[40]

4. *The Principle Of Inviolability Of Diplomatic And Consular Premises*

The inviolability of the diplomatic mission is absolute. So strongly does the Soviet Union adhere to this principle that even "the possible threat to property through failure to deal with an emergency promptly was far less formidable than the danger of embittering relations between states through the failure to respect the inviolability of premises of the diplomatic mission. Respect for such inviolability must take precedence over all other considerations."[41] In addition, the archives of the mission, whether confidential or not, are inviolable.[42]

An attack on the Rumanian Embassy in Switzerland, "the Bern Incident of 1955," offered the occasion for an article by Soviet academician David B. Levin on the duties of states to guarantee inviolability of diplomatic mission. Legislative, executive and judicial measures must be taken by the receiving state to (1) "prevent any encroachment whatsoever on diplomatic officials, premises of diplomatic representatives, their papers and property;" (2) "resolutely to cut short such encroachments when they arise;" and (3) "strictly to punish the persons guilty of such encroachments." These actions, according to the article, were not taken by Swiss authorities (as they did not prevent the attack on the Rumanian Embassy) and, therefore, the Swiss Government has violated customary principles of international law.[43]

With equal vigor, although with less supporting evidence, Soviet spokesmen assert that consular premises are also absolutely inviolable as a matter of customary law. "Any exception," noted Mr. Zabigailo (Ukrainian SSR Delegate to the 1963 U.N. Conference on Consular Relations), would be an "infringement on the principles of inviolability."[44] "Absolutely inviolable" was a derivative of national sovereignity. As to archives and documents, they too were inviolable and not subject to *subpoena duces tecum*. All papers, official or not, within the consulate were immune from search or seizure. "If those authorities could scan or handle archives and documents in order to establish whether they were official ones connected with consular relations there could be no effective inviolability."[45] There were, to be sure, two recognized limitations: first, official documents must be kept separate from private papers, and second, they must be kept in the consulate.

The Soviet Union has never made use of honorary consuls, citizens of the receiving state who carry on consular duties for a sending state. Concerning inviolability of the premises of honorary consuls, the Soviet Government having no experience, summarizes what it believes to be the practice of other states. Those states are reluctant, Moscow feels, to extent inviolability to the premises of honorary consuls as it would be "difficult for that state to accept the proposition that one of its own citizens should occupy premises which were inviolable to the local authorities."[46] To Soviet thinking, such premises would not be inviolable, although archives and documents of a consular nature would be. The honorary consul would have to be especially diligent in maintaining the consular records separate from his own. The principle of inviolability as applied to honorary consuls is not absolute but limited.

The "Kasenkina Case" is an exceptional example of Soviet reliance solely upon customary international law. At the time of the unfolding of the panoply of events, there existed no consular treaty between the United States and the Soviet Union.[47] The Soviet Government had to rely upon the practice of states, upon custom-based law.

A Russian national, Mrs. Kasenkina, was brought to the United States by the Soviet Government as a schoolteacher. When in July 1948, the school closed she refused to return to the Soviet Union. The Soviet Consul-General of New York sought her out, found her, and convinced her to return with him to the consulate. After six days without contact with the police or other authorities who wished to speak with her, a writ of *habeas corpus* was issued by Justice Dickstein of the New York Supreme Court[48] commanding the Soviet Consul-General to produce Mrs. Kasenkina in the courtroom the following morning. The writ was served on the doorstep of the consulate as Mr. Lomankin, the Consul-General, was exiting from his automobile to enter the building.

A spokesman for the consulate informed the press that "Mr. Lomankin will not appear in any court. He will not produce the woman. He didn't receive any papers."[49] The following morning the Soviet Ambassador, Mr. Panyushkin, addressed a note to the State Department which read in part (as paraphrased by the *New York Times*), "the writ was in complete contradiction of the rights its foreign consulates enjoy and should enjoy, and that the judicial organs of a country in which a consul resides may not impose on him obligations to secure the appearance in court of citizens of the country he represents . . . "[50] These rights were asserted in the absence of a consular treaty.

Mrs. Kasenkina was not produced in court that morning. Before the judicial process could take further action, Mrs. Kasenkina leaped from a third story window of the consulate. Police arrived, an ambulance was summoned for Mrs. Kasenkina, an inspection was made of her room in the consulate in routine fashion as suicide was suspected, and a letter was taken but later returned unopened.[51] On August 14, 1948, a short note of protest was sent by the Soviet Ambassador to the U.S. State Department,

On August 12, 1948, at 4:20 P.M., two New York City policemen, taking advantage of the fact that employees of the Consulate General had opened the door to the courtyard of the building occupied by the Consulate General where O.S. Kasenkina had jumped from a window, arbitrarily burst into the building of the Consulate General. At 4:30 P.M. four inspectors of the New York police headed by Deputy Chief Inspector of Police, Conrad Rotingast, came to the Consulate General to learn from the Consul-General, Y.M. Lomankin, the circumstances of Kasenkina's attempted suicide. However, instead of dealing with the Consul-General the police inspectors, inspite of his protests, seized one of Kasenkina's personal letters which was in her personal bag. The aforesaid persons attempted to search Kasenkina's room and to question employees of the Consulate General.

By such acts the representatives of the New York police authorities violated the extra-territoriality of the building of the Consulate General of the USSR in New York, the need for the observance of which is derived from *international custom* and from the norms of international law.[52]

The note ended by characterizing the action of the New York Police Department as "illegal" and requested prompt corrective measures by the Government of the United States. On August 19, Under-Secretary of State Lovett responded to the Soviet note. He indicated that the Soviet Government misunderstood customary law.[53] Lovett concluded his note to the Soviet Ambassador by informing him that Consul-General Lomankin's *exequatur* had been revoked and that the United States expected him to leave the country within a reasonable time.

The Soviet Government, on August 25, 1948, rejected Lovett's statement and reiterated that the United States was acting contrary to the accepted practice of states and notified the U.S. Government that it was closing its consulates in New York and San Francisco as it had become impossible for them to carry on their functions and that, on the basis of reciprocity, the Soviet Government expected the United States to close its consulates in Vladivostok and Leningrad.[54]

As there existed no consular treaty between the United States and the Soviet Union, the delicate political issue raised in the "Kasenkina Case" had to be formulated in terms of customary law. The United States, however, took the position that in the absence of treaty, inviolability could not be claimed. The United States did not claim such exemption for its consulates without treaty and neither could the Soviet Union, that is, so the U.S. asserted.

5. *The Principle Of Free Communication*

There are many aspects of this principle. One aspect of free communication which is basic is the right of every sovereign state to establish foreign relations with other states. *Ipso facto,* a subject of international law possesses the "right of legation". From this right flows the right of communication among states. Although each state has the right, every other state possesses the right to refuse to establish relations — this latter "right" to refuse to establish relations has been subject increasingly to criticism especially in the light of the United Nations Charter and the peaceful relations among states concept.[55]

A second aspect of this principle is the absolute inviolability of the diplomatic pouch. This right, in the Soviet view, ensures to the mission free unobstructed communications with the sending state. Admittedly there are abuses of this right. Neither Soviet nor western writers believe this justifies modification of the practice of states granting inviolability. The dangers of abuse weighed against the benefits derived from an unconditional right are so great as not to justify departure. If difficulties arise, if the receiving state has any doubts as to the contents of the pouch, it may not detain or open it but it must use other diplomatic remedies to secure satisfaction. Grigorii Tunkin (USSR) summed up the Soviet position when he said, "The diplomatic bag. . .remained the most important means of communication between Governments and their missions." He concluded, "Although the scope and volume of diplomatic correspondence has greatly increased in recent years," that change did not justify "making exceptions to the rule of inviolability."[56]

Another aspect of this principle is the right of a consul to communicate with his nationals. One of the tasks of consuls is the protection of nationals abroad and this responsibility can be discharged only if communication with them is guaranteed. This right has been described by the

Soviets as "inalienable and undisputed."[57] The United States has, nonetheless, disputed this right, not in principle but in application. Washington's position is that consuls do not possess an absolute right of communication with nationals, in so far as they do not possess the right to follow a rebellious citizen to the four-corners of the world and, when found, to force that citizen to return home against his will. The Soviet Union has vigorously disputed this point.[58]

In addition to the absolute right, as reflected in the practice of states, of a government to be in contact with its nationals abroad through its consular officers, Mr. Tsyba (Ukrainian SSR) asserted, "A person who requested asylum from the receiving state nevertheless needed the assistance of the sending state for he had left a family and property in his country. He might need documents. Why therefore should he be deprived of the help of his consul?"[59] The interest of nationals seeking asylum must also be considered. The U.S. Government's position has been to let the national himself decide whether he wishes his consul's help or not (in the absence of a treaty stipulation to the contrary). The Soviet position, contrarily, is that customary law gives the consul the right to be present.[60]

If a national is arrested the receiving state is obligated to inform the consulate of the detention without delay. The Soviet Union dismissed the argument that the consul should be informed only if the person detained so desired. Mr. Konshukov (USSR) at the 1963 U.N. Conference on Consular Relations asked the following rhetorical question, "What guarantee was there that the person concerned had been informed of his right, that he had refused to request that his consulate should be informed, or that he had not been the victim of undue influences?"[61] Only the notification of the consul could protect nationals in the Soviet view. This aspect of the principle of free communications is concerned with securing the communications link between consul and national. Politically it serves the purpose of supplying the Soviet Union with a legal basis for contact with all of its nationals abroad whether it is with those who seek asylum, those who are arrested, or just for the sake of keeping in touch.

6. Summary

Moving from a position of rejecting diplomacy with the fervor of a revolutionary Marxist, the USSR has become a strong proponent of diplomatic and consular law. Today the Soviet Union is in general accord with western states about this law (with the major exception of consular law). For Soviet as for western jurists, these principles are custom-based. In recent years, however, the Soviet Union along with other states, has been laboring to codify into treaty form these principles of the law of nations.

Two draft conventions have been prepared by the International Law Commission (ILC) and submitted to states for ratification. They are the Vienna Convention on Diplomatic Relations and the Vienna Convention on Consular Relations.

The first of these, the Vienna Convention on Diplomatic Relations was deposited with the Secretary-General of the United Nations for ratification in 1961. By April 1964, enough states had ratified in accordance with Article 51 of the Draft Convention for the treaty to enter into binding force. As of December 1967, 65 states had ratified including: Byelorussian SSR (signed April 18, 1961, ratified May 14, 1964); Ukrainian SSR (signed April 18, 1961, ratified June 12, 1964); and the USSR (signed April 18, 1961, ratified March 25, 1964).[62]

For the Soviet Union as for other ratifying states the treaty is in force and the principles contained therein, as Soviet practitioners see it, are treaty-based. Although treaty is becoming a more important source of law in this area, custom remains of great significance because, first, where there is a hiatus in the diplomatic law set down in "black letter" in the Convention, customary law will be relied upon to fill in the gaps; second, where there is a need to interpret the "black letter" wording of the Convention either because of an unfortunate turn of phrase or because of state disagreement customary law will be called upon; and third, as for the states who have as yet not ratified the Convention, the principles remain custom-based.

It should be noted that in ratifying the Convention on Diplomatic Relations, Byelorussia, the Ukraine and the USSR each called attention "to the discriminatory nature of Article 48 and 50 of the Convention, under the terms of which a number of states [particularly, it may be inserted, the People's Republic of China] are precluded from acceding to the Convention. The Convention deals with matters which affect the interests of all states and should therefore be open for accession of all states. In accordance with the principle of sovereign equality no state has the right to bar other states from accession to a convention of this nature."[63] This is a reiteration of the "all states" principle discussed in Chapter IV.

The second proposed treaty of the International Law Commission (ILC) is the Vienna Convention on Consular Relations. This Draft Convention was deposited with the Secretary-General in 1963 for ratification. On Marcy 19, 1967, that treaty entered into force in accordance with Article 77 of that Convention. Twenty-seven states had ratified as of December 1967. Byelorussia, the Ukraine and the USSR were not among them.[64] If it is recalled that, unlike the principles of diplomatic law upon which jhere is little disagreement betweenthe USSR and the West, there is a wide disagreement concerning most of the principles of consular law, Soviet failure to ratify is not surprising. The Soviet Union and the United States have disputed several points of consular law. It was not until 1968 that the first consular treaty was concluded between them. Since the Soviet Union has not ratified the Convention on Consular Relations, principles of consular law remain custom-based for the USSR.

NOTES

[1]The codification work of the International Law Commission and its effect on custom-based principles of diplomatic and consular intercourse are not overlooked. Attention is given to the ILC, where appropriate, throughout this chapter.

On the subject of custom as a source of law for principles of diplomatic and consular intercourse see: Mr. Abushjevich (Byelorussian SSR), Sixth (Legal) Committee of the U.N. General Assembly, A/C.6/SR571/20 (October 30, 1958), p. 101; John N. Hazard, "Soviet Union and International Law," *Illinois Law Review*, Vol. 18 (November-December 1948), p. 595; Akademii nauk, Institut gosudarstva i prava, *International Law*, translated by Dennis Ogden, (Moscow: Foreign Languages Publishing House, n. d.), pp. 292-301; David B. Levin, *O neprikosnovesnosti diplomaticheskik i ih personaia* (Diplomatic Immunity of Envoys and Their Staff), (Moscow: 1946), p. 11; and Grigorii I. Tunkin, *Droit International Public* (Public International Law), (Paris: A. Pedone, 1965), pp. 169-170.

[2]I.P. Blishchenko and V.N. Durdenevskii, *Diplomaticheskoe i konsulskoe pravo* (Diplomatic and Consular Law), (Moscow: 1962), pp. 11-12.

[3]David B. Levin, *op. cit.*, p. 25.

[4]The organization of this chapter differs somewhat from other chapters. Since, in the Soviet view, the source of all of the principles considered herein are alike in origin and development, in order to avoid needless repetition, the source of all these principles is considered together at the end of the chapter, rather than as in other chapters, immediately following the discussion of the meaning of the principle.

[5]Vladimir I. Lenin, *Sobr. Soch.* (Collected Works), Vol. 15 (July 15, 1918), p. 356.

[6]See Akademii nauk SSSR, Institut gosudarstva i prava, *International Law, op. cit.*, pp. 302-303.

[7]*Ibid.*, p. 289.

[8]See Grigorii I. Tunkin, U.N. *Yearbook of the International Law Commission*, A/CN.4/SR 390/59 (May 3, 1957), p. 35.

[9]David R. Deemer, "Some Problems of the Law of Diplomatic Immunity," *American Journal of International Law*, Vol. 50 (1956), pp. 117-118.

[10]See Evgenii A. Korovin, "Latest Lawless Action of the American Authorities," *Literaturnaya gazeta* (Literary Newspaper), April 29, 1949, p. 4; and Ilya P. Trainin, "Legal Aggression," *Literaturnaya gazeta* (Literary Newspaper), May 21, 1949, p. 4.

[11]*U.S. v. Coplon and Gubitchev*, 88 F. Supp. 472 (1949), reargued, 88 F. Supp. 915 (1950).

[12]See Grigorii I. Tunkin, 1961 U.N. Conference on Diplomatic Intercourse and Immunities, A/CONF.20/C.1/SR7/26 (March 9, 1961), p. 76; and David B. Levin, *Diplomaticheskii immunitet* (Diplomatic Immunity), (Moscow-Leningrad, 1959).

[13]Mr. Cruz Ocampo (Chile), Sixth (Legal) Committee of the U.N. General Assembly, A/C.6/SR135 (December 3, 1948), pp. 727-728. Mr. Cruz Ocampo, Chilean Representative to the Sixth Committee is the father of Mr. Alvaro Cruz who was, in 1946, Chilean Ambassador to Moscow.

[14]Mr. Pavlov (USSR), Sixth (Legal) Committee of the U.N. General Assembly, A/C.6/SR 136 (December 6, 1958), p. 743. See also Mr. Khomusko (Ukrainian SSR), Sixth (Legal) Committee of the U.N. General Assembly, A/C.6/SR138 (December 7, 1948), p. 761; and Grigorii I. Tunkin (USSR), U.N. *Yearbook of the International Law Commission*, A/CN.4/SR403/32 (May, 1957), p. 99.

[15]See Grigorii I. Tunkin, U.N. *Yearbook of the International Law Commission*, A/CN.4/ SR407/65 (May 29, 1957), p. 122; A/CN.4/SR408/61 (May 31, 1957), p. 128; A/CN.4/SR 410/58-60 (June 4, 1957), p. 138; and A/CN.4/SR462/5-7 (June 12, 1958), pp. 161-162.

[16]"Non-diplomatic staff" is a term which Soviet jurists employ to refer to administrative, technical and servant staff of the mission.

[17]See A.H. Heller and Manley O. Hudson, *A Collection of the Diplomatic and Consular Laws and Regulations of Various Countries*, (Washington: Carnegie Endownment for International Peace, 1933), Vol. 2, p. 1218.

[18]Oliver J. Lissitzyn, "The Soviet Union and International Law," *International Conciliation*, 542 (March), pp. 26-27.

[19]See Grigorii I. Tunkin, U.N. *Yearbook of the International Law Commission*, A/CN.4/ SR408/62-63 (May 31, 1957), p. 128; and Grigorii I. Tunkin, "Some Developments in International Law Concerning Diplomatic Privileges and Immunity," *International Affairs* (Moscow), no. 12 (1957), p. 70.

[20]See Grigorii I. Tunkin, U.N. *Yearbook of the International Law Commission*, A/CN.4/ SR463/70-72 (June 13, 1958), p. 173.

[21]See Grigorii I. Tunkin, 1961 U.N. Conference on Diplomatic Intercourse and Immunities, A/CONF.20/C.1/SR29/7 (March 24, 1961), p. 175.

[22]Grigorii I. Tunkin, U.N. *Yearbook of the International Law Commission*, A/CN.4/SR405 /32 (May 27, 1957), p. 111.

[23]See A.H. Heller and Manley O. Hudson, *op. cit.*, "USSR, Regulations Concerning . . . Consular Institutions, Approved January 24, 1927," Vol. 2, p. 1220.

[24]See Akademii nauk SSSR, Institut gosudarstva i prava, *International Law, op. cit.*, pp. 315-316. Among the basic Soviet Regulations reflecting customary practice, excluding consular agreements concluded with foreign governments, are the Consular Statute of the USSR adopted January 8, 1926 *(Code of Laws of the USSR*, 1926, no. 11, Article 78), the Statute of Diplomatic Missions and Consulates of Foreign States on the Territory of the USSR, approved January 14, 1927 *(Code of Laws of the USSR*, 1927, no. 5, Article 48), and the Code of Commercial Navigation of the USSR, June 14, 1929 *(Code of Laws of the USSR*, 1929, no. 41, Article 366).

[25]See Grigorii I. Tunkin, U.N. *Yearbook of the International Law Commission*, A/CN.4/ SR496/44 (May 19, 1959), p. 78.

[26]Grigorii I. Tunkin, U.N. *Yearbook of the International Law Commission*, A/CN.4/SR508 /34-36 (June 4, 1959), p. 131.

[27]Not every consular treaty to which the USSR is a party provides for personal inviolability. See: Consular Convention between the USSR and Hungary of August 24, 1957, (Article 5); USSR and Czechoslovakia of October 1957, (Article 4); and the USSR and the People's Republic of China of June 23, 1959, (Article 6). "Consular Intercourse and Immunities," A/CN.4/131, Vol. 2 (1960), p. 15.

[28]Honorary consuls (a consul who is a national of the host state), is an exception to this statement. See Grigorii I. Tunkin, U.N. *Yearbook of the International Law Commission* A/CN.4/SR451/60-61 (May 28, 1957), pp. 104-105; and A/CN.4/SR554/94-95 (June 3, 1960), p. 191.

[29]See Grigorii I. Tunkin, U.N. *Yearbook of the International Law Commission*, A/CN.4/ SR599/37 (May 30, 1961), p. 108; U.L. Sanchov, *Uchebnik konsulskogo prava* (Textbook on Consular Law), 2nd edition, (Moscow-Leningrad: 1926), pp. 38-39; and A.V. Sabanin,

Posolskoe i konsulskoe pravo(Ambassadorial and Consular Law), (Moscow: 1930).

[30]Such provisions occur in the conventions between the USSR and the Federal Republic of Germany of June 23, 1959 (Article 8, para. 3); and between the USSR and Austria of February 28, 1959 (Article 7, para. 3).

[31]See Mr. Yakimenko (Ukrainian SSR), Sixth (Legal) Committee of the U.N. General Assembly, A/C.6/SR706/23 (November 2, 1961), p. 86.

[32]Grigorii I. Tunkin, U.N. *Yearbook of the International Law Commission*, A/CN.4/SR517 /43-47 (June 17, 1959), pp. 172-173.

[33]See Grigorii I. Tunkin, *U.N. Yearbook of the International Law Commission*, A/CN.4/SR 452/54 (May 29, 1958), p. 111. Note also, Kazimierz Grzybowski, *Socialist Commonwealth of Nations*, (New Haven: Yale University Press, 1964), p. 19.

[34]See the Soviet Statute on Trade Delegations (Law of December 13, 1933, *Sob. Zak. SSSR*, Vol. 1, no. 59, item 354, 1933). See also, Akademii nauk SSSR, Institut gosudarstva i prava, *International Law, op. cit.*, pp. 303-307; David B. Levin, *Diplomaticheskii immunitet* (Diplomatic Immunity), *op. cit.*
   "The Arcos Raid" of May 12, 1927, when British police entered the building of Arcos and the Soviet Trade Delegation, searched the premises and employees, no doubt has influenced Soviet reasoning. See: *Raid on Arcos Ltd. and the Trade Delegation of the USSR, Facts and Documents*, printed by the Anglo-Parliamentary Committee, London, May 1927; and "The Arcos Raid," in Louis Fischer, *The Soviets in World Affairs* (Princeton: Princeton University Press, 1951), Vol. 2, p. 683.

[35]Grigorii I. Tunkin, U.N. *Yearbook of the International Law Commission*, A/CN.4/SR 452/39-42 (May 29, 1958), pp. 110-111.

[36]Grigorii I. Tunkin, U.N. *Yearbook of the International Law Commission*, A/CN.4/SR582 /54 (May 3, 1961), p. 4; see also, Grigorii I. Tunkin, *U.N. Yearbook of the International Law Commission*, A/CN.4/SR497/15 (May 20, 1959), p. 79; and A/CN.4/SR497/55 (May 20, 1959), p. 83; and A/CN.4/SR576/12-13 (June 29, 1960), p. 323.

[37]Grigorii I. Tunkin, U.N. *Yearbook of the International Law Commission*, A/CN.4/SR582 /51 (May 3, 1961), p. 7.

[38]Grigorii I. Tunkin, U.N. *Yearbook of the International Law Commission*, A/CN.4/SR394 /76 (May 9, 1957), p. 51.

[39]See Grigorii I. Tunkin, U.N. *Yearbook of the International Law Commission*, A/CN.4/SR 459/68-69 (June 9, 1958), p. 148; and Akademii nauk SSSR, Institut gosudarstva i prava, *International Law, op. cit.*, p. 300.

[40]Grigorii I. Tunkin, 1961 U.N. Conference on Diplomatic Intercourse and Immunities, A/ CONF.20/C.1/SR13/17 (March 14, 1961), p. 102.

[41]Grigorii I. Tunkin, U.N. *Yearbook of the International Law Commission*, A/CN.4/SR455 /65 (June 3, 1958), p. 128. For the Soviet position on the "right of asylum," see, International Law Commission Draft Convention on Diplomatic Relations.

[42]See Grigorii I. Tunkin, U.N. *Yearbook of the International Law Commission*, A/CN.4/ SR397/40 (May 14, 1957), p. 70.

[43]David B. Levin, "Attack on the Rumanian Diplomatic Mission in Bern and Its Assessment in the Light of International Law," *1963 Sovetskii ezhegodnik mezhdunarodnogo prava* (1963 Soviet Yearbook of International Law), pp. 291-302.

[44]Mr. Zabigailo (Ukrainian SSR), 1963 U.N. Conference on Consular Relations (Vienna), A/CONF.25/SR8/29 (April 11, 1963), pp. 23-24. See also Mr. Khlestov (USSR), 1963 U.N. Conference on Consular Relations (Vienna), A/CONF.25/SR9/14 (April 16, 1963), p. 26; and V.N. Durdenevskii and S.B. Krylov, *Mezhdunarodnoe pravo* (International Law), (Moscow: 1947), p. 328.

[45]Grigorii I. Tunkin, U.N. *Yearbook of the International Law Commission*, A/CN.4/SR 554/42 (June 3, 1960), pp. 187-188.

[46]See Grigorii I. Tunkin, U.N. *Yearbook of the International Law Commission*, A/CN.4/SR553/15 (June 2, 1960), p. 179.

[47]See generally on the "Kasenkina Case," W.W. Bishop, Jr., *International Law*, 2nd edition, (Boston: Little Brown and Company, 1962), pp. 601-606; and Lawrence Preuss, "Consular Immunities: The Kasenkina Case (US-USSR)," *American Journal of International Law*, Vol. 43 (January 1949), pp. 37-56.

[48]The New York Supreme Court is the lowest state court in New York.

[49]*New York Times*, August 12, 1948.

[50]*New York Times*, August 13, 1948.

[51]See *New York Times*, August 16, 1948.

[52]Note of Ambassador Panyushkin to the U.S. Department of State, *Department of State Bulletin*, Vol. 19, no. 478 (August 14, 1948), p. 255. Emphasis supplied.

[53]Note of Under-Secretary of State Lovett to Ambassador Panyushkin, *Department of State Bulletin*, Vol. 19 (August 19, 1948), p. 251.

[54]See *New York Times*, August 25, 1948. *The Washington Post* reported on June 15, 1968, that the United States Senate had ratified a consular treaty between the US and the USSR. The treaty would re-establish consular relations between the two countries after 20 years, but this time on a treaty-basis.

[55]Grigorii I. Tunkin, U.N. *Yearbook of the International Law Commission*, A/CN.4/SR 385/2 (April 26, 1957), p. 10. See also, Mr. Tsyba (Ukrainian SSR), 1963 U.N. Conference on Consular Relations (Vienna), A/CONF.25/C.1/SR26 (March 6, 1963), p. 104.

[56]Grigorii I. Tunkin, U.N. *Yearbook of the International Law Commission*, A/CN.4/SR 399/21 (May 16, 1957), p. 80. See also, Grigorii I. Tunkin, U.N. *Yearbook of the International Law Commission*, A/CN.4/SR425/85 (June 25, 1957), p. 208; and A/CN.4/SR596/89 (May 25, 1961), p. 95. In addition, see Grigorii I. Tunkin, 1961 U.N. Conference on Diplomatic Intercourse and Immunities, A/CONF.20/C.1/SR25/67 (March 22, 1961), p. 159.

[57]Mr. Tsyba (Ukrainian SSR), 1963 U.N. Conference on Consular Relations (Vienna), A/CONF.25/C.1/SR25/36 (March 21, 1963), p. 220.

[58]See discussion of "Kasenkina Case," *supra*, pp. 193-196.

[59]Mr. Tsyba (Ukrainian SSR), 1963 U.N. Conference on Consular Relations (Vienna), A/CONF.25/C.1/SR25/35 (March 21, 1963), p. 220.

[60]See Grigorii I. Tunkin, U.N. *Yearbook of the International Law Commission*, A/CN.4/SR535/28 (May 9, 1960), p. 51; and A/CN.4/SR536/3 (May 10, 1960), p. 53.

[61]Mr. Konshukov (USSR), 1963 U.N. Conference on Consular Relations (Vienna), A/CONF. 25/SR11/13 (April 17, 1963), p. 37. See also, Grigorii I. Tunkin, U.N. *Yearbook of the International Law Commission*, A/CN.4/SR536/47 (May 10, 1960), p. 58.

[62]*Multilateral Treaties In Respect of Which the Secretary-General Performs Depository Functions: List of Signatures, Ratifications, Accessions, etc., As of 31 December 1967* (United Nations: New York, February 1968), ST/LEG/SER.D/1, "Vienna Convention on Diplomatic Relations," pp. 43-47.

[63]*Ibid.*, pp. 45-47. The Vienna Convention on Diplomatic Relations, Article 48 provides, "The present convention shall be open for signature by all states members of the United Nations or any of the specialized agencies or parties to the Statute of the International Court on Justice, and by any other state invited by the General Assembly of the United Nations to become a party to the convention. . ." Article 50 provides, "The present convention shall remain open for accession by any state belonging to any of the four categories mentioned in Article 48. The instruments of accession shall be deposited with the Secretary-General of the United Nations." *United Nations Treaty Series* (UNTS), Vol. 500, p. 124.

[64]*Ibid.*, pp. 51-52.

CHAPTER VI.
TERRITORY AND POPULATION

Many norms of international law dealing with territory (and "non-territory"[1] such as the high seas and outer space) as well as population are custom-based. These principles are the cause of numerous difficulties for the Soviet Union. "The integrity of the territory of all states has always been and remains," remarked Andrei Gromyko in 1960, "a major and generally recognized principle of international law."[2] The general principles of territorial law developed for the most part through custom. There are few treaties of a multilateral nature.[3] Difficulties arise as a result of uncertainty of practice. Outer space law is an example. Since the laun‚hing of Sputnik, Soviet scholars have been struggling to find agreeable answers to the legal nature of the cosmos. On a broader perspective there is the need to achieve community agreement on space law. To Russia uncertainty is one of the chief evils of customary law and outer space law is the example that proves the case.

Territorial law suggests several theoretical difficulties. In the Chapter on "Subjects of International Law," concepts of the "state" and "sovereignty" were defined by Soviet spokesmen as unassailable and as the basis of fundamental principles of customary law. It follows that territory, the geographical area occupied by a state, should be equally inviolable. Territorial law seeks to define and guarantee rights, duties and obligations of one state toward the territory of another. Yet, according to traditional Marxism, in a classless society the state will "wither away" and national territorial circumscriptions will lose their significance. The proletariat has no fatherland. With the successes in Russia in 1917, the proletariat captured the Tsarist State apparatus which Lenin and his companions found they had to defend as their fatherland until the spread of the revolution was universalized. Practicality was an important consideration. Territory played and plays a crucial role in that consideration. The Soviets thus accepted as binding the customary principles of international law with respect to territory — even though philosophies differed among communists and non-communist states and even though Marxism had to be redefined. As Timothy A. Taracouzio noted in 1935, "Both in their legislation and in international intercourse the Soviets have proved that the principles of international law relative to state domain, be it land, water, or air space, are fully recognized and almost without exception followed by the Communist authorities."[4]

A similar difficulty exists with respect to citizenship and nationality law. Marxism emphasizes the socialization of man, the creation of mass-men. Domestically such attempts have been made but on the international scene, the Soviet Union has, as much as any other nation, stressed the significance of political allegiance. A Soviet citizen or national must be loyal to the Soviet Union and the Soviet State must be able to decide who are its citizens and nationals and who are not. Again general principles of customary international law have been accepted.

In this chapter principles of territory, "non-territory" and population are reviewed. "Territory—non-territory," includes land, sea (territorial waters and high seas), and air (air space and outer space). "Population" includes citizens, nationals, aliens, refugees, statelessness, extradition and the like. The principles discussed are those of *usque ad coelum*, outer space as *res communis* (?), the high seas as *res communis*, territorial waters as part of the littoral state, discovery and occupation as a basis for land acquisition, and the status of population as within domestic jurisdiction.

1. *The Principle of "Usque Ad Coelum"*

(a) *Meaning*

The old maxim expressing the traditional state of air law is *cujus est solum, ejus est usque ad coelum*, whose is the land, his it is also up to the sky. The Soviet Government has consistently supported the *usque ad coelum* principle. In 1956, the often cited article of Professors A. Kislov and S.B. Krylov appeared, in which they asserted the exclusive sovereignty of the subjacent state to air space above its land territory *ad infinitum*. In their words, "But the ceiling question has long since been settled in international law and in international practice. As long ago as 1913 the French lawyer Clunet wrote, 'The right of the sovereignty of each country to its territorial atmosphere must theoretically (it was not a practical question at the time — authors) extends *usque ad coelum* (right to the skies, that is to infinity — authors), as they used to say in olden times.' Contemporary British lawyers, interpreting the expression 'complete and exclusive' sovereignty over air space point out that 'complete' signifies 'without limit,' that is, there is 'no limit on height'."[5] Air space may be characterized as (1) part of the territory of the underlying state, (2) as subject to the exclusive sovereignty of that state and (3) as extending indefinitely, *i.e.*, without limits, upwards.[6]

The Soviet Air Code of 1935 incorporates this view in Article 1,

The Union of Soviet Socialist Republics exercises full and exclusive sovereignty over the airspace of the Union of Soviet Socialist Republics.

Airspace of the Union of Soviet Socialist Republics shall mean the airspace above the land and water territory of the Union of Soviet Socialist Republics including territorial waters, as determined by the Union of Soviet Socialist Republics and international agreements, entered into by the Union of Soviet Socialist Republics.[7]

The Code did not define "air space" in terms of altitudinal limitations.[8]

With the advent of Sputnik in 1957, adherence to the traditional principle of *usque ad coelum* (sovereignty to infinity), became practically an impossibility. The *usque ad coelum* formula had to be modified otherwise the hurling of Sputnik into orbit by the USSR would be a violation of the territorial integrity of every state over which it passed. After Sputnik, without exception, every Soviet writer implicitly or explicitly rejected the "to infinity" concept.

The first article to appear was written by G. Zadorozhnyi and was appropriately enough entitled, "The Artificial Satellite and International Law."[9] The theme of the article was that the new satellite was whirling through free space. Sovereignty was not to be extended above the level where air space could be effectively utilized. Zadorozhnyi, while stressing that outer space was not subject to state sovereignty, at the same time he wished to stress that the state continued to exercise jurisdiction over air space. High altitude balloons, for example, would still violate state sovereignty if they passed over state territory. In 1956, there had been considerable discussion among Soviet authorities about the legality of United States weather ballons and the conclusion of that inquiry was that Washington should be condemned for violating Soviet territorial integrity.[10]

Authoritatively in 1958, A. Galina, a noted Soviet specialist on air law, rejected the extension of sovereignty to outer space when she called for acceptance of the principle that "no state has the right to subject parts of cosmos space to its own legislation, administration and jurisdiction."[11] The principle of *usque ad coelum* was limited to air space. How high is air space? High altitude balloons are included, satellites of 100 miles altitude are excluded. The absence of a definition of the upward limit is not a unique problem in Soviet legislation or writing on the subject. It is a universal problem.

The question of how high up does sovereignty extend took on substantive form in the political incident over the U-2. The Soviet Government presented its case to the Military Division of the Supreme Court of the USSR by stating,

The principle whereby 'each state has full and exclusive sovereignty over the air space above its territory' was anchored in the multipartite Paris Convention on the Regulation of Air Navigation of October 13, 1919, taken up in the Havana Convention of 1928, concluded by a number of American States, and reproduced in Article 1 of the Convention on International Civil Aviation concluded in Chicago on December 7, 1944.

The same principle of complete and exclusive sovereignty of a state over its air space found expression also in the national legislation of various countries, including the Soviet Union and the United States (the Air Commerce Act of the U.S. Congress of 1926 and the Civil Aeronautics Act of the U.S. Congress of 1938).

. . .

This principle of sovereignty is sacred and immutable in international relations.[12]

The U-2 flight, alleged the Soviet Government, violated the sovereignty of the USSR and the United States was guilty of an international delict, a violation of international law.[13]

115

In the Security Council of the United Nations all states agreed that the flight of the U-2 had violated Soviet territory. Only Poland, however, agreed with the Soviet position that the flight should be characterized as "aggression". Nationalist China, France, Great Britain and Italy sought to minimize — not to deny — the seriousness of the American violation by positing the question of the impact of satellites on international law.[14]

The United States did not put forward as a defense in justification of the U-2 flight that Sputnik had unsettled the law. The altitude of the U-2 flight, the United States may have asserted, did not violate Soviet sovereignty. But the U.S. did not protest the Soviet trial of Francis Gary Powers which suggests that the U.S. recognized that Soviet jurisdiction extended at least to the height of the U-2 flight. In the words of Professor Lissitzyn, "The failure of the United States to protest against the action of the Soviet authorities toward Powers and the plane he was flying provides additional evidence that national sovereignty in air space is a rule of customary international law and that it applies to the Soviet Union."[15]

For years the United States has been laboring to obtain from the USSR some relaxation of its view of absolute jurisdiction over air space. American attempts at "freedom of the air" have been resisted. In line with the Soviet position on air space, the Kremlin rejected the Eisenhower "open skies" policy.[16] Through treaty agreement between the US and the USSR, the Soviet Government has permitted reciprocal commercial travel (air). Yet, Soviet leaders continue to jealously guard their rights in this area. There can be no utilization of Soviet air space without Soviet permission.

(b) Source

Usque ad coelum is a customary principle of international law, universally recognized. The Soviet Union, not willing to compromise its absolute sovereignty over air space in general treaty, has refused to become a party to the 1944 Chicago Air Convention,[17] or of any other multilateral convention on air space. There exists no treaty for this principle. For Moscow, the practice of states is the source of law.[18]

The customary practice in the area of air law underwent change as Sputnik altered the old ways of doing and thinking. The space age, so the Soviets assert and as others agree, has called for a rethinking of the old view that state sovereignty extends to infinity. A limit to the upward reaches of the jurisdiction of terrestrial states was required. Almost instantaneously as space was intruded, the law ordering relations among states no longer sufficed to order those relations. Such is eloquent testimony of the nature of custom. With change has come uncertainty in the law. Custom can rapidly change with revolutionary events — scientific or otherwise — but the course of its change is not always immediately discernible.

Custom may be "established" after a short period of state practice.

The Soviet Foreign Ministry cites the last twenty years as a sufficient period for the creation of customary practice limiting the altitude of allied aircraft approaching the city of Berlin *via* the Berlin Corridor to 10,000 feet.[19] Western scholars have questioned whether "ancient usage has gradually ripened" into custom in this instance. This claim by the Kremlin illustrates a number of points: first, the problem of selecting evidence to prove the creation of a new customary norm; and second, the Soviet Union's willingness to utilize custom — even to the point of creating new principles to achieve political ends. This technique is not limited to the Soviet State but, placed in the perspective of Soviet dislike of custom, it takes on a special import.

2. *The Principle of Outer Space As "Res Communis?"*

(a) *Meaning*

The concept of *usque ad coelum* (sovereignty to infinity) has been thoroughly rejected by every Soviet writer with respect to outer space.[20] What principle of law governs activity in outer space? Soviet scholars divide into various schools of thought on the subject as each characterization has its own particular advantages and disadvantages.

The *res communis* school which believes that cosmic space is a "thing common to all" and analogizes outer space to the high seas holds center stage and has served as the catalyst for other theoretical conceptions. Members of this school include G.Y. Zadorozhnyi, S.V. Molodtsov and more recently Evgenii A. Korovin. Opposing this school of thought, however, is a formidable group including F.N. Kovalev, I.I. Cherpov, G.A. Osnitskii (formerly A. Galina, ranking Soviet specialist on air law) and G. Zhukov. Because of the discussion among Soviet scholars and their indecision, a "question-mark" has been placed after the section title, *supra*. With such disagreement one can only say that the principle regulating outer space, if there is one, is of doubtful character. A summary of Soviet views on the subject will at least illustrate what the Soviet Union is striving for in the way of a principle.

As with diplomatic and consular law, advocates of a principle of outer space law have relied upon the functional approach. What matters is that the principle guarantee the security of the subjacent state. Thus Zadorozhnyi writes, "the right of a state to destroy a spy-satellite and generally any space ship threatening the security of the state is undeniable."[21] He added as a *caveat* that the "destruction of a spy-satellite or of a satellite-aggressor beyond the area of air space under the sovereignty of a state cannot mean the extension of the sovereignty of that state to the sphere in which the satellite is flying."[22] The functional approach calls for a principle which on the one hand does not require the extension of sovereignty to cosmic space and, on the other hand, provides

117

security. Soviet writers suggest that such a principle can evolve only from an application of the general principles of contemporary international law, namely, peaceful coexistence and the sovereign equality of states.[23]

The first scholarly article on the régime of outer space appeared in January 1959 and was written by Evgenii A. Korovin. He argued that the status of the cosmos ought to be the reverse of air space and accordingly concluded that cosmic space was a "legal vacuum."[24] In defense of this view Kovalev and Cheprov declared that, "The concept of a 'legal vacuum' renders senseless the very foundation of the question whether other states must permit the launching of satellites."[25] Summing up they claimed that "the space in which the orbits of the first sputniks lay was, therefore, outside the sphere of law regulation, i.e., in what may be termed a 'legal vacuum'."[26]

But the "legal vacuum" principle (or non-principle) contained obvious defects. Not only did it legitimize Sputnik but any and all satellites (including offensive military and spy-satellites) of any and all states. This principle did not meet the needs of the functional requirement of security. In July 1960, Kovalev and Cheprov, original advocates of outer space as a "legal vacuum," criticized that view as a "completely artificial" application of international law to outer space.[27]

Korovin also realized the unsatisfactory nature of the "legal vacuum" approach. At the Moscow Space Policy Symposium he denied the *in vaccuo* principle and announced himself as a proponent of the application of *res communis* to outer space. He explained:

Of the possible conceptions of outer space — either as "no one's," belonging to no one (*res nulles*), or as an object of common use (*res communis omnium*) we, in my opinion, should choose the second one, naturally, if the other states take the same stand. Indeed, if we grant that outer space and what it contains are "no one's," have "no owner," from that inevitably follows the conclusion that it is possible to "occupy," to take possession of one or another part of outer space, for a thing that belongs to no one, according to the general [customary] rule, becomes the property of the one who first takes possession of it (*primi occupantis*).

And conversely, proceeding from the conception of outer space as an object of common use for all mankind, it is necessary to recognize that the forms and methods of this "common possession" can be established only by the mutual consent of all users, i.e., as a result of international agreement among all the states interested in the exploration and use of outer space.[28]

In his closing remarks, Korovin emphasized that the Soviet Government had steadily followed the path of viewing outer space as *res communis*. In terms of the development of custom, these remarks could be taken to mean that as far as Soviet practice was concerned the Moscow Government had acted so as to support the evolution of a customary principle of outer space as *res communis*. In that respect, Korovin could point not only to Soviet practice concerning satellites but also to Premier Nikita Khrushchev's hasty announcement that the USSR did not claim the moon as a result of implanting the hammer and sickle on its surface.

At the same time, however, Korovin was astute to add that a customary principle could evolve only when "other states take the same stand."

In asserting that outer space was *res communis* Korovin gave expression to the earlier thoughts of G.Y. Zadorozhnyi who wrote in 1958, "By analogy to the principle of freedom of the open sea, which beyond the limits of territorial waters and special maritime zones do not belong to anyone and are in general use by all nations, the upper atmosphere, which is beyond the limit of effective air control by states, can likewise be considered a zone of open air, in general use by all nations."[29] Analogizing outer space to the high seas has several advantages. V.P. Meshara (USSR) pointed out that as a condition precedent to the settlement of the status of outer space, especially neutralization (*i.e.*, demilitarization), the question of the régime of the high seas would have to be settled by agreement as well, as they were similar situations.[30]

But S.V. Molodtsov, Soviet specialist on admiralty law and a sympathetic supporter of the *res communis* analogy, warned against "the mechanical transfer of the régime of the high seas to outer space." Such would engender serious disadvantages. "It is possible," he noted, "to borrow some principles, some individual rules of sea law, for example, the rule about the exclusive jurisdiction of the flag state over its ships. . . But, on the whole, the régime of the open seas must not be carried over to outer space, because in the open seas there exist the practice of using the space of the open seas for military purposes."[31] Molodtsov's concern was with military weapons in outer space if the law applicable thereto were the same as the law of the high seas. Security is the underlying theme.

Other critics of the *res communis* principle are less charitable. Writes G. A. Osnitskii (formerly A. Galina), "suffice it to recall the principle of the freedom of the open seas, for example, pre-supposes freedom of navigation for warships, in time of war the open seas are a theatre of military operations. It would, therefore, be hazardous for the cause of peace to accept so broad an interpretation of the present practice of launching rockets and satellites for scientific research."[32]

Osnitskii proposes as an alternative to *res communis* that the principle to be applied ought to be freedom of outer space with the possibility of international restraints for security purposes: a ban on offensive weapons and spy-satellites. The advantage of this view is that it is more "principled" in that it shifts the emphasis away from mechanical rules of traditional international law as applied to the high seas to the development of unique rules for a unique situation. The difficulties in this view materialize when inquiries are made into how this "new" principle will be developed. Sovereignty and peaceful coexistence rank high as criteria for measurements. Also Osnitskii suggested the extension of vertical jurisdiction as a possible solution to security.[33] The defect in this suggestion is that it avoids the issue and the extension of sovereignty might equally interfere with scientific research as with military activities of the USSR. Professor Petr Romashkin spoke the fears of every scholar when he said, "A declaration of sovereignty over this space could only hinder the conduct of the very valuable investigations and the acquisition of very important information about the Universe and lead to the aggravation of the international situation."[34]

Another suggested analogy was to that of Antarctica. This view did not acquire much force until after the conclusion of the 1959 Treaty on Antarctica. Some Soviet scholars would like to apply portions of the Antarctica treaty to outer space. Chief among those provisions is the "agreed solution" principle, which is another way of expressing the right of veto. Ambassador V. Zorin (USSR) stated at the United Nations, "If the principle of unanimity could be applied in the Antarctic, there is no reason why it could not in outer space activities."[35]

(b) *Source*

In recent years a number of multilateral treaties have been negotiated creating legal rights and obligations in outer space. Chief among them are the Nuclear Test Ban Treaty[36] and the Treaty on Principles Governing the Activities of States in the Exploration and Use of Outer Space, Including the Moon and Other Celestial Bodies.[37] The Soviet Union and the United States are signatories and ratifying powers of both of these treaties. The Soviets favor treaty-based space law. G. Zhukov (USSR) at the 1964 Tokyo Meeting of the International Law Association called for the Association to "authoritatively speak up in favor of the creation of space law by way of treaty."[38]

At the present time, Soviet scholars assert that it may be premature to say that any customary principles regarding the nature of outer space have come to be recognized by states.[39] The few treaties which have been negotiated are relied upon. Should the occasion arise, the Soviet Union may be willing to argue that non-signatories are bound to the principles expressed in these treaties because these treaties represent the announced practice of states, that is, the developed custom of international law. Such an occasion has not yet occurred. Primarily, space law is treaty law for the Soviet Union.

3. *The Principle Of The High Seas As "Res Communis"*

(a) *Meaning*

In the Soviet view, the high seas are *res communis*, open to all states on a basis of equality. "Disrespect for the flag of any state is an unfriendly act in relation to that state and is a violation of international law."[40] No state may claim sovereignty over any part of the high seas nor the air space above it. To do so would be to act to the detriment of other states

120

and to violate international law.[41]

According to Soviet spokesmen France violated international law in February 1961, when French fighters intercepted a Soviet transport plane 80 miles off the coast of Morocco over the Mediterranean in what France called their "zone of identification". Aboard the Soviet aircraft was the Chairman of the Presidium of the Supreme Soviet and other officials. French interceptors fired warning shots at the aircraft claiming it to be off course and to close to Algeria. The Soviet Government replied in a sharp note that the aircraft was on course. The note centered on the rhetorical *quo warranto* question:

But first of all it is permissible to ask: Who gave the French authorities the right to engage in "identification" of other states' aircraft flying in airspace over the high seas? It should be well known to the French Government that the generally accepted norms of international law provide for freedom of flight in the airspace over the high seas, and no state, if it does not wish to be a violator of international law has the right to limit this freedom and to dictate arbitrarily for the aircraft of other states any routes over international waters.[42]

At the time of this incident the Geneva Convention on the High Seas was not in force.[43] No universal treaty law regulated the relations of states concerning the high seas in 1961. The Soviet Union was asserting its rights under customary international law.

The permissibility of military vessels on the high seas was alluded to in the discussion of outer space, *supra*. Although the *res communis* principle does not outlaw military activities on the high seas, Soviet scholars assert that when military operations are of such a nature as to effect the extension of state sovereignty over the high seas, such activities violate customary principles of international law. Pacific Ocean themonuclear testing by the United States subjected large portions of the high seas to American sovereignty, reason Soviet jurists. Navigation, fishing, as well as human life were endangered. Such testing "undoubtedly constituted a violation of the principle of freedom of the seas."[44] In like manner, naval maneuvers on the high seas "was clearly illegal under existing international law, since the designation of training areas by a state was tantamount to subjecting a part of the high seas to its sovereignty."[45]

The attitude of the Soviet Union toward "hot pursuit" is similar to that in the West. "Hot pursuit" is a legal rule which permits pursuing a vessel guilty of violating the laws of the littoral state into the open seas if the pursuit is continuous and the pursued vessel does not enter the territorial waters of another state. Article 27 of the Statute of the Protection of the USSR provides:

The pursuit of a vessel which has not complied with the orders of the coast guard within territorial waters. . .may be continued beyond these waters on the high seas, but in any case must be suspended when the pursued vessel enters the waters of a foreign state, and must cease completely when the [pursued] vessel flying a foreign flag enters a foreign port.[46]

The Soviet Union has entered into international agreements containing hot pursuit provisions.[47]

Concerning piracy on the high seas the Soviet Union has a broader conception of the term than does the western world. To continue to view piracy in the traditional way, as acts by private ships and aircraft, is too restrictive, Soviet spokesmen claim. They seek to expand the piracy concept to include acts committed on the high seas, encouraged or initiated, by a state. This was considered by the Soviets as a logical extension of the Nyon Agreement of September 14, 1937, on improper submarine activity.[48]

(b) *Source*
On September 30, 1962, the Geneva Convention on the High Seas entered into force according to Article 39 of the text. Forty states have ratified this Convention as of December 31, 1967, including Byelorussian SSR (signed October 30, 1958, ratified February 27, 1961), Ukrainian SSR (signed October 30, 1958, ratified January 12, 1961), and the USSR (signed October 30, 1958, ratified November 22, 1960).[49] In ratifying the Convention each of the three Soviet entities took exception to Article 9 which did not recognize the immunity of state-owned vessels doing commercial service.[50] In addition, each declared that the definition of piracy was inadequate as provided in the Convention because the Convention did not cover certain acts "which under contemporary international law should be considered as acts of piracy" and therefore the Convention "does not serve to ensure freedom of navigation of international sea routes."[51] A reiteration of the Soviet dislike for the traditional concept of piracy.

The impact of the Geneva Convention on the High Seas on the body of customary law of the high seas is similar to the impact of the Vienna Convention on Diplomatic Relations on the body of customary international law.[52]

4. *The Principle Of Territorial Waters As Part Of The Littoral State*

(a) *Meaning*
From its first days the Soviet State has not hesitated to make use of international law concerning territorial waters. Lenin complained of the unauthorized entry of foreign warships as part of the capitalist military intervention into Russian waters.[53] Percy Corbett wrote of the Soviet complaint, "Merely to assert the illegality of intervention and the distinction between open sea and territorial waters of course logically implied acceptance to that extent of a system of international law."[54]

A.N. Nikolayev defined "territorial waters" as, "A maritime belt of definite width along the coast of the state, this belt being a part of the state's territory and being subject to its sovereignty."[55] A state exerts absolute sovereignty over its coastal waters.[56] Soviet territorial waters are the property of the Soviet State. V.N. Durdenevskii expressed the purpose of territorial seas, "Territorial waters have basically a dual significance for the coastal state: economic, as a source of maritime resources and as the route of navigation, and militarily, as a defensive maritime belt against hostile actions from the sea."[57]

Every littoral state has the right to extend its sovereignty over areas adjacent to its coasts, subject to the right of innocent passage. Every littoral state, therefore, has the right to determine in its national interest, in the Soviet view, what the width will be of its territorial seas.[58] The only limitation is one of reasonableness. Grigorii I. Tunkin suggested that within the range of 3 to 12 nautical miles would be reasonable. Beyond that a state would be acting unreasonably.[59]

Soviet scholars feel certain, and many western scholars agree, that there is no customary rule of a three-mile limit.[60] According to A.N. Nikolayev in 1954, of the 70 maritime states which were or desired to be members of the United Nations, more than 30 applied a limit greater than three nautical miles. The width of Soviet territorial waters is at present 12 nautical miles."[61] Soviet spokesmen at the U.N. and elsewhere have made it clear that the USSR intends to continue to claim 12 nautical miles.[62] Soviet scholars point to decrees (ukazes) of the Tsars as historical evidence of their position.[63]

Soviet writers, in addition, point with constant satisfaction to the decision of the International Court of Justice (ICJ) in the Anglo-Norwegian Dispute of 1951.[64] The case arose when the British Government labelled as illegal the Norwegian action of including as part of its territorial waters the West Fjord (whose distance inter fauces terrae is greater than 30 miles) and other fjords. The main British argument was that Norway's action was not recognized in international practice especially since international law did not permit the inclusion of bays and gulfs as territorial waters of the littoral state if the width inter fauces terrae exceeded 10 miles. The Court rejected the British view holding that there did not exist a 10 mile rule for bays and gulfs and that because of the nature of the Norwegian coast the fjords were a part of Norway's territorial waters.[65]

The American scholar Zigurds Zile acknowledged that "This decision certainly had added force to the unilateral Soviet claim to a 12 mile limit of territorial waters and to the denial of the existence of a rule of international law governing the 10 mile maximum width of an entrance to a national bay."[66] Sergei B. Krylov (USSR) speaking at a meeting of the International Law Commission (ILC) said that he "strongly depreciated any effort to undermine the case-law created by the Court. Norway was not the only state which possessed a deeply indented coastline as he has had the opportunity of seeing for himself when travelling near Murmansk and along the Finnish coast."[7]

Other categories of territorial waters are gulfs and internal seas. Unlike the Soviet claim in the Baltic, Moscow's argument here focuses on history. The rule for gulfs and bays is: the water of gulfs and bays are territorial waters if the width of the entrance does not exceed twice the width of the territorial waters of the state concerned or, if the width is wider, a claim on the basis of "historic bays" is possible.[68] A.N. Nikolayev in his work, *Problema territorialnykh vod v mezhdunarodnom prave* (The Problems of Territorial Waters in International Law), discussed the "historic bays" of the Soviet Union,

The author of this work is in full agreement with Soviet scholars who regard as "historic" and subject to the régime of the internal waters of the USSR the seas which form bays in the Siberian Coast: the Sea of Kora, the Laptev Sea, the East Siberian Sea, and the Chukchi Sea. [9]

The most ambitious claim is to the Bay of Peter the Great as a historical inland sea. The distance *inter fauces terrae* between Tuman Ula and the Cape of Povorontu is 108 miles.[70] The Bay of Peter the Great is viewed as a historic bay because of the activities of Russian Admiral Poutiatin in that region in 1854 and Russian Count Mouraviev-Amourskii in 1859 and his naming of the bay for the Russian Tsar in 1860.[71]

Another question is the "right of innocent passage" through territorial waters. Merchant vessels have the right to innocent passage, in the Soviet view, if they are sailing customary sea lanes.[72] Imentov's view[73] that innocent passage is an unqualified right of merchant vessels has been categorically denied. Passage is limited to *innocent* passage of merchant vessels plying customary routes only. These vessels may be regulated by the littoral state as to navigation, revenue, sanitation and the like. Merchant vessels passing under the right may not anchor unless necessitated by ship malfunction or disaster.

The right of innocent passage of merchant vessels is complicated by the issue of which waterways are subject to the right. International straits connecting two parts of the high seas come within this right. Sergei B. Krylov expressed doubt as to whether a body of water, the only means of access to another's port, would come within the right. The issue was raised at a meeting of the International Law Commission (ILC) by the Israeli Delegation reflecting, without doubt, their concern over the Gulf of Aquba. Since the Soviet Union is not involved in a similar situation Krylov was able to suggest that the International Court of Justice (ICJ) might consider the issue.[74]

Taking a position different from that of the West, Soviet authorities believe that warships do not have the right of innocent passage. In the mid-1930's Sheptovitskii and Pashukanis expressed the underlying reason why military ships were denied such passage. Passage of warships threaten the safety of the coastal state.[75] In order to pass, a warship must obtain the consent of the littoral state, the decision of the ICJ in the *Corfu Channel Case* notwithstanding.[76] In his dissent in the *Corfu Chan-*

nel Case (Merits), Judge Krylov wrote that there was neither custom nor convention which gave warships the right of innocent passage. Corfu was not regulated by convention and Krylov was not willing to give credence to a customary principle to that effect. Instead Krylov quoted Gidel as an accurate reporter of the state of customary law, "The passage of foreign warships through territorial waters is not a right but a tolerance."[77] Soviet spokesmen uniformly dismiss the view that warships irrespective of their gun positions and sailing formation have the right of innocent passage.

The Chairman of the Soviet Delegation to the U.N. Conference on the Law of the Sea (1958), Grigorii Tunkin, summarized his delegation's view on the right of innocent passage:

It is generally recognized under international law that merchant and other non-military vessels have the right of unhindered passage through the territorial waters of a foreign state, provided they use the customary shipping routes. The coastal state has the right to lay down any rules it wishes regarding the passage of warships, including a requirement that preliminary notification be given or permission obtained.[78]

A special area of the law has developed since the 19th Century concerning the littoral state's right to regulate foreign vessels in its port. International custom gives to the captain of the ship the power to maintain internal order. However, should the vessel or any of its crew violate the local ordinances, the coastal state may take appropriate measures against the offender. When vessels are subject to search, seizure or arrest the consul, according to the practice of states in the Soviet view, must be notified without undue delay.[79]

Merchant vessels which are the property of the state, even if operated for commercial purposes, cannot be searched, seized or arrested. They enjoy the same immunity as a military vessel. They are to be considered as having a "special status" flowing from the sovereignty of the flag state.[80] Such state-owned and operated vessels like a man-of-war is expected to obey harbor regulations — to do otherwise would be, in the Soviet view, to violate customary international law.

(b) *Source*

It is a long standing international practice, records a Soviet law text, "that a littoral state itself customarily determines the line from which territorial waters begin and itself lays down the limit (width) of its territorial waters."[81] Platon D. Morozov (USSR) put it this way, "historically, the breadth of the territorial sea has always been decided by the coastal state itself. . ."[82]

On September 10, 1964, the Geneva Convention on the Territorial Sea and Contiguous Zones entered into force in accordance with Article 29. Among the 33 ratifying powers were the Byelorussian SSR (signed October 30, 1958, ratified February 27, 1961), the Ukrainian SSR (signed October 30, 1958, ratified January 12, 1961), and the USSR (signed October 30, 1958, ratified November 20, 1960).[83] The question is to what extent does the Geneva Convention replace or supplement customary international law? Articles 3 through 13 deal with the methods for determining where and how to draw base lines from which to measure the width of the territorial sea. For the Soviet Union, as a ratifying power, these provisions supercede customary law. But where there are gaps in the Convention or where interpretation of the instrument becomes necessary, the Soviet Union must rely on customary practice. Because of the disagreement among states as to the width of the territorial sea, no limit was included in the Convention. In the words of Platon D. Morozov (USSR), "The fact that no decision had been reached at Geneva regarding the breadth of territorial waters in no way signified, as some had tried to contend in the Committee, that a state of judicial vacuum had been created."[84] Custom remained the North Star. Where Soviet diplomats are unable to obtain agreement from the international community on a principle, e.g., 12 mile limit, which they advocate, they would rather have no principle adopted and, as much as they prefer treaty to custom, rely on custom as ordering international relations.

The Geneva Convention, Articles 14 through 23, set forth the law of innocent passage. To this part of the Convention the USSR as well as Byelorussia and the Ukraine have filed with the Secretary-General of the U.N. two reservations. The first expressed Soviet concern over nonrecognition of the "special status" of government owned commercial vessels,

The Government of the Union of Soviet Socialist Republics considers that government ships in foreign waters have immunity and that the measures mentioned in this article [Article 20] may therefore be applied to them only with the consent of the flag state.[85]

The other reservation concerned Article 23, subsection D, rule of innocent passage applicable to warships,

The Government of the Union of Soviet Socialist Republics considers that a coastal state has the right to establish procedures for the authorization of the passage of warships through its territorial waters.[86]

Exempting itself from these Convention provisions, the USSR consequently expresses its preference for customary international law, as Soviet statesmen view it.

As for the right of the littoral state to regulate fishing in specified zones, on March 20, 1966, the Geneva Convention on Fishing and Conservation of Living Resources on the High Seas went into force in accordance with Article 18. The USSR, Byelorussia and the Ukraine are not among the 25 ratifying powers.[87] Thus, for them, custom continues to govern.

A third convention is the Geneva Convention on the Continental Shelf which entered into force on June 10, 1964, in accordance with Article 11.

Among the 37 ratifying states, without reservation or declaration, were the Byelorussian SSR (signed October 31, 1958, ratified February 27, 1961), the Ukrainian SSR (signed October 31, 1958, ratified January 12, 1961), and the USSR (signed October 31, 1958, ratified November 22, 1960).[88] The limitations inherent in written law, the need for interpretation and the like, apply in this instance as well.

5. The Principle of Discovery And Occupation As A Basis For Land Acquisition

(a) Meaning

Land and its subsoil comprise a most important part of the territory of a state. The inviolability of the land territory of a state is a primary principle of international law. According to Soviet jurists land may be properly acquired in several ways: discovery and occupation, accretion, prescription, cession, annexation and plebicite.[89]

Focusing specifically on discovery and occupation, the Soviet Union has relied upon this method in putting forth its claim to Antarctica. Antarctica is a continent comprising 1/6th of the world's land surface and a successful claim to any portion of it by the USSR could only be viewed as a major political-economic victory.

The Soviet Geographical Society resolution of 1949 expressed "the historical right" of the USSR vis-à-vis the self-sacrifices of Russian navigators Bellingshausen and Lazarev, who in 1819-1821 circumnavigated Antarctica, to participate in a solution of the question of the régime of this territory.[90] In the words of Professor Kalesnik, "Russia has never renounced her rights, and the Soviet Government has never consented for anyone to dispose of territory discovered by the Russian navigators."[91] Komsomolskaya pravda (Komsomol Truth), in 1950, stated the Soviet claim in these words, "Our country is the lawful heir to the outstanding Russian geographical discoveries made in the South Polar Seas at the beginning of the 19th Century. Historically the right of priority in the discovery and exploration of a number of Antarctic lands remain eternally with Russia and, by succession, with the USSR."[92]

In addition to discovery there must be occupation. Occupation evidences the desire of the discovering state to extend its sovereignty to the area in question. In the case of Antarctica, Soviet scholars reject the notion of "effective occupation" is required. S.V. Molodtsov cites Lawrence, Higgins, Hyde and Fauchille and others to support the view that because of the nature of the South Polar region, all that is required is exercise of minimum control over the region and not effective occupation. Molodtsov points to other examples where "effective occupation" was not required because of the nature of the land involved — Palmas Islands, Clipperton Islands, Eastern Greenland and parts of Africa.[93] Minimum control (which the Soviets claim they have exercised in Antarctica) plus discovery under international law yeilds a Soviet claim to that region.

Another issue which the Soviet Union has had to deal in order to protect its claim is the suggestion that the "sector theory" applicable to the Arctic be applied to the Antarctic. If the sector theory were applied to the Antarctic the USSR would be out in the cold. Molodtsov's argument is representative of Soviet analysis concerning the applicability of the "sectory theory,"

The Arctic regions are located near population centers of the adjoining Arctic states and, therefore, the possession of the Arctic has also an exclusive . . . economic value: For the population of the Arctic states the Arctic region represents sources of existence. Therefore, the Arctic territories are inseparable from their base, that is, the territory of the adjoining state. Antarctica, however, does not possess such a base and, therefore, cannot have such economic importance for any one of the world states, which certain regions of the Arctic may have for each of the adjoining countries.[94]

As a footnote, the Soviet Union partially achieved its objective when on December 1, 1959, the Antarctic Treaty went into effect ratified by Argentina, Australia, Belgium, Chile, France, Japan, New Zealand, Norway, Union of South Africa, USSR, United Kingdom and the United States. By the provisions of the treaty, the USSR was recognized as one of the powers which had a claim to the continent and the "sector theory" was put aside. The treaty placed all claims into abeyance and froze the *status quo*, as "no new claim, or enlargement of existing claims, to territorial sovereignty in Antarctica shall be asserted while the present Treaty is in force."[95]

(b) *Source*
As a universal customary principle discovery and occupation as a means of acquiring land has evolved through state practice.[96] There is no universal multilateral convention on the subject (no doubt because of the decreasing importance of the principle in contemporary international relations inasmuch as the greater portion of the surface of the earth has already been claimed). There are bilateral and multilateral (not universal) treaties between various states which reflect the practices of the international community. States expect that, if they first discover and then peacefully occupy a piece of land territory with the intent of claiming it, they have some legal right to extend their sovereignty to it.

6. *The Principle Of The Status Of Populations As Within The Jurisdiction Of Municipal Law*

(a) *Meaning*
According to general international law, the legal status of individuals (whether citizens, nationals, aliens, refugees or stateless persons) is de-

termined by the municipal legislation of the state in which they are domiciled.[97] There is no rule of international law governing citizenship and nationality except the rule that local state law is controlling. "Under international law," records a Soviet law text, "citizenship means the particular legal link between a physical person and a definite state, expressed in the aggregate of his rights and obligations to that state. The rights and duties of the citizen of any state are laid down by its legislation — by its constitution — its citizenship laws and other regulations."[98] The term "national" is broader than "citizen" and comprises all those persons who owe allegiance to the state but who do not necessarily possess the rights of citizens. The sovereignty of the state reaches to citizens and nationals alike, within the territorial domain and abroad. For determination of such questions as the effect of marriage upon nationality, the nationality of children, *jus soli* (citizenship by place of birth) and *jus sanquinis* (citizenship by parentage), the laws of the USSR are the source of authority.

Because of the closeness of Europe and the shifting boundaries and movements of populations, dual nationality problems have been created. Dual nationality means that two sovereigns have a claim to the same person. Most dissatisfying to the Soviet Union is this conflict of loyalty. Consequently the USSR has entered into treaty relations to clarify this matter. In a protocol attached to the 1945 Czech-Soviet Agreement, persons of Czech or Slovak nationality living in the Ukraine and persons of Ukrainian or Russian nationality living in Czechoslovakia had the right to opt (with the consent of the two governments) for either Soviet or Chech nationality.[99] Treaties were also concluded with Hungary (August 27, 1957), Albania (September 18, 1957), Rumania (September 4, 1957), Bulgaria (December 12, 1957), North Korea (December 16, 1957), Poland (January 21, 1958), and Mongolia (August 25, 1958).[100] Professor John Hazard summarizes the importance of these treaties as representing "a full recognition of the concept of sovereignty over people with concern to avoid any conflict of jurisdiction. It is a classic concept to be enforced even more rigorously than in some states where dual citizenship is tolerated under limited circumstances, especially during the minority of a child."[101]

Statelessness is the reverse of dual nationality. A stateless person is one who is without nationality. Until World War I, statelessness was virtually unknown. In numbers of persons, the Soviet Union has been a major contributor to the status of stateless persons. The RSFSR by decree of December 15, 1921, and the USSR by decree of November 13, 1925, ordered mass denationalization.[102] When Latvia, Estonia and Lithuania were annexed in 1940, the USSR by decree of September 7, 1940, extended Soviet nationality to these areas. Nationals of these former states abroad were requested to register with Soviet diplomatic and consular officers. Failing to do so, they were denied Soviet nationality and became stateless.[103] Whatever the cause, the Soviet Union has consistently held that the matter "fell purely with domestic jurisdiction."[104] A state could enter into treaties with other states to solve the problem. But as Platon D. Morozov (USSR) said of the New York Draft Convention on the Reduction of Statelessness, it contained a number of provisions which conflicted with the principle that "nationality was a matter of domestic jurisdiction and national questions had to be resolved by states independently."[105]

The refugee problem has its roots in the same causes as statelessness — war, revolution and its aftermath. In fact many refugees are *de facto,* if not *de jure,* stateless persons.[106] The firm Soviet position is that the handling of refugees like stateless persons is a matter of domestic jurisdiction.[107]

The entry and exit of aliens to and from a foreign state is a matter regulated solely by municipal law. "The right of a state," notes a Soviet law text, "to permit or refuse entry and to lay down rights and obligations for aliens flows from the generally recognized principle of contemporary international law — the principle of state sovereignty."[108] While in a foreign country aliens must obey its laws or be prosecuted for violation. A foreign state has a general right under international law to expel undesirable aliens. The expelling state need give no reason, but discriminatory ejection of aliens may give rise to similar reprisals.[109] Concerning extradition, it is "a sovereign right of a state." Under international law there is no requirement that criminals be surrendered. A state's right to demand that another state extradite a criminal usually arises only on the basis of an extradition treaty between the states concerned.[110]

Populations within a state (as well as citizens and nationals abroad) are subject to the domestic jurisdiction of that state and that state determines their status, rights, duties and obligations in the Soviet view. In the words of T.A. Taracouzio, "The Soviet Union finds no other way of settling the problems arising from conflicts between states interested in their respective citizens than to resort to the rules of international law accepted by other civilized nations."[111]

(b) *Source*

The principle that the status of populations is a matter of domestic jurisdiction is a generally recognized principle of customary international law in the Soviet view.[112] There is no universal multilateral convention which expresses that principle. The New York Convention on the Reduction of Statelessness is not in force as only one state, the United Kingdom, has thus far ratified.[113] For the Soviet Union control of populations within its territory (and of its citizens and nationals abroad) is of prime importance and a matter to be administered, in accord with customary international law, by the laws of the USSR.

7. *Summary*

The principles discussed in this chapter are another illustration of Soviet acceptance of customary law. As perhaps the strongest advocate of state sovereignty, the Soviet Union wholeheartedly embraces traditional customary law to secure territory and population with a few embellishments suggested by Soviet diplomats. Both territory and population are essential to a state entity.

The uncertainty in air and cosmic law is troublesome to Soviet jurists. The thread which runs through Soviet writings on the subject is "the striving for security." The same thread can be found in Soviet writings about the high seas and territorial waters. In contrast with air and cosmic law, the law of the high seas and territorial waters have been subject to a great deal of scrutiny by the International Law Commission (ILC). Although there are a number of conventions concerning cosmic space, the high seas and territorial waters (which the USSR has ratified — with a number of reservations), custom remains a significant source of law. Additionally, the principle of land acquisition by discovery and occupation and the principle relating to the status of populations is entirely custom-based (*i.e.*, the general principles).

NOTES

[1]The term "non-territory" refers to that which is not subject to occupation, *i.e.*, non-exclusive.

[2]Andrei Gromyko, remarks in *U.N. Review*, July 1960, p. 44

[3]Multilateral conventions include: Convention on the Territorial Sea and Contiguous Zone (entry into force September 10, 1964), Convention on the High Seas (entry into force September 30, 1962), Convention on Fishing and Conservation of Living Resources of the High Seas (entry into force March 20, 1966), Convention on the Continental Shelf (entry into force June 10, 1964), and the Convention on the Reduction of Statelessness (entry into force not achieved, insufficient number of ratifying states). *Multilateral Treaties in Respect of Which the Secretary-General Performs Depository Functions: List of Signatures, Ratification, Accessions, etc., As of December 31, 1967* (United Nations: New York, February 1968), ST/LEG/SER.D.1.

[4]Timothy A. Taracouzio, *The Soviet Union and International Law: A Study Based on the Legislation, Treaties and Foreign Relations of the Union of Soviet Socialist Republics*, New York: Macmillian, 1935), pp. 78-79.

[5]A. Kislov and S.B. Krylov, "State Sovereignty in Air Space — A Generally Accepted Principle of International Law," *Mezhdunarodnaia zhizn* (International Affairs), no. 3, March 1956, pp. 42-43. See for western discussion of this passage: John N. Hazard, "Legal Terminology For the Upper Regions of the Atmosphere are for Space Beyond the Atmosphere," *American Journal of International Law*, Vol. 51 (1957), p. 367; Robert D. Crane, "Soviet Attitudes Toward International Space Law," *American Journal of International Law*, Vol. 56 (1962), p. 688; and U.S. Document (Senate) No. 26, *1961 Senate Symposium: Legal Problems of Space Exploration*, 87th Congress, 1st Session, March 1961, p. 1037.

[6]See Akademii nauk SSSR, Institut gosudarstva i prava, *International Law*, translated by Dennis Ogden, (Moscow: Foreign Languages Publishing House, n. d.), p. 241

[7]See Dennis A. Cooper, *The Air Code of the USSR*, (Charlottesville: The Michie Company, 1966), pp. 37-38.

[8]See G.A. Osnitskii (formerally A. Galina), "International Law Problems of the Conquest of Space," *1959 Sovetskii ezhegodnik mezhdunarodnogo prava* (1959 Soviet Yearbook of International Law), p. 66.

[9]G. Zadorozhnyi, "The Artifical Satellite and International Law," *Sovetskaya Rossiya* (Soviet Russia), October 17, 1957, p. 3.

[10]*Ibid.*, See also, A. Kislov and S.B. Krylov, *loc. cit.*, p. 43.

[11]A. Galina, "On the Question of Inter-Planetary Law," *Sovetskoe gosudarstvo i pravo* (Soviet State and Law), 1959, p. 58.

[12]*The Trial of the U-2; Exclusive Authorized Account of the Proceedings of the Case of Francis Gary Powers, Heard Before the Military Division of the Supreme Court of the USSR, Moscow, August 17-19, 1960*. Introduction by Harold Berman (Chicago: Translation World Publishers, 1960), pp. 6-7.

[13]See Evgenii A. Korovin, "Aerial Espionage and International Law," *International Affairs* (Moscow), June 1960.

[14]See U.N. Security Council *Records*, May 24-27 and July 26, 1960, SOC S/P v858, 861, 863 and 883. See also Oliver J. Lissitzyn, "Some Legal Implications of the U-2 and RB-47 Incidents," *American Journal of International Law*, Vol. 56 (1962), p. 138; and Quincy Wright, "Legal Aspects of the U-2 Incident," *American Journal of International Law*, Vol. 54 (1960), p. 842.

[15]Oliver J. Lissitzyn, *loc. cit.*, pp. 136-137.

[16]See E.Y. Chernomordik, "Air Space in International Law," *Izvestiia akademii nauk SSSR, otdelenie ekonomiki i prava* (News of the Academy of Sciences of the USSR, Department of Economics and Law), 4/1948, p. 243; and Ronald Christensen, *Soviet Views on Space: A Comparative and Critical Analysis*, American Rocket Society, Space Flight Report to the Nation, October 1961, p. 51.

[17]61 Stat. 1180; TIAS no. 1591.

[18]See G.A. Osnitskii (formerally A. Galina), *loc. cit.*, p. 66; and Akademii nauk SSSR, Institut gosudarstva i prava, *International Law, op. cit.*, p. 244.

[19]See Urban G. Whitaker Jr., *Power and Politics*, (New York: Harper and Row, 1964), p. 67.

[20]See generally G.A. Osnitskii (formerally A. Galina), *loc. cit.*, pp. 66-68.

[21]G.Y. Zadorozhnyi, "The Basic Problems of the Science of Cosmic Law," *Cosmos and International Law*, (Moscow: 1962), p. 53.

[22]*Ibid.*, p. 55. See also, Petrov, "Spy-Satellites and International Law," *Cosmos and International Law*, (Moscow: 1962), p. 171; Evgenii A. Korovin, "Peaceful Coexistence in Space," *International Affairs* (Moscow), p. 63; and G. Zhukov, "Space Espionage Plans and International Law," U.S. Document (Senate), no. 26, *1961 Senate Symposium: Legal Problems of Space Exploration*, 87th Congress, 1st Session, March 1961, p. 1095.

[23]See remarks of Professor I.P. Blishchenko (USSR), *Report of the 51st Conference, Tokyo, 1964*, International Law Association, p. 627; and Vladimir M. Koretskii (USSR), *Report of the 49th Conference, Hamburg, 1960*, International Law Association, pp. 255-256.

[24]Evgenii A. Korovin, "International Status of Cosmic Space," *International Affairs* (Moscow), no. 1 (January, 1959), p. 54.

[25]F.N. Kovalev and I.I. Cheprov, "Artifical Satellites and International Law," *1958 Sovetskii ezhegodnik mezhdunarodnogo prava* (1958 Soviet Yearbook of International Law), p. 131.

[26]*Ibid.*, p. 146.

[27]F.N. Kovalev and I.I. Cheprov, "Solving the Legal Problems of Outer Space," *Sovetskoe gosudarstvo i pravo* (Soviet State and Law), no. 7 (July 1960), pp. 136-137.

[28]Evgenii A. Korovin, Moscow Space Policy Symposium, October 1959 as reproduced in U.S. Document (Senate) No. 26, *1961 Senate Symposium: Legal Problem of Space Exploration*, 87th Congress, 1st Session, March 1961, p. 1075.

[29]G.Y. Zadorozhnyi, "The Artifical Satellite and International Law," *loc. cit.*, p. 3.

[30]V.P. Meshara at the February 1959 meeting of the Soviet International Law Association as reported, *1959 Sovetskii ezhegodnik mezhdunarodnogo prava* (1959 Soviet Yearbook of International Law), p. 409.

[31]S.V. Molodtsov, *1959 Sovetskii ezhegodnik mezhdunarodnogo prava* (1959 Soviet Yearbook of International Law), pp. 432-433.

[32]G.A. Osnitskii (formerally A. Galina), *loc. cit.*, p. 67. See also, G. Zhukov, "Space Espionage Plans and International Law," *International Affairs* (Moscow), no. 10 (1960), p. 53.

[33]G.A. Osnitskii (formerally A. Galina), at the 1959 meeting of the Soviet International Law Association as reported, *1959 Sovetskii ezhegodnik mezhdunarodnogo prava*, (1959 Soviet Yearbook of International Law), p. 409; G.A. Osnitskii (formerally A. Galina), "International Law Problems of the Conquest of Space," as reproduced in U.S. Document (Senate), no. 26, *1961 Senate Symposium: Legal Problems of Space Exploration*, 87th Congress, 1st Session, March 1961, p. 1091; and F.N. Kovalev and I.I. Cheprov, "Artifical Satellites and International Law," *loc. cit.*, p. 128.

[34]Petr Romashkin, "Technological Progress and Soviet Law," *Sovetskoe gosudarstvo i pravo* (Soviet State and Law), January 1960, p. 22.

[35]Ambassador V. Zorin (USSR), December 4, 1961, Verbatim Record of the U.N. First Committee, Discussion of the Report of the Committee on Peaceful Uses of Outer Space, DOC. A/C.1/SR1210, pp. 41-42.

[36]*United States Treaty and Other International Agreements*, Vol. 14, p. 1313; or *Treaties and Other International Acts Series* (TAIS), p. 5433; or *United Nations Treaty Series* (UNTS), Vol. 48, p. 43.

[37]"Treaty on Principles Governing the Activities of States in the Exploration and Use of Outer Space, Including the Moon and Other Celestial Bodies, January 27, 1967," *American Journal of International Law*, Vol. 61 (1967), p. 644.

[38]Memorandum, Dr. G. Zhukov (USSR), *Report of the 51st Conference, Tokyo, 1964*, International Law Association, p. 648.

[39]Akademii nauk SSSR, Institut gosudarstva i prava, *International Law, op. cit.*, p. 219.

[40]Akademii nauk SSSR, Institut gosudarstva i prava, *International Law, op. cit.*, p. 219.

[41]See Keilin (USSR), 1958 U.N. Conference on the Law of the Sea, A/CONF.13/SR15/44 (March 25, 1958), p. 39. See also, Article 1 of the Protocol of April 22, 1926 between Finland, Estonia and the RSFSR, *League of Nations Treaty Series* (LNTS), Vol. 45, p. 184.

[42]*Pravda*, February 12, 1961. For a rendition of events see *New York Times*, February 10-12, 1961; and *Pravda*, February 11-13, 1961.

[43]Geneva Convention on the High Seas entered into force on September 30, 1962. *Multilateral Treaties In Respect of Which The Secretary-General Performs Depository Functions: List of Signatures, Ratifications, Accessions, etc., As Of 31 December 1967* (United Nations: New York, February 1968), ST/LEG/SER.D/1, pp. 324-327.

[44]See Grigorii I. Tunkin, 1958 U.N. Conference on the Law of the Sea, A/CONF.13/C.1/SR12/11 (March 12, 1958), p. 2; Grigorii I. Tunkin, 1958 U.N. Conference on the Law of the Sea, A/CONF.13/C.2/SR8/11 (March 11, 1958); S.V. Molodtsov, "Some Questions on the Regulations of the Law of the Open Sea," *1959 Sovetskii ezhegodnik mezhdunarodnogo prava* (1959 Soviet Yearbook of International Law), p. 340; and Evgenii A. Korovin, "U.S. Violation of the Principle of Freedom of the Seas," *Mezhdunarodnaia zhizn* (International Affairs), no. 3 (March 1955), pp. 52-65.

[45]Pushkin (Ukrainian SSR), 1958 U.N. Conference on the Law of the Sea, A/CONF.13/C.2/SR16/41 (March 26, 1958), p. 43. See also Grigorii I. Tunkin (USSR), 1958 U.N. Conference on the Law of the Sea, A/CONF.13/C.2/SR8/12 (March 11, 1958), p. 10.

[46]Decree of the Central Executive Committee and the Council of People's Commissars of June 5, 1927, *Sobr. Zak. i Rasp. SSSR*, 1927, pp. 1223-1224. See also, Akademii nauk SSSR, Institut gosudarstva i prava, *International Law, op. cit.*, p. 220.

⁴⁷See Article 9, International Convention Regarding the Suspension of Contraband Traffic in Alcoholic Liquors, August 19, 1925, *Sbom. Deistv Dogov.* Vol. 5 (1930), p. 46ff. or *League of Nations Treaty Series* (LNTS), Vol. 88, p. 327.

⁴⁸See S.B. Krylov, U.N. *Yearbook of the International Law Commission*, A/CN.4/SR289/14 (May 11, 1955), p. 32; Mr. Zabigailo (Ukrainian SSR), Sixth (Legal) Committee of the U.N. General Assembly, A/C.6/SR496/55 (December 12, 1956), p. 88; Grigorii I. Tunkin, 1958 U.N. Conference on the Law of the Sea, A/CONF.13/SR10/20 (April 23, 1958), p. 21; and Akademii nauk SSSR, Institut gosudarstva i prava, *International Law, op. cit.*, p. 221.

⁴⁹Geneva Convention on the High Seas entered into force September 30, 1962. *Multilateral Treaties in Respect of Which the Secretary-General Performs Depository Functions: List of Signatures, Ratifications, Accessions, etc., As Of 31 December 1967.* (United Nations; New York, February 1968), ST/LEG/SER D/1. pp. 324-327.

⁵⁰Article 9, "Ships owned or operated by a state and used only in government non-commercial service shall, on the high seas, have complete immunity from the jurisdiction of any state other than the flag state." Convention on the High Seas, Done at Geneva April 29, 1958. *The Work of the International Law Commission*, (United Nations: New York, 1968), 67.V.4, p. 105.

⁵¹Soviet Declaration upon ratifying the Geneva Convention on the High Seas. *Multilateral Treaties in Respect Of Which the Secretary-General Performs Depository Functions; List of Signatures, Ratifications, Accessions, etc., As Of 31 December 1967*, (United Nations: New York, February 1968), ST/LEG/SER. D/1, p. 327.

⁵²See discussion concerning the Vienna Convention on Diplomatic Relations, Chapter V, *supra*.

⁵³See Joseph Stalin, *Voprosy Lennizma* (Problems of Leninism), 10th edition, p. 359. Among the early treaties between the RSFSR and other states containing provisions on the territorial sea, see Article 3 of the Treaty of Dorpat (between the RSFSR and Finland), October 14, 1920, *League of Nations Treaty Series* (LNTS), Vol. 3, p. 66; and Article 9 of the Provisional Agreement between the RSFSR and the Ukraine and the Austrian Republic, December 7, 1921, *Sbom. Deistv. Dogov.* Vol. 1, 1924, p. 38.

⁵⁴Percy E. Corbett, *Law in Diplomacy* (Princeton: Princeton University Press, 1959), pp. 88-89.

⁵⁵A.N. Nikolayev as quoted by V.N. Durdenevskii, review of Nikolayev's book *Problema territorialnykh vod v mezhdunarodnom prave* (Problems of Territorial Waters in International Law), (Moscow: 1954), in *Sovetskoe gosudarstvo i pravo* (Soviet State and Law), no. 7 (1955), p. 141.

⁵⁶Of course writes V.N. Durdenevskii, "A state may accept some limitations of its rights over the territorial waters because of reciprocity or for other serious reasons. The USSR has done it, agreeing for instance with other states not to proceed with the health inspection of ships which merely pass through their territorial waters and do not stop in their ports or by their shore." *Sovetskoe gosudarstvo i pravo* (Soviet State and Law), no. 7 (1955), p. 142.
An additional example of the Soviet Union accepting limitation on its rights is the Soviet-British Treaty of May 25, 1956, permitting British registered vessels to fish within three miles of the Soviet coast. The Soviet Government indicated explicitly that by this act she did not recognize a three mile limit, on the contrary, this act was a direct concession to the United Kingdom. Sergei B. Krylov (USSR), U.N. *Yearbook of the International Law Commission*, A/CN.4/SR362/3 (June 7, 1956), p. 166.

⁵⁷V.N. Durdenevskii, in book review of A.N. Nikolayev's book, *loc. cit.*, p. 141.

⁵⁸See Sergei B. Krylov (USSR), U.N. *Yearbook of the International Law Commission*, A/CN.4/SR313/32 (June 16, 1955), p. 180; Sergei B. Krylov (USSR), U.N. *Yearbook of the*

International Law Commission, A/CN.4/SR362/12 (June 7, 1956), p. 167; and Akademii nauk SSSR, Institut gosudarstva i prava, *International Law, op. cit.,* p. 84.

[59]See Grigorii I. Tunkin, ". . .international law did not permit extension beyond twelve miles, in other words, it allowed the breadth of the territorial sea to be fixed within a limit of twelve miles." 1958 U.N. Conference on the Law of the Sea, A/CONF.13/SR14/35 (April 25, 1958), p. 37.

At the 1958 U.N. Conference on the Law of the Sea, the Soviet Delegation introduced the following draft of Article 3, "Each state shall determine the breadth of its territorial waters in accordance with established practice within the limits, as a rule, of three to twelve miles, having regard to historical and geographical conditions, economic interests, and the interests of the security of the coastal state and the interests of international navigation." Vol. 2, Document A/CONF.13/L30, p. 126.

[60]Grigorii I. Tunkin, 1958 U.N. Conference on the Law of the Sea, A/CONF.13/SR14/35 (April 25, 1958), p. 37; and Akademii nauk SSSR, Institut gosudarstva i prava, *International Law, op. cit.,* p. 212.

The U.N. Conference on the Law of the Sea (Geneva, 1958), was unable to reach agreement on the breadth of the territorial sea. No provision setting forth the limits of the territorial sea appear in the Convention on the Territorial Sea and Contiguous Zone as submitted to the Secretary-General of the United Nations for state ratification. *Work of the International Law Commission,* (United Nations: New York, 1967), 67.V. 4, pp. 97-104.

[61]A.N. Nikolayev, *Problema territorialnykh vod v mezhdunarodnom prave* (Problems of Territorial Waters in International Law), (Moscow: 1954), p. 204.

[62]See Fedor I. Kozhevnikov (USSR), U.N. *Yearbook of the International Law Commission,* A/CN.4/SR197/28 (June 18, 1953), p. 81; Fedor I. Kozhevnikov (USSR), U.N. *Yearbook of the International Law Commission,* A/CN.4/SR210/38 (July 7, 1953), p. 166; Sergei B. Krylov (USSR), U.N. *Yearbook of the International Law Commission,* A/CN.4/SR309/6 (June 10, 1955), p. 156; and Platon D. Morozov (USSR), Sixth (Legal) Committee of the U.N. General Assembly, A/C.6/SR488, p. 36.

[63]See Arthur H. Dean, "The Second Geneva Conference of the Law of the Sea: The Fight For Freedom of the Seas," *American Journal of International Law,* Vol. 54 (1960), p. 761.

[64]See *Anglo-Norwegian Fisheries Case,* 1951 ICJ Reports, p. 116.

[65]See Akademii nauk SSSR, Institut gosudarstva i prava, *International Law, op. cit.,* pp. 205 and 395.

[66]Zigurds L. Zile, "Soviet Contribution to International Adjudication: Professor Krylov's Jurisprudential Legacy," *American Journal of International Law,* Vol. 58 (April 1964), p. 371.

[67]Sergei B. Krylov, U.N. *Yearbook of the International Law Commission,* A/CN.4/SR317/10 (June 22, 1955), p. 202. See also, Sergei B. Krylov, U.N. *Yearbook of the International Law Commission,* A/CN.4/SR316/40 (June 21, 1955), p. 371.

The Swedish-Danish dispute with the USSR over Soviet territorial sea claims in the Baltic is an example of Soviet application of the Anglo-Norwegian Case. See Gene Glen, "The Swedish-Soviet Territorial Sea Controversy in the Baltic," *American Journal of International Law,* Vol. 59 (July 1965), p. 948.

[68]Akademii nauk SSSR, Institut gosudarstva i prava, *International Law, op. cit.,* pp. 204-205. See also, Fecor I. Kozhevnikov (USSR), U.N. *Yearbook of the International Law Commission,* A/CN.4/SR164/22 (July 15, 1952), p. 144; and Sergei B. Krylov (USSR), U.N. *Yearbook of the International Law Commission,* A/CN.4/SR365/64-66 (June 12, 1956), pp. 192-193.

[69]A.N. Nikolayev, *op. cit.*, pp. 207-108. See also, Sergei B. Krylov (USSR), U.N. *Yearbook of the International Law Commission*, A/CN.4/SR375/51-52 (June 26, 1956); and France de Harting, *Les Conceptions Soviétique du Droit International de la Mer* (Soviet Conceptions of the International Law of the Sea), (Paris: R. Pichon and R. Durand-Auzias, 1960), p. 30.

[70]*New York Times*, July 21, 1957, p. 1, col. 1.

[71]See A.N. Nikolayev, *op. cit.*

[72]See Grigorii I. Tunkin, 1958 U.N. Conference on the Law of the Sea, A/CONF.13/C.1/SR2/9 (March 22, 1960), p. 39; and Akademii nauk SSSR, Institut gosudarstva i prava, *International Law*, *op. cit.*, p. 214, "International practice shows that littoral countries do not customarily make the innocent passage of foreign merchant vessels through their territorial waters subject to special permission." See also, Vladimir M. Koretskii quoting V.N. Durdenevskii, "Custom recognized the right of innocent passage for foreign merchant ships through territorial waters," *Mezhdunarodnomu prave* (International Law), (Moscow: 1951), pp. 302-303; and A.N. Nikolayev, *op. cit.*, p. 51.

[73]Imentov, *Sovetskoe morskoe i ryboivnoe pravo* (Soviet Sea and River Law), (Moscow: 1951), p. 21.

[74]Sergei B. Krylov, U.N. *Yearbook of the International Law Commission*, A/CN.4/SR366/101 (June 13, 1956). See also, Sergei B. Krylov, U.N. *Yearbook of the International Law Commission*, A/CN.4/SR308 (June 8, 1955)/19-21/ p. 150.

[75]See Sheptovitskii, *Morskoe pravo* (Sea Law), (Leningrad: 1936), p. 34; and Evgenii B. Pashukanis, *Ocherki po mezhdunarodnomu pravu* (Essays on International Law), (Moscow: 1935), p. 120. See also, Grigorii I. Tunkin, "His delegation could not agree with the contention that foreign warships could pass through the territorial sea without the consent of the coastal state, because that could entail a security risk for the latter and had in practice given rise to abuse." 1958 U.N. Conference on the Law of the Sea, A/CONF.13/C.1/SR12/10 (March 12, 1958), p. 32; A.N. Nikolayev, "Every coastal state could claim the right to subject foreign warships wishing to enter its territorial waters to the requirement of prior authorization," 1958 U.N. Conference on the Law of the Sea, A/CONF.13/SR20/29 (April 27, 1958), p. 67; Akademii nauk SSSR, Institut gosudarstva i prava, *International Law*, *op. cit.*, "A littoral state which exercises sovereignty over territorial waters naturally has the right, in the interest of its own security and defense, completely to close its territorial waters to foreign men-of-war."

[76]*Corfu Channel Case (Merits)*, 1949 ICJ Reports, "Dissenting Opinion of Judge Krylov," pp. 68-77; and see Akademii nauk SSSR, Institut gosudarstva i prava, *International Law*, *op. cit.*, p. 394.

[77]Judge Krylov quoting Gidel, *Corfu Channel Case (Merits)*, 1949 ICJ Reports, "Dissenting Opinion of Judge Krylov," p. 74. See additionally, Sergei B. Krylov, U.N. *Yearbook of the International Law Commission*, A/CN.4/SR307/13 (June 8, 1955), p. 145 and A/CN.4/SR368/3, 7, 11-13 (June 15, 1956), pp. 212-213; and A.N. Nikolayev, 1958 U.N. Conference on the Law of the Sea, A/CONF.13/C.1/SR42/9 (April 11, 1958), p. 130.

[78]Grigorii I. Tunkin, "The Geneva Conference on the Law of the Sea," *International Affairs* (Moscow), no. 7 (1958), p. 48.

[79]See Akademii nauk SSSR, Institut gosudarstva i prava, *International Law*, *op. cit.*, pp. 207-210.

[80]See Sergei B. Krylov, U.N. *Yearbook of the International Law Commission*, A/CN.4/SR306/50-52, 75 (June 7, 1955), pp. 141-142; A/CN.4/SR367/81 (June 14, 1956), p. 209; and Akademii nauk SSSR, Institut gosudarstva i prava, *International law*, *op. cit.*, p. 208.

[81]Akademii nauk SSSR, Institut gosudarstva i prava, *International Law, op. cit.*, p. 211. See also, Platon D. Morozov (USSR), Sixth (Legal) Committee of the U.N. General Assembly, A/C.6/SR585/26 (November 16, 1958), p. 174.

[82]Platon D. Morozov (USSR), Sixth (Legal) Committee of the U.N. General Assembly, A/C.6/SR488/19 (December 3, 1956), pp. 36-37.

[83]See *Multilateral Treaties In Respect of Which the Secretary-General Performs Depository Functions: List of Signatures, Ratifications, Accessions, etc., As of 31 December 1967*, (United Nations: New York, February 1968), ST/LEG/SER.D/1, pp. 319-321.

[84]Platon D. Morozov (USSR), Sixth (Legal) Committee of the U.N. General Assembly, A/C.6/SR583/62 (November 17, 1958, p. 164.

[85]See *Multilateral Treaties In Respect of Which The Secretary-General Performs Depository Functions: List of Signatures, Ratifications and Accessions, etc., As of 31 December 1967*, (United Nations: New York, February 1968), ST/LEG/SER.D/1, p. 321.

[86]*Ibid.*

[87]*Ibid.*, p. 329.

[88]*Ibid.*, p. 311.

[89]See Akademii nauk SSSR, Institut gosudarstva i prava, *International Law*, (Moscow: 1951), pp. 260-266.

[90]See USSR Geographical Society resolution of February 10, 1949, reprinted by D. Golubev, *Russie v Antarktike* (Russians in Antarctica), (Moscow: 1949), pp. 68-69. See also, S.V. Molodtsov, *Sovremennoe mezhdunarodno-pravovoe polozhenie Antarktiki* (Contemporary Legal Status of Antartica), (Moscow: 1954), p. 43; and A.P. Movchan, "The Legal Status of Antartica: An International Problem," *1959 Sovetskii ezhegodnik mezhdunarodnogo prava* (1959 Soviet Yearbook of International Law), pp. 342-359.

[91]S. Kalesnik, "Russian Discoveries in Antarctica," *Slavyanye*, no. 4 (April 1949), p. 22.

[92]"Russians Discovered Antarctica," *Komsomolskaya pravda* (Komsomol Truth), January 28, 1950, p. 4.

[93]S. V. Molodtsov, *op. cit.*, pp. 30-35.

[94]*Ibid.*, pp. 36-37. See also, A.I. Andreyev, "New Facts Concerning the Discovery of Antarctica," *Pravda*, April 1, 1949, p. 4.

[95]See Akademii nauk SSSR, Institut gosudarstva i prava, *International Law, op. cit.*, p. 194.

[96]*Ibid.*, pp. 176-177.

[97]See Akademii nauk SSSR, Institut gosudarstva i prava, *International Law, op. cit.*, pp. 173-174.

[98]*Ibid.*, p. 143. See Fedor I. Kozhevnikov (USSR), U.N. *Yearbook of the International Law Commission*, A/CN.4/SR156/53-56 (July 3, 1952), p. 107; and A/CN.4/SR159/13 (July 8, 1952), p. 120; and western writer Kazimierz Grzybowski, *Socialist Commonwealth of Nations* (New Haven: Yale University Press, 1964), pp. 12-13.

[99]*Ibid.*, pp. 147-148. See also, "Nationality, Including Statelessness," Doc. A/CN.4/44, Annex 1, "Nationality in General," Vol. 2 (1952), pp. 9-10.

[100]See Kazimierz Grzybowski, *op. cit.*, p. 15.

[101]John N. Hazard, *1959 Proceedings of the American Society of International Law*, p. 38.

[102]See "Nationality, including Statelessness," Doc. A/CN.4/44, Annex 1, "Nationality in General," Vol. 2. (1952), p. 10.

[103]*Ibid.*, p. 9. See also, G.Y. Vilkov, "International Legal Regulation of the Question of Statelessness," *1963 Sovetskii ezhegodnik mezhdunarodnogo prava* (1963 Soviet Yearbook of International Law), p. 269.

[104]Fedor I. Kozhevnikov, U.N. *Yearbook of the International Law Commission*, A/CN.4/SR163/2 (July 14, 1952), p. 137. See also, "Soviet law recognizes and defined the concept of statelessness," Fedor I. Kozhevnikov, U.N. *Yearbook of the International Law Commission*, A/CN.4/SR159/12 (July 8, 1952), p. 120; Abushkevich (Byelorussia SSR), Sixth (Legal) Committee of the U.N. General Assembly, A/C.6/SR399 (October 6, 1954), p. 12; and G.Y. Vilkov, *loc. cit.*, p. 270.

[105]Platon D. Morozov (USSR), Sixth (Legal) Committee of the U.N. General Assembly, A/C.6/SR401/51 (October 12, 1954), pp. 24-25.

[106]There are two types of refugees: one type comprises the refugees from other states seeking refuge in the Soviet Union and the other type are refugees or refugee-exiles of the Soviet Union seeking refuge elsewhere. This statement applies equally to both.

[107]See Georg Ginsburg, "The Soviet Union and the Problem of Refugees and Displaced Persons," *American Journal of International Law*, Vol. 51 (1957), pp. 327-361.

[108]Akademii nauk SSSR, Institut gosudarstva i prava, *International Law, op. cit.*, p. 159.

[109]See Khlestov (USSR), 1963 U.N. Conference on Consular Relations A/CONF.25/SR12/4 (April 17, 1963), p. 40; and Akademii nauk SSSR, Institut gosudarstva i prava, *International Law, op. cit.*, p. 162.

[110]Akademii nauk SSSR, Institut gosudarstva i prava, *International Law, op. cit.*, p. 167.

[111]Timothy A. Taracouzio, *op. cit.*, p. 164.

[112]Akademii nauk SSSR, Institut gosudarstva i prava, *International Law, op. cit.*, pp. 173-174.

[113]See *Multilateral Treaties in Respect of Which the Secretary-General Performs Depository Functions: List of Signatures, Ratifications and Accessions, etc., As of 31 December 1967*, (United Nations: New York, February 1968), ST/LEG/SER. D/1.

CHAPTER VII.
PEACEFUL SETTLEMENT OF DISPUTES AND THE LAWS OF WAR

The Soviet Union has uniformly asserted that only voluntary negotiation, arbitration and /or adjudication can be the rule of law. To hold otherwise would be to erode away national sovereignty. The theme is "voluntariness" in the selection of means for the peaceful settlement of disputes.

This chapter is concerned with the volatile issues of the peaceful settlement of disputes and the laws of war. Five principles are considered: the "principle" of *nemo debet esse judex in propria causa* (third party judgment); the principle of peaceful settlement of disputes by voluntary negotiation, arbitration and/or adjudication; the principle of self-help; the principle of non-aggression; and the principle of the inviolability of civilian populations in time of war.

1. The "Principle" Of Nemo Debet Esse Judex In Propria Causa (Third Party Judgment)

The Soviet Foreign Ministry subscribes to the view that states ought to settle their disputes amicably but holds as completely contrary to the principles of international law any idea of compulsory third party judgment. *Nemo debet esse judex in propria causa* is not, in the Soviet view, a binding principle of law. Because of comity states may go to a third party, but not because the law requires it. "Surely, the head of state," noted Grigorii Tunkin, "could not be regarded as superior to the two states directly concerned in the dispute. Naturally they could leave it to him to settle the entire procedure if they wished, but, that was a matter of courtesy not law."[1]

Several arguments have been made against application to international relations of the principle of third party judgments. Fedor I. Kozhevnikov stressed that advocates of the principle "start out from a false premise, namely, that no trust could be placed in the good will of states. He would submit that it was wrong to build up a system of international law on that premise."[2] In addition, compulsory third party judgment would violate the principle of sovereign equality of states. One sovereignty could not be raised above two others in order to fix a settlement to a dispute between them without their consent.[3]

Additionally, the USSR refuses to accept the possibility of "impartiality". It makes no difference whether the third party is another sovereign or an international panel of arbitrators or a court of judges. In Litvinov's words, spoken at The Hague in 1922, "only an angel could be unbiased in judging Russian affairs."[4] Korovin explained, "The indispensable minimum and fundamental postulate of any arbitration is a community of legal views and normative criteria. Failing such community, every attempt to find an arbitral authority between two halves of humanity speaking different languages is *a priori* hopeless."[5] Perhaps this feeling of partiality of men sitting as third party judges has lessened in the last forty years. It remains true, however, that the East and West speak "different languages" although these differences may no longer be "hopeless" as long as all parties understand and can deal with these differences. Nonetheless, the Soviet Union remains reluctant to relinquish control of the decision-making process — compulsory third party judgment remains unacceptable.

At times the Soviet Union has, through treaty, agreed to third party judgment when it was offered no other alternative.[6] Nonetheless, Moscow has striven in practice to avoid the presence of the third party. In boundary dispute treaties, as an example, entered into with Turkey, Afghanistan, Poland, Finland, Rumania and Hungary, the procedures for settlement were the establishment of a commission of two plentipotentiaries, one from each of the disputing parties.[7] One of the earliest of such bilateral treaties with Latvia in 1932 called for a "permanent" commission (actually created in an *ad hoc* fashion as disputes arose) with four members, two named from each state.[8] Direct agreement between the parties is infinitely more satisfying to the Soviet Foreign Ministry than a decision reached by an outsider. *Nemo debet esse judex in propria causa* (third party judgment) is neither a treaty nor a customary principle of international law in the Soviet view.[9]

2. *The Principle Of Peaceful Settlement Of Disputes By Voluntary Negotiation, Arbitration And/Or Adjudication*

(a) *Meaning*
Soviet diplomats believe there is a principle which commands that nations employ peaceful means on a voluntary basis for the achievement of the settlement of disputes. The Soviet Union is proud of what it feels is its "good faith" tradition. A Soviet law text quoted with satisfaction the words of Professor Martens of the University of St. Petersburg (Imperial Russia), "History knows no other civilized people who have made so many efforts to insure the peaceful settlement of matured questions of international law and order."[10]

At the 1961 meeting of the International Law Association, the Soviet Branch submitted a report which in part said, "The parties are free to choose any form for the peaceful settlement of their disputes."[11] The Soviet report favored diplomatic negotiation as the paramount and most appropriate method of settling disputes. This position was taken even

141

though several other branches pointed out that negotiation unduly favored the powerful nation and weakened the sovereignty of an already weak nation.

Other specific procedures which take a second place to negotiation are voluntary arbitration and judicial settlement.[12] For many of the same reasons that Moscow rejects compulsory arbitration and judicial settlement, it is cool toward voluntary settlement by these means. As already noted, Soviet diplomats deny the existence of a principle of compulsory arbitration or adjudication. Moscow is willing to admit that states may consent to these methods recognizing that "resort to arbitration is voluntary" while "an arbitration award is binding."[13] It is the *res judicata* nature of arbitral awards, their finality, that is most distasteful. The Soviet aim is to preserve its discretion at every stage of the settlement proceedings and this is lost even when arbitration or adjudication is voluntarily entered into. In part also, Soviet fears are those of a minority in the international community, a minority reluctant to rely upon the impartiality of the majority to settle tough questions of East-West conflict. Americans should appreciate this view as the United States has expressed similar attitudes toward arbitration. The role of law in the settlement of disputes was described by Leo Gross, speaking of the Soviet preference for "voluntariness", "International law need not be excluded and may indeed offer a useful starting or bargaining position, but law is not the dominant factor in the process. The object is a settlement acceptable to the parties. It should be noted that the role of politics may be strongest and that law weakest in negotiation, and this may well be the reason why great powers show a penchant for this procedure."[14]

A theme which dominates the Soviet postion on free choice of the means for peaceful settlement is state sovereignty. Voluntariness and sovereignty go hand in hand. As Fedor I. Kozhevnikov told the International Law Commission, "it was clearly an abuse of sovereignty and free will for a party to be able to drag another party into a dispute against its will."[15] The Soviet Union defends the classical principle and has resisted every attempt to elevate a supernational authority above the nation-state.[16] It is important to note the full meaning of this principle of voluntary peaceful settlement of disputes. On the one hand states may select the means of peaceful settlement. On the other, states are obligated to settle peacefully. Acknowledgment that non-peaceful means are improper is the keystone of the U.N. Charter.

Concerning arbitration and adjudication there is a half-way house, namely, voluntary acceptance of compulsory jurisdiction in a limited area. The Soviets have been willing to agree to such a procedure when "the recognized evil [such as narcotics control] called for strong measures" but otherwise "the remedy of compulsory arbitration was out of proportion to the issues at stake."[17] For that reason, Sergei Krylov vigorously opposed the inclusion of a compulsory arbitration clause as the way to resolve disputes concerning the conservation of the resources of the sea and of fisheries.[18] Arbitration and adjudication were too strong a measure for the issues at hand.

Actually the test may be phrased: if the Soviet Union can avoid committing itself to compulsory arbitration or adjudication it will do so; if not, it will yeild if political interests so demand. When ratifying the Genocide Convention the USSR submitted a reservation refusing to accept the jurisdiction of the International Court of Justice (ICJ) as adjudicator of disputes under the Convention.[19] In 1954, when the Soviet Union attempted to ratify the International Labor Organization Convention with a similar reservation, the Soviet Government was informed that the Convention contained no provision which permitted reservations. Either Moscow had to accept the Convention in its entirety (with a compulsory jurisdiction clause) or not at all. The Soviet Union ratified, without reservation, on April 26, 1954. Likewise the USSR accepted the compulsory jurisdiction clauses in the International Atomic Energy Statute (Article 17); the Supplementary Convention on Slavery (Article 10); and the UNESCO Convention (Article 14); as well as the World Health Organization and World Meteorological Conventions.[20]

In contrast the Soviet Union has eschewed the compulsory jurisdiction of the International Court of Justice. This position is consistent with Soviet hostility toward general acceptance of compulsory jurisdiction.[21] The USSR entered the League of Nations with a reservation, "In as much as Article 12 and 13 of the Covenant propose that states consider settling disputes through arbitration or judicial procedure, the Soviet Government deems it necessary to make it clear that, in its opinion such a procedure cannot be applied relating to questions arising before its entrance into the League."[22] The USSR did not adhere to the Statute of the Permanent Court of International Justice (PCIJ) and a Soviet judge never sat on its bench. No doubt the Soviet Union was plagued by the memory of the *Eastern Carelia Case* brought before the PCIJ in 1923 (prior to Soviet membership in the League) by the League Council which requested that the Court decide whether the 1920 Treaty of Dorpat and an annexed declaration thereto regarding the autonomy of Eastern Carelia had created an obligation on the part of Russia to Finland. The Soviet Government refused to participate, but the League Council continued to press for a decision and it was only after the Court declined to render the opinion requested that the case was dropped. The Soviet Union did not give credit to the PCIJ for the dismissal.[23] To avoid political friction, the Soviet Union has taken the position that the International Court of Justice (ICJ) of the United Nations is not the successor to nor a continuation of the Permanent Court of International Justice (PCIJ) of the League of Nations.[24]

Political reasons have induced the Soviet Union to play a larger role in the work of the ICJ. A Soviet national has continuously occupied a seat on the Court since its "inception" in 1946. Political reasons have also lead the Soviet Union to refuse to submit to the compulsory jurisdiction of the Statutes of the World Court. These have already been alluded to: (1) lack of a belief in impartial judges,[25] (2) finalized decisions, (3) yeilding control of the settlement process, and (4) fear of the influence of the Court.[26]

Only on one occassion has a communist state, Albania, submitted to the jurisdiction of the ICJ. The decision rendered by the Court in that case, the *Corfu Channel Case (Merits)*, was not altogether satisfying.[27] There have been decisions of the ICJ which Moscow has praised, such as the *Anglo-Norwegian Fisheries Case*, the *Anglo-Iranian Oil Co. Case (Preliminary Objections)*, and the *Interpretation of Peace Treaties (Second Phase)*. There are also a number of ICJ decisions which the Soviet Government has found unsatisfactory, in addition to the *Corfu Channel Case (Merits)*. They are the *Interpretation of Peace Treaties*, the *International Status of South-West Africa*, and the *Case Concerning Rights of Nationals of the United States in Morocco*.[28]

Should the Soviet Union submit *ad hoc* to the ICJ a legal problem would then arise. The Moscow Government recognizes only treaty and custom as sources of international law. Article 38 of the Statute (of the ICJ) recognizes, in addition to these sources, general principles of law recognized by civilized nations. This additional source is not acknowledged by the USSR as an independent source of international law. A difficult legal issue could confront the Court as to applicable law.

The Soviet Union has acted cautiously toward the Court. Moscow has not only refused to submit to the compulsory jurisdiction provision of the Statute but also has challenged the Court's exercise of jurisdiction in cases brought before it by other states in an attempt to circumscribe its power to give decisions in those instances.

(b) *Source*

The Preamble of the Charter of the United Nations sets forth as one of the purposes of the Organization, "to ensure, by acceptance of principles and its institution of methods, that armed force shall not be used, save in the common defense." To achieve these ends Chapter VI (Articles 33-38) of the Charter was inserted.

To the Soviets, this codification of the principle of peaceful settlement of disputes by voluntary negotiation, arbitration and/or adjudication was achieved. "The United Nations Charter," wrote Tunkin, "is an unusual treaty. In the first place, it is the legal basis for the functioning of the world organization for peace and security. In the second place, states have given it pre-eminence over all treaties."[29] Principles set forth in the Charter are universal principles of international law. They are binding on U.N. members as treaty signatories. Custom is not altogether excluded.

For non-signatories of the Charter, this principle remains custom-based. Moreover, custom may re-enter the picture as a body of law develops around the 1945 Charter principles. "The Soviet Union declared outright that it does not acknowledge the right of the General Assembly to adopt a resolution on the establishment and utilization of armed forces."[30] Written law modifications of 1945 Charter principles is denied by way of General Assembly resolutions. In terms of this principle, in the Soviet view, treaty is the more important source, but not the exclusive source.

3. The Principle Of Self-Help

(a) Meaning
"[A]ll actions taken by an individual state against those violating the rules of international law for the purpose of self-preservation are embraced by a single concept of international law" termed self-help, according to a Soviet author.[31] The principle of self-help must operate, in the Soviet view, within the framework of contemporary international law which includes the principles of peaceful settlement of disputes and non-aggression. The post-1945 self-help principle has no commonality with the 19th Century, and earlier, self-help concept which, in essence, permitted any response including a declaration of war. Today the principle of self-help, caution Soviet writers, is a limited right of response. To excede the proper response is to act illegally. A special case of self-help is self-defense. The United Nations Charter sets forth the limitations in this respect. Armed force may be employed only in the instance of direct armed aggression. No case will justify its use otherwise. The historical evolution of this principle portrays the results in the struggle to narrow the occasions for the use of force.[32] In addition to the use of armed force self-help may include economic and political measures as the response of the defending state to economic aggression, ideological and political subversion (terroristic acts, sabotage, espionage and the like). Among the economic measures are reprisals, embargo and boycott. Political measures include the lodging of diplomatic protests and the severing of diplomatic and/or consular relations.

(b) Source
Soviet scholars believe[33] that the modern principle of self-help is to be found in Article 51 of the United Nations Charter. Self-help has been codified to the extent that self-help means the right to use armed force in self-defense.[34] As for the economic and political self-help measures, they are regulated by the United Nations Charter to the extent that that instrument imposes an obligation for peaceful settlement of disputes. Beyond that, such self-help measures are those that have evolved through the practice of states, the customary practice of reprisals, embargo and the severing of diplomatic and consular relations.

4. *The Principle Of Non-Aggression*

(a) *Meaning*
Modern international law prohibits the use of force as a means of settling disputes even when hostilities are preceded by a declaration of war. "Under international law," according to a Soviet law text, "any state which is the *first* to declare war upon another state, or to invade with its armed forces, even without a declaration of war, the territory of another state, is recognized as the assailant — that is, the aggressor. In this way, a declaration of war not only no longer frees a state from international liability but forms part of the conception of aggression."[35] The status of war is not equal to the status of peace. Contrary to the law in the days of Grotius, "The starting of war constitutes, according to contemporary international law, the gravest breach of international law involving, side by side with the responsibility of a state which resorts to such a war, also personal responsibility of the perpetrators of the war."[36]

Soviet scholars speak of the "unqualified" principle of non-aggression. They do not consider support of wars of national liberation as an infringement on that principle.[37] K.A. Bagninian (USSR) placed these two notions into a unified whole, "According to the Soviet definition of aggression only states, *i.e.*, subjects of international law, may become aggressors or victims of aggression. The concept of aggression does not apply to domestic conflicts and civil wars which are fought between various groups and parties within the frontiers of one and the same state. Internal conflicts and civil wars belong to the domestic affairs of states . . ."[38]

This analysis permits a favorable interpretation of the activities of domestic communists within a state. But the analysis has its difficulties too. Take the Viet-Nam situation as an example. If the Soviet Union takes the position that there are two independent sovereign states, North and South Viet-Nam, then the principle of aggression may be applied and the Saigon Government may be subject to condemnation. But if the Soviet Union recognizes only one legitimate Government of Viet-Nam, then the actions of the South Vietnamese cannot be condemned as aggression. This, of course, says nothing about the role of the United States.[39]

Colonies are sovereign and as such are protected by international law in the Soviet view. Under the principle of non-aggression if a colony wishes to sever its ties with the mother country and if the mother country, according to Soviet thinking, resists, the mother country commits aggression. If the colony has to repel "aggression", it acts in self defense.

The work of the United States Information Agency (USIA) and Radio Free Europe are criticized by Soviet diplomats as a violation of the principle of non-aggression. Non-aggression includes a prohibition against "war propaganda". War propaganda incites hatreds among peoples and is an instrument for the preparation of aggression. Platon D. Morozov (USSR) called attention to General Assembly Resolution 110 (II) which defined "war propaganda" as "all forms of propaganda, in whatsoever country conducted, which is either designed or likely to provoke or encourage any threat to the peace, breach of the peace, or an act of aggression."[40]

Soviet spokesmen hold to the view of "responsibility of states for acts of aggression."[41] This was a new development, as they saw it. The concept of state responsibility had evolved primarily as the liability of states for damage caused to aliens in the country of the respondent state. The focus was upon problems of denial of justice, exhaustion of local remedies, responsibility for *ultra vires* actions and reparations. "In modern international law," recorded G.I. Tunkin at a meeting of the International Law Commission (ILC), "state responsibility arose not so much out of the treatment of aliens, as out of actions which endangered, or could endanger international peace or friendly relations between states and out of breaches of the United Nations Charter as developed by General Assembly Resolution 1514 (XV) of 14 December 1960, the declaration granting of independence to colonial countries and peoples. Accordingly, the very concept of state responsibility in international law needed to be re-examined in the light of those developments."[42] A re-examination would show, Tunkin believed, that the problem of sanctions and the responsibility for breaches of the rules of international law had become more prominent than the responsibility of states to aliens.[43]

(b) *Source*

Platon D. Morozov (USSR) expressed the view of Soviet scholars as to the source of the principle of non-aggression when he said,

The Charter of the United Nations not only prohibited aggressive war but Article 2, paragraph 4, also banned the threat of force "against the territorial integrity or political independence of any state." The principle of non-aggression, as defined in the United Nations Charter, should be considered a generally accepted principle of the international law of the day. It has been affirmed in the Bandung Declaration of 1955, the Declaration of the Heads of State and Government of the Non-Aligned Countries, issued on the occasion of the Belgrade Conference of 1961, and the 1963 Charter of the Organization of African States.[44]

Of course, for non-members of the United Nations, the principle of non-aggression was, from the Soviet viewpoint, a customary norm. Morozov hints in his statement that the principle "should be" accepted, indicating that there is (at least in his own mind) some doubt as to whether it has been accepted by states *via* the United Nations Charter. He continued by pointing to other evidences of the restatement of the principle by states. This analysis strongly suggests that Morozov may be arguing for the principle of non-aggression as a customary norm of contemporary international law.

On the other hand, Morozov may have intended by his statement that the principle of non-aggression, codified in the U.N. Charter, has only been reaffirmed and supplemented by subsequent state practice. A supplement to the principle of non-aggression may well be the addition of "state responsibility" or a "just wars of national liberation" corollary. No where, to the knowledge of this writer, have Soviet publicists claimed that the "just wars" concept eminates from the United Nations Charter. They have written only that the principle of non-aggression may flow from the Charter and that that principle does not deny "just wars." If "just wars" are legally permissible, the source of that legality must be viewed, by Soviet scholars, as a customary practice of states in the Twentieth Century.

Whichever position Morozov intended to take, custom plays a significant role. As for the analytical confusion, in more recent years Soviet writers have not shed any new light on the subject.

In the area of state responsibility, Soviet diplomats have asserted that the Charter of the United Nations does not codify new development along these lines. Several sessions of the International Law Commission (ILC) were devoted to the "Draft Convention on Rights and Duties of States" in an effort to codify state responsibility. In 1949, a report containing a proposed Draft was submitted by the Commission to the General Assembly.[45] The Soviet Delegate on the Commission at the time, Vladimir M. Koretskii, vigorously dissented from the report because of its shortcomings, i.e., the encroachment on national sovereignty which the Draft imposed.[46] The General Assembly, after deliberation, recommended that the Commission continue to work on state responsibility.[47] To date, the International Law Commission (ILC) has proposed no new draft convention on the subject. As a result, any new development concerning state responsibility for aggression must be found in custom.

5. The Principle Of The Inviolability Of Civilian Populations In Time Of War

(a) Meaning

Since international fighting does take place, the laws of war continue to have relevance. Professor Castrén of the University of Helsinki (Finland) verbalized the feelings of the overwhelming majority of all writers when he admitted that, "only a few of the laws of war and neutrality now in force are suited to present-day conditions, and belligerents do not pay much regard to them."[48] One principle which the Soviet Union believes to be in force and well-suited to the Twentieth Century is that military operations may be conducted only against the armed forces of the enemy. Unfortunately, the United States has violated this principle, wrote A.I. Poltorak and L.I. Savinskii, in their execution of military operations in Viet-Nam.[49]

Contemporary laws and customs of war, assert Soviet publicists, draw a distinction between combatants and civilian populations. It is groundless to assert that "in modern war the conception of military operations

148

has extended so far that virtually every person is a potential combatant, while the development of military technology has advanced so far that it is allegedly in practice impossible to adhere to the principle of the inviolability of the civilian populations."[50]

The principle of inviolability of civilian populations in time of war prohibits the use of nuclear weapons. O.V. Bogdanov, Senior Research Associate of the Institute of State and Law of the USSR Academy of Sciences, wrote that "the use of nuclear weapons violates . . . the customary principle of international law of the prohibition of the direction of military activities against the peaceable civilian populace."[51]

(b) Source

The principle of the inviolability of civilian populations in time of war is a universal principle of international law.[52] It is a customary norm whose antecedents, in the Soviet view, stretch back to the Nineteenth Century practice of states. Petr Romashkin, Director of the Institute of State and Law of the USSR Academy of Sciences, outlined the legal developments which culminated in the outlawing of the uses of nuclear weapons (and reflects the principle of the inviolability of civilian populations).

> They [nuclear weapons] produce effects comparable to those chemical and bacteriological weapons, and therefore the arguments on the disposition of such weapons should justifiably be extended to them. There are international documents, such as the St. Petersburg Declaration of 1868, which proclaimed the existence of technical frontiers before which the claims of humanity overrode the claims of war; the appendices to the Hague Convention of 1907 concerning the laws and customs of war on land forbid the use of poisons or toxic weapons as well as weapons, machines or substances capable of unnecessary suffering, and the Geneva Protocol of 1925 bans the use in time of war of asphyxiating, toxic or similar gases together with bacteriological weapons. Under these conventions, which have been signed by many countries and have received world-wide approval the same prohibition shall apply to nuclear weapons.[53]

A procession of conventions reaching back to the mid-1800's are aimed at the protection of non-combatants. The Hague Convention of 1907 placed non-combatants under the protection of international law. This was affirmed by the Geneva Conventions of 1949.[54] Soviet scholars believe that undeniably the inviolability of non-combatants is a customary principle of international law.[55]

7. Summary

While the laws of war do not proceed from the U.N. Charter the principles of peaceful settlement of disputes, in the Soviet view, does eminate from the U.N. Charter. Peaceful settlement of disputes (voluntary selection of the means) and the principle of non-aggression are "codified" as are the principles of peaceful coexistence, non-intervention and national self-determination of states in the U.N. Charter. Yet it is clear that custom, even with respect to these principles, plays an important role — explaining the "bindingness" of new developments in the law since 1945.

These principles of peaceful settlement of disputes and the laws of war are of a highly political nature. Few principles could be more closely related to the life or death of a nation. Few principles are under as much stress and strain in today's world. There are increasing numbers of written conventions in this area of the law, but custom — the practice of nations, remains, in the Soviet view, a chief source of the law.

NOTES

[1]Grigorii I. Tunkin, U.N. *Yearbook of the International Law Commission,* A/CN.4/SR442/ 68 (May 13, 1958), p. 56. See also, Fedor I. Kozhevnikov, U.N. *Yearbook of the International Law Commission,* A/CN.4/SR218/104 (July 17, 1953), p. 228.

[2]Fedor I. Kozhevnikov, U.N. *Yearbook of the International Law Commission,* A/CN.4/SR 202/59 (June 25, 1953), p. 116.

[3]See Fedor I. Kozhevnikov, U.N. *Yearbook of the International Law Commission,* A/CN.4/ SR146/61 (June 19, 1952), p. 53; and A/CN.4/SR202/59 (June 25, 1953), p. 116.

[4]M. Litvinov's statement at the Conference on Russian Affairs, The Hague, July 12, 1922, as quoted by Louis B. Sohn, *Cases and Materials on World Law,* (Brooklyn, 1950), p. 1046.

[5]Evgenii A. Korovin, *Mezhdunarodnoe pravo perekhodnogo vremeni* (International Law During the Transitional Period), (Moscow: 1924), pp. 47-48.

[6]The Soviet Union has accepted the compulsory jurisdiction provisions in the Charters of the International Atomic Energy Agency (IAEA), International Labor Organization (ILO), United Nations Educational, Scientific and Cultural Organization (UNESCO), World Health Organization (WHO), World Meteorological Organization (WHO), as well as the Supplementary Convention on the Abolition of Slavery.

[7]See Akademii nauk SSSR, Institut gosudarstva i prava, *International Law,* translated by Dennis Ogden, (Moscow: Foreign Languages Publishing House, n. d.), p. 199.

[8]Treaty between Latvia and the USSR dated June 18, 1932, *Sobraine deistvuiushchikh dogovorov SSSR,* Vol. 8; *League of Nations Treaty Series* (LNTS), Vol. 147, p. 129. For a study of Soviet emphasis on direct settlement of disputes see, Samuel Pisar, "Soviet Conflicts of Laws in International Commercial Relations," *Harvard Law Review,* Vol. 70 (1957), pp. 593-656.

[9]See "Soviet Branch Report," *Report of the 50th Conference, Tokyo, 1962,* International Law Association, p. 359.

[10]Professor Martens as quoted by Akademii nauk SSSR, Institut gosudarstva i prava, *International Law, op. cit.,* p. 52. Fedor I. Kozhevnikov criticized Evgenii A. Korovin for stating that the USSR was absolutely opposed to arbitration, see, Fedor I. Kozhevnikov, *Sovetskoe gosudarstvo i mezhdunarodnoi pravo* (Soviet State and International Law), (Moscow: 1948), p. 376.

[11]"Soviet Branch Report," *Report of the 50th Conference, Tokyo, 1962,* International Law Association, p. 359.

[12]See Akademii nauk SSSR, Institut gosudarstva i prava, *International Law, (Mezhdunarodnoe pravo)* edited by Fedor I. Kozhevnikov, (Moscow: 1957), pp. 377-379.

[13]Akademii nauk SSSR, Institut gosudarstva i prava, *International Law, op. cit.,* p. 385. See also, Platon D. Morozov (USSR), "no state could be compelled to submit to arbitration; the state's consent was an essential condition," Sixth (Legal) Committee of the U.N. General Assembly, A/C.6/SR495/17 (December 11, 1956), p. 78; Mr. Abushkevich (Byelorussian SSR), "There could be no arbitration without the consent of the parties to submit the dispute to arbitration . . . Thus the principle of the autonomy of the will of the parties had entered into the practice of states, it was laid down in international agreements, and it was accepted in legal doctrine." Sixth (Legal) Committee of the U.N. General Assembly, A/C.6 /SR554/27 (October 2, 1958), p. 25.

[14]Leo Gross, "Some Observations on the International Court of Justice," *American Journal of International Law,* Vol. 56 (January 1962), p. 41.

[15]Fedor I. Kozhevnikov, U.N. *Yearbook of the International Law Commission*, A/CN.4/SR 228/40 (July 31, 1953), p. 298.

[16]See Fedor I. Kozhevnikov, U.N. *Yearbook of the International Law Commission*, A/CN.4 /SR185/80 (June 3, 1950); and A/CN.4/SR191/59 (June 11, 1953), p. 43. See also, Grigorii I. Tunkin, "The Soviet Union's view was not that national sovereignty prevailed over the law of nations, but the basis of any principle of international law was agreement and that states were bound only by that to which they subscribed." 1958 U.N. Conference on the Law of the Sea, A/CONF.13/SR13/18 (April 15, 1958), p. 32; and Mr. Russin (Ukrainian SSR), "His delegation . . . was prepared to defend the classical principles of arbitration . . . " Sixth (Legal) Committee of the U.N. General Assembly, A/C.6/SR556/34 (October 7, 1958), p. 34.

[17]Sergei B. Krylov, U.N. *Yearbook of the International Law Commission*, A/CN.4/SR360/ 53 (June 5, 1956), p. 153.

[18]See Sergei B. Krylov, U.N. *Yearbook of the International Law Commission*, A/CN.4/SR 353/62-63 (May 24, 1956), p. 99; Grigorii I. Tunkin, 1958 U.N Conference on the Law of the Sea, A/CONF.13/9-10 (April 15, 1958), p. 31; S.V. Molodtsov, "Codification and Further Development of the Law of the Sea," *1958 Sovetskii ezhegodnik mezhdunarodnogo prava* (1958 Soviet Yearbook of International Law), pp. 340-341; and Akademii nauk SSSR, Institut gosudarstva i prava, *International Law, op. cit.*, p. 224.

[19]USSR reservation to the Genocide Convention, December 16, 1949, *Sobranie deistvuiushchikh dogovorov SSSR* (Collection of Treaties of the USSR), Vol. 16, p. 70; *United Nations Treaty Series* (UNTS), Vol 78, p. 277. See also, S. Volodin, "Convention on the Prevention and Punishment of the Crime of Genocide," *Sovetskoe gosudarstvo i pravo* (Soviet State and Law), 1955, pp. 125-128; and V.F. Gubin, "The Soviet Union and Reservations to International Treaties," *1959 Sovetskii ezhegodnik mezhdunarodnogo prava* (1959 Soviet Yearbook of International Law), pp. 137-138.

The Soviet Union would prefer provisions for settlement of disputes similar to that in the Antarctic Treaty which provides for negotiation, inquiry, mediation, conciliation, arbitration and judicial settlement at the choice of the parties and only if these methods should fail may the dispute "with the consent, in each case, of all the parties to the dispute" be adjudicated by the International Court of Justice. For text see, "A Treaty for Antarctica," *International Conciliation*, 531 (1961).

[20]International Labor Organization (ILO): F. Ivanov, "Enforcement of the International Labor Organization Convention," *1958 Sovetskii ezhegodnik mezhdunarodnogo prava* (1958 Soviet Yearbook of International Law), p. 445.

International Atomic Energy Agency (IAEA): *Sob. deistv. dog. SSSR.* (Collection of Treaties of the USSR), Vol. 15, p. 195.

Supplementary Convention on Slavery; *Sob. deistv. dog. SSSR* (Collection of Treaties of the USSR), Vol. 19, p. 146; *United Nations Treaty Series* (UNTS), Vol. 266, p. 3.

UNESCO Convention: *Sob. deistv. dog. SSSR*(Collection of Treaties of the USSR), Vol. 16, pp. 583-595; *United Nations Treaty Series* (UNTS), Vol. 4, pp. 275-301.

World Health Organization (WHO): Does not appear in *Sob. deistv dog. SSSR* (collection of Treaties of the USSR). Appears in *Belorussaia SSR v mezhdunarodnykh otnosheniiakh* (Byelorussian SSR in International Relations), 1960, p. 425.

World Meteorological Organization (WMO): Does not appear in *Sob. deistv. dog. SSSR* (Collection of Treaties of the USSR). Appears in *Belorussaia SSR v. mezhdunarodnykh otnosheniiakh* (Byelorussian SSR in International Relations), 1960, p. 775.

[21]See "Memorandum of Soviet Branch" prepared by David B. Levin, N.I. Petrenko and N.A. Ushakov, "The viewpoint of the Committee of the Soviet Association of International Law on the essence of the problem is as follows: 1. The operating Charter of the United Nations and the Statute of the International Court of Justice records the principle of optionality . . . states voluntarily recognize the compulsory jurisdiction of the International Court on some definite question. The Committee holds that at the present stage of international

relations such a situation is justified both judically and politically." *The 51st Conference, Brussels, 1964*, International Law Association, p. 97. See additionally, Grigorii I. Tunkin, U.N. *Yearbook of the International Law Commission*, A/CN.4/SR465/60 (June 17, 1958), p. 184, and A/CN.4/SR447/47 (May 21, 1958), pp. 81-82; and Mr. Feodorov (USSR), 1964 U.N. Special Committee on Principles of International Law Concerning Friendly Relations and Cooperation Among States, A/CN.119/SR20 (September 11, 1964), p. 7.

[22]Letter from the People's Commissar for Foreign Affairs to the President of the Assembly of the League of Nations, *Sob. deistv. dog. SSSR* (Collection of Treaties of the USSR), Vol. 2, p. 36.

[23]*Eastern Carelia Case*, PCIJ, Series C, no. 3, p. 67; Series B, no. 5, p. 12.

[24]See N.N. Polianskii, *Mezhdunarodnyi sud* (The International Court of Justice), (Moscow: 1951), pp. 48-53.

[25]See Fedor I. Kozhevnikov, "It goes without saying that under all circumstances there will remain unchanged that general principles of Soviet Foreign Policy, under which Soviet diplomacy will always seek to obtain such a bench for the arbitration tribunals or for other similar agencies as will guarantee to the USSR the same measure of disinterestedness and justice as is assumed to other states." *Uchebnoe posobie po mezhdunarodnomu publichnomu pravy (Ocherki)*, (Teaching Aid in International Public Law — Essays), (Moscow: 1947), p. 204.

See American writers on the subject, John N. Hazard, "Soviet Union and International Law," *Soviet Studies* (University of Glasgow), Vol. 1, no. 3 (January 1950), p. 197; and Zigurds L. Zile, "Soviet Contribution to International Adjudication: Professor Krylov's Jurisprudential Legacy," *American Journal of International Law*, Vol. 58 (April 1964), p. 387.

[26]Arthur Larson, "The Soviets, however, fear more than particular decisions of the Court; they fear the influence of the Court in world affairs in general." Arthur Larson, "Soviet Impact on International Law," U.S. State Department, External Research Paper no. 156, May 1964, p. 7. See also, Charles de Visscher, "Reflections on the Present Prospects of International Adjudication," *American Journal of International Law*, Vol. 50 (July 1956), p. 474.

[27]*Corfu Channel Case (Merits)*, "Dissenting Opinion of Judge Krylov," ICJ Reports, 1949, pp. 68-77.

[28]*Anglo-Norwegian Fisheries Case*, ICJ Reports, 1951, p. 116; *Anglo-Iranian Oil Co. Case (Preliminary Objections)*, ICJ Reports, 1952, p. 93; *Interpretation of Peace Treaties (Second Phase)*, ICJ Reports, 1950, p. 65; *Corfu Channel Case (Merits)*, ICJ Reports, 1949, "Dissenting Opinion of Judge Krylov," pp. 68-77; *Interpretation of Peace Treaties*, ICJ Reports 1950, "Dissenting Opinion of Judge Krylov," pp. 105-113; *International Status of South-West Africa*, ICJ Reports 1950, "Dissenting Opinion of Judge Krylov," pp. 191-192; and the *Case Concerning Rights of Nationals of the United States in Morocco*, ICJ Reports 1952, p. 176.

See also S. Borisov (pseud. Sergei B. Krylov), "International Court's Violation of Iran's Sovereignty," *Sovetskoe gosudarstvo i pravo* (Soviet State and Law), no. 1 (January 1952), pp. 69-73; and S. Borisov (pseud. Sergei B. Krylov), "Two Cases Before the World Court of the United Nations in 1952," *Sovetskoe gosudarstvo i pravo* (Soviet State and Law), no. 4 (1953), pp. 152-157.

[29]Grigorii I. Tunkin, "The United Nations 1945-1965 (Problems of International Law)," *Sovetskoe gosudarstvo i pravo* (Soviet State and Law), no. 10 (1965) as translated in *Soviet Law and Government*, Spring 1966/Vol. 2, no. 4, p. 8.

[30]*Ibid.*, p. 10. See also Evgenii A. Korovin, *Pravovaia priroda i iuridicheskaia sila reshenii Generalnoi Assamblai OON* (Legal Nature and Legal Force of the Decisions of the General Assembly of the UNO), (Moscow: 1962).

[31]G.V. Sharmazanashvilli, "The Conception of Self-Help in International Law," *1959 Sovetskii ezhegodnik mezhdunarodnogo prava* (1959 Soviet Yearbook of International Law), p. 310.

[32]K.A. Bagninian, "Permanent Neutrality, the Right of Self-Defense and the Regional System in Light of the U.N. Charter," *Sovetskoe gosudarstvo i pravo* (Soviet State and Law), no. 6 (1956), pp. 102-106; and S.A. Malinin, "Participation of the Great Powers in Regional Treaties," *Uchenye zapiski* (Scientific Report), no. 255 (1958), pp. 86-98.

[33]G.V. Sharmazanashvilli, *loc. cit.*, p. 310.

[34]Treaty is the source of law for the USSR as a signatory of the Charter; but custom remains the source of law for non-signatories.

[35]Akademii nauk SSSR, Institut gosudarstva i prava, *International Law, op. cit.*, p. 420. Emphasis supplied. See also, K.A. Bagninian, *Borba Sovetskogo Soiuza protiv agressii* (The Struggle of the Soviet Union Against Aggression), (Moscow: 1959).

[36]Grigorii I. Tunkin, *Droit International Public* (Public International Law), translated from *Voprosy teorii mezhdunarodnoe prava* (Theoretical Problems of International Law), (Paris: A. Pedone, 1965), pp. 66-67.

[37]Writes Samson Soloveitchik, "The contradiction between the justification of a war 'for the liberation of a nation from the slavery of capitalism' and the unqualified repudiation of intervention is apparent but it cannot trouble a Communist. For him this contradiction is solved quite easily: an intervention carried out by a Communist Government is justified as 'just war,' while an intervention carried out by a non-communist government is 'by its very nature, a deep violation of the principle of sovereignty and of international co-operation.' What is good for 'world revolution' is 'progressive,' what is bad for it, is 'reactionary.'" Samson Soloveitchik, "International Law as 'an Instrument of Politics'," *University of Kansas City Law Review*, Vol. 21 (Summer 1953), p. 177. This analysis is somewhat "rough" and misses the fine points of Soviet "legalism."

[38]K.A. Bagninian, "The Question of the Definition of Aggression," *Sovetskoe gosudarstvo i pravo* (Soviet State and Law), no. 1 (1955), p. 61.

[39]See Platon D. Morozov (USSR), Sixth (Legal) Committee of the U.N. General Assembly, A/C.6/SR234/84-85 (November 6, 1950), p. 157; Platon D. Morozov (USSR), Sixth (Legal) Committee of the U.N. General Assembly, "Draft Code of Offenses Against the Peace and Security of Mankind," Doc. A/CN.4/ Vol. 2 (1951), p. 55; V.S. Polrovskii, "Just and Unjust Wars," *Marksizm-Leninism o voine, armii i voennoi nauke, sbornik statei* (Marxism-Leninism on War, Armies and Military Science, Collection of Articles), 1955, pp. 34-43; Kubatov, "Marxism-Leninism on Justs and Unjust Wars," *Propaganda i agitatsiga* (Propaganda and Agitation), Vol. 12 (1951), pp. 42-49; and Chuvikov, "The Teachings of Lenin and Stalin on Just and Unjust Wars," *Bolshevik*, Vols. 7-8 (1945), pp. 14-26.

[40]Platon D. Morozov (USSR), Sixth (Legal) Committee of the U.N. General Assembly, A/C. 6/SR802/27 (October 29, 1963), p. 111.

[41]Grigorii I. Tunkin, Annex 1 of the "Report of the Commission to the General Assembly," Doc. A/CN.4/152: "Report of Mr. Robert Ago (Italy), Chairman of the Subcommittee on State Responsibility, 4th Meeting (January 1963)," U.N. *Yearbook of the International Law Commission*, Vol. 2 (1963), p. 233.

[42]Grigorii I. Tunkin, U.N. *Yearbook of the International Law Commission*, A/CN.4/SR634 /49-50 (May 2, 1962), p. 37.

[43]See Sergei B. Krylov, U.N. *Yearbook of the International Law Commission*, A/CN.4/SR 372/30 (June 21, 1956), p. 242; Grigorii I. Tunkin, U.N. *Yearbook of the International Law Commission*, A/CN.4/SR634/51-52 (May 2, 1962), pp. 37-38; and A/CN.4/SR635/2 (May 3, 1962), p. 40.

[44]Platon D. Morozov (USSR), Sixth (Legal) Committee of the U.N. General Assembly, A/C.6/SR802/25 (October 29, 1963), p. 110. See also, Akademii nauk SSSR, Institut gosudarstva i prava, *International Law, op. cit.*, p. 377.

[45]"Draft Convention on Rights and Duties of States," text in *Work of the International Law Commission* (United Nations: New York, 1967), 67 V. 4, pp. 61-62.

[46]Vladimir M. Koretskii (USSR), dissent, footnote 21, "Report to the General Assembly," Part II: Draft Declaration on the Rights and Duties of States, 1949 *Yearbook of the International Law Commission*, p. 287.

[47]See the following resolutions of the General Assembly, 799 (VIII) of December 7, 1953; 1686 (XVI) of December 18, 1961; 1902 (XVIII) of November 18, 1963; and 2167 (XXI) of December 6, 1966.

[48]E. Castrén, *The Present Law of War and Neutrality*, (Helsinki: 1954), p. 5.

[49]A.I. Poltorak and L.I. Savinskii, "USA Lawlessness and Iniquity in Vietnam," *Sovetskoe gosudarstvo i pravo* (Soviet State and Law), no. 12 (December 1966), pp. 3-11.

[50]Akademii nauk SSSR, Institut gosudarstva i prava, *International Law, op. cit.*, p. 426.

[51]O.V. Bogdanov, *Vseobshcheii i polnoe rasoruzhenie (mezhdunarodno-pravovye voprosy)*, (General and Complete Disarmament — Problems of International Law), (Moscow: 1964), pp. 165-191.

[52]See Akademii nauk SSSR, Institut gosudarstva i prava, *International Law, op. cit.*, p. 422.

[53]Petr Romashkin, "Legal Problems Arising From the Development and Utilization of Atomic Power," *Proceedings of the 2nd Commission*, VIIth Congress of the International Association of Democratic Lawyers, Sofia, October 10-14, 1960, p. 22.

[54]See O.V. Bogdanov, *op. cit.*, pp. 165-191; and A.I. Poltorak and L.I. Savinskii, *op. cit.*, pp. 3-11.

[55]An interesting fact to which the reader's attention is directed is that the United Nations Charter was ratified two months *prior* to the dropping of the A-bomb on Japan.

CHAPTER VIII.
NEW MYTHS AND NEW REALITIES

Soviet and western scholars alike admit that the law must be built on the shifting sands of custom as well as on the rock of the written law. Custom provides a method for maintaining continuity in the law, of balancing stability with change. But custom is not always certain and clear. Customary law is linked to practice and as practice undergoes transformation so too may custom be transformed. Shifts in practice are not always lucid, the path is not always clearly marked. At times custom is hidden in the fuliginous obscurity of diverging practices and seeming contradictions and it is not an easy task to define at what point or when a practice is of such a nature as to be recognized as "required by law."

Revolutionary states do not make the task any easier. Greater uncertainty as to what the practice of states is materializes for uncertainty is heightened as disagreements as to what "the law" is arises. Initially the Bolshevik Régime was hostile toward customary law and diplomacy. Moscow disliked, if not distrusted, principles of law which evolved entirely out of the practice of capitalist states in their dealings with one another. But international conditions required that the new Soviet State negotiate treaties, exchange ambassadors, and claim and protect territory. Custom provided many of the rules for doing so.

Today the USSR accepts custom. It is in part because international life requires it. In part it is because Soviet fears about the bourgeois origins of customary law have been allayed. Over the last 50 years the Soviet Union, through its practice, has been contributing to the body of that law. In part it is because custom has proven useful in achieving the narrow foreign policy interests of the Soviet State.

What impact has customary law had on Soviet ideology? What is the Soviet conception of the legal nature of customary international law? What impact has international custom had on Soviet foreign policy? Conversely, what has been the impact of the Soviet Union on customary international law? These are the central questions.

Impact on Soviet Ideology

Soviet scholars have not been able to reconcile traditional Marxism with customary international law. How can law, as a "superstructure," have a common existence for fundamentally different social systems? How can a single body of customary international law apply equally to socialist and capitalist states? Men of the caliber of Stuchka, Korovin, Sabinin, Pashukanis, Vyshinskii, Kozhevnikov, Krylov and Tunkin have been unable to formulate a satisfactory answer. Today Soviet theoreticians are admonished by Grigorii I. Tunkin, chief spokesman in the field of international law, to free themselves "from dogmatism, from the use of citations [of Marx] instead of creative thought, from crying hallelujah, and from the isolation from actual reality which interferes with the development of the science of international law."[1] Energies are to be directed toward a legal analysis of pragmatic issues and away from the ideological questions.

Tunkin recognized the influence of ideology on Soviet thinking about customary law when he cautioned Soviet scholars to "free themselves from dogmatism" and engage in more "creative thought". Apparently he believed that "the isolation from actual reality which interferes with the development of the [Soviet] science of international law" was attributable to a lack of legal analysis resulting from an excess in ideology. Because his statement took the form of a warning to his colleagues rather than a polemic directed toward the West, especial credence may be attached to his evaluation that ideology not only played a role in Soviet thinking about international custom and treaty law but, in his view, it played too great a role.

Illustrative also of the continuing relevance of Soviet ideology is the manner in which ideological discussions have infected legal analysis of custom. In part ideology must be recognized as having influenced Soviet academicians to put forward the "consensus doctrine", to assert the rule of "new" states and "old" norms, and to evaluate, in the way in which they have, the importance of custom as a source of law in the contemporary world. The "consensus doctrine" provided an ideological explanation, not altogether satisfactory to be sure, of how customary international law could rest on a single superstructure and at the same time bind diverse social systems. Ideological considerations of how a proletarian state could accept bourgeois customary norms provided a basis and reinforced the legal argument of Soviet lawyers for the rule of "new" states and "old" norms while the very characterization of traditional customary norms as "bourgeois" contributed to Soviet judgment as to the relative importance of custom as compared to treaty-law. By understanding Soviet ideology greater insight is possible into Soviet legal analysis.

Soviet Conception of the Legal Nature of Customary International Law

The Soviet Union has expressed displeasure over the uncertainties of customary law, uncertainties which arise from the very nature of unwritten law linked to practice. With the aim of reducing uncertainty through clarity, no doubt in the belief that the knife of uncertainty can cut two ways, while seeking to maximize a guaranteed immunization from unwanted principles, Soviet writers espouse the "consensus doctrine" for the formation and termination of binding customary norms. This doctrine requires that before the Soviet Union can be bound by a customary principle, that principle must be "accepted" by the Soviet Union. Consequently a veto is created. But unlike other vetoes which the Soviet Union possesses, this one has not been exercised to any appreciable extent. To understand why this is so customary international law must be looked at from the viewpoint of the policy-maker in the Kremlin: which customary principles may be rejected out of hand as "unwanted"? This question confronts the Soviet policy-maker not in terms of applying a specific principle to a particular foreign policy situation (that will be discussed later) but in abstract terms, whether the Soviet Union can afford to reject forever and in all cases a principle of law. Can the principles of recognition be rejected? What of the principle of *pacta sunt servanda?* national self-determination? diplomatic immunity? *usque ad coelum?* The fundamental all-important character of customary principles themselves have resulted in an unexercised veto.

Why then do Soviet lawyers feel that "agreement" is the essential element in custom formation? Several reasons may be suggested. First, the "agreement" requirement offers the USSR security against future unwanted principles which other states may assert and which the Soviet Union may not wish to embrace. Second, the "consensus doctrine" offers, as mentioned already, ideological solace as a possible explanation of how a single international law can bind diverse social systems. Finally, a strong position on national sovereignty, which Moscow has long advocated, almost demands that "agreement" be made the decisive ingredient in norm-creation.

The fundamental character of customary principles and the growing stake of the Soviet Union in the international system also explains why the right of "new" states to review "old" norms cannot be an unqualified right. If a new state, according to the Soviet view, enters into relations with other states "without reservation" it is presumed to have accepted the existing international legal system. It is likely that a "new" state may lose this right before it ever realized that it had it. At one time, of course, this right directly served the foreign policy interests of the Soviet State, but the USSR is no longer a "new" state. Torn between espousal of an unqualified right of review for the benefit of newly emerging nations in the mid-Twentieth Century and a restricted view in the interest of international order, the Soviet Union has clearly opted for the latter. The right of "new" states to review "old" norms like the "consensus doctrine" contained potential seeds of revolutionary change for international law but Soviet application has made Soviet and western positions on the process of customary norm-creation nearly indistinguishable.

Having accepted custom along with treaty-law as the only primary sources of international law, Soviet writers hasten to add that of the two sources custom is of lesser importance. Does this mean that treaties will always override custom when there is a conflict of law? What about *jus cogens?* Does it mean that treaty principles are inherently more fundamental than customary principles? What could be more fundamental than *pacta sunt servanda?* Does it mean that on the whole treaty principles are more fundamental than customary principles? Or are becoming so?

Soviet writers advance the thesis that because of uncertainty in character and the slowness of development of custom (not to mention its bourgeois character) the trend of modern international law is away from custom and toward treaty. The work of the International Law Commission (ILC), where Soviet representatives have been active participants, lends credence to this view. Yet the question must be asked: can there exist an international legal system in which custom will not play an important role? Such a system would be difficult to conceive. It would be a system in which all principles were codified, in which every principle was clearly stated, in which the practice of states would count for nothing because there would be no hiatus in the law for custom to fill, no evolutionary practice not already reflected in treaty. The unique function of custom would be difficult to replace by treaty-law especially since at the international level the law-making process remains primitive indeed. Yet it cannot be denied that great strides have been made. The United Nations Charter and international conventions concerning the "high seas", "consular relations", "diplomatic intercourse and immunities", and recently "the law of treaties" stand as examples of achievement. But a balanced view requires an admission that much remains undone and that, in fact, the U.N. Charter and other international conventions have and probably will continue to create new customary law in what may be an endless process. Perhaps the Soviet thesis stands for the proposition that the process will not be endless. Be that as it may, for the present at least, Soviet scholars and practitioners recognize that custom is an important source of international law.

Impact on Soviet Foreign Policy

To understand the restraining influence of customary international law, custom must be approached from the vantage point of the Soviet policy-maker. Does he feel at all restrained by custom? Does he espouse custom with the intent of binding others and not himself, of restraining the foreeign policy of other states but not his own, or does he feel, in fact, an obligation to the law? In short, where and when does the law fit into his constellation of policies?

As a framework for analysis, it is important to recognize as do Soviet policy-makers, that customary law has an ordering and a provocative function. Customary law performs an ordering function when serving the broad interests of the international community. It performs a provocative function when used to advance the narrow national interests of a particular state. This does not mean that the ordering and the provocative functions are mutually exclusive. They rarely are. More frequently the two functions are coincidental in some degree. National interest and community interest join to provoke order and to order provocation. In this way customary law becomes a restraint on, as well as, an instrument of foreign policy. Conjointed function is the strength of international law and goes a long way toward explaining Soviet acceptance of customary law. Like all states the Soviet Union will follow custom either because of self-restraint arising from a sense of duty pure and simple, or because of self-restraint arising from a calculation of interests, or because of actual use or threat of use of force or reprisal. To fully comprehend the admixture of Soviet motives for accepting custom, a closer look at the ordering and provocative functions is required.

The evidence is clear that Moscow not only recognizes but accepts the ordering function of customary international law. Soviet diplomats have with remarkable uniformity defended the principle of *pacta sunt servanda*. Consistency on this principle has lead them to narrowly interpret the principle of *res inter alios gesta* (state succession), to openly express dislike for the alleged "principle" of *clausula rebus sic stantibus*, and to convert the right of "new" states to review "old" norms into a qualified right of limited usefulness although there were strong factors pressuring for a different result. Commitment to international order has also contributed to Soviet acceptance of other customary norms of an ordering nature relating to diplomatic immunity, air space, the high seas, outer space, territory, population and recognition.

Why has the Soviet Union felt it necessary to accept customary norms of an ordering nature? First, the Soviet Government cannot isolate itself from political realities, from the inter-state system, and from the "rules of the game" regulating that system. From the very beginning Soviet leaders recognized this fact of international life as they negotiated treaties, settled boundaries, arranged peace, granted recognition and exchanged diplomats. International law, of which custom is a part, corresponds to the belief that international "society" for all its competitiveness should also entail orderly relations. New realities of the mid-Twentieth Century have not only confirmed but accented the need for order. The nuclear age cries out for accommodation or chaos and the USSR has clearly expressed preference for order over nuclear holocaust.

Second, the Soviet Union has a stake in the international system. Customary norms provide a basis for conducting relations among states — for ordering expectations. The Soviet Government relies on these norms for that purpose. As a great power the USSR has obtained many advantages in the world stretching from Egypt to Finland, from Cuba to Afghanistan. Many of these relationships are, for example, firmly established on the basis of treaty arrangements grounded on the principle of *pacta sunt servanda*. To jeopardize that principle is to jeopardize those relations. Soviet coolness toward the "principle" of *clausula rebus sic stant-*

ibus is a recognition of this. In the same vein the need to preserve customary principles underlying Soviet relations is an explanation of Soviet qualification of the right of "new" states to review "old" norms and in Soviet non-use of the "consensus doctrine" (to reject established customary norms), to any appreciable extent.

Closely related to the second point, is a third, that the Soviet Union observes customary law because of reciprocity. The great majority of rules of custom are generally observed by all nations without actual compulsion because it is in the interest of each state concerned to honor its international obligations. The Soviet Union will observe the law concerning diplomatic privileges and immunities because of an identical interest in having other states observe the same law. In like manner, the Soviet Union will observe treaty arrangements because of a similar interest in having other states do likewise. Mutual benefit provides a basis for observance and self-enforcement.

The need for international order, a stake in the international system and recognition of reciprocity have motivated the Soviet Union to accept customary norms of an ordering nature. So strong do these pressures appears to be that acceptance has come notwithstanding the inability of Soviet academicians to reconcile custom with traditional Marxist teachings. Given a choice between ideological consistency and political reality Moscow has chosen without doubt the latter course. Having reviewed the record one is lead inevitably to the conclusion that former Premier Nikita S. Khrushchev was speaking sincerely when he said in 1959, "We are deeply conscious that without the observance of the norms of international law, without the fulfillment of undertakings assumed in relations between states, there can be no trust and without trust there can be no peaceful coexistence."[2] What is revealing about this statement and many others like it is not that Soviet officials claim to be "law-abiding" but rather that they recognize the importance of law observance by all states, including their own country, in order to make the international system work.

In order to maintain a proper perspective it must be recalled that in addition to the ordering function of customary law there is also the provocative. A recognition of the provocative function is an admission that law exists in a political environment, that nations use the law to achive narrow national interests. Some customary principles lend themselves more readily to provocative purposes than do others. As a result three broad categories may be suggested. The first of these is composed of customary principles of primarily an ordering nature of which the principle of *pacta sunt servanda* is an example. The second category is composed of customary principles of primarily a provocative nature and the juridical principle of peaceful coexistence is an example. An intermediate category is composed of customary principles which can serve, without too great an effort, either a provocative or an ordering purpose. The principle of national self-determination is an example of this latter category. The importance of these categories rest in the fact that the more provocative and less ordering is a principle the greater the dispute is likely to be with respect to its meaning. Soviet and western spokesmen completely agree on the meaning of the principle of *pacta sunt servanda*. At the same time these spokesmen widely differ over the meaning of the juridical principle of peaceful coexistence. It is, of course, the malleability of a principle's meaning that contributes to its provocative use.

Because of the provocative function of customary law a dimension of freedom is given to Soviet foreign policy. Support of policy can be achieved through interpretation of principles. "What does a principle mean?" That frequently is the crucial question which if answered properly by the legal adviser can orient the law favorably toward narrow national objectives. To be sure the Soviet Union is not exceptional in this regard. Widespread practice lead Jean Giradoux to wittingly conclude that international law is the most powerful training ground for the imagination. What is unique about Soviet exercise of imagination in support of foreign policy is the extent to which it is exercised.

The Soviets have a penchant for what may be termed "legalism" which arises out of an inclination to put forward every conceivable argument in favor of Soviet policy. As a result, and not infrequently, rather complex legal positions are advocated. Illustrative of this point was the argument made by Soviet lawyers that a customary norm had evolved since 1945 limiting the ceiling of the air corridors into the city of Berlin to 10,000 feet. If the purpose of the argument, namely to restrict western ingress and egress to Berlin, could not be appreciated the ingenuity of the argument could. What western lawyer would ever attempt such an argument? When confronted with the trial of Francis Gary Powers, the United States for example, offered no legal defense but instead sought to justify the U-2 flight purely on political grounds. In a similar situation the Soviet Union might well have argued that the launching of satellites had so unsettled the law regarding the altitudinal limits of *usque ad coelum* as to make the flight, at best, within the law, and at worse, an honest mistake. Characteristic also of "legalism" were Soviet arguments based on the principle of sovereign equality of states to justify Soviet actions toward Finland (1939), Poland (1939), Germany (1945), Hungary (1956) and Czechoslovakia (1968).

Candidly it is to be admitted that such provocative uses of custom do not advance international law but are an abuse of it. But realization of this fact does not obfuscate Soviet acceptance of the ordering function of international custom. Soviet policy-makers must balance in their own minds and ultimately in their policies the provocative and the ordering functions as they acknowledge both as serving the interests of the Soviet State.

Grigorii I. Tunkin recognized the restraint on foreign policy flowing from an acceptance of the ordering function of custom when he wrote,

"This [the provocative function] of course, does not mean that international law can be an instrument of any policy. The norm of international law can be an instrument of the policy of states only within the limits determined by their substance, *i. e.*, the substance of the agreement between states which have brought these norms into being."[3] A balanced approach was necessary. Exploitation of the provocative function should not be pushed to the point of endangering the ordering function. The probity of Tunkin's statement rests on the acknowledged importance by the Soviet State of the ordering function: the need for international order, a stake in the international system and a recognition of reciprocity. To that extent, to the extent that the ordering function of customary law must be protected, the Soviet State must — and as the evidence shows, restrain its foreign policy.

Impact on Customary International Law

The old customary norms have never been seriously put in doubt. One need only recall the areas of the law concerned with the binding effect of treaties *(pacta sunt servanda)*, the extent and limit of territorial integrity, the law governing nationality, the extent and limit of national jurisdiction (immunities), and the law of recognition. The Soviet Union has not only bolstered old principles of customary law which have continuing value in the contemporary world but has given vigorous support to such principles. The USSR has staunchly defended, for example, the principle of sovereign equality of states. So firm has been the Soviet position that it has given the USSR the image of a conservative power.

While taking a conservative position on some principles, the Soviet Union is radical and innovative in other areas. The very existence of a Great Power representing a new social system is bound to have an effect on traditional institutions and rules of international law. Soviet spokesmen have been waging a continuous struggle for what they term "the law of peaceful coexistence." In addition to interjecting new content into old form *vis* "the law of peaceful coexistence," Soviet diplomats propose wholly new principles such as unequal treaties, national self-determination and the "all states" principle.

The Soviet Union has rejected some traditional principles of customary law which they view as manifestly harmful or out of keeping with Soviet foreign policy. Rejected are *clausula rebus sic stantibus* (fundamental change of circumstances) and *nemo debet esse judex in propria causa* (third party judgment). Concerning these there is much doubt, notwithstanding the Soviet position, that they were ever principles of international law. Apparently most nations appraised them in the same manner as did the USSR. In recent years, there have been indications that the Soviet Union, as well as other states, may be willing to accept a restricted "principle" of *rebus sic stantibus*, restricted in such a manner that the order

163

provided by *pacta sunt servanda* will not be undermined. Among the principles which the Soviet Union rejects and traditional international law plainly accepted is innocent passage of warships. There are also principles of traditional customary law which the Soviet Foreign Ministry has attempted to modify, such as the extension of immunity to all government owned vessels and the extension of the width of the territorial sea to 12 miles.

The chart below summarizes the extent to which the Soviet Union has accepted or rejected international custom:

SUMMARIZATION OF PRINCIPLES AND SOURCE
(Treaty (1) U. N. Charter; (2) ILC Convention; (3) Other)

Principle	Source
SUBJECTS OF INTERNATIONAL LAW	
1. Peaceful Coexistence	Treaty(1) + Custom
2. Sovereign Equality of States	Treaty(1) + Custom
3. National Self-Determination	Treaty(1) + Custom
4. Non-Intervention	Treaty(1) + Custom
5. Recognition Principles	Custom
INTERNATIONAL TREATIES	
6. *Pacta Sunt Servanda*	Custom
7. *Clausula Rebus Sic Stantibus*	(status uncertain)
8. Unequal Treaties	(source uncertain)
9. *Res Inter Alios Gesta* (State Succession)	Custom
10. "All States" Principle	(source uncertain)
11. *Jus Cogens*	Custom
DIPLOMATIC AND CONSULAR INTERCOURSE:	
PRIVILEGES AND IMMUNITIES	
12. Diplomatic Immunity	Treaty(2) + Custom
13. Consular Immunity	Custom
14. *Persona Non Grata* (Diplomatic)	Treaty(2) + Custom
14a. *Persona Non Grata* (Consular)	Custom
15. Inviolability of Premises (Diplomatic)	Treaty(2) + Custom
15a. Inviolability of Premises (Consular)	Custom
16. Free Communication (Diplomatic)	Treaty(2) + Custom
16a. Free Communication (Consular)	Custom
TERRITORY AND POPULATION	
17. *Usque Ad Coelum*	Custom
18. Outer Space As *Res Communis?*	Treaty(3) + Custom
19. High Seas As *Res Communis*	Treaty(2) + Custom
20. Territorial Waters As A Part Of The Littoral State	Treaty(2) + Custom
21. Status Of Populations As Within The Jurisdiction Of Municipal Law	Custom

164

22. Discovery And Occupation As A Basis For Land Acquisition	Custom
PEACEFUL SETTLEMENT OF DISPUTES AND THE LAWS OF WAR	
23. *Nemo Debet Esse Judex In Propria Causa* (Third Party Judgment)	(not recognized)
24. Peaceful Settlement Of Disputes By Voluntary Negotiation, Arbitration And/Or Adjudication	Treaty(1) + Custom
25. Self-Help	Treaty(1) + Custom
26. Non-Aggression	Treaty(1) + Custom
27. Inviolability Of Civilian Populations In Time Of War	Treaty(1) + Custom

The Soviet Union has had an impact on traditional customary international law in terms of the Soviet conception of old principles and in terms of advocating new principles. But international custom has had an impact on Soviet ideology and foreign policy as well. The USSR, under the pressure of a new reality, the nuclear age and great power status, has adopted the course of action of working within the legal system rather than assaulting the system from without in the tradition of a revolutionary firebrand. Soviet ideologues have labored to construct new myths to meet these new realities. Soviet diplomats have had to take law into their policy considerations. Time works changes, brings into existence new conditions and purposes, tempers revolutionary zeal.

NOTES

[1]Grigorii I. Tunkin, "The 22nd Congress of the CPSU and the Tasks of the Soviet Science of International Law," *Sovetskoe gosudarstvo i pravo* (Soviet State and Law), no. 5 (1962), translated in *Soviet Law and Government*, Vol. 1, no. 3, (Winter 1962/63), p. 20.

[2]Nikita S. Khrushchev, *Pravda*, September 1, 1959.

[3]Grigorii I. Tunkin, "Coexistence and International Law," *Recueil des Cours* (Collection of Lectures), Vol. 95 (1958-III), p. 72.

APPENDICES

APPENDIX A
SOVIET REPRESENTATION IN PUBLIC AND PRIVATE INTERNATIONAL ORGANIZATIONS[1]

I. *Soviet Judge on the International Court of Justice.*
Sergei Borisovich Krylov. February 1946- February 5, 1952.
Sergei Aleksandrovich Golunskii. February 5, 1952- February 5, 1954. (Because of ill health Judge Golunskii never assumed his seat on the Court.)
Fedor Ivanovich Kozhevnikov. February 5, 1954- February 5, 1961.
Vladimir Mikhailovich Koretskii. February 5, 1961- February 5, 1970.
Platon D. Morozov. February 5, 1970-

II. *Soviet Representative to the International Law Commission.*
Vladimir Mikhailovich Koretskii (USSR). 1949-1952. (Mr. Koretskii was absent, 1950-1951).
Fedor Ivanovich Kozhevnikov (Ukrainian SSR). 1952-1953. (Mr. Kozhevnikov was absent from the 1953 Session).
Sergei Borisovich Krylov (USSR). 1953-1956. (Mr. Krylov was absent from from the 1954 Session).
Grigorii Ivanovich Tunkin (USSR). 1956-1961; re-elected 1961-1967.
Nicholai Aleksandrovich Ushakov (USSR). 1967-

III. *Officers of the International Law Commission.*
1st Session (1949). Vladimir Mikhailovich Koretskii (USSR). 1st Vice-Chairman.
5th Session (1953). Fedor Ivanovich Kozhevnikov (Ukrainian SSR). 2nd Vice-Chairman.
7th Session (1955). Sergei Borisovich Krylov (USSR). 1st Vice-Chairman.
10th Session (1958). Grigorii Ivanovich Tunkin (USSR). 2nd Vice-Chairman.
13th Session (1961). Grigorii Ivanovich Tunkin (USSR). Chairman.
16th Session (1964). Grigorii Ivanovich Tunkin (USSR). 2nd Vice-Chairman.

IV. *United Nations Special Committee on Principles of International Law Concerning Friendly Relations and Co-Operation Among States.* Mexico City. August 27-October 2, 1964. Soviet Delegates:
Mr. O. Khlestov (USSR).
Mr. Fedorov (USSR).
Mr. Kazantsev (USSR).

V. *United Nations Special Committee on Principles of International Law Concerning Friendly Relations and Co-Operation Among States.* New York. June 1966. Soviet Delegates:
Mr. P. D. Morozov (USSR).
Mr. A. P. Movchan (USSR).
Mr. Y. D. Ilyin (USSR).

VI. *United Nations Conference on Consular Relations.* Vienna. March 4- April 22, 1963.
(a) Byelorussian SSR Delegation:
Mr. A. Rassolko, Head of the Protocol and Consular Department, Ministry of Foreign Affairs (Chairman of the Delegation).
Mr. M. Avakov, Professor of Law and Jurisprudence of the State Institute of Political Economy.
Mr. Y. Ilyin, 3rd Secretary, International Relations Section, Ministry of Foreign Affairs (Adviser and Secretary).
(b) Ukrainian SSR Delegation:
Mr. V. Tsyba, Head of Protocol and Consular Questions, Ministry of Foreign Affairs (Chairman of the Delegation).
Mr. K. Zabigailo, Ministry of Foreign Affairs.
Mr. V. Gapon, 2nd Secretary, Ministry of Foreign Affairs (Adviser).
(c) USSR Delegation:
H.E. Mr. V. Avilov, Ambassador to Austria (Chairman of the Delegation).
Mr. O. Khlestov, Deputy Head of the Legal and Treaty Department, Ministry of Foreign Affairs (Deputy Chairman of the Delegation).
Mr. I. Konshukov, Deputy Head of Consular Department, Ministry of Foreign Affairs.
Mr. E. Leonidow, 1st Secretary, Ministry of Foreign Affairs (Adviser).
Mr. I. Gorodetskaia, Legal and Treaty Department, Ministry of Foreign Affairs (Adviser).
Mr. M. Kurishchew, Consul (Adviser).
Mr. A. Abramov, Consular Department, Ministry of Foreign Affairs (Adviser).
Mr. N. Petrenko, Legal and Treaty Department, Ministry of Foreign Affairs (Adviser).
Mr. N. Turov, 2nd Secretary (Adviser).
Mr. Y. Schaposchnikov, Press Attaché (Adviser).
Mr. W. Tscherkasov, Attaché (Adviser).
Mr. V. Shigulenkov, Attaché (Adviser).
Mrs. I. Stepanova, Ministry of Foreign Affairs (Interpreter).

VII. *United Nations Conference on Diplomatic Intercourse and Immunities.* Vienna. March 2- April 14, 1961.
(a) Byelorussian SSR Delegation:
Mr. S.T. Shardyko, Chairman Supreme Court of Byelorussia (Chairman of the Delegation).
Mr. N.P. Sherdyukov, Ministry of Foreign Affairs.
Mr. I.P. Dedyulia (Secretary-General of the Delegation).
(b) Ukrainian SSR Delegation:
Mr. K.S. Zabigailo, Ministry of Foreign Affairs, Kiev (Chairman of the Delegation).
Mr. D.T. Yakovenko, Kiev University.
Mr. Y.I. Nikolski (Secretary-General of the Delegation).

(c) USSR Delegation:

Mr. G.I. Tunkin, Head of the Treaty and Legal Department, Ministry of Foreign Affairs (Chairman of the Delegation).

Mr. G.N. Mikheev, Minister Counsellor, USSR Embassy, Vienna.

Mr. V.A. Romanov, 1st Secretary, Ministry of Foreign Affairs.

Mr. A.P. Movchan, 1st Secretary, Ministry of Foreign Affairs.

Mr. V.I. Khamanev, Assistant, Treaty and Legal Department, Ministry of Foreign Affairs (Adviser).

Mr. I.P. Blishchenko, Academy of Sciences of the USSR (Adviser).

Mr. N.A. Ushakov, Academy of Sciences of the USSR (Adviser).

Mr. S.A. Kondrashev, 1st Secretary, USSR Embassy, Vienna (Adviser).

Mr. Y.N. Granov, 1st Secretary, USSR Embassy, Vienna (Adviser).

Mrs. N.M. Frantsuzova, Ministry of Foreign Affairs (Interpreter).

Mrs. T.M. Korolyuk, Ministry of Foreign Affairs (Interpreter); (Verbatim Reporter).

VIII. *United Nations Conference on the Law of the Sea.* Geneva. March 17-April 26, 1960.

(a) Byelorussian SSR Delegation:

Mr. G.A. Povetiev, State University, Minsk (Chairman of the Delegation).

Mr. A.N. Sheldov, 2nd Secretary (Adviser).

(b) Ukrainian SSR Delegation:

Mr. V.M. Koretskii, Member of the Academy of Sciences of the Ukraine (Chairman of the Delegation).

Mr. K. Zabigailo, 1st Secretary, Ministry of Foreign Affairs.

Mr. I. Denesenko, Vice-Chairman of the Fishery Department, Department of State Plan.

(c) USSR Delegation:

Mr. G.I. Tunkin, Head, Treaty and Legal Department, Ministry of Foreign Affairs (Chairman of the Delegation).

Mr. A. Nikoleav, Deputy Head, Treaty and Legal Department, Ministry of Foreign Affairs (Vice-Chairman of the Delegation).

Mr. A. Keilin, Professor, Institute of Foreign Trade; Legal Adviser, Ministry of Foreign Trade.

Mr. A. Shudro, Head of the Legal Section, Ministry of Merchant Marine Fleet.

Mr. G. Izhevskii, Senior Scientific Officer, Scientific Research Institute of Sea Fisheries and Oceanography.

Mr. D. Kolesnik, 2nd Secretary, Ministry of Foreign Affairs (Adviser).

Mr. V. Khamanev, Assistant, Treaty and Legal Department, Ministry of Foreign Affairs (Adviser).

Col. P. Borabolia, Naval Legal Service (Adviser).

IX. *United Nations Conference on the Law of the Sea.* Geneva. February 24-April 27, 1958.

(a) Byelorussian SSR Delegation:

Mr. I.E. Geronin (Chairman of the Delegation).

Mr. G.A. Povetiev (Adivser).

Mr. A.N. Sheldon (Adviser).

(b) Ukrainian SSR Delegation:

Mr. V.M. Koretskii, Professor, Member of the Ukrainian Academy of Sciences (Chairman of the Delegation). Mr. Koretskii was elected Rapporteur of the Conference's First Committee on "Territorial Sea and Contiguous Zone."

Mr. K.S. Zabigailo, 1st Secretary, Ministry of Foreign Affairs.

Mr. A.A. Pushkin, Lecturer, Judicial Institute, Karkov (Adviser).

Mr. Y:A. Lepanov (Secretary to the Delegation).

(c) USSR Delegation:

Mr. G.I. Tunkin, Head, Treaty and Legal Department, Ministry of Foreign Affairs (Chairman of the Delegation).

Mr. A.N. Nikolaev, Deputy Head, Treaty and Legal Department, Ministry of Foreign Affairs (Vice-Chairman of the Delegation).

Capt. A.A. Saveliev, Member of the Board, Chief of Department, Ministry of Merchant Marine Fleet.

Mr. A.D. Keilin, Professor, Institute of Foreign Trade, Legal Adviser, Ministry of Foreign Trade.

Mr. S.B. Krylov, Professor, Institute of Foreign Relations, Legal Adviser, Ministry of Foreign Affairs.

Mr. A.K. Zhudro, Head of Legal Section, Ministry of Merchant Marine Fleet (Adviser).

Mr. Berzrukov, Professor, Laboratory Director, Oceanographic Institute, Academy of Sciences (Adviser).

Mr. G.I. Izhevskii, Senior Scientific Officer, Scientific Research Institute for Sea Fisheries and Oceanography (Adviser).

Mr. S.V. Molodtsov, Senior Scientific Officer, Legal Institute, Academy of Sciences (Adviser).

Capt. K.P. Ryzhkov, USSR Navy (Adviser).

Mr. V.L. Borisov, Permanent Mission to the European Office of the United Nations (Adviser).

Mr. D.N. Kolesnik, 2nd Secretary, Ministry of Foreign Affairs (Adviser).

Mr. V.I. Khamanov, Assistant, Treaty and Legal Department, Ministry of Foreign Affairs (Expert).

Mr. V.A. Romanov, 3rd Secretary, Ministry of Foreign Affairs (Expert).

Mr. Busarov, Ministry of Foreign Affairs (Secretariat).

Mrs. E.S. Nikolaeva, Ministry of Foreign Affairs (Secretariat).

Mrs. Y.V. Pavlova, Ministry of Foreign Affairs (Secretariat).

Mrs. T.M. Korolyuk, Ministry of Foreign Affairs (Secretariat).

X. *Soviet Representatives to the United Nations General Assembly's Sixth (Legal) Committee.* 1st session (1946)—21st session (1966).

The numbers following each name indicate the sessions attended by each delegate. Delegation lists were provided in United Nations records of the Sixth Committee for the 1st through the 14th sessions. From the 15th session on, delegation lists were compiled from Committee records on the basis of those delegates who participated in discussion.

(a) Byelorussian SSR Delegation:

Mr. V.I. Formashev, 1.

Mr. M.F. Dechko, 2.
Mr. F.P. Shmigov, 2.
Mr. N.M. Khomusho, 3, 4, 5.
Mr. M.T. Kustov, 6.
Mr. Y.A. Varnakov, 6.
Mr. G.A. Povetyev, 7, 8, 17.
Mr. V.V. Grekov, 7.
Mr. Kiselyov, 7.
Mr. K.N. Abushevich, 9, 10, 13.
Mr. L.I. Maksimov, 9.
Mr. L.I. Sheldon, 10, 11, 12.
Mr. G.F. Basov, 11, 12.
Mr. A.R. Sitnikov, 13, 14, 15, 17.
Mr. S.T. Sharsyko, 14 (elected Rapporteur).
Mr. Kachan, 15.
Mr. Oorogin, 16.
Mr. Stanevich, 20, 21.
(b) Ukrainian SSR Delegation:
Mr. V.M. Koretskii, 1.
Mr. V.I. Shiganskii, 1.
Mr. V.P. Kovalenko, 2, 3, 4, 6, 7.
Mr. A.I. Galagan, 4.
Mr. P.P. Udovichenko, 5.
Mr. G.P. Stadnik, 5.
Mr. V.I. Sapozhnikov, 8, 9, 13, 20.
Mr. G.E. Buvailik, 10.
Mr. K.S. Zabigailo, 11, 12, 14, 18 (elected Rapporteur).
Mr. V.P. Rusin, 13.
Mr. P.Y. Nedbalio, 14, 15 (elected Rapporteur), 17.
Mr. Yakimenko, 16, 21.
Mrs. Zgurskaya, 18.
Mr. I.M. Pedanyuk, 20 (died during 20th session).
Mr. Maksimenko, 21.
(c) USSR Delegation:
Mr. S.B. Krylov, 1.
Mr. V.N. Durdenevskii, 1, 2.
Mr. K.K. Rodionov, 2.
Mr. V.M. Koretskii, 2, 4.
Mr. A. Bogomolov, 3.
Mr. P.D. Morozov, 3, 5, 6, 7, 8, 9, 10, 11, 12, 13, 14, 15, 16, 17, 18, 19, 20.
Mr. A.G. Abramov, 3.
Mr. A.F. Sokirkin, 5, 7.
Mr. A.V. Zhukov, 6, 8, 9.
Mr. A. Ia. Vyshinskii, 7.
Mr. Baranovskii, 7, 8.
Mr. V. Kamenev, 8.
Mr. A.N. Nikolaev, 10.
Mr. B.P. Pisarev, 10, 11, 12, 13.
Mr. V.V. Kuznetsov, 10.

Mr. V.S. Romanov, 11, 12.
Mr. Y.A. Ostrovskii, 11.
Mr. I.G. Usachev, 12.
Mr. A.M. Belonogov, 12.
Mr. V.I. Sapozhnikov, 14.
Mr. V.N. Travkin, 14.
Mr. A.P. Movchan, 15, 17, 18.
Mr. G.I. Tunkin, 16 (Mr. Tunkin first appeared in an advisory capacity as Chairman of the International Law Commission, 13th session 1961, and remained as a member of the USSR Delegation).
Mr. Chkhikvadze, 20.
Mr. A.A. Bybakov, 20, 21.
Mr. O.N. Khlestov, 21.
Mr. Piradov, 21.

XI. *Soviet Branch of the International Law Association.* Founded October 12, 1957.
   (a) Officers of the Soviet Branch:
      (i) President
         Mr. G.I. Tunkin, 1957-
      (ii) Vice-Presidents
         Mr. E.A. Korovin, 1957-1963.
         Mr. S.B. Krylov, 1957-1959.
         Mr. V.M. Koretskii, 1959-
         Mrs. G.P. Kaluznaja, 1963-1966.
         Mr. N.A. Ushakov, 1966-
      (iii) Executive Committee
         Mr. K.K. Bakhtov, 1957-1961.
         Mr. V.N. Durdenevskii, 1957-1963.
         Mr. G.E. Žtvania, 1957-1959.
         Mr. F.I. Kozhevnikov, 1957-1963.
         Mr. V.M. Koretskii, 1957-1959.
         Mr. L.M. Maksudov, 1957-1959.
         Mr. G.E. Zhavanija, 1959-1965.
         Mr. R.L. Bobrov, 1961-
         Mr. M.I. Lazarev, 1961-1966.
         Mr. A.T. Uustal, 1961-1965.
         Mr. L.A. Aleksidze, 1965-
         Mr. A.D. Keilin, 1965-
         Mr. I.I. Lukashuk, 1965-
         Mr. G.I. Morozov, 1965-1966.
         Mr. V.S. Semenov, 1965-
         Mr. O.N. Khlestov, 1966-
         Mr. L.A. Lunts, 1966-
      (iv) Honorary Secretary
         Mr. S.V. Molodtsov, 1957-1963.
         Mr. O.V. Bogdanov, 1963-
      (v) Learned Secretary
         Mr. G.I. Morozov, 1957-1961.

Mrs. L.V. Korbut, 1961-
(b) Members of the Soviet Branch:
Mr. L.A. Aleksidze, 1963-
Mr. A.B. Amelin, 1957-1963.
Mr. V.N. Avilin, 1965-
Mr. K.K. Bakhtov, 1957-1963.
Mr. K.A. Bagninian, 1957-1963.
Mr. R.L. Bobrov, 1963-
Mr. O.V. Bogdanov, 1957-
Mr. V.N. Durdenevskii, 1957-1965.
Mrs. G.P. Kaluznaja, 1963-1966.
Mr. A.D. Keilin, 1957-
Mrs. R.O. Khalfina, 1961-
Mrs. L.V. Korbut, 1963-
Mr. V.M. Koretskii, 1957-1965.
Mr. E.A. Korovin, 1957-1965.
Mr. F.I. Kozhevnikov, 1957-
Mr. A.M. Ladyzhenskii, 1957-
Mr. M.I. Lazarev, 1957-
Mr. D.B. Levin, 1965-
Mr. I.I. Lukashuk, 1957-
Mr. L.A. Lunts, 1957-
Mr. L.M. Maksudov, 1957-1963.
Mr. V.F. Meshera, 1957-
Mrs. L.A. Modzhoriyan, 1957-
Mr. S.V. Molodtsov, 1957-1966.
Mr. P.S. Romashkin, 1957-
Mr. V.S. Semenov, 1963-
Mr. V.M. Shurshalov, 1957-
Mr. G.I. Tunkin, 1957-
Mr. N.A. Ushakov, 1963-
Mr. G.E. Zhvanija, 1957-1963.
Mr. O.N. Khlestov, 1966-
Mr. G.I. Talalaev, 1966-
(c) Present Members and Addresses of the Soviet Branch (as of the 52nd Conference of the International Law Association, Helsinki, 1966).
Aleksidze, L.A. pr. Chavchavadze 1, Tbilisskii Universitet, Juridicheskii Facultet, Tbilissi.
Avilin, V.N. Publishing House of Legal Literature, ul. Chkalova 38, Moskva.
Bobrov, R.L. Leningradskii Universitet, Juridicheskii Facultet, Smolnogo 3, Leningrad.
Bogdanov, O.V. Institut Gosudarstva i Prava, Akademii Nauk SSR, ul. Frunze 10, Moskva.
Keilin, Professor A.D. Legal Adviser, Ministerstvo Vneshnej Torgovli.
Khalfina, Professor Madame Rahisa O. Institut Gosudarstva i Prava, Akademii Nauk SSR, ul. Frunze 10, Moskva.
Khlestov, O.N. Ministerstvo Inostranih Del SSR, Smolenskaja Sennaja pl. d. 32, Moskva.

175

Korbut, Madame L.V. Sovetskaja Associasija Mezhdunarodnogo Prava, ul. Frunze 10, Moskva.

Koretskii, Judge Vladimir M. ul. Lenina 42, kv. 5 Kiev.

Kozhevnikov, Judge Fedor I. Institut Mezhdunarodnich Otnostenij, Metrostroevskaja 53, Moskva.

Ladyzhenskii, Professor A.M.B. Konjushkovskaja ul., d. 8, kv. 1, Moskva.

Lazarev, Professor M.I. Frunzenskaja nab 28, kv. 79, Moskva.

Levin, Professor D.B. Institut Gosduarstva i Prava, Akademii Nauk SSR, ul. Frunze 10, Moskva.

Lukashuk, Professor I.I. Universitet, Juridicheskii Facultet, Kiev.

Lunts, Professor L.A. Vsesojuznij Nauhtychno-Issledovatelskii Institut Sovetskogo Zakonodatelstva, Kutuzovskii pr. 37/45, Moskva.

Meshera, Professor V.F. ul. Orzhonikidze 13, kv. 54, Leningrad.

Modzhorijan, Professor Madame Lidija A. Frunzenskaja nab. 28, kv. 30, Moskva.

Morozov, Professor G.J. Institut Mirovoi Ekhononiki i Mezhdunarodnich Otnoshenij, Akademii Nauk SSSR, Vtoraja Jaroslavskaja, ul. 3 Korpus 8, Moskva.

Romashkin, Professor Petr S. Institut Gosudarstva i Prava, Akademii Nauk SSSR, ul. Frunze 10, Moskva.

Semenov, V.S. Kharkovskii Juridicheskii Institut, Pushkinskaja 77, Kharkov.

Shurshalov, V.M. Institut Gosudarstva i Prava, Akademii Nauk SSSR, ul. Frunze 10, Moskva.

Talalaev, Professor G.I. Moskovskii Universitet, Juridicheskii Facultet, ul. Herzena 11, Moskva.

Tunkin, Professor G.I. ul. Herzen 32, Moskovskii Universitet Juridicheskii Facultet, Moskva.

Ushakov, N.A. Institut Gosudarstva i Prava, Akademii Nauk SSSR, ul. Frunze 10, Moskva.

Uustal, Abner T. Juridicheskii Facultet, Tarusskii Gosudar. Universitet, ul. Julikooli d. 18, Tartu, Est. USSR.

XII. *Sixth Congress of the International Association of Democratic Lawyers.* Brussels, May 22-25, 1956.

(a) Byelorussian SSR Delegation:

Mr. Ivan Vetrov, Minister of Justice, Byelorussia.

(b) Ukrainian SSR Delegation:

Mr. Fedor Glouk, Minister of Justice, Ukraine.

(c) USSR Delegation:

Mr. Sergei Golunskii, Professor of Criminal Law; Corresponding Member, USSR Academy of Sciences.

Mr. Victor Gorchkov, Member of the Moscow Bar.

Mr. Kadmus Ionessian, General-Procurator of the Armenian Soviet Republic.

Mr. Petr Kudriavtsev, Vice-Minister of Justice, USSR.

Mr. L.A. Lunts, Professor, Institute of Legal Sciences, USSR.

Mr. Murat Sherliev, Minister of Justice, Uzbekistan SSR.

Mr. Vladimir Babkin, Member of the Moscow Bar.

APPENDIX B
OFFICERS AND MEMBERS: SOVIET DOMESTIC ASSOCIATIONS AND EDITORIAL BOARDS OF PRINCIPAL PUBLICATIONS CONCERNED WITH INTERNATIONAL LAW[2]

I. *Executive Committee of the Soviet Association of International Law.*
   (a) Chairman:
   Mr. G.I. Tunkin, 1958-
   (b) Deputy Chairmen:
   Mr. E.A. Korovin, 1958-1962.
   Mr. V.M. Koretskii, 1958-
   Mrs. G.P. Kalushnaya, 1962-1966.
   Mr. N.A. Ushakov, 1966-
   (c) Learned Secretary:
   Mrs. L.V. Korbut, 1960-
   (d) Members:
   Mr. K.K. Bakhtov, 1958-1962.
   Mr. V.N. Durdenevskii, 1958-1963.
   Mr. G.E. Zhvanaiya, 1958-1962.
   Mr. F.I. Kozhevnikov, 1958-1962.
   Mr. V.M. Koretskii, 1958-1962.
   Mr. L.M. Maksudov, 1958-1962.
   Mr. S.V. Molodtsov, 1958-1962.
   Mr. P.S. Romashkin, 1958-1962.
   Mr. L.A. Aleksidze, 1962-
   Mr. R.L. Bobrov, 1960-
   Mr. A.D. Keilin, 1962-
   Mr. O.V. Bogdanov, 1962-
   Mr. M.I. Lazarev, 1960-1966.
   Mr. A.T. Uustal, 1960-1962.
   Mr. I.I. Lukashak, 1962-
   Mr. G.I. Morozov, 1962-1966.
   Mr. V.S. Semenov, 1962-
   Mr. L.A. Lunts, 1966-
   Mr. O.N. Khlestov, 1966-

II. *Editorial Board of Sovetskii ezhegodnik mezhdunarodnogo prava (Soviet Yearbook of International Law), 1958, 1959, 1960, 1961, 1962, 1963, 1964-1965 editions.*
   The dates following each name indicate the volume(s) on which each labored.
   (a) Editor-in-Chief:
   Mr. S.B. Krylov, 1958.
   Mr. G.I. Tunkin, 1959, 1960, 1961, 1962.
   Mr. V.K. Sobakin, 1963.
   Mr. N.A. Ushakov, 1964-1965.

(b) Assistant Editors:

Mr. O.V. Bogdanov, 1959.
Mr. N.A. Ushakov, 1960, 1961, 1962, 1963.
Mr. V.K. Sobakin, 1963.
Mr. V.N. Avilin, 1963, 1964-1965.

(c) Members of the Board:

Mr. O.V. Bogdanov, 1958, 1960, 1961, 1962.
Mr. A.D. Keilin, 1958, 1959, 1960, 1961, 1962.
Mr. E.A. Korovin, 1958, 1959, 1960, 1961, 1962.
Mr. M.I. Lazarev, 1958, 1959.
Mr. L.A. Lunts, 1958, 1959, 1960, 1961, 1962, 1963, 1964-1965.
Mr. V.F. Meshera, 1958, 1959, 1960, 1961, 1962, 1963, 1964-1965.
Mrs. L.A. Modzhorijan, 1958, 1959, 1960, 1961, 1962, 1963, 1964-1965.
Mr. G.I. Morozov, 1958, 1959, 1960, 1961, 1962, 1963.
Mr. E.M. Semerikin, 1958, 1959, 1960, 1961, 1962.
Mr. G.I. Tunkin, 1958.
Mr. D.B. Levin, 1959, 1960, 1961, 1962, 1963, 1964-1965.
Mr. M.M. Boguslavskii, 1960, 1961, 1962, 1963, 1964-1965.
Mr. O.N. Khlestov, 1960, 1961, 1962.
Mr. I.I. Lukashuk, 1960, 1961, 1962.
Mrs. L.V. Korbut, 1963, 1964-1965.
Mr. F.I. Kozhevnikov, 1963, 1964-1965.
Mr. S.V. Molodtsov, 1963, 1964-1965.
Mr. A.P. Movchan, 1963, 1964-1965.
Mr. V.M. Shurshalov, 1963, 1964-1965.
Mrs. N.N. Ulyanova, 1963, 1964-1965.
Mr. E.T. Usenko, 1963, 1964-1965.
Mr. M.V. Janovskii, 1963, 1964-1965.

III. *Editorial Board of Sovetskoe gosudarstvo i pravo (Soviet State and Law), January 1946- March 1968.* (°Subsequently elected as members of the board).

(a) Editor:

Mr. A. Ia. Vyshinskii, 1/1946-3/1950.
Mr. F.I. Kozhevnikov, 3/1950-3/1953°
Mr. V.V. Evgenev, 3/1953-8/1955.
Mr. I.V. Pavlov, 8/1955-1/1959°
Mr. S.A. Golunskii, 1/1959-1/1962.
Mr. A.I. Leieshkii, 1/1962-6/1965.
Mr. S.A. Ivanov, 6/1965-

(b) Assistant Editors:

Mr. I.P. Trainin, 1/1946-7/1949 (died).
Mr. E.A. Korovin, 10/1948-3/1953.
Mr. M.R. Kareva, 3/1953-2/1954°
Mr. S.N. Bratus, 3/1953-1/1959.
Mr. N.G. Subarikov, 2/1954-5/1956.
Mr. G.A. Aksenenok, 1/1959-3/1960°
Mr. I.F. Pankratov, 3/1960-5/1962.
Mr. E.M. Vorozheinkin, 7/1962-11/1963°

(c) Members of the Board:

Mr. M.A. Arzhanov, 1/1946-3/1953.

Mr. S.A. Golunskii, 1/1946-3/1953.

Mr. I.T. Golyakov, 1/1946-3/1953; 1/1955-1/1959.

Mr. K.I. Gorshenin, 1/1946-3/1953; 1/1959-10/1965.

Mr. M.G. Gribanov (Sec.), 1/1946-1/1949.

Mr. A.N. Trainin, 10/1948-3/1953.

Mr. V.M. Chkhikvabze, 10/1948-1/1959.

Mr. E.P. Meleshko, 9/1951-3/1953.

Mr. M.V. Grobovenko (Sec.), 3/1953-4/1954.

Mr. M.G. Zhuravkov, 3/1953-1/1956.

Mr. D. Karev, 3/1953-1/1955; 1/1959-4/1962.

Mr. Yu. A. Kalenkov, 3/1953-1/1959.

Mr. F.I. Kozhevnikov, 3/1953-1/1959.

Mr. P.E. Orlovskii, 3/1953-10/1965.

Mr. A.N. Siborov, 3/1953-2/1954.

Mr. M.P. Kareva, 2/1954-1/1959.

Mr. N.S. Ryabov, 2/1954-1/1956.

Mrs. E.A. Panova (Sec.), 4/1954-1/1956.

Mr. G.I. Morozov (Sec.), 1/1956-8/1957.

Mr. P.I. Barbin, 1/1956-4/1962.

Mr. G.I. Tunkin, 1/1956-

Mr. S.S. Stubenikin, 5/1956-12/1957 (died).

Mr. V.F. Kotok, 9/1958-10/1965.

Mr. P.I. Kubryavtsev, 9/1959-4/1962.

Mr. G.I. Petov, 9/1958-4/1962.

Mr. P.S. Romashkin, 9/1958-10/1965.

Mr. I.V. Pavlov, 1/1959-4/1962.

Mr. F.I. Kaliychev, 1/1959-4/1962.

Mr. M.S. Strogovich, 1/1959-4/1962.

Mr. V.S. Tabevosyan,.1/1959-4/1962.

Mr. G.A. Aksenenok, 3/1960-10/1965.

Mr. G.Z. Anashkim, 4/1962-10/1965.

Mr. S.F. Kechekyan, 4/1962-10/1965.

Mr. V.V. Kulikov, 4/1962-10/1965.

Mr. V.A. Tumanov, 4/1962-10/1965.

Mr. A.F. Shebanov, 4/1962-

Mr. I.F. Pankratov, 5/1962-7/1962.

Mr. A.S. Pankratov, 12/1962-

Mr. E.M. Vorozheikin, 11/1963-10/1965.

Mr. I.A. Azovkin, 10/1965-

Mr. V.P. Efimochkin, 10/1965-

Mr. V.P. Kazimirchuk, 10/1965-

Mr. M.I. Kozyr, 10/1965-

Mr. A.P. Kositsyn, 10/1965-

Mr. M.A. Krutogolov, 10/1965-

Mr. A.I. Leieshkin, 10/1965-

Mr. A.E. Lunev, 10/1965-

Mr. A.N. Mishutin, 10/1965-

Mr. A.A. Pointkovskii, 10/1965-

Mr. O.N. Sabikov, 10/1965-
Mr. N.F. Chistyakov, 10/1965-
Mr. G. Kh. Shakhazarov, 10/1965-
Mr. A.M. Yakovlev, 10/1965.

APPENDICES A & B

[1]Appendix A was compiled from the following sources: SECTION I, International Court of Justice, *Reports;* SECTIONS II and III, International Law Commission, *Yearbooks* (A/CN.4/); SECTIONS IV and V, United Nations General Assembly, Special Committee on Principles of International Law Concerning Friendly Relations and Co-Operation Among States, *Summary Records* (A/AC.119); SECTION VI, United Nations, Conference on Consular Relations, *Official Records* (A/Conf. 25/); SECTION VII, United Nations, Conference on Diplomatic Intercourse and Immunities, *Official Records* (A/Conf. 20/); SECTION VIII, United Nations, Conference on the Law of the Sea (1960), *Official Records* (A/Conf. 19/); SECTION IX, United Nations, Conference on the Law of the Sea (1958), *Official Records* (A/Conf. 13/); SECTION X, United Nations General Assembly, Sixth (Legal) Committee, *Summary Records* (A/C.6/); SECTION XI, International Law Association, *Reports* (47th-52nd Conferences); and SECTION XII, International Association of Democratic Lawyers, *Proceedings* (6th Congress).

[2]Appendix B was compiled from the following sources: SECTIONS I and II from *Sovetskii ezhegodnik mezhdunarodnogo prava* (Soviet Yearbook of International Law), 1958, 1959, 1960, 1961, 1962, 1963, and 1964-1965 editions; and SECTION III from *Sovetskoe gosudarstvo i pravo* (Soviet State and Law), 1946-*seriatim.*

APPENDIX C
WHO'S WHO: SOVIET SCHOLARS OF INTERNATIONAL LAW

ALEKSIDZE, L. A.

Professor, Law Faculty, Tbilisi University. Member of the Executive Committee of the Soviet Branch of the International Law Association (ILA) since 1965. Member of the Soviet Branch of the ILA since 1963. Member of the Executive Committee of the Soviet Association of International Law since 1962.

AVAKOV, M. M.

Professor of Law and Jurisprudence at the State Insitute of Political Economy. Byelorussian Delegate to the 1963 United Nations Vienna Conference on Consular Relations.

AVILIN, V. N.

Member of the Soviet Branch of the International Law Association (ILA) since 1965. Assistant Editor, 1963 and 1964-1965 editions of the *Sovetskii ezhegodnik mezhdunarodnogo prava* (Soviet Yearbook of International Law). Presently associated with the Publishing House of Legal Literature.

BAGNINIAN, K. A.

Doctor of Laws. Member of the Soviet Branch of the International Law Association (ILA), 1957-1963. Presently associated with the Institute of Law, Academy of Sciences of the USSR. Among his works: *Borba Sovetskogo Soiuze protiv agressii* (The Struggle of the Soviet Union Against Aggression), 1960.

BAKHTOV, K. K.

Chief of the Legal Department, Ministry of Foreign Trade (USSR). Member of the Soviet Branch of the International Law Association (ILA), 1957-1963. Member of the Executive Committee of the Soviet Association of International Law, 1958-1962.

BLISHCHENKO, I. P.

Member of the Academy of Sciences (USSR). Adviser to the USSR Delegation to the 1961 United Nations Vienna Conference on Diplomatic Intercourse and Immunities. Among his works are: *Mezhdunarodnoe i vnutrigosudanstvennoe pravo* (International and Municipal Law), 1960; and *Diplomaticheskoe i konsulskoe pravo* (Diplomatic and Consular Law), 1962.

BOBROV, R. L.

Professor, Law Faculty, Leningrad University. Member of the Soviet Branch of the International Law Association (ILA) since 1961. Member of the Executive Committee of the Soviet Association of International Law since 1960. Among his works are: *Sovremennoe mezhdunarodnoe pravo: obektivnye predposylki i sotsialnoe nazachenie* (Present-Day International Law: Its Objectives, Premises and Social Purposes), 1962.

BOGDANOV, O. V.

Member, Institute of State and Law, Academy of Sciences of the USSR. Member of the Soviet Branch of the International Law Association (ILA) since 1957; Chief Secretary to the Branch since 1963. Member of the Executive Committee of the Soviet Association of International Law since 1962. Assistant Editor, 1959 edition; member of the Editorial Board, 1958, 1960, 1961, and 1962 editions of the *Sovetskii ezhegodnik mezhdunarodnogo prava* (Soviet Yearbook of International Law).

BOGUSLAVSKII, M. M.

Member of the Editorial Board, 1960, 1961, 1962, 1963 and 1964-1965 editions of *Sovetskii ezhegodnik mezhdunarodnogo prava* (Soviet Yearbook of International Law). His works include: *Immuntet gosudarstva* (State Immunity), 1962.

DURDENEVSKII, VSEVOLOD NIKOLAEVICH

Born 1889, Moscow. Graduated 1911 with Silver Medal, from Law Faculty, University of Moscow. 1915, became Assistant Professor, University of Moscow. June 1917, became Professor at Perm. According to Soviet sources, he was an active participant in the Socialist construction (elaboration of legal questions). March 7, 1946, awarded Doctor of Laws. Areas of specialization: consular and diplomatic law, territorial problems, international treaties and international organizations.

January 1944, named expert-consultant, Treaty Department, USSR Ministry of Foreign Affairs. June 15, 1947, conferred diplomatic rank of Minister, Class II.

Participated in drafting 1926 USSR Consular Regulations. 1947-1948, participated as Soviet expert at Potsdam Conference, Paris Peace Conference, Second Session of the General Assembly of the UN, Belgrade Conference on the régime for the navigation of the Danube. He also participated in 1954 Geneva Conference, 1954 Berlin Conference, 1955 Warsaw Conference and 1956 London Conference on Suez. 1957, named a member of Soviet Delegation to the Hague Court of Arbitration. Member of the Executive Committee of the Soviet Branch of the International Law Association (ILA), 1957-1965. Member of the Executive Committee of the Soviet Association of International Law, 1958-1963. Attended first (1946) and second (1947) sessions of the UN General Assembly, Sixth (Legal) Committee as USSR Delegate.

Simultaneously with public service, he continued teaching and researching. Among his works: *Foreign Consular Law* (1925); *Soviet Administrative Law* (1940), *International Law* (1946, 1947); and the *History of State and Law* (1947, 1957). Compiled under his direction by L.A. Modzhoryan and V.K. Sobakin was the three volume work, *International Law Through Selected Documents,* a collection on legal procedure of chief political conferences of the 20th century.

December 26, 1957, elected to the RSFSR Academy of Sciences. Awards: Worker's Order of the Red Banner and the Badge of Honor.

GOLUNSKII, SERGEI ALEKSANDROVICH

Born 1895. Since 1954, Professor of Law, University of Moscow. From 1923 to 1939, he worked in the Procurator's Office. Joined the Communist Party in 1941. 1939-1943, Chairman of the Military Law Academy, USSR Academy of Sciences. From 1943 to 1945, expert-consultant to the Treaty Department, USSR

People's Commissariat of Foreign Affairs. 1945-1952, Head of the Treaty Department. 1952-1954, judge, International Court of Justice (ICJ) of the United Nations. During the "war years," he served as adviser to the Soviet Delegation to the 1943 Moscow Conference, the 1944 Dumbarton Oaks Conference, the 1945 San Francisco Conference, the 1945 Yalta Conference and the 1945 Potsdam Conference. From 1946 to 1948, State Prosecutor for the USSR at the international trials of Japanese war criminals at Tokyo. In 1954, expert at the Berlin Conference of Foreign Ministers. A member (and since 1958, Vice-President) of the USSR Association for Co-Operation with the United Nations. Member, USSR Delegation to he Sixth Congress of the International Association of Democratic Lawyers (Brussels, 1956).

1959-1962, Editor, *Sovetskoe gosudarstvo i pravo* (Soviet State and Law). Among his works: *Manual of the Judicial System* (1939); *Criminal Law* (1939); *Judicial System of the USSR* (1946); *New Principles of Criminal Legal Procedure in the USSR and the Union Republics* (1950).

GRABAR, VLADIMIR EMMANUILOVICH

Doctor of International Law. Professor. Born, January 22, 1865. Died, November 26, 1956. 1888, graduated, Faculty of Law, Kiev. Became member, Faculty of Law, University of Moscow. His first work, *On International Rivers*, won him the University's Gold Medal.

After his graduate in 1888, he traveled abroad, assuming the Chair of International Law at Tartu University (which he held for a quarter of a century). After the revolution, he became Professor of International Law. University of Moscow; and adviser to the People's Commissariat of Foreign Affairs of the USSR and the People's Commissariat of Foreign Trade of the USSR. Retired on pension, 1929. Continued research study at the University of Moscow; Institute of Law of the Academy of Sciences and occupied, as an honorary member, the Chair of International Law at the University of Moscow.

Wrote more than 135 works in Russian, Ukrainian, French, German and Latin. Among his principal works are: *Roman Law in the History of International Scholarship* (1901); *De Legatarum Jure* (1918); *The Role of Hugo Grotius in the Scientific Development of International Law* (1925); and *Materials on Historical Literature on International Law* (1957).

Awards: Worker's Order of the Red Banner.

ILYIN, Y. O.

Third Secretary, International Relations Section, Ministry of Foreign Affairs. Adviser and Secretary to the Byelorussian Delegation to he 1963 United Nations Vienna Conference on Consular Relations.

IVANOV, S. A.

Doctor of Laws. Editor, *Sovetskoe gosudarstvo i pravo* (Soviet State and Law), since 1965.

JANOVSKII, M. V.

Member, Editorial Board, 1963 and 1964-1965 editions of *Sovetskii ezhegodnik mezhdunarodnogo prava* (Soviet Yearbook of International Law).

KALUZNAYA, Madame G. P.

Professor. Member and Deputy Chairman, Soviet Branch of the International Law Association (ILA), 1963-1966. Vice-President, Soviet Association of International Law, 1962-1966.

KEILIN, A. D.

Professor. Legal adviser, Institute of Foreign Trade, Ministry of Foreign Trade of the USSR. Member, USSR Delegation to the 1958 and 1960 United Nations Geneva Conferences on the Law of the Sea. Member, Editorial Board, 1958, 1959, 1960, 1961, 1962 editions of *Sovetskii ezhegodnik mezhdunarodnogo prava* (Soviet Yearbook of International Law). Member, Soviet Branch of the International Law Association (ILA) since 1957. Member, Executive Committee, Soviet Association of International Law since 1962.

KHALFINA, Madame RASHISA O.

Member, Academy of Sciences of the USSR. Member, Soviet Branch of the International Law Association (ILA) since 1962.

KHLESTOV, O. N.

Deputy Head, Legal Department, Ministry of Foreign Affairs. Deputy Chairman, USSR Delegation to the 1963 United Nations Vienna Conference on Consular Relations. Chairman, Soviet Delegation, 1964 Mexico City Conference of the UN Special Committee on Principles of International Law Concerning Friendly Relations and Co-Operation Among States. Member, Editorial Board, 1960, 1961, and 1962 editions, *Sovetskii ezhegodnik mezhdunarodnogo prava* (Soviet Yearbook of International Law). Member, Executive Committee, Soviet Association of International Law since 1966. Attended 21st (1966) session of the UN General Assembly; USSR Delegate, Sixth (Legal) Committee.

KORBUT, Madame L. V.

Learned Secretary, Soviet Association of International Law since 1960. Member, Soviet Branch of the International Law Association (ILA) since 1963. Member and Executive Secretary, Editorial Board, 1963 and 1964-1965 editions of *Sovetskii ezhegodnik mezhdunarodnogo prava* (Soviet Yearbook of International Law).

KORETSKII, VLADIMIR MIKHAILOVICH

Doctor of Laws since 1939. Full member, Ukrainian Academy of Sciences since 1948. Deputy Chairman, Soviet Association of International Law since 1958. Member, Executive Committee, Soviet Association of International Law, 1958-1959. Deputy Chairman, Soviet Branch of the International Law Association (ILA), 1957-1959. Member, Soviet Branch of the International Law Association (ILA) since 1957. Judge, International Court of Justice (ICJ) of the UN since 1961. Honorary Scientific Worker of Ukrainian SSR since 1947.

Born 1890. Graduated, Law Faculty, Kharkov University, 1916. Began teaching. 1920-1930, instructor, Kharkov Institute of National Economy. 1930-1937, Kharkov Institute of Soviet Construction and Law. 1937-1941 and 1944-1949, Kharkov Law Institute. 1941-1944, Tashkent Law Institute. Since

1949, Head, State and Law Section, Ukrainian Academy of Sciences. Chairman, Legal Section and Board Member, Ukrainian Society of Friendship and Cultural Relations with Foreign Countries. Member, Editorial Board, *Ukrainska radyanska entsyklopedia* (Ukrainian Soviet Encyclopedia). Adviser, Soviet delegations at three sessions of the UN General Assembly and Security Council. Delegate to the first (1946) through third (1948) sessions of the UN General Assembly's Sixth (Legal) Committee. 1946 attended Paris Peace Conference. Honorary member since 1950, Indian Society of International Law. Participated in work of UN Committee on Progressive Development and Codification of International Law; Human Rights Commission. 1956 adviser, Geneva Conference for Drafting a Convention for the Abolition of Slavery and Slave Trafficking. Attended 1949-1952 sessions of the International Law Commission (Vice-Chairman of 1949 session). 1957 attended UNESCO Conference in Munich. 1958 and 1960 headed Ukrainian Delegation to UN Geneva Conferences on the Law of the Sea. Attended 14th session of Assembly of World Federation of Associations for Co-Operation with the United Nations. Member since 1959, Polish-Norwegian Permanent Conciliation Commission.

Awards: Order of Lenin; Medal "for Valiant Labor in the Great Patriotic War;" Ukrainian Supreme Soviet's Presidium, Scroll of Honor.

KOROVIN, EVGENII ALEKSANDROVICH

Born, October 12, 1892. Died, Autumn 1965. Professor. Corresponding Member, Academy of Sciences of the USSR. Honored Worker of Science of the RSFSR. Honored Worker of Science of the Uzbek SSR.

Worked with the Red Cross, 1918-1919. Member, Preparatory Commission for the UN. Attended international conferences at London, Paris, Warsaw, Prague and Geneva. 1957, named member, Hague Permanent Court of Arbitration.

Deputy Chairman, Soviet Branch of the International Law Association (ILA), 1957-1963. Member, Soviet Branch of ILA from 1957 until his death in 1965. Deputy Chairman, Soviet Association of International Law, 1958-1962. Member, Editorial Board, 1958, 1959, 1960, 1961 and 1962 editions of *Sovetskii ezhegodnik mezhdunarodnogo prava* (Soviet Yearbook of International Law). Assistant Editor, *Sovetskoe gosudarstvo i pravo* (Soviet State and Law), 1948-1953. Elected, Council of UNESCO. Director of the International Institute on Cosmic Law. Member, of the Council of the International Fund named for Hugo Grotius. Lectured, University of Paris and the Hague Academy of International Law.

Areas of chief interest: (according to Soviet sources): the concept of international law, the concept of sovereignty, the problem of socialist international law, the relation of international law to the present-day struggle of peoples for peace, the role of the masses of peoples in the history of international law, the formation of international law, and the dynamic development of peaceful coexistence.

Member, Soviet Association for the Advancement of the UN. Member, Editorial Board, *Diplomatic Dictionary, International Affairs* (Moscow), and *New Times.*

Among his works are: 13 books, 16 phamplets and more than 200 articles. His principal works include: *International Law During the Transitional Period* (1923); *Present-Day International Law* (1926); *Fundamental Problems of Contemporary International Relations* (1959); *Japan and International Law* (1936) and *Disarmament* (1930).

Awards: Order of Lenin; Order of the Red Banner of Labor; Order of the Badge of Honor; 1943, named "honorary reader," by the Presidium of the Supreme Soviet of Turkmenstan SSR; 1948, awarded the Grotius Medal by the International Fund named for Hugo Grotius for "great merit in developing international space law;" and 1963, a medal from the International Federation of Astronomers (at their Paris Conference).

KOZHEVNIKOV, FEDOR IVANOVICH

Born 1903. Doctor of Laws. Lawyer. Professor. 1952-1961, Judge, International Court of Justice (ICJ). Member, Soviet Branch of the International Law Association (ILA) since 1957. Member, Executive Committee, Soviet Branch of the ILA, 1957-1963. Member, Executive Committee, Soviet Association of International Law, 1958-1962. Member, Editorial Board, 1963 and 1964-1965 editions of the *Sovetskii ezhegodnik mezhdunarodnogo prava* (Soviet Yearbook of International Law). Editor (1950-1953) and Member, Editorial Board (1953-1959), of *Sovetskoe gosudarstvo i pravo* (Soviet State and Law). Expert, Commission on Legal Sciences, USSR Ministry of Higher Education. Member (1952-1953), UN International Law Commission (2nd session, Vice-Chairman). Member, Soviet Committee for the Defense of Peace. Member, Auditing Commission, Union Society for Friendship and Cultural Relations with Foreign Countries. Board member, Soviet-American Institute.

Awards: Badge of Honor; World Peace Council, Scroll of Honor.

KRYLOV, SERGEI BORISOVICH

Born January 1, 1888. Graduated, Faculty of Law, University of Leningrad in 1910. Doctoral thesis in law entitled, *International Conferences and Radio-Electricity*.

Professor at Leningrad in comparative and international law (1911-1942). Director of the Institute at Leningrad, 1930-1939. Adviser, Commissariat of Foreign Affairs since 1942. Professor of international law at the Advance School of Diplomacy and the Institute of International Relations at Moscow since 1942. Deputy Chairman, Soviet Branch of the International Law Association (ILA), 1957-1959.

Delegate, Dumbarton Oaks Conference (1944), and the San Francisco Conference (1945). Adviser to the sessions of the Committee on Jurists, Washington, D.C. (1945). 1946-1952, Judge, International Court of Justice (ICJ). Delegate, first session (1946), UN General Assembly's Sixth (Legal) Committee. 1953-1956, member, International Law Commission (1955 session, first Vice-Chairman). Member, USSR Delegation to the 1958 UN Geneva Conference on the Law of the Sea.

Soldier World War I. Wounded during 1916 offensive. Took part in the defense of Leningrad, 1941-1942. Deputy, Leningrad Municipal Soviet.

Among his works: *Fundamentals of Budgetary Law in the Soviet Federal System* (1928); *Manual of International Private Law* (1930); *Air Law* (1933); *Manual of International Private Law*, co-authored with M. Pereterskii (1933); and *Manual of International Public Law*, co-authored with V. Durdenevskii (1945). Editor, 1958 edition, *Sovetskii ezhegodnik mezhdunarodnogo prava* (Soviet Yearbook of International Law).

In writing he has, at times, used the pseudonym S. Borisov.

KUDRIATSEV, PETR IVANOVICH

Government Official. Legal adviser, Class I. Colonel-General, Armed Forces Legal Services. Kazakstan Procurator-General since 1962. Member USSR College of Procurators since 1959. Until 1956, Vice-Minister of Justice of the USSR. 1956-1961, USSR Deputy Procurator-General. 1955, headed Soviet lawyers delegation to Rumania. 1956, headed Soviet lawyers delegation to the Sixth Congress of the International Law Association (Brussels). 1957, elected Vice-President of the Association. 1958 took part in discussions with lawyers from Rumania, Bulgaria, GDR and Hungary on conclusion of agreement on legal aid in civil and criminal suits.

Among his works: *Iuridicheskii slovar* (Legal Dictionary), co-authored (1956) and *Inogo vykhoda net: problemy mirnogo sosushchestvovaniia i mezhdunarodnoe pravo* (There is No Other Way: International Law and the Problem of Peaceful Coexistence), co-authored with E. M. Rozental (1961).

LADYZHENSKII, ALEKSANDR MIKHAILOVICH

Lawyer. Doctor of Laws since 1947. Professor since 1922. Chairman, Auditing Commission, Soviet Association of International Law. Member, Soviet Branch of International Law Association (ILA) since 1957. Born 1892, Yurev (now Tartu). Graduated 1914, Faculty of Law, University of Moscow. 1915-1917, lecturer at the People's University. Since 1917, lecturer at the University of Moscow. Member, Moscow Institute of International Relations, Institute for Foreign Trade, Institute of State and Law of the USSR Academy of Sciences and other higher legal educational establishments. Former Chairman, North Caucasian Regional Society of History, Archeology and Ethnography. Former Secretary Rostov-on-Don Philosophical Society. Legal consultant to major institutions. Published more than 150 works.

LAZAREV, M. I.

Doctor of Laws. Professor. Member, Soviet Branch of the International Law Association (ILA) since 1957. Member, Executive Committee, Soviet Branch of ILA, 1961-1966. Member, Executive Committee of the Soviet Association of International Law, 1960-1966. Member, Editorial Board, 1958 and 1959 editions of *Sovetskii ezhegodnik mezhdunarodnogo prava* (Soviet Yearbook of International Law).

Among his principal works: *Kongress narodov v zashchito mira i osnovnye printsipy mezhdunarodnogo prava* (Congress of Peoples of Peace and Basic Principles of International Law), (1953); *Imperialisticheshie voennye razy na chuzikh territoriiakh i mezhdunarodnoe pravo* (Imperialist Military Bases in Foreign Countries and International Law), (1963); and *Tekhnicheskii progress i sovremennoe mezhdunarodnoe pravo* (Technical Progress and Present-Day International Law), (1963).

LEVIN, DAVID B.

Doctor of Laws. Professor. Member, Institute of State and Law, USSR Academy of Sciences. Member, Soviet Branch of the International Law Association (ILA) since 1965. Member, Editorial Board, 1959, 1960, 1961, 1962, 1963 and 1964-1965 editions of *Sovetskii ezhegodnik mezhdunarodnogo prava* (Soviet Yearbook of International Law).

Among his works: *Diplomaticheskii immunitet* (Diplomatic Immunity), (1949); *Lenin o mezhdunarodnoi politike i mezhdunarodnom prave* (Lenin on International Politics and International Law), (1958); *Osnovynye problemy sovremenno-go mezhdunarodnogo prava* (Fundamental Problems of Contemporary International Law), (1958); *O sovremennykh burzhkaznykh teoriiakh mezhdunarodnogo pravo* (On Present-Day Bouregois Theory of International Law), (1959); and *Istoriia mezhdunarodnogo prava* (History of International Law), (1962).

LUKASHUK, I. I.
Doctor of Laws. Professor, Judicial Faculty, University of Kiev. Member. Soviet Branch of the International Law Association (ILA) since 1957. Member, Executive Committee, Soviet Association of International Law. Member, Editorial Board, 1960, 1961 and 1962 editions of *Sovetskii ezhegodnik mezhdunarodnogo prava* (Soviet Yearbook of International Law).

LUNTS, LSAR ADOLFOVICH
Born in Dorpat (now Tartu) in 1892. Since 1896, domiciled in Moscow. In 1917, graduated, Faculty of Law, University of Moscow. Since 1918, lecturer at the same Faculty and later at the Institute of Foreign Trade (now Institute of Foreign Relations), on civil and private international law. Between 1918 and 1941, legal adviser to the People's Commissariat for Finance. Awarded Doctor of Laws in 1947. From 1939 on, senior collaborator at the All-Union Institute of Judicial Sciences (now, All-Union Institute of Soviet Law). Member, Soviet Branch of the International Law Association (ILA) since 1957. Member, Executive Committee, Soviet Branch of ILA since 1966. Member, Editorial Board, 1958, 1959, 1960, 1961, 1962, 1963 and 1964-1965 editions of *Sovetskii ezhegodnik mezhdunarodnogo prava* (Soviet Yearbook of International Law). Member, USSR Delegation to the Sixth Congress of the International Association of Democratic Lawyers (Brussels, 1956).

Among his principal works: *Uchebnik mezhdunarodnogo chastnogo prava* (Handbook on Private International Law), (1949); *Voprosy mezhdurarodnogo chastnogo prava* (Problems of Private International Law), (1956); *Kurs mezhdunarodnogo chastnogo prava* (A Treatise on Private International Law), (1959); and *Kurs mezhdunarodnogo chastnogo prava* (A Treatise on Private International Law), (1963).

MAKSUDOV, L. M.
Member, Eastern Institute, Central-Asian University. Member, Soviet Branch of the International Law Association (ILA), 1957-1963. Member, Executive Committee, Soviet Branch of ILA, 1957-1959. Member, Executive Committee, Soviet Association of International Law, 1958-1962.

MESHERA, V. F.
Professor. Member, Soviet Branch of the International Law Association (ILA) since 1957. Member, Editorial Board, 1958, 1959, 1960, 1961, 1962, 1963, and 1964-1965 editions of the *Sovetskii ezhegodnik mezhdunarodnogo prava* (Soviet Yearbook of International Law).

MINASIAN, N. M.

Professor, Rostov State University. Student of the late Evgenii A. Korovin.

Among his principal works: *Istochniki sovremennogo mezhdunarodnogo prava* (Sources of Present-Day International Law), (1960); and *Sushchnost sovremennogo mezhdunarodnogo pravo* (The Essence of Present-Day International Law), (1962).

MODZHORIJAN, Madame LIDIJA A.

Doctor of Laws. Professor. Member, Soviet Branch of the International Law Association (ILA) since 1957. Member, Editorial Board, 1958, 1959, 1960, 1961, 1962, 1963 and 1964-1965 editions of *Sovetskii ezhegodnik mezhdunarodnogo prava* (Soviet Yearbook of International Law).

Among her principal works: *Mezhdunarodnoe pravo i izbrannykh dokumentakh* (International Law and Selected Documents), co-authored with S.K. Sobakin, (1957); *Subekty mezhdunarodnogo prava* (Subjects of International Law), (1958); *Voprosy teorii i praktiti mezhdunarodnogo prava* (Theoretical and Practical Problems of International Law), co-authored with V.N. Durdenevskii, (1959); *Voprosy teorii i praktiti sovremennogo mezhdunarodnogo prava* (Theoretical and Practical Problems of Contemporary International Law), (1960); and *Osnovnye prave i obiazannosti gosudarstv* (Fundamental Rights and Duties of States), (1965).

MOLODTSOV, STEPHAN V.

Doctor of Laws. Since 1958, Senior Scientific Officer, Legal Institute, USSR Academy of Sciences. Adviser to USSR Delegation to the 1958 United Nations Geneva Conference on the law of the Sea. Honorary Secretary, Soviet Branch of the International Law Association (ILA), 1957-1963. Member, Soviet Branch of the ILA, 1957-1966. Member, Executive Committee, Soviet Association of International Law, 1958-1962. Member, Editorial Board, 1963 and 1964-1965 editions of *Sovetskii ezhegodnik mezhdunarodnogo prava* (Soviet Yearbook of International Law).

MOROZOV, G. I.

Professor, Institute of World Economy and International Relations. Assistant Secretary, Soviet Branch of the International Law Association (ILA), 1957-1961. Member, Soviet Branch of the ILA since 1957. Member, Executive Committee, Soviet Association of International Law, 1965-1966. Member and Chief Secretary, Editorial Board, 1958, 1959, 1960, 1961, 1962 editions of *Sovetskii ezhegodnik mezhdunarodnogo prava* (Soviet Yearbook of International Law). Member and Secretary, Editorial Board, *Sovetskoe gosudarstvo i pravo* (Soviet State and Law), 1956-1957.

MOVCHAN, A. P.

First Secretary, Ministry of Foreign Affairs of the USSR. Member, USSR Delegation to the 1961 United Nations Vienna Conference on Diplomatic Intercourse and Immunities. Attended 15th (1960), 17th (1962), and 18th (1963) sessions of the UN General Assembly's Sixth (Legal) Committee as USSR Delegate. Member, Editorial Board, 1963 and 1964-1965 editions of *Sovetskii ezhegodnik mezhdunarodnogo prava* (Soviet Yearbook of International Law).

NEDBAILO, P. Y.
Doctor of Laws. Professor. Attended 14th (1959), 15th (1960), and 17th (1962) UN General Assembly's Sixth (Legal) Committee as Ukrainian Delegate (elected Rapporteur at 15th session).

NIKOLAYEV, ANATOLY NIKOLAEVICH
Diplomat with rank of Ambassador Extraordinary and Plentipotentiary. USSR Ambassador to Thailand, 1960-1965. Born 1915. Diplomatic posts since 1948. 1953-1955 and 1957-1960, Head, Treaty and Legal Board, USSR Ministry of Foreign Affairs. 1955-1957, adviser to Soviet Mission to the UN. 1957, member Soviet Delegation at meeting for concluding statutes on legal status of Soviet troops in Hungary and Rumania. Vice-Chairman, USSR Delegation to the 1950 UN Geneva Conference on Law of the Sea.

PASHUKANIS, EVGENII BRONISLAVOVICH
Born in the city of Staritsa in Tver Guberniya, near the headwaters of the Volga on February 10, 1891. He attracted little attention until he published in 1924, a work entitled, "General Theory of Law and Marxism." Shortly thereafter he became Vice-President of the Communist Academy and Director of the Institute of Soviet Construction and Law. In the late 1920's and early 1930's he was severely criticized for his views, therefore, he modified them somewhat in 1931, in order to allay his adversaries. Seemingly successful, he replaced P.I. Stuchka (1930), as editor of the leading official law journal, *Sovetskoe gosudarstvo i revoliutsiia prava* (Soviet State and Revolutionary Law). He was made Vice-Commissar of Justice in 1936. He participated actively in the formulation of the 1936 "Stalin" Constitution. However, on the morning of January 20, 1937, an article by P. Yudin (see biographical sketch, *infra*), in the Principal Party newspaper, *Pravda*, unleashed a vigorous attack upon Pashukanis as an "enemy of the people." Finally in 1938, Andrei Ia. Vyshinskii (see biographical sketch, *infra*), summed up the attack against him. After 1937, facts about Pashukanis are unknown.
Among his principal works: *Imperialism and Colonial Policy* (1920); *For A Marxist-Leninist Theory of the State and the Law* (1931); *Essays on International Law* (1935); and *Textbook on Soviet Economic Law* (n.d.).

RADBIL, O. S.
Professor. MD. Writes on International medical law.

REISNER, MIKHAIL ANDREEVICH
Born in Siberia in 1868 and educated at Tomsk University (his doctoral dissertation was entitled, *The State and the Church* which was published after the revolution in January 1919). Reisner participated, as an expert, in the trial of Karl Liebkneckt in Königsberg (now Kaliningrad) in 1904 and joined the Bolshevik wing of the Russian Social Democratic Labor Party in 1905. He attended the University of St. Petersburg in 1906 and became a professor of Public Law in 1907. He was likewise Professor of Public Law at the Psychoneurological Institute. He retained these positions until 1917. Some biographical sources indicate that after the revolution he became Chief of the Section for Legislative Drafting of the Commissariat of Justice, although he left this post to serve at the front during the civil war.

Reisner was violently attacked by Andrei Ia. Vyshinskii (see biographical sketch, *infra*) in 1938 and by Sergei A. Golunskii (see biographical sketch, *supra*) and by Mikhail S. Strogovich (see biographical sketch, *infra*) in 1940 for what they believed were errors in his application of Marxism.

Among his principal works: *The State of Bourgeoisie and the RSFSR* (1923); *The Ideology of the East* (1927); and *The History of Political Studies* (1929).

ROMASHKIN, PETR SEMENOVICH

Lawyer. Doctor of Laws since 1957. Professor, Chair of Criminal Law, Faculty of Law, University of Moscow since 1952. Corresponding Member, USSR Academy of Sciences since 1958. Member, Executive Committee, Union for the Defense of People's Rights since 1958. Member, Executive Board, *Sovetskoe gosudarstvo i pravo* (Soviet State and Law), 1958-1965. Member, Communist Party since 1939. Member, Soviet Branch of the International Law Association since 1957. Member, Executive Committee, Soviet Branch of ILA, 1957-1965. Member, Executive Committee, Soviet Association of International Law, 1958-1962.

Born 1915. Graduated, 1936, Kazan Law Institute. Specialist in criminal law, particularly criminal legislation in pre-revolutionary Russia and criminal responsibility for international crimes. 1939-1958, assisted USSR Council of Ministers. 1943-1952, lecturer, Department of Criminal Law, Faculty of Law, University of Moscow. 1958-1964, Director, Institute of State and Law, USSR Academy of Sciences.

RYBANOV, A. A.

Candidate of Law. Attended 20th (1965) and 21st (1966) sessions of the UN General Assembly's Sixth (Legal) Committee as USSR Delegate.

SABIKOV, O. N.

Candidate of Law. Member, Editorial Board, *Sovetskoe gosudarstvo i pravo* (Soviet State and Law) since 1965.

SEMENOV, V. S.

Candidate of Law. Member, Soviet Branch of the International Law Association (ILA) since 1963. Member, Executive Committee, Soviet Branch of the ILA since 1965. Member, Executive Committee, Soviet Association of International Law since 1962. Lecturer, Kharkov Judicial Institute.

SEMERIKIN, E. M.

Lecturer, Faculty of Law, State University of Minsk. Member, Soviet Branch of the International Law Association (ILA), 1957-1963. Member, Editorial Board, 1958, 1959, 1960, 1961, and 1962 editions *Sovetskii ezhegodnik mezhdunarodnogo prava* (Soviet Yearbook of International Law).

SHURSHALOV, V. M.

Candidate of Law. Corresponding Member, Institute of State and Law, USSR Academy of Sciences. Member, Soviet Branch of the International Law Association (ILA) since 1957. Member, Editorial Board, 1963 and 1964-1965 editions *Sovetskii ezhegodnik mezhdunarodnogo prava* (Soviet Yearbook of International Law).

Among his principal works: *Osnovaniia deistvitelnosti mezhdunarodnykh dogovorov* (Essays on Existing International Treaties), (1957); and *Osnovnye voprosy teorii mezhdunarodnogo dogovora* (Essays on Theoretical Questions of International Treaties), (1959).

SOBAKIN, V. K.

Editor-in-Chief, 1963 edition, *Sovetskii ezhegodnik mezhdunarodnogo prava* (Soviet Yearbook of International Law). Co-authored with Madame L.A. Modzhorijan, *Mezhdunarodnoe pravo v izbrannykh dokumentakh* (International Law and Selected Documents), compiled under direction of V.N. Durdenevskii,(1957).

STROGOVICH, MIKHAIL SOLOMONOVICH

Born 1894. Member, USSR Academy of Sciences since 1939. Head, Criminal Law and Litigation Section, Institute of State and Law, USSR Academy of Sciences. Member, Communist Party since 1943. Since 1959, full member of the Polish Academy of Sciences. Member, Editorial Board, *Sovetskoe gosudarstvo i pravo* (Soviet State and Law), 1959-1962. Expert in criminal litigation and theory of state and law.

Among his principal works: *The Question of Material Truth in Criminal Legislation* (1947); *Criminal Prosecution in Soviet Criminal Litigations* (1951); and *The Verification of the Legality and Justification of Legal Sentences* (1956).

STUCHKA, PAVEL IVANOVICH

Born, Riga, August 14, 1865 of peasant stock. 1888-1897, he was editor of the *Lativian Social Democrat*. He was exiled to the upper reaches of the Volga in Vyatka Guberniya when his newspaper was closed in 1897. Five years later he returned from exile and in 1907, he moved to St. Petersburg. In 1917, with the abdication of the Tsar, he became a member of the Petrograd Soviet. In March of 1918, he became Commissar of Justice. Stuchka organized the "Section of General Theory of Law and the State" in the Communist Academy (later to become the Institute of Soviet Construction and Law of the Communist Academy in 1929 and ultimately in 1937, the Institute of Law of the USSR Academy of Sciences). Other directors of this institute were Evgenii Pashukanis (see biographical sketch, *supra*), Andrei Ia. Vyshinskii (see biographical sketch, *infra*), and Ilya Trainin (see biographical sketch, *infra*). 1920-1921, member of the Central Committee of the CPSU. 1921, he was reduced to an alternate member and then finally released entirely from that powerful body.

Among his principal works: *The Revolutionary Part Played by Law and the State: A General Doctrine of the Law* (1921); *The Study of the State and the Constitution of the USSR* (1922); *The Class State and Civil Law* (1924); *The Study of the Soviet State and Its Constitution — The USSR and the RSFSR* (1929); and *A Treatise on Soviet Civil Law* (1927-1929).

TRAININ, ILYA PAVLOVICH

Born 1887. Died June 27, 1949. Relatively unknown until World War II. During the War, Trainin assumed the position of Director of the Institute of Law of the USSR Academy of Sciences. Assistant Editor, *Sovetskoe gosudarstvo i pravo* (Soviet State and Law) until his death. On his 60th birthday, awarded Order of the Red Banner of Labor for his work in the field of law.

TUNKIN, GRIGORII IVANOVICH

Diplomat with rank of Envoy Extraordinary and Plentipotentiary. Doctor of Laws. Professor of International Law. Born October 13, 1906 in Arkhangelsk region, USSR. Graduate of the Institute of Law, Moscow, 1935. Post-graduate work, same institute, 1935-1938. Scientific collaborator at the Institute of Law, USSR Academy of Sciences, 1938-1939. Entered the diplomatic service in 1939. Since that time occupied different posts in the Ministry of Foreign Affairs of the USSR and abroad. 1952, Head, Treaty and Legal Section, USSR Ministry of Foreign Affairs. Chairman, Soviet Association of International Law since 1957. President and member of the Executive Committee, Soviet Branch of the International Law Association (ILA) since 1957. Editor-in-Chief, 1959, 1960, 1961 and 1962 editions of *Sovetskii ezhegodnik mezhdunarodnogo prava* (Soviet Yearbook of International Law). Member, Editorial Board, *Sovetskoe gosudarstvo i pravo* (Soviet State and Law) since 1956. Since 1947, Head, First Eastern Department (China), USSR Ministry of Foreign Affairs. 1956, attended the conclusion of Soviet-Polish Treaty on the legal status of Soviet troops in Poland. 1956-1961, re-elected 1961-1967, Soviet Representative, UN International Law Commission (1958 and 1964 sessions, elected 2nd Vice-Chairman of the Commission, 1961 elected Chairman). Head, USSR Delegation, 1958 and 1960 United Nations Geneva Conferences on the Law of the Sea. Head, USSR Delegation, 1961 United Nations Vienna Conference on Diplomatic Intercourse and Immunities. Attended 16th (1961) session, UN General Assemnly's Sixth (Legal) Committee as USSR Delegate. Head, USSR Delegation, 1959 international conference at Washington, D.C., held to draft a treaty on the use of Antarctica for scientific purposes. Hold chair of theory and history of state and law, USSR Academy of Sciences, 1948-1954. 1965, withdrew as Head, Treaty and Legal Section, USSR Ministry of Foreign Affairs to assume the Chair of International Law held by the late Evgenii A. Korovin (see biographical sketch, *supra*), at the University of Moscow.

Among his recent principal works are: *Osnovy sovremennogo mezhdunarodnogo prave* (Principles of Present-Day International law), (1956); *Voprosy mezhdunarodnogo prava* (Questions of International Law), editorship, (1960); and *Voprosy teorii mezhdunarodnoe prava* (Theoretical Questions of International Law), (1962).

ULYANOVA, N. N.

Candidate of Laws. Member, Editorial Board, 1963 edition, *Sovetskii ezhegodnik mezhdunarodnogo prava* (Soviet Yearbook of International Law).

USHAKOV, NICHOLAI ALEXSANDROVICH

Candidate of Laws. Member, Institute of State and Law, USSR Academy of Sciences. Member, Soviet Branch of the International Law Association (ILA) since 1963. Deputy-Chairman of the Soviet Association of International Law since 1966. Editor-in-Chief, 1964-1965 edition, *Sovetskii ezhegodnik mezhdunarodnogo prava* (Soviet Yearbook of International Law). Assistant Editor, 1960, 1961, 1962 and 1963 editions, *Sovetskii ezhegodnik mezhdunarodnogo prava* (Soviet Yearbook of International Law). Adviser, USSR Delegation, 1961 United Nations Vienna Conference on Diplomatic Intercourse and Immunities. Soviet Representative, UN International Law Commission, succeeding G.I. Tunkin (see biographical sketch, *supra)*, as of January 1, 1967.

UUSTAL, ABNER T.

Professor, Law Faculty, Tartu State University. Member, Soviet Branch of the International Law Association (ILA) since 1957. Member, Executive Committee, Soviet Branch of ILA, 1961-1965. Member, Executive Committee, Soviet Association of International Law, 1960-1962.

Among his works: *Mezhdunarodnoe pravo* (International Law), (1963).

VYSHINSKII, ANDREI IANUARYEVICH

Born, Odessa in 1883. Died, November 1954. He received a legal education at the College of Law, University of Kiev. Joined the Social Democratic Movement in 1902 but was associated with the Menshevik faction until the revolution. From 1923 to 1925, Prosecutor of the RSFSR and Professor of Law, University of Moscow. From 1936 to 1938, Prosecutor of the USSR performing his duties at the trials of Zinoviev, Kamenev, Trotskii (in absentia), Bukharin, Radek and others. When Pashukanis (see biographical sketch, *supra)* was ousted as Head, Institute of Law, USSR Academy of Sciences. Vyshinskii became its new director. He retained the post until he became USSR Minister of Foreign Affairs. Editor of *Sovetskoe gosudarstvo i pravo* (Soviet State and Laws), 1946-1950. Attended 7th (1952) session of UN General Assembly's Sixth (Legal) Committee as USSR Delegate.

Among his principal works: *Voprosy teorii gosudarstva i prava* (Theoretical Problems of State and Law), (1938); *The Law of the Soviet State*, translated into English, Hugh W. Babb, (1948); *Diplomaticheskii slovar* (Diplomatic Dictionary) with S.A. Lozovskii, (1948), (1950); and *Voprosy mezhdunarodnogo prava i mezhdunarodnoi politiki* (Problems of International Law and International Politics), (1951).

YUDIN, PAVEL FEDOROVICH

Philosopher. Full member, USSR Academy of Sciences since 1953. Member of the CPSU since 1918. Born in 1899 in village in Apraksino (now Gorky Oblast). Graduated, Leningrad Communist University, 1924. 1931 graduate, Institute of Red Professors, Moscow. 1917-1919, lathe operator in locomotive workshop. 1919-1921, member, Red Army Regiment. 1932-1938, director, Institute of Philosophy of Red Professors. Editor of various journals and instructor in philosophy and Communist Party history at above Institute. 1937-1946, Head, RSFSR Joint State Publishing House. 1938-1944, Director, Institute of Philosophy, USSR Academy of Sciences. 1937-1947, Head, Chair of Marxism-Leninism, Univeristy of Moscow. 1947, Chief Editor, newspaper *"Trud"* (Labor). 1947-1950, Chief Eidtor, Cominform newspaper, *"Za prochny mir, za narodnuyu demokratiyu"* (For a Lasting Peace, For People's Democracies). 1950-1953, political adviser, Soviet Control Commission in Germany. 1953-1959, USSR Ambassador to China. 1960, Presidum Member, USSR Academy of Sciences. 1952-1961, members Central Committee, CPSU. Deputy, USSR Supreme Soviet, 1950 and 1954 convocations.

Awards: Order of Lenin, Order of the Red Banner of Labor.

Medals: Stalin Prize, 1943.

ZABIGILO, K.

First Secretary, Ukrainian Ministry of Foreign Affairs. Member, Ukrainian Delegation, 1963 United Nations Vienna Conference on Consular Relations. Member, Ukrainian Delegation, United Nations 1961 Vienna Conference on Diplomatic Intercourse and Immunities. Member, Ukrainian Delegation, 1960 United Nations Geneva Conference on the Law of the Sea. Attended 11th (1956), 12th (1957), 14th (1959), and 18th (1963) sessions of the UN General Assembly's Sixth (Legal) Committee as Ukrainian Delegate.

ZHAVANIYA, GRIGORII E.

Member, Soviet Branch of the International Law Association, 1957-1963. Member, Executive Committee, Soviet Branch of ILA, 1959-1963. Member, Executive Committee, Soviet Association of International Law, 1958-1962.

Among his works: *Mezhdunarodnopravovye garantii zashchity natsionykh menshinstv: istoricheskii ocherk* (International Legal Protection of Minorities: A Historical Study), (1959).

ZHUKOV, G. P.

Candidate of Law. Deputy-Chairman, USSR Space Law Commission.

Among his works: *Kritika estestvenno-pravobykh teorii mezhdunarodnogo prava* (Critique of the Natural Law Theory of International Law), (1961).

BIBLIOGRAPHY

The bibliography is divided into four parts. The first, containing source materials on the Soviet Union and International law, is subdivided into three sections: public documents, books and articles. Materials in English, Russian and French have been included. English translations of all Russian and French titles have been provided, in parentheses, following the foreign language title.

The remainder of the bibliography contains selected source material on subjects and issues connected secondarily with the international law focus of the work. Part two lists materials on Soviet domestic law; part three, material on ideology; and part four, material on the foreign policy of the U.S.S.R.

I. INTERNATIONAL LAW

Public Documents

United Nations. Conference on Consular Relations. *Official Records.* Vienna, March 4 - April 22, 1963. A/Conf.25/.

United Nations. Conference on Diplomatic Intercourse and Immunities. *Official Records.* Vienna, March 2 - April 14, 1961. A/Conf.20/.

United Nations. Conference on the Law of the Sea. *Official Records.* Geneva, 1958. A/Conf.13/.

United Nations. Conference on the Law of the Sea. *Official Records.* Geneva, 1960. A/Conf.19/.

United Nations. General Assembly. International Law Commission. *Official Yearbooks.* 1st Session (1949)-.

United Nations. General Assembly. International Law Commission. "Memorandum of the Soviet Doctrine and Practice With Respect to the Law of Treaties." Prepared by the Secretariat. November 21, 1950. A/CN.4/37.

United Nations. General Assembly. Sixth (Legal) Committee. *Official Summary Records.* 1st Sessions (1946)-. A/C.6/.

United Nations. General Assembly. Special Committee on Principles of International Law Concerning Friendly Relations and Co-Operation Among States. *Summary Records,* Mexico City Meeting, August 27-October 2, 1964. A/AC 119.

United Nations. General Assembly. Special Committee on Principles of International Law Concerning Friendly Relations and Co-Operation Among States. *Report,* 1966 New York Meeting. March 8 - April 25, 1966. A/AC125.

United Nations. International Court of Justice.

Barcelona Traction, Light and Power Company, Limited. Preliminary Objection. ICJ Reports 1964. "Declaration of Judge Koretsky." p. 6.

Case Concerning the Northern Cameroons (Cameroons v. United Kingdom), Preliminary Objection. ICJ Reports 1963. "Declaration of Judge Koretsky." p. 15.

Case of Certain Expenses of the United Nations (Article 17, paragraph 2 of the Charter). ICJ Reports 1962 (Advisory Opinion). "Dissenting Opinion of Judge Koretsky." pp. 253-287.

Concerning Right of Passage Over Indian Territory (Merits). ICJ Reports 1960. "Declaration of Judge Kozhevnikov." p. 6.

Interhandel Case (Switzerland v. The United States of America), Preliminary Objection. ICJ Reports 1959. "Declaration of Judge Kozhevnikov." p. 6.

Case Concerning the Application of the Convention of 1902 Governing the Guardianship of Infants (Netherlands v. Sweden). ICJ Reports 1958. "Declaration of Judge Kozhevnikov." p. 55.

Judgment of the Administrative Tribunal of the ILO Upon Complaints Made Against UNESCO. ICJ Reports 1956. (Advisory Opinion). "Declaration of Judge Kozhevnikov." p. 77.

Admissibility of Hearings of Petitioners by the Committee on South West Africa. ICJ Reports 1956. (Advisory Opinion). "Declaration of Judge Kozhevnikov." p. 23.

South West Africa — Voting Procedure. ICJ Reports 1955. (Advisory Opinion). "Declaration of Judge Kozhevnikov." p. 67.

International Status of South West Africa. ICJ Reports 1950. (Advisory Opinion). "Dissenting Opinion of Judge Krylov." pp. 191-192.

Interpretation of Peace Treaties. ICJ Reports 1950. (Advisory Opinion). "Dissenting Opinion of Judge Krylov." pp. 105-113.

Reparations For Injuries in the Service of the United Nations. ICJ Reports 1949. (Advisory Opinion). "Dissenting Opinion of Judge Krylov." pp. 217-218.

Corfu Channel Case (Merits). ICJ Reports 1949. "Dissenting Opinion of Judge Krylov." pp. 68-77.

Admission of a State to the United Nations (Article 4 of the Charter). ICJ Reports 1948. (Advisory Opinion). "Dissenting Opinion of Judge Krylov." pp. 107-115.

Corfu Channel Case: Judgment on Preliminary Objections. ICJ Reports 1948. "Separate Opinion by Judge Basdevant, Alvarez, Winarski, Zoricič, de Visscher, Badawi Pasha, and Krylov." pp. 31-32.

Books

Akademiia nauk SSSR. Institut gosudarstva i prava. *International Law: Textbook For Use in Law School.* Translated by Dennis Ogden. Moscow: Foreign Languages Publishing House, n.d.

Akademiia nauk SSSR. Institut prava. *Mezhdunarodnoe pravo* (International Law). Moskva: Gos. izd-vo IUrid. lit-ry, 1957.

Avakov, Mirza M. *Pravopreemstvo Sovetskogo gosudarstva* (Succession of the Soviet State). Moskva: Gosizdat. IUrid. lit., 1961.

Baade, Hans W. (ed). *The Soviet Impact on International Law.* New York: Oceana Publications, 1965.

Bagninian, K.A. *Borba Sovetskogo Soiuza protiv agressii* (The Struggle of the Soviet Union Against Aggression). Moskva: izd-vo sotsialno-ekon. lit-ry, 1959.

Baratashvili, D.I. *Amerikanskii teorii mezhdunarodnogo prava* (American Theories of International Law). Moskva: Gos. Izd-vo. IUrid. lit-ry, 1956

Blishchenko, I.P. *Mezhdunarodnoe i vnutrigosudarstvenno pravo* (International and Municipal Law). Moskva: Gosizdat IUrid. lit., 1960.

Blishchenko, I.P. and Durdenevskii, Vsevolod Nikolaevich. *Diplomaticheskoe i konsulskoe pravo* (Diplomatic and Consular Law). Moskva: Institut Mezhdunarodnykh Otnoshenii, 1962.

Bobrov, R.L. *Sovremennoe mezhdunarodnoe pravo: obektivnye predposylki i sotsialnoe nazachenie* (Present Day International Law: Its Objective, Premises and Social Purposes). Leningrad: Izd-vo Leningrad Univ., 1962.

Boguslavskii, M.M. *Immunitet gosudarstva* (State Immunity). Moskva: Institut Mezhdunarodnykh Otnoshenii, 1962.

Briggs, Harold. *The International Law Commission.* Ithaca: Cornell University Press, 1965.

Calvez, Jean-Ives. *Droit International et Souveraineté en URSS: L'Evolution de L'Idéologie Juridique Depuis La Revolution D'Octobre* (International Law and Sovereignty as Viewed by the USSR: The Evolution of a Judicial Ideology Since the October Revolution). Paris: A. Colin, 1953.

Carlston, Kenneth Smith. *Law and Organization in World Society.* Urbana: University of Illinois Press, 1962.

Chernogolovkin, N.V. *Formy kolonialnoi zavistmosti* (Forms of Colonial Dependencies). Moskva: Gosizdat. IUrid. lit., 1956.

_____. *Krushenie kolonializma i mezhdunarodnoe pravo* (Bankruptcy of Colonialism and International Law). Moskva: Gosiurizdat, 1963.

Christensen, Ronald. *Soviet Views on Space: A Comparative and Critical Analysis*. American Rocket Society. Space Flight Report to the Nation. October 1961.

Cooper, Dennis A. *The Air Code of the USSR*. Charlottesville: Michie Company, 1966.

Corbett, Percy E. *Law in Diplomacy*. Princeton: Princeton University Press, 1959.

Dallin, Alexander. *The Soviet Union and the United Nations*. New York: Praeger, 1962.

de Visscher, Charles. *Theory and Reality in Public International Law*. Translated by Percy E. Corbett. Princeton: Princeton University Press, 1957.

Durdenevskii, Vsevolod Nikolaevich and Krylov, Sergei B. (eds.) *Mezhdunarodnoe pravo* (International Law). Moskva: IUridicheskoe izd., 1947.

Durdenevskii, Vsevolod Nikolaevich and Modzhorian, Lidija A. *Voprosy teorii i praktiki mezhdunarodnogo prava* (Theoretical and Practical Problems of International Law). Moskva: izd-vo, Institut Mezhdunarodnykh Otnoshenii, 1959.

Falk, Richard A. and Mendlovitz, Saul H. (eds). *Strategy of World Order*. Vol. II, *International Law*. New York: World Law Fund, 1966.

Feldman, D.I. *Priznanie pravitelstv v mezhdunarodnom prave* (Recognition of Governments in International Law). Kazan: Izd. Kazanakogo Universiteta, 1961.

_____. *Sovremennye teorii mezhdunarodno-pravovogo priznaniya* (Contemporary Theory of International Legal Recognition). Kazan: Izd-vo Kazan, in-ta, 1963.

Filippov, S.V. *Ogovorki v teorii i praktike mezhdunarodnogo dogovora* (Reservations in the Theory and Practice of International Treaties). Moskva: Izd. Institut Mezhdunarodnykh Otnoshenii, 1958.

Friedmann, Wolfgang Gaston. *The Changing Structure of International Law*. New York: Columbia University Press, 1964.

Grabar, Vladimir Emmanuilovich. *Materialy k istorii literatury mezhdunarodnogo prava v Rossii* (Material on the Historical Literature of International Law in Russia). Moskva: Izd. Akademii nauk SSSR, 1958.

Grzybowski, Kazimierz. *Socialist Commonwealth of Nations*. New Haven: Yale University Press, 1964.

Guggenheim, Paul. *Traité* de Droit International Public (Treatise on International Public Law). Geneve: Libraire de L'Universite, Georg and Cie S.A., 1953.

Hazard, John N. *Law and Social Change in the USSR*. Toronto: Carswell, 1953.

Higgins, Rosalyn. *Conflict of Interest: International Law in a Divided World*. Chester Springs: Dufour Edition, 1965.

_____. *The Development of International Law Through the Political Organs of the United Nations*. New York: Oxford University Press, 1963.

Ioffe, Olimpiad Solomonovich. *Sovetskoe grazhdanskoe pravo* (Soviet Citizenship Law). Leiningrad, 1958.

Ioffe, Olimpiad Solomonovich and Shargorodskii, M.D. *Voprosy teorii prava* (Theoretical Questions of Law). Moskva: Gosiurizdat, 1961.

Jenks, Clarence Wilfred. *The Common Law of Mankind*. New York: Praeger, 1968.

_____. *International Law in a Changing World*. Dobbs Ferry: Oceana Publications, 1963.

_____. *Prospects of International Adjudication*. Dobbs Ferry: Oceana Publications, 1963.

Jessup, Philip C. *Transnational Law*. New Haven: Yale University Press, 1956.

Kabes, Vladimir and Sergot, Alfons. *Blueprint for Deception: Character and Record of the International Association of Democratic Lawyers*. Netherlands: Mouton and Company, 1957.

Kelsen, Hans. *The Communist Theory of Law*. New York: Praeger, 1955.

Klimenko, Boris Mikhailovich. *Demilitarizatsiia i neitralizatsiia v mezhdunarodnoe pravo* (Demilitarization and Neutralization in International Law). Moskva: Institut Mezhdunarodnykh Otnoshenii, 1963.

Koretskii, Vladimir Mikhailovich. *"Obshchie printsipy prava" v mezhdunarodnom prave* ("General Principles of Law" in International Law). Moskva: Gosiurizdat, 1957.

_____. *Ocherki anglo-amerikanskoi doktrinky i praktiki mezhdunarodnogo chastnogo prava* (An Essay on Anglo-American Doctrines and Practice of International Private Law). Moskva: IUridicheskoe izd., 1948.

Korovin, Evgenii Aleksandrovich *et al* (eds.) *International Law*. Moscow: Foreign Languages Publishing House, n.d.

Korovin, Evgenii Aleksandrovich. *Kratkii kurs mezhdunarodnogo prava* (Short Course in International Law). Part II. Moskva: 1944. (This work was the Red Army Manual. Part I was never published.)

_____. (ed). *Mezhdunarodnoe prava* (International Law). Moskva: Gosizdat. IUrid. lit., 1951.

_____. *Mezhdunarodnoe pravo perekhodnogo vremeni.* (International Law During the Transitional Period). Moskva: 1924.

_____ . *Mezhdunarodnoe pravo perekhodnogo vremeni.* (International Law During the Transitional Period). Moskva: 1924.

_____. *Pravovaia priroda i iuridicheskaia sila reshenii Generalnoi Assamblai OON.* (Legal Nature and Legal Force of the Decisions of the General Assembly of the UN). Moskva: Mosk. Univ., 1962.

_____. *Sovremennoe mezhdunarodnoe publichnoe pravo.* (Contemporary International Public Law). Moskva: Gosizdat, 1926.

_____. *Voprosy mezhdunarodnogo prava v teorii i praktike S.Sh.A.* (Problems of International Law in Theory and Practice of the USA). Moskva: Izd-vo Instituta Mezhdunarodnykh Otnoshenii, 1957.

Kozhevnikov, Fedor Ivanovich (ed). *Mezhdunarodnoe pravo.* (International Law). Moskva: Gosizdat Iurid. lit., 1957. (English edition: *International Law*. Moscow: Foreign Languages Publishing House, n.d.).

_____. *Sovetskoe gosudarstvo i mezhdunarodnoe pravo 1917-1947.* (Soviet State and International Law, 1917-1947). Moskva: IUridicheskoe izd., 1948.

_____. *Velikaia otechestvennaia voina Sovetskogo Soiuza i nekotorye voprosy mezhdunarodnogo prava.* (The Great Patriotic War of the Soviet Union and Some Problems of International Law). Moskva: Izd-vo. Moskovskogo Universitet, 1954.

Krylov, Sergei Borisovich. *Mezhdunarodnoe pravo.* (International Law). Moskva: 1950.

_____. *Mezhdunarodnyi sud organizatsii obedinennykh natsii.* (The International Court of Justice). Moskva: Gosizdat IUrid. lit., 1958.

Kudriavtsev, Petr I. *et al* (eds). *IUridicheskii slovar* (Legal Dictionary). 2nd edition. 2 vols. Moskva: Gosizdat IUrid. lit., 1956.

Kudriavtsev, Petr I. and Rozental, E.M. *Inogo vykhoda net: problemy mirnogo sosushchestvovaniia i mezhdunarodnoe pravo.* (There is no Other Way: International Law and the Problem of Peaceful Coexistence). Moskva: Gosiurizdat, 1961.

Kunz, Josef L. *Changing Law of Nations: Essays on International Law.* Columbus: Ohio State University, 1965.

Ladyzhenskii, Alexandr Mikhailovich and Blishchenko, I.P. *Mirnye sredstva razresheniia sporov mezhdu gosudarstvarni.* (Peaceful Means of Settling Disputes Among Nations). Moskva: Gosiurizdat, 1962.

LaFavre, Wayne R. (ed). *Law in Soviet Society.* Urbana: University of Illinois Press, 1962.

Lapenna, Ivo. *Conceptions Soviétiques de Droit International Public.* (Soviet Conceptions of Public International Law). Paris: A. Pedone, 1954.

Larson, Arthur. *When Nations Disagree: A Handbook on Peace Through Law.* Baton Rouge: Louisanna State University Press, 1961.

Larson, Arthur and Jenks, Clarence Wilfred. *Sovereignty Within the Law.* Dobbs Ferry: Oceana Publishers, 1965.

Lazarev, M.I. *Imperialisticheshie voennye bazy na chuzikh territoriiakh i mezhdunarodnoe pravo.* (Imperialist Military Bases in Foreign Countires and International Law). Moskva: Institut Mezhdunarodnykh Otnoshenii, 1963.

_____. *Kongress narodov v zashchitu mira i osnovnye printsipy mezhdunarodnogo prava.* (Congress of Peoples for Peace and the Basic Principles of International Law). Moskva: gos. izd-vo. IUrid. lit-ry., 1953.

_____. *Tekhnicheskii progress i sovremennoe mezhdunarodnoe pravo.* (Technical Progress and Present-Day International Law). Moskva: Gosiurizdat, 1963.

Levin, David B. *Diplomaticheskii immunitet* (Diplomatic Immunity). Moskva: Izd-vo Akademiia nauk SSSR, 1949.

_____. *Istoriia mezhdunarodnogo prava.* (History of International Law). Moskva: Izd-vo Institut Mezhdunarodnykh Otnoshenii, 1962.

_____. *Lenin o mezhdunarodnoi politike i mezhdunarodnom prave.* (Lenin on International Polictics and International Law). Moskva: Izd-vo, Institut Mezhdunarodnykh Otnoshenii, 1958.

_____. *O sovremennykh burzhuaznykh teoriiakh mezhdunarodnogo prava.* (Present Day Bourgeois Theory of International Law). Moskva: vses. IUrid. lit., 1958.

_____. *Osnovnye problemy sovremennogo mezhdunarodnogo prava.* (Basic Problems of Present-Day International Law). Moskva: Gosizdat. IUrid. Lit., 1958.

Levin, I.D. *Suverenitet.* (Sovereignty). Moskva: IUrid. Izd., 1948.

Lisovskii, V.I. *Mezhdunarodnoe pravo.* (International Law). [Kiev?]: Izd-vo. Kievskogo gos. univ., 1955.

Lissitsyn, Oliver J. *International Law Today and Tomorrow.* Dobbs Ferry: Oceana Publishers, 1965.

Lukin, Petr Ivanovich. *Istochniki mezhdunarodnogo prava.* (Sources of International Law). Moskva: Akademiia nauk SSSR, 1960.

Lunts, Lasar Adolfovich. *Voprosy mezhdunarodnogo chastnogo prava.* (Problems of Private International Law). Moskva: Gos. izd-vo. IUrid. lit-ry., 1956.

McDougal, Myres and Burke, William T. *The Public Order of the Oceans.* New Haven: Yale University Press, 1962.

McDougal, Myres and Feliciano, Florentino P. *Law and Minimum World Public Order.* New Haven: Yale University Press, 1961.

McDougal, Myres and Lasswell, Harold D. *Studies in World Public Order.* New Haven: Yale University Press, 1960.

McDougal, Myres and Lasswell, Harold D. and Vlassic, Ivan A. *Law and Public Order in Space.* New Haven: Yale University Press, 1963.

McWhinney, Edward (ed). *Law, Foreign Policy and East-West Detente.* Toronto: University of Toronto Press, 1965.

_____. *"Peaceful Coexistence" and Soviet-Western International Law.* Leyden: A.W. Sythoff, 1964.

Minasian, N.M. *Istochniki sovremenogo mezhdunarodnogo prava.* (Sources of Present-Day International Law). Rostov-na-Donu: Izd-vo Rostovskogo Univ., 1960.

_____. *Pravo mirnogo sosushchestvovaniia.* (The Law of Peaceful Coexistence). Rostov-na-Donu: Izd-vo Rostovskogo Univ., 1966.

_____. *Suschnost sovremennogo mezhdunarodnogo pravo.* (The Essence of Present-Day International Law). Rostov-na-Donu: Rostovskii gos. univ., 1962.

Modzhorian, Lidija A. *Osnovnye prava i obiazannosti gosudarstv* (The Fundamental Rights and Duties of States). Moskva: IUridicheshaia literaturs, 1965.

_____. *Subekty mezhdunarodnogo prava.* (Subjects of International Law). Moskva: Gos. izd-vo IUrid. lit-ry, 1958.

_____. *Voprosy teorii i praktiki sovremennogo mezhdunarodnogo prava.* (Theoretical and Practical Questions of Present-Day International Law). Moskva: Institut Mezhdunarodnykh Otnoshenii, 1960.

Modzhorian, Lidija A. and Sobakin, V.K. *Mezhdunarodnoe pravo v izbrannykh dokumentakh* (International Law in Selected Documents). 3 vols. Moskva: Institut Mezhdunarodnykh Otnoshenii, 1957.

Nikolayev, A.N. *Problema territorialnykh vod v mezhdunarodnom prava.* (Problems of Territorial Waters in International Law). Moskva: Gos. Izd-vo, IUrid. lit-ry, 1957.

Nogee, Joseph L. *Soviet Policy Toward International Control of Atomic Energy.* Notre Dame: University of Notre Dame, 1961.

Pashukanis, Evgenii Bronslavovich. *Ocherki po mezhdunarodnomu pravu.* (Essays on International Law). Moskva: 1935.

Polianskii, N.M. *Mezhdunarodnyi sud.* (International Court). Moskva: Izd-vo, Akademii nauk SSSR, 1951.

Povolny, Majmir. *The Basic Assumptions of the Soviet Doctrine of International Law.* Lenden: Czechoslavakia Foreign Institute in Exile, Section of International Relations, 1950.

Ramundo, Bernard A. *The (Soviet) Socialist Theory of International Law.* Washington, D.C.: George Washington University Press, 1964.

_____. *Peaceful Coexistence: International Law And The Building of Communism.* Baltimore: Johns Hopkins Press, 1967.

Rashba, Evsey S. *Soviet Doctrines and Practices in International Law.* New York: New York University Press, Vol. I (1953), Vol. II (1959).

Röling, Bernard Victor Aloysius. *International Law in an Expanded World.* Amsterdam: Djambatan, 1960.

Rosenne, Shabtai. *International Court of Justice.* Dobbs Ferry: Oceana Publications, 1963.

_____. *The Law and Practice of the International Court.* Leyden: A.W. Sijthoff, 1965. Vols I & II.

Schwarzenberger, Georg. *The Frontiers of International Law.* London: Stevens, 1962.

Shurshalov, V.M. *Osnovaniia deistvietelnosti mezhdunarodnykh dogovorov.* (Essays on Existing International Treaties). Moskva: Izd. Akademii nauk SSSR, 1957.

_____. *Osnovnye voprosy teorii mezhdunarodnogo dogovora.* (Essays on Theoretical Questions of International Law). Moskva: Izd. Akademii nauk SSSR, 1959.

Speranskaia, L.V. *Printsip samo-opredeleniya natsii v mezhdunarodnom prave.* (The Principle of National Self-Determination in International Law). Moskva: gosiurizdat, 1961.

Starushenko, G.B. *The Principle of National Self-Determination in Soviet Foreign Policy.* Moscow: Foreign Languages Publishing House, [1963?].

Stone, Julius. *Quest For Survival: The Role of Law and Foreign Policy.* Cambridge: Harvard University Press, 1961.

Strohl, Mitchell P. *The International Law of Bays.* The Hague: Martinus Nijhoff, 1963.

Syatauw, J.J.G. *Decisions of the International Court of Justice.* Leyden: A.W. Sythoff, 1962.

Talalaev, A.N. *IUridicheskaia priroda mezhdunarodnogo dogovora.* (Legal Nature of International Treaties). Moskva: Institut Mezhdunarodnykh Otnoshenii, 1963.

Tandon, M.P. *Public International Law.* Allahabad: Allahabad Law Agency, Law Publishers, 1965. 10th edition.

Taracouzio, Timothy A. *The Soviet Union and International Law: A Study Based on the Legislation, Treaties and Foreign Relations of the Union of Soviet Socialist Republics.* New York: Macmillan, 1935.

Telberg, Ina. *Soviet-English Dictionary of Legal Terms and Concepts.* New York: Telberg Book Company, 1961.

Thomas, Ann (Van Wynen). *Communism Versus International Law: Today's Clash of Ideals.* Dallas: Southern Methodist University Press, 1953.

Triska, Jan and Slusser, Robert M. *The Theory, Law and Policy of Soviet Treaties.* Stanford: Stanford University Press. 1962.

Tunkin, Grigorii Ivanovich. *Droit International Public.* (International Law). Translation of *Voprosy teorii mezhdunarodnogo prava*(Theoretical Questions of International Law). Paris: A. Pedone, 1965.

_____. *Osnovy sovremennogo mezhdunarodnogo prava: uchebnoe posibie*

(Principles of Present-Day International Law). Moskva: vysshaia partiinaia shkola pri TkS KPSS, 1956.

_____. (ed). *Problemy mezhdunarodnogo prava.* (Problems of International Law). Moskva: Foreign Languages Publishing House, 1961.

_____. (ed). *Voprosy mezhdunarodnogo prava.* (Questions of International Law). Moskva: Institut Mezhdunarodnykh Otnoshenii, 1960.

_____. *Voprosy teorii mezhdunarodnogo prava.* (Theoretical Questions of International Law). Moskva: Gosizday. IUrid. lit., 1962.

Uustal, Abner T. *Mezhdunarodnoe pravo.* (International Law). Tarti: Tartiskii gos. un-m., 1963.

Vyshinskii, Andrei Ianuaryevich. *Voprosy mezhdunarodnogo prava i mezhdunarodnoi politiki.* (Questions of International Law and International Relations). Moskva: Gos. izd-vo. IUrid. lit-ry, 1951.

Vyshinskii, Andrei Ianuaryevich and Kareva, M. *Soviet Socialist Law.* Translated by Arthur Prudden Coleman. Austin, Texas: University of Texas, Department of Government, 1950. (Reproduced from typewritten copy).

Vyshinskii, Andrei Ianuaryevich and Lozovskii, S.A. (eds). *Diplomaticheskii slovar.* (Diplomatic Dictionary). 2 vols. Moskva: Gospolitizdat, 1948, 1950.

Wolfke, Carol. *Custom in Present International Law.* Wroclaw: Zaklad Norodowy im Ossolwskich, 1964.

Zadorozhnyi, G.P. *Mirnoe sosushchestvovanie i mezhdunarodnoe pravo.* (Peaceful Coexistence and International Law). Moskva: Institut Mezhdunarodnykh Otnoshenii, 1964.

Zhavaniya, Grigorii E. *Mezhdunarodnopravovye garantii zashchity natsionnykh menshinstv: istoricheskii ocherk.* (International Legal Protection of Minorities: A Historical Study). Tbilisi: Izd-vo, Akademiia nauk SSSR, 1959.

Zhukov, G.P. *Kritika estestvenno-pravobykh teorii mezhdunarodnogo prava.* (Critique of the Natural Law Theory of International Law). Moskva: Gosiurizday, 1961.

Articles

Achilles, Theodore C. "Peaceful Coexistence and United States National Security," *Department of State Bulletin.* vol. 46 (1962), p. 324.

American Journal of International Law. Washington: American Society of International Law. 1949-*seriatim.*

Anisimov, A.A. "Illegality of the Atlantic Pact," *Sovetskoe gosudarstvo i pravo* (Soviet State and Law). no. 1 (January 1952), pp. 62-68.

Annuaire Française de Droit International, (French Annual of International Law). Paris: Centre National de la Recherche Scientifique. vol. 1 (1955)-*seriatim*.

"Atomic and Thermonuclear Explosions and the Law," *Nir nauki* (Scientific World). no. 2 (1957), pp. 27-33.

Avakov, M.M. and Ilyin, Y.D. "Vienna Conference on Consular Relations," *1963 Sovetskii ezhegodnik mezhdunarodnogo prava* (1963 Soviet Yearbook of International Law), pp. 271-290.

Bagninian, K.A. "Permanent Neutrality, the Right of Self-Defense, and the Regional System in the Light of the U.N. Charter," *Sovetskoe gosudarstvo i pravo* (Soviet State and Law), no. 6 (1956), pp. 102-106.

_____. "The Question of the Definition of Aggression," *Sovetskoe gosudarstvo i pravo* (Soviet State and Law). no. 1 (1955), pp. 59-67.

Baratashvik, D.I. "Positive Neutrality in Present-Day International Law," *Sovetskoe gosudarstvo i pravo* (Soviet State and Law). no. 6 (June 1963), pp. 95-103.

Baresgov, IU.G. "Inviolability of Territorial Rights is One of the Principles of Peaceful Coexistence," *Sovetskoe gosudarstvo i pravo* (Soviet State and Law). no. 9 (September 1957), pp. 25-31.

Barnet, Richard J. "Coexistence and Cooperation in International Law," *World Politics*. vol. 18 (October 1965), pp. 82-91.

Bekker, John A. "Soviet Conceptions of International Law," *Duquesne Review*. vol. 3 (Spring 1958), pp. 55-67.

Berman, Harold J. "Force Majeure and the Denial of an Export License Under Soviet Law: A Comment on Jordan Investments Ltd. v. Soiuznefteksport," *Harvard Law Review*. vol. 73 (April 1960), pp. 1128-1146.

_____. "Human Rights and the Soviet Union," *Howard Law Journal*. vol. 11 (Spring 1965), pp. 333ff.

Blishchenko, I.P. "Definition of Present-Day International Law," *Uchenye zapiski* (Faculty Report). Kafedra mezhdunarodnogo prava.

_____. "International Law and Peaceful Settlement of Disputes," *Novoe vremia* (New Times). vol. 21 (February 19, 1964), pp. 9-11.

_____. "The Nature of International Law of Our Time and the Struggle of the Two Systems," *Voprosy filosofii* (Problems of Philosophy). vol. 19, no. 1 (1965), pp. 28-36.

Bobrov, R.L. "The Concept of Modern General International Law," Ministerstvo vysshego i srednego spetsialnogo obrazovaniia. *Izvestiia vysshikh uchebnykh zavedenii: pravovedenie* (Ministry of Higher and Secondary Specialized Education. Bulletin of the Institute of Higher Learning: Jurisprudence). vol. 9, no. 3 (1965), pp. 167-169.

_____. "The Great October Revolution and International Law," Ministerstvo vysshego i srednego spetsialnogo obrazovaniia. *Izvestiia vysshikh uchebnykh zavedenii: pravovedenie* (Ministry of Higher and Secondary Specialized Education. Bulletin of the Institute of Higher Learning: Jurisprudence). vol. 1, no. 1 (1957), pp. 87-99.

_____. "International Law and the Historical Process," *Sovetskoe gosudarstvo i pravo* (Soviet State and Law). no. 12 (December 1963), pp. 3-11.

_____. "The Objective Basis of Modern International Law," Leningrad Universitet. *Vestnik* (University Review). vol. 11, no. 5 (1956), pp. 111-123.

_____. "The Principle of Equal Right of Two Political Systems in Present-Day International Law," *Sovetskoe gosudarstvo i pravo* (Soviet State and Law). no. 11 (November 1960), pp. 42-50.

Bogdanov, O.V. "American International Law Doctrine in the Service of Imperial Expansion," *Sovetskoe gosudarstvo i pravo* (Soviet State and Law). no. 5 (May 1952), pp. 70-73.

_____. "Bourgeois International Law Doctrine in the Problem of International Collaboration," *Sovetskoe gosudarstvo i pravo* (Soviet State and Law). no. 4 (1955), pp. 97-108.

_____. "The Peaceful Coexistence of States and International Law," *Novoe vremia* (New Times). vol. 13, no. 33 (August 1955), pp. 6-9.

_____. "Security of Individual States in a Disarmed World and International Law," *Sovetskoe gosudarstvo i pravo* (Soviet State and Law). no. 9 (September 1963), pp. 62-71.

_____. "The Soviet Plan of General Disarmament and International Law," *Sovetskoe gosudarstvo i pravo* (Soviet State and Law). no. 2 (February 1960), pp. 46-56.

Boguslavskii, M.M. and Keilin, A.D. "Immunity of Foreign States," *Sovetskoe gosudarstvo i pravo* (Soviet State and Law). no. 7 (July 1963), pp. 153-154.

Boguslavskii, M.M. and Kolodkin, A.L. "State Immunity," Ministerstvo vysshego i srednego spetsialnogo obrazovaniia. *Izvestiia vysshikh uchebnykh zavedenii: pravovedenie* (Ministry of Higher and Secondary Specialized Education. Bulletin of the Institute of Higher Learning: Jurisprudence). vol. 7, no. 2 (1963), pp. 184-185.

Bonatt, E. "International Law and the Plebiseite in Eastern Poland, 1939," *Journal of Central European Affairs*. vol. 5 (January 1946), pp. 378-393.

Borisov, S. [pseud. Krylov, Sergei Borisovich]. "International Court's Violation of Iran's Sovereign Rights," *Sovetskoe gosudarstvo i pravo* (Soviet State and Law). no. 1 (January 1952), pp. 69-73.

_____. "Sovereign Rights of Governments Participating in Multilateral Pacts to Claim Reservations," *Sovetskoe gosudarstvo i pravo* (Soviet State and Law), no. 4 (April 1952), pp. 64-69.

_____. "Two Cases Before the World Court of the United Nations in 1952," *Sovetskoe gosudarstvo i pravo* (Soviet State and Law). no. 4 (1953), pp. 152-157.

Briggs, Harold W. "Columbian-Peruvian Aslyum Case and Proof of Customary International Law," *American Journal of International Law*. vol. 45 (October 1951), pp. 728-731.

_____. "Official Interest in the Work of the International Law Commission: Replies of Governments to Requests for Information or Comment," *American Journal of International Law*. vol. 48 (October 1954), pp. 603-612.

British Yearbook of International Law. London: H. Milford, Oxford University Press. 1953-*seriatim*.

Butler, William E. "Soviet Concepts on Innocent Passage," *Harvard International Law Club Journal*. vol. 7, no. 1 (Winter 1965), pp. 113-130.

Caflisch, L.C. "Recent Judgment of the International Court of Justice in the Case Concerning the Aerial Incident of July 27, 1955, and the Interpretation of Article 36 (5) of the Statutes of the Court," *American Journal of International Law*. vol. 54 (October 1960), pp. 855-868.

The Canadian Yearbook of International Law. Vancouver: Publications Center, University of British Columbia. vol. 1 (1963)- *seriatim*.

Carlston, Kenneth S. "Interpretation of Peace Treaties With Bulgaria, Hungary and Rumania, Advisory Opinion of the International Court of Justice," *American Journal of International Law*. vol. 44 (October 1950), pp. 728-737.

Chakste, Mintavts. "Soviet Concepts of State, International Law and Sovereignty," *American Journal of International Law*. vol. 43 (January 1949), pp. 26-30.

Chayes, Abram. "Progress Toward International Law," *Proceedings of the American Society of International Law*. 55th year (1966), pp. 202-205.

Chiu, Hungdah. "Communist China's Attitude Toward International Law," *American Journal of International Law*. vol. 60 (April 1965), pp. 245-267.

Chizhov, F.IA. "American Imperalism, Violator of International Law," *Sovetskoe gosudarstvo i pravo* (Soviet State and Law). no. 2 (February 1952), pp. 52-59.

_____. "Two World Markets and Present-Day International Law," *Sovetskoe gosudarstvo i pravo* (Soviet State and Law). no. 1 (January 1953), pp. 36-51.

"Conditions of Admission of a State to Membership in the United Nations," *American Journal of International Law.* vol. 43 (April 1949), pp. 288-303.

"The Conquest of Outer Space and the Several Problems of International Relations," *Mezhdunarodnaia zhizn'* (International Affairs). vol. 6, no. 11 (November 1959), pp. 116-125.

"Contemporary International Law and the Individual," *Zapiski obshichestva Russkikh zarubezhnykh iuristov* (Records of the Society of Russian Lawyers Abroad). nos. 5-8 (August 1948), pp. 97-99.

Coplin, W.D. "International Law and Assumptions About the State System," *World Politics.* vol. 17 (July 1965), pp. 615-634.

Crane, Robert D. "Soviet Attitudes Toward International Space Law," *American Journal of International Law.* vol. 56 (1962), pp. 710-713.

de Visscher, Charles. "Reflections on the Present Prospects of International Adjudications," *American Journal of International Law.* vol. 50 (July 1956), pp. 467-474.

Dillard, Hardy Cross. "Conflict and Change: The Role of Law," *Proceedings of the American Society of International Law.* 57th year (1963), pp. 50-67.

"A Discussion of the Problems of the Theory of International Law," *Sovetskoe gosudarstvo i pravo* (Soviet State and Law). no. 2 (1955), pp. 74-84.

Domke, Martin. "The Israeli-Soviet Oil Arbitration," *American Journal of International Law.* vol. 53 (1959), pp. 787-806.

Durdenevskii, Vsevolod Nikolaevich. "The Most Important Problems Following the Establishment of a New State," *Uchenye zapiski* (Faculty Report). no. 2 (1959), pp. 27-29.

Durdenevskii, Vsevolod Nikolaevich and Krylov, Sergei Borisovich. "Violation of the Principle of Observance of International Treaties by the Imperialist Governments," *Mezhdunarodnaia zhizn'* (International Affairs). no. 2 (February, 1955), pp. 56-63.

Eugenev, V.V. "Legal Status, Sovereignty, and Non-Intervention in International Law," *Sovetskoe gosudarstvo i pravo* (Soviet State and Law). no. 2 (1955), pp. 74-84.

Falk, Richard A. "The Reality of International Law," *World Politics.* vol. 14 (1961-1962), pp. 353-363.

Fedynskii, J. "Sovietization of an Occupied Area Through the Medium of the Courts (Northern Bukovina)," *American Journal of International Law.* vol. 12 (February 1953), pp. 44-56.

Feldman, D.I. "Some Forms and Methods of International Legal Recognition of New States," *1963 Sovetskii ezhegodnik mezhdunarodnogo prava* (1963 Soviet Yearbook of International Law). pp. 129-149.

Feldman, D.I. and Farukshin, M.Fh. "Bankruptcy of the Colonial System and Some Legal Problems Relating to International Recognition and Succession," Ministerstvo vysshego i srednego spetsialnogo obrazovaniia. *Izvestiia vysshikh uchebnykh zavedenii :pravovedenie* (Ministry of Higher and Secondary Specialized Education. Bulletin of the Institute of Higher Learning: Jurisprudence). vol. 6, no. 2 (1962), pp. 115-123.

Fernando, E.M. "An International Law of Human Dignity: A Review of McDougal's Studies in World Public Order," *Philippine International Law Journal.* vol. 1 (1962), pp. 178-195.

"For An Authoritative Scientific Reworking of the Root Questions of the Science of the History of the Soviet State and Law," *Sovetskoe gosudarstvo i pravo* (Soviet State and Law), no. 6 (1956), unsigned editorial.

For the Rule of Law. The Hague: International Commission of Jurists. vol. 1 (1955)-*seriatim.*

Foscaneánu, Lazar. "Les 'cinq principles' de Coexistence et le Droit International," (The Five Principles of Coexistence and International Law). *Annuaire Français de Droit International* (French Annual of International Law). 1956, pp. 150-180.

"Founding the International Law Association of the USSR," *Sovetskoe gosudarstvo i pravo* (Soviet State and Law). no. 8 (August 1957), p. 130.

"The Fourth Session of the Soviet International Law Association," *Sovetskoe gosudarstvo i pravo* (Soviet State and Law). no. 6 (June 1961).

Frendl, Louis. "Soviet Conception of International Law," *World Justice.* vol. 2 (December 1960), pp. 199-227.

Friedmann, Wolfgang Gaston. "Modern Trends in Soviet Law," *University of Toronto Law Journal.* vol. 10 (1965), pp. 87-92.

_____. "Some Impacts of Social Organizations on International Law," *American Journal of International Law.* vol. 50 (1956), pp. 475-513.

Ginsburgs, Georg. "Case Study in the Soviet Use of International Law: Eastern Poland 1939," *American Journal of International Law.* vol. 52 (January 1958), pp. 69-84.

_____. "Option of Nationality in Soviet Treaty Law: The War Time and Post War Time Record," *Iowa Law Review.* vol. 49 (Summer 1954), pp. 1130ff.

_____. "Soviet Citizenship Legislation and Statelessness As A Consequence of the Conflict of Nationality Laws," *International and Comparative Law Quarterly.* vol. 15 (January 1966), pp. 1-54.

_____. "The Soviet Union and the Problem of Refugees and Displaced Persons 1917-1956," *American Journal of International Law.* vol. 51 (1957), pp. 325-361.

_____. "Soviet Union, the Neutrals and International Law During W.W. II," *International and Comparative Law Quarterly.* vol. 11 (January 1962), pp. 171ff.

_____. "The Validity of Treaties in the Municipal Law of 'Socialist' States," *American Journal of International Law.* vol. 59 (July 1965), pp. 523-544.

Glenn, Gene. "The Swedish-Soviet Territorial Sea Controversy in the Baltic," *American Journal of International Law.* vol. 50 (1956), pp. 942-949.

Gore, Albert. "Principles of International Law Concerning Friendly Relations Among States," *Department of State Bulletin.* vol. 47 (1962), pp. 972ff.

Gross, L. "Expenses of the United Nations for Peace-Keeping Operations: The Advisory Opinion of the International Court of Justice," *International Organization.* vol. 17 (Winter 1963), pp. 1-35.

_____. "Limitations Upon the Judicial Function (Case of the Cameroons v. the United Kingdom)," *American Journal of International Law.* vol. 58 (April 1964), pp. 415-431.

_____. "Some Observations on the International Court of Justice," *American Journal of International Law.* vol. 56 (January 1962), pp. 33-62.

Grotius: Annuaire International (Grotius: International Annual). The Hague: M. Nijhoff. 1955-*seriatim.*

Grzybowski, Kazimierz. "In Quest of the Counterpoise: Principle and Policy," *Review of Metaphysics.* vol. 17 (December 1963), pp. 243-256.

_____. "Socialist Judges on the International Court of Justice," *Duke Law Journal.* 1964, pp. 536-549.

Gubin, V.F. "The Soviet Union and Reservations to Multilateral Treaties," *1959*

Sovetskii ezhegodnik mezhdunarodnogo prava (1959 Soviet Yearbook of International Law). pp. 126-143.

Guggenheim, Paul. "Contribution à l'Histoire des Sources du Droit des Gens," (The Contribution to History of the Sources of the Law of Nations). *Recueil des Cours.* vol. 94 (1958-II), pp. 3-81.

Harvard International Law Club Journal. Cambridge: Harvard University, vol. 1 (Spring 1959)-*seriatim.*

Hazard, John N. "Book Review and Notes: Review of N.M. Minasian's *Pravo mirnogo sosushchestvovaniia* (The Law of Peaceful Coexistence)," *American Journal of International Law.* vol. 61 (January 1967), pp. 230-233.

──────────. "Codifying Peaceful Coexistence," *American Journal of International Law.* vol. 55 (1961), pp. 109-120.

──────────. "Coexistence Bows Out," *American Journal of International Law.* vol. 59 (January 1965), p. 59.

──────────. "Coexistence Codification Reconsidered," *American Journal of International Law.* vol. 57 (1963), pp. 88-97.

──────────. "General Principles of Law (Soviet System of Law)," *American Journal of International Law.* vol. 52 (January 1958), pp. 91-96.

──────────. "Legal Research on 'Peaceful Coexistence," *American Journal of International Law.* vol. 51 (January 1957), pp. 63-71.

──────────. "Pashukanis Is No Traitor," *American Journal of International Law.* vol. 51 (1957), pp. 385-388.

──────────. "A Pragmatic View of New International Law," *Proceedings of the American Society of International Law.* 57th Year (1963), pp. 79-83.

──────────. "Quelques Aspects du Droit Sovietiquè Tel Qu'il Apparait à un Juriste Anglo-Saxon," (Several Aspects of Soviet Law as are Apparent to an Anglo-Saxon Jurist). *Revue Internationale de Droit Comparé.* (Review of International and Comparative Law). vol. 2, no. 2 (April-June 1950), pp. 237-249.

──────────. "Sixth Committee and New Law," *American Journal of International Law.* vol. 57 (July 1963), pp. 604-613.

──────────. "Socialist Law and the International Encyclopedia (of Comparative Law: On Whether Or Not Topics in the Law of Marxist Socialist Countries Can Be Integrated With The Law of Other Legal Systems Under Appropriate Subject Headings, Or Whether Such Topics Must Be Treated In A Separate Volume Devoted Solely To Their Various East European and Asian Forms)." *Harvard Law Review.* vol. 79 (December 1965), pp. 278-302.

_____. "Soviet Law and Its Assumptions," *Ideological Differences and World Order.* Edited by F.S.C. Northrop. New Haven: Yale University Press, 1949, pp. 192-207.

_____. "Soviet Socialism As A Public Order System," *Proceedings of the American Society of International Law.* 53rd year (1959), pp. 30ff.

_____. "Soviet Socialism and the Conflict of Laws," *Military Law Review.* vol. (January 1963), pp. 69-79.

_____. "Soviet Union and International Law," *Illinois Law Review.* vol. 18 (November-December 1948), pp. 591-607.

_____. "Soviet Union and International Law," *Soviet Studies.* (University of Glasgow). vol. 1, no. 3 (January 1950), pp. 189-199.

_____. "Soviet Union and A World Bill of Rights," *Columbia Law Review.* vol. 47, no. 7 (November 1947), pp. 1095-1117.

Hoffman, Stanley. "International Systems and International Law," *World Politics.* vol. 14 (October 1961), pp. 205-237.

Horono, J. "The Slogan 'Toward Universal Peace Through Law' and Its Real Meaning," *Sovetskaia iustitsiia* (Soviet Justice). no. 23 (December 1961), pp. 25-27.

Honig, F. "Progress in the Codification of International Law," *International Affairs* (London). vol. 36 (January 1960), pp. 62-72.

"An Important Contribution to Peaceful Coexistence," Editorial. *International Affairs* (Moscow). no. 6 (1956), pp. 12-16.

The Indian Journal of International Law. New Delhi. vol. 1 (July 1960)-*seriatim.*

The Indian Yearbook of International Law. Madias. vol. 1 (1952)-*seriatim.*

International Association of Democratic Lawyers. Brussels Meeting, May 1956. *Proceedings* (General Meetings).

Proceedings of the Commission on Legal Principles of Peaceful Coexistence.

Proceedings of the Commission on Penal Procedure.

Proceedings of the Commission on Private International Law.

International Association of Democratic Lawyers. Sofia Meeting, October 1960. *Proceedings of the Second Commission on "Legal Problems Arising From The Development and Utilization Of Atomic Weapons.*

215

International Law Association (Brussels). *Reports*. 1956-*seriatim.*

"International Law and the Problem of Frontiers," *Kommunist* (Communist) JPRS 23,628, pp. 40-48.

"International Protection of Human Rights," *Zapiski obshchestva Russkikh zarubezhnykh iuristov* (Records of the Society of Russian Lawyers Abroad). no. 1 (October 1949), p. 28.

Ivanov, F. "Fourth Session of the UN Commission on International Law," *Sovetskoe gosudarstvo i pravo* (Soviet State and Law). no. 11 (November 1952), pp. 72-78.

Ivanov, F. and Volodin, S. "Fifth Session of the UN International Law Commission," *Sovetskoe gosudarstvo i pravo* (Soviet State and Law). no. 7 (1953), pp. 88-100.

Ivanova, I.M. "The 'Nuremburg Principles' of International Law," *Sovetskoe gosudarstvo i pravo* (Soviet State and Law). no. 8 (August 1960), pp. 83-90.

_____. "The United Nations and the Problems of an International Criminal Court," *Uchenye zapiski* (Faculty Report). no. 2 (1959), pp. 124-144.

The Japanese Yearbook of International Law. Tokyo: International Law Association. vol. 1 (1951)-*seriatim.*

Jenks, Clarence Wilfred. "Craftsmanship in International Law," *American Journal of International Law*. vol. 50 (January 1956), pp. 32-60.

Jessup, Philip C. "Diversity and Uniformity in the Law of Nations," *American Journal of International Law*. vol. 58 (April 1964), pp. 341-358.

_____. "International Law Association Meeting At Dubrovnik," *American Journal of International Law*. vol. 51 (1957), pp. 89-94.

Johnson, D.H.N. "The Case Concerning the Northern Cameroons," *International and Comparative Law Quarterly*. vol. 13 (October 1964), pp. 1143-1192.

Jowitt, Rt. Hon. Viscount. "The Value of International Law in the Establishment of Co-Operation Among Nations," *International Law Quarterly*. vol. 1 (1947), pp. 295-300.

Justice Dans le Monde (World Justice). Louvain: Research Centre For International Social Justice. vol. 1 (September 1959)-*seriatim.*

Jully, L. "Arbitration and Judicial Settlement: Recent Trends," *American Journal of International Law*. vol. 48 (July 1954), pp. 380-407.

Kaplan, Morton A. and Katzenbach, Nicholas DeB. "Patterns of International

Politics and International Law," *American Political Science Review*. vol. 53 (September 1959), pp. 693-712.

Karpets, I. and Levin, David B. "International Law and the War Criminals," *International Affairs* (Moscow). 1964, pp. 40-45.

Karpov, Victor P. "The Soviet Concept of Peaceful Coexistence and Its Implications for International Law," *The Soviet Impact on International Law*. Edited by Hans W. Baade. New York: Oceana Publications, 1965, pp. 14-20.

Kerley, Ernest L. "United Nations Contribution to Developing International Law," *Proceedings of the American Society of International Law*. 56th year (1962), pp. 99-105.

Khlestov, O.N. "International Law Is On the Side Of Panama (In Its Dispute With the United States)," *International Affairs* (Moscow). April 1964. pp. 92-93.

Kiralfy, A.K.R. "A Soviet Approach to Private International Law," *International Law Quarterly*. vol. 4 (1951), pp. 120-125.

Klimenko, B.M. "Critique Of the Bourgeois Theories of International Servitudes," *1963 Sovetskii ezhegodnik mezhdunarodnogo prava* (1963 Soviet Yearbook of International Law). pp. 219-235.

_____. "The Third Annual Meeting of the Soviet International Law Association," *Sovetskoe gosudarstvo i pravo* (Soviet State and Law). no. 6 (June 1960), pp. 124-127.

Klooz, M.S. "Role of the General Assembly of the United Nations in the Admission of Members," *American Journal of International Law*. vol. 43 (April 1949), pp. 256-261.

Kokhokhin, B.I. "Decline of the Colonial System of Imperialism and Present-Day International Law," Leningrad Universitet. *Vestnik* (University Review). no. 23 (1958), pp. 116-124.

Kopelmans, Lazare. "Custom As A Means of Creation of International Law," *British Yearbook of International Law*. vol. 18 (1937), pp. 127-151.

Korovin, Evgenii Aleksandrovich. "Atomic Weapons and International Law," *Mezhdunarodnaia zhizn'* (International Affairs). no. 5 (May 1955), pp. 48-49.

_____. "International Law Today," *International Affairs* (Moscow). July 1961. pp. 18-22.

_____. "More Attention To International Law," *Sovetskoe gosudarstvo i pravo* (Soviet State and Law). no. 3 (March 1962), pp. 131-132.

217

_____. "Peace Through the Rule of Law: Two Interpretations," *Mezhdunarodnaia zhizn'* (International Affairs). no. 7 (July 1963), pp. 130-132.

_____. "The Role of the Masses in the Development of International Law," *Sovetskoe gosudarstvo i pravo* (Soviet State and Law). no. 3 (1956), pp. 50-60.

_____. "The Second World War and International Law," *American Journal of International Law*. vol. 40 (1946), pp. 742-755.

_____. "Several Basic Problems in the Contemporary Theory of International Law," *Sovetskoe gosudarstvo i pravo* (Soviet State and Law). no. 6 (October 1954), pp. 34-44.

_____. "We Should Eliminate the Harmful Results of the Cult of the Personality from International Law," *Sotsialiaticheskaia zakonnost'* (Socialist Legality). vol. 39, no. 8 (August 1962), pp. 46-49.

Korovin, Evgenii Aleksandrovich and Chkhivadze, V. "The Norms of International Law," *Kommunist* (Communist). no. 15 (October 1964), pp. 126-128.

Korovin, Evgenii Aleksandrovich and Kozhevnikov, Fedor I. "Peaceful Coexistence and International Law," *Izvestia* (News). April 18, 1962, p. 5.

Korowicz, Marek Stanislaw. "Protection and Implementation of Human Rights Within the Soviet Legal System," *Proceedings of the American Society of International Law*. 53rd year (1959), pp. 248ff.

Kovalev, F.N. and Cheprov, I.P. "Artifical Satellites and International Law," *1958 Sovetskii ezhegodnik mezhdunarodnogo prava* (1958 Soviet Yearbook of International Law). pp. 128-149.

Kozhevnikov, Fedor Ivanovich. "Basic Tasks of the Soviet Science of International Law," *Sovetskoe gosudarstvo i pravo* (Soviet State and Law). no. 10 (1952), pp. 34-44.

_____. "Concerning the Most Backward Sector of Soviet Law," *Sovetskoe gosudarstvo i revolutsiia prava* (Soviet State and Revolutionary Law). no. 3 (1930), pp. 147ff.

_____. "The Great October Socialist Revolution and the International Significance of the First Legal Acts Of the Foreign Policy of the Soviet State," *Sovetskoe gosudarstvo i pravo* (Soviet State and Law). no. 11 (November 1957), pp. 50-60.

_____. "International Law," *Bolshaia Sovetskaia entsiklopediia* (The Great Soviet Encyclopedia). columns 635-643. Moskva: 1940.

_____. "Some Legal Problems Relating to the Work of the International Court of Justice in 1959," *Sovetskoe gosudarstvo i pravo* (Soviet State and

Law). no. 3 (March 1960), pp. 95-104.

_____. "Universally Recognized Principles and Rules of International Law," *Sovetskoe gosudarstvo i pravo* (Soviet State and Law). no. 12 (December 1959), pp. 15-24.

Kozhevnikov, Fedor Ivanovich and Movchan, A.P. "The UN Charters Incorporates the Generally Recognized Prinicples of International Law," *Sovetskoe gosudarstvo i pravo* (Soviet State and Law). no. 6 (1955), pp. 3-7.

Krylov, Sergei Borisovich. "A Contribution to the Discussion of Questions of the Theory of International Law," *Sovetskoe gosudarstvo i pravo* (Soviet State and Law). no. 7 (November 1954), pp. 74-79.

_____. "Discussion on the Theory of International Law," *Sovetskoe gosudarstvo i pravo* (Soviet State and Law). no. 7 (1954), pp. 74-79.

_____. "Les Notions Principales du Droit des Gens (La Doctrine Soviétique du Droit International)," (The Principal Notions of the Law of Nations: The Soviet Doctrine of International Law). Recueil des Cours. vol. 70 (1947-I), pp. 407-476.

_____. "Private Codification of International Law," *Sovetskoe gosudarstvo i pravo* (Soviet State and Law). no. 6 (June 1959), pp. 106-111.

_____. "Unofficial Codification of International Law," *Sovietskoe gosudarstvo i pravo* (Soviet State and Law). no. 4 (April 1957), pp. 129-130.

Kudriavtsev, Petr I. "International Law," *Sovetskaia kniga* (Soviet Book), no. 1 January 1952), pp. 80-84.

Kulski, Wladyskaw W. "Soviet Comments on International Law," *American Journal of International Law*. vol. 45 (April 1951), pp. 347-353; vol. 45 (October 1951), pp. 762-770; vol. 46 (1952), pp. 131-140; pp. 333-341; pp. 542-549; pp. 716-726; vol. 47 (1953), pp. 125-134; pp. 308-314; pp. 485-491; vol. 48 (1954), pp. 148-151; pp. 307-313; pp. 474-479; pp. 640-646; and vol. 49 (1955). pp. 518-534.

_____. "Trends in Soviet International Law," *Proceedings of the American Society of International Law*. 47th year (1953), pp. 1-121.

Kunz, Josef L. "Changing Law of Nations," *American Journal of International Law*. vol. 51 (January 1957), pp. 77-83.

_____. "The Nature of Customary International Law," *American Journal of International Law*. vol. 47 (October 1953), pp. 662-669.

_____. "Pluralism of Legal and Value Systems and International Law," *American Journal of International Law*. vol. 49 (July 1955), pp. 370-376.

————. "Systematic Problem of the Science of International Law," *American Journal of International Law.* vol. 53 (April 1959), pp. 379-385.

Lapenna, Ivo. "International Law in the Soviet Union," *Solicitor.* vol. 27 (December 1960), pp. 368-371.

Lasswell, Harold D. "A Brief Discourse About Method in Current Madness," *Proceedings of the American Society of International Law.* 57th year (1963), pp. 72-78.

Lauterpacht, Hersch. "Codification and Development of International Law," *American Journal of International Law.* vol. 49 (January 1955), pp. 16-43.

"Law and Soviet Society," (Symposium). *University of Illinois Law Forum.* Spring 1964. pp. 1-318.

Lazarev, M.I. "A Book Entitled: 'Contemporary International Law: Collection of Documents'," *Sovetskoe gosudarstvo i pravo* (Soviet State and Law). no. 9 (September 1965), pp. 149-150.

————. "The Guantanamo Military Base of the USA and Present International Law," *Voprosy mezhdunarodnogo prava* (Questions of International Law). no. 4 (1962), pp. 117-147.

————. "International Legal Aspects of the People's Movement For Peace," *1963 Sovetskii ezhegodnik mezhdunarodnogo prava* (1963 Soviet Yearbook of International Law). pp. 45-69.

————. "Technological Progress and Present-Day International Law," *Sovetskoe gosudarstvo i pravo* (Soviet State and Law). no. 12 (December 1962), pp. 102-110.

Lee, Luke T. "International Law Commission: Re-Examined," *American Journal of International Law.* vol. 59 (July 1965), pp. 545-569.

————. "The Mexico City Conference of the United Nations Special Committee on Principles of International Law Concerning Friendly Relations and Co-Operation Among States," *International and Comparative Law Quarterly.* October 1965, pp. 1296-1313.

Levin, David B. "Attack on the Rumanian Diplomatic Mission in Bern and Its Assessment in the Light of International Law," *1963 Sovetskii ezhegodnik mezhdunarodnogo prava* (1963 Soviet Yearbook of International Law). pp. 291-302.

————. "Concepts and System of Contemporary International Law," *Sovetskoe gosudarstvo i pravo* (Soviet State and Law). no. 5 (May 1947), pp. 7-21.

————. "Falsification of International Law Concepts by Bourgeois Pseudo-

Science," *Sovetskoe gosudarstvo i pravo* (Soviet State and Law). no. 4 (April 1952), pp. 55-63.

_____. "International Law in the Present World," Ministerstvo vysshego vysshikh i sredneog spetsialnogo obrazovaniia. *Izvestiia vysshikh uchebnykh zavedenii: pravovedenie* (Ministry of Higher and Secondary Specialized Education. Bulletin of the Institute of Higher Learning: Jurisprudence). no. 2 (1964), pp. 112-120.

_____. "The Main Trends of Contemporary Bourgeois Theories of International Law," *1959 Sovetskii ezhegodnik mezhdunarodnogo prava.* (1959 Soviet Yearbook of International Law). pp. 88-125.

_____. "Peaceful Coexistence of Two World Systems and International Law," Ministerstvo vysshego i srednego spetsialnogo obrazovaniia. *Izvestiia vysshikh uchebnykh zavedenii: pravovedenie* (Ministry of Higher and Secondary Specialized Education. Bulletin of the Institute of Higher Learning: Jurisprudence). no. 1 (1958), pp. 95-106.

_____. "The Preservation of Peace and the Basic Principles of International Law," *Sovetskoe gosudarstvo i pravo* (Soviet State and Law). no. 6 (June 1958), pp. 31-40.

_____. "The Principle of Self-Determination of Nations in International Law," *1962 Sovetskii ezhegodnik mezhdunarodnogo prava* (1962 Soviet Yearbook of International Law). pp. 25-48.

Levin, David B. "What Does the Theory of 'Primacy' of International Law Over Domestic Law Conceal," *Sovetskoe gosudarstvo i pravo* (Soviet State and Law). no. 7 (1955), pp. 115-120.

Levitsky, Serge L. "Khrushchev vs. Grotius At Geneva," *America.* vol. 99, p. 105.

Liang, Y. "Reparations For Injuries Suffered in the Service of the United Nations," *American Journal of International Law.* vol. 43 (July 1949), pp. 460-478.

Lipson, Leon. "Peaceful Coexistence," *Law and Contemporary Problems.* vol. 29 (1964), pp. 871-881.

Lissitzyn, Oliver J. "Recent Soviet Literature on International Law," *American Slavic Review.* vol. 11 (December 1952), pp. 275-277.

_____. "Some Legal Implications of the U-2 and RB-47 Incidents," *American Journal of International Law.* vol. 56 (1962), pp. 135-142.

_____. "The Soviet Union and International Law," *International Conciliation.* 542 (March), pp. 14-26.

Lukashuk, I.I. "The National Liberation Movement and Some Problems of Present-Day International Law," Ministerstvo vysshego i srednego spetsialnogo obrazovaniia. *Izvestiia vysshikh uchebnykh zavedenii: pravovedenie* (Ministry of Higher and Secondary Specialized Education. Bulletin of the Institute of Higher Learning: Jurisprudence). no. 3 (1962), pp. 92-100.

_____. "The Nature of Present-Day International Law," *Sovetskoe gosudarstvo i pravo* (Soviet State and Law). no. 8 (1954), pp. 87-89.

_____. "Problem of the 'Object' of International Law," *Sovetskoe gosudarstvo i pravo* (Soviet State and Law). no. 3 (March 1958), pp. 104-111.

_____. "The Soviet Union and International Treaties," *1959 Sovetskii ezhegodnik mezhdunarodnogo prava* (1959 Soviet Yearbook of International Law). pp. 16-50.

Luntz, Lasar Adolfovich. "Conflict of Laws in International Sales: Theory and Practice of Socialist Countries," *Recueil des Cours.* vol. 114 (1965-I), pp. 5-55.

_____. "International Private Law," Moskva. Vsesoiuznyi institut iuricheskikh nauk. *Uchenye zapiski* (All Union Institute of Judicial Studies. Faculty Report). no. 3 (1955), pp. 20-29.

McDougal, Myres S. "Law and Power," *American Journal of International Law.* vol. 46 (January 1952), pp. 102-114.

McDougal, Myres S. and Lasswell, Harold D. "The Identification and Appraisal of Diverse Systems of Public Order," *American Journal of International Law.* vol. 53 (January 1959), pp. 1-29.

McDougal, Myres S., Lasswell, Harold D. and Vlasic, Ivan A. "Toward a Public Order of Space: Common Interests in Inclusive and Exclusive Uses and Competences," *Philippine International Law Journal.* vol. 2 (1963), pp. 29-77.

MacGibbon, I.C. "Customary International Law and Acquiescence," *British Yearbook of International Law.* vol. 33 (1957), pp. 115-145.

_____. "The Scope of Acquiescence in International Law," *British Yearbook of International Law.* vol 30 (1954), pp. 143-186.

McNair, Lord. "The General Principles of Law Recognized By Civilized Nations," *British Yearbook of International Law.* vol. 33 (1957), pp. 1-19.

McWhinney, Edward. "Changing International Law Methods and Objectives in the Era of the Soviet-Western Detente," *American Journal of International Law.* vol. 59 (January 1965), pp. 1-15.

_____. "International Law in the Nuclear Age: Soviet-Western, Inter-Bloc International Law," *Proceedings of the American Society of International Law.*

57th year (1963), pp. 68-71.

_____. "The 'New' Countries and the 'New' International Law: The United Nations' Special Conference on Friendly Relations and Co-Operation Among States," *American Journal of International Law*. vol. 60 (January 1966), pp. 1-33.

_____. "Peaceful Coexistence and Soviet-Western International Law," *American Journal of International Law*. vol. 56 (October 1962), pp. 951-970.

_____. "Soviet and Western International Law and the Cold War in the Era of Bipolarity: Inter-Bloc Law in a Nuclear Age," *Canadian Yearbook of International law*. 1963, pp. 40ff.

Mai, S. "Legal Conditions for the Development of International Trade," *Vneshniaia tongovlia* (Foreign Trade). no. 4 (April 1952), pp. 27-30.

Malinin, S.A. "The Criteria of Legality of the Resolution of the General Assembly of the United Nations," Ministerstvo vysshego i srednego spetsialnogo obrazovaniia. *Izvestiia vysshikh uchebnykh zavedenii: pravovedenie* (Ministry of Higher and Secondary Specialized Education. Bulletin of the Institute of Higher Learning: Jurisprudence). no. 2 (1965), pp. 113-123.

_____. "Participation of the Great Powers in Regional Treaties." *Uchenye zapiski* (Scientific Records). no. 255 (1958), pp. 86-98.

Margolis, Emanuel. "Soviet Views on the Relationship Between National and International Law," *International and Comparative Law Quarterly*. vol. 4 (January 1955), pp. 116-128.

Mason, G.M. "Towards Indivisible International Law? The Evolution of Soviet Doctrine," *Social Research*. vol. 23 (Spring 1956), pp. 57-88.

Melekhin, B.I. "The Influence of World Opinion Upon Contemporary International Law," *Sovetskoe gosudarstvo i pravo* (Soviet State and Law). no. 2 (February 1963), pp. 75-83.

Menton, C.A. "Russo-American Convergence: Fact or Fantasy?" *Oklahoma Bar Association Journal*. vol. 35 (September 1964), pp. 1639ff.

Miller, Richard W. "Comparison of the Basic Philosophies Underlying Anglo-American Criminal Law and Russian Criminal Law," *University of Kansas City Law Review*. vol. 23 (Fall 1954), pp. 62-93.

Minasian, N.M. "Concept of Present-Day International Law," Ministerstvo vysshego i srednego spetsialnogo obrazovaniia. *Izvestiia vysshikh uchebnykh zavedenii: pravovedenie* (Ministry of Higher and Secondary Specialized Education. Bulletin of the Institute of Higher Learning: Jurisprudence). no. 2 (1959), pp. 120-129.

223

Modzhorian, Lidija A. "Identity, Continuity, and Legal Succession of Subjects of International Law," *Sovetskoe gosudarstvo i pravo* (Soviet State and Law). no. 9 (September 1958), pp. 61-70.

_____. "The Notion of Sovereignty in International Law," *Sovetskoe gosudarstvo i pravo* (Soviet State and Law). no. 1 (February 1955), pp. 68-76.

_____. "Reactionary Jurists in the Service of American Aggressors," *Sovetskoe gosudarstvo i pravo* (Soviet State and Law). no. 10 (1952), pp. 85-90.

_____. "The Restoration of China's Legitimate Rights in the UN," *1959 Sovetskii ezhegodnik mezhdunarodnogo prava* (1959 Soviet Yearbook of International Law). pp. 202-211.

Molodtsov, Stephan V. "Downfall of the Colonial System and its Influences on International Law," *Sovetskoe gosudarstvo i pravo* (Soviet State and Law). no. 5 (1956), pp. 79-86.

_____. "The Frontiers of International Law," *International Affairs* (Moscow). April 1964. pp. 9-14.

Morozov, G.I. "Hostile Propaganda Among States Is Opposed to International Law," *Sovetskoe gosudarstvo i pravo* (Soviet State and Law). no. 2 (1956), pp. 99-107.

Movchan, A.P. "Codification of the International Legal Principles of Peaceful Coexistence," *1963 Sovetskii ezhegodnik mezhdunarodnogo prava* (1963 Soviet Yearbook of International Law). pp. 15-30.

_____. "The Significance of the Codification of the Rules of International Law," *Sovetskoe gosudarstvo i pravo* (Soviet State and Law). no. 1 (January 1965), pp. 46-55.

Muszkat, Marjan. "Some Legal Aspects of Peaceful Coexistence," *Mezhdunarodnaia zhizn'* (International Affairs), no. 9 (September 1956), pp. 37-46.

Nedbailo, P.Y. "Codification of the International Law of Peaceful Coexistence," *Radianske pravo* (Soviet Law). no. 5 (September-October 1963), pp. 25-36.

Nedbailo, P.Y. and Zabigailo, K. "Let's Enhance the Role of International Law in the Struggle for Peace," *Radianske pravo* (Soviet Law). no. 4 (July-August 1961), pp. 138-141.

Nesterov, V.S. "Conference of the Soviet Association of International Law," *Sovetskoe gosudarstvo i pravo* (Soviet State and Law). no. 6 (June 1958). pp. 149-152.

Northrop, F.S.C. "Contemporary Jurisprudence and International Law (Analysis of the Major Contemporary Theories of Jurisprudence and Their Bearing on

International Law and Concludes that an Attempt Further To Improve International Relations by Legal Means Is Both Practical and Necessary). *Yale Law Journal*. vol. 61 (May 1952), pp. 623-654.

Osnitskaya, G.A. "Colonialist Concepts of Equal and Unequal Subjects of International Law in the Theory and Practice of the Imperialist States," *1962 Sovetskii ezhegodnik mezhdunarodnogo prava* (1962 Soviet Yearbook of International Law). pp. 49-63.

Osnitskii, G.A. "International Law Problems of the Conquest of Space," *1959 Sovetskii ezhegodnik mezhdunarodnogo prava* (1959 Soviet Yearbook of International Law). pp. 51-71.

"Peaceful Coexistence and International Law," Ministerstvo vysshego i srednego spetsialnogo obrazovaniia. *Izvestiia vysshikh uchebnykh zavedenii: pravovedenie* (Ministry of Higher and Secondary Specialized Education. Bulletin of the Institute of Higher Learning: Jurisprudence). no. 4 (1963), pp. 14-21.

Piradov, A.S. "Military Bases and International Law," *Mezhdunarodnaia zhizn'* (International Affairs). vol. 11, no. 5 (May 1964), pp. 140-142.

Piradov, A.S. and Starushenko, G.B. "Non-Intervention and Contemporary International Law," *1958 Sovetskii ezhegodnik mezhdunarodnogo prava* (1958 Soviet Yearbook of International Law). pp. 230-251.

Pisar, Samuel. "Soviet Conflict of Laws ir. International Commercial Relations," *Harvard Law Review*. vol. 70 (1957), pp. 593-656.

Pokrovskii, V.S. "Treaty of Novogorod the Great With Gotland and German Cities of 1189-1195 As An Act of International Law," Ministerstvo vysshego i srednego spetsialnogo obrazovaniia. *Izvestiia vysshikh uchebnykh zavedenii: pravovedenie* (Ministry of Higher and Secondary Specialized Education. Bulletin of the Institute of Higher Learning: Jurisprudence). no. 1 (1959), pp. 90-100.

Polyanskii, N.N. "The Principle of Sovereignty in the Secruity Council," *Sovetskoe gosudarstvo i pravo* (Soviet State and Law). no. 3 (1946), pp. 30ff.

Potter, P.B. "Liberal and Totalitarian Attitudes Concerning International Law and Organizations," *American Journal of International Law*. vol. 45 (April 1951), pp. 327-329.

_____. "Obstacles and Alternatives to International Law," *American Journal of International Law*. vol. 53 (July 1959), pp. 647-751.

Preobrazhenskaia, V.V. "Trade Delegations of the USSR in Foreign Countries Are An Outstanding Contribution of the Soviet State to International Law," Lvov University. *Naukovi zapipskii* (Scientific Records). vol. 38 (1956), pp. 33-38.

Proceedings of the American Society of International Law. Washington: American Society of International Law. 1955-*seriatim.*

Preuss, Lawrence. "Consular Immunities: The Kasenkina Case (US-USSR)," *American Journal of International Law.* vol. 43 (January 1949), pp. 37-56.

Quiason, C.D. "Brief Examination of Fundamental Soviet Legal Principles,"*Philippine Law Journal.* vol. 29 (December 1954), pp. 668-685.

Quigley, John B. "The New Soviet Approach to International Law," *Harvard International Law Club Journal.* vol. 7, no. 1 (Winter 1965), pp. 1-32.

Ramundo, Bernard A. "Soviet Criminal Legislation in Implementation of the Hague and Geneva Conventions Relating to the Rules of Land Warfare," *American Journal of International Law.* vol. 57 (1963), pp. 73-84.

Ramzaitsev, D.F. "Problems of Private International Law in the Practice of the Arbitration Committee of Foreign Trade," *Sovetskoe gosudarstvo i pravo* (Soviet State and Law). no. 9 (September 1957), pp. 50-60.

Ramzaitsev, I. "Application of Private International Law in Soviet Foreign Trade Practice," *Journal of Business Law.* October 1961. pp. 343ff.

Rapaport, M.IA. "Against Bourgeois Theories of International Law," *Sovetskoe gosudarstvo i pravo* (Soviet State and Law). nos. 1-2 (1937), pp. 94ff.

_____. "Basic Principles of the Peaceful Coexistence of Different States as a Criteria for the Observance of Present-Day International Law," Ministerstvo vysshego i srednego spetsialnogo obrazovaniia. *Izvestiia vysshikh uchebnykh zavedenii: pravovedenie* (Ministry of Higher and Secondary Specialized Education. Bulletin of the Institute of Higher Learning: Jurisprudence). no. 4 (1960), pp. 89-99.

Recueil des Cours (Collection of Lectures). Hague: Academy of International Law. 1955-*seriatim.*

"A Review of the Discussion of Problems in the Thoery of Contemporary International Law," *Sovetskoe gosudarstvo i pravo* (Soviet State and Law). no. 5 (1955), pp. 45-50.

Revue Egyptienne de Droit International (Egyptian Review of International Law). Alexander; Société Egyptienne de Droit International. 1955-*seriatim.*

Revue Hellénique de Droit International (Greek Review of International Law). Athènes. 1955-*seriatim.*

Rosenne, Shabtai. "Court and the Judicial Process," *International Organization.* vol. 19 (Summer 1965), pp. 518-536.

Rosseau, Charles. "Principle of Acquired Rights," *Principles Généraux du Droit International* (General Principles of International Law). vol. 1 (1944), pp. 901-906.

Sabanin, Andrei. "The First Soviet Course on International Law," *Mezhdunarodnaia zhizn'* (International Affairs). no. 2 (1925), pp. 119-120.

Salter, L.M. "US and USSR: Convergence and/or Confrontation," *Canadian Law Journal*. vol. 69 (March 1964), pp. 59ff.

Schich, F.B. "Cuba and International Law," *Mezhdunarodnaia zhizn'* (International Affairs). no. 9 (September 1963), pp. 85-94.

Schlesinger, Rudolf. "Research on the General Principles of Law Recognized by Civilized Nations," *American Journal of International Law*. vol. 51 (1957), pp. 734-753.

Schwarts, Mortimer, Hogan, John C. and Krieger, F.J. "Soviet Attacks on the Western Legal Order," *Oklahoma Law Review*. vol. 10 (1957), pp. 302-316.

Schwarzenberger, Georg. "The Impact of the East-West Rift on International Law," *Grotius Society Transactions*. vol. 36 (1950), pp. 229-269.

"The Second Conference of the Soviet Association of International Law," *Sovetskoe gosudarstvo i pravo* (Soviet State and Law). no. 5 (May 1959), pp. 140-142.

Serbov, S. "Sixth and Seventh Sessions of the Commission of International Law," *Sovetskoe gosudarstvo i pravo* (Soviet State and Law). no. 8 (1955), pp. 108-112.

Shargorodskii, M.D. "International Criminal Law," *Sovetskoe gosudarstvo i pravo* (Soviet State and Law). no. 3 (1947), pp. 24-32.

Sharma, Surya P. "Professor Edward McWhinney's 'Peaceful Coexistence and Soviet-Western International Law'," *Indian Journal of International Law*. vol. 5 (1965), pp. 52-55.

Sharmazanashvili, G.V. "The Conception of Self-Help in International Law," *1959 Sovetskii ezhegodnik mezhdunarodnogo prava* (1959 Soviet Yearbook of International Law). pp. 300-311.

——————. "Peaceful Solution of International Conflicts Is An Important Principle of International Law," *Sovetskoe gosudarstvo i pravo* (Soviet State and Law). no. 1 (January 1962), pp. 71-79.

Shurshalov, V.M. "International Law Principles of the Co-Operation of Socialist States," *Sovetskoe gosudarstvo i pravo* (Soviet State and Law). no. 7 (July 1962), pp. 95-105.

_____. "Judicial Content of the Principle of *Pacta Sunt Servanda* And Its Realization In International Relations," *1958 Sovetskii ezhegodnik mezhdunarodnogo prava* (1958 Soviet Yearbook of International Law). pp. 150-168.

_____. "Some Problems of the Theory of International Law," *Sovetskoe gosudarstvo i pravo* (Soviet State and Law). no. 8 (1954), pp. 89-92

Simmonds, K.R. "The UN Assessments Advisory Opinion," *International and Comparative Law Quarterly.* vol. 13 (July 1964), pp. 854-898.

Snyder, Earl A. and Bracht, Hans Werner. "Coexistence and International Law," *International and Comparative Law Quarterly.* vol. 7 (January 1958), pp. 54-71.

Soloveitchik, Samon. "International Law as 'An Instrument of Politics'," *University of Kansas City Law Review.* vol. 21 (Summer 1953), pp. 169-183.

Sφrensen, M. "International Court of Justice: Its Role In Contemporary International Relations," *International Organizations.* vol. 14 (Spring 1960), pp. 261-276.

Sovetskaia iustitsiia (Soviet Justice). Moskva. 1957-*seriatim.*

Sovetskii ezhegodnik mezhdunarodnogo prava (Soviet Yearbook of International Law). Moskva: Akademiia nauk SSSR. 1958, 1959, 1960, 1961, 1962, 1963 and 1964-1965.

Sovetskoe gosudarstvo i pravo (Soviet State and Law). Moskva: Akademiia nauk, Institut pravo. 1955-*seriatim.* (Previous titles of this journal: 1925-1929, *Revoliutsiia prava;* 1930-1931, *Sovetskoe gosudarstvo i revoliutsiia prava;* and 1932-1938, *Sovetskoe gosudarstvo.)*

"Soviet Draft Codes of Peaceful Coexistence," *International Law Association Report of the Fifthieth Conference.* Brussels. 1961.

"Soviet Impact on International Law," *Law and Contemporary Problems.* vol. 29 (Autumn 1964), pp. 845-1018.

Soviet Law and Government. New York: International Arts and Science Press. vol. 1 (Summer 1962)-*seriatim.*

Spender, Percy. "Law, Morality, and the Communist Challenge," *Proceedings of the American Society of International Law.* 46th Year (1952), pp. 190-195.

Starushenko, G.B. "The National Liberation Movement and the Struggle for Peace," *International Affairs* (Moscow). 1963. pp. 3-8.

Storey, Robert G. "Law and Lawyers in a Divided World," *Washington University Law Quarterly.* June 1958. pp. 247ff.

Sulkowski, J. "Competence of the International Labor Organization Under the United Nations System: Jurisdiction of the World Court," *American Journal of International Law*. vol. 45 (April 1951), pp. 306-313.

"Summary Work of the International Court of Justice: Year of the Court," *American Journal of International Law*. vol. 46 (January 1952), pp. 1-19; vol. 47 (January 1953), pp. 1-19; vol. 48 (January 1954), pp. 1-22; vol. 49 (January 1955), pp. 1-15; vol. 50 (January 1956), pp. 1-17; vol. 51 (January 1957), pp. 1-17; vol. 52 (January 1958), pp. 1-15; and vol. 53 (April 1959), pp. 318-323.

"Summary Work of the International Law Commission," *American Journal of International Law*. vol. 47 (Supplement, January 1953), pp. 1-28; vol. 48 (Supplement, January 1954), pp. 1-70; vol. 49 (Supplement, January 1955), pp. 1-45; vol. 50 (January 1956), pp. 190-192; vol. 51 (January 1957), pp. 154-155; vol. 52 (January 1958), pp. 177-209; vol. 53 (January 1959), pp. 230-300; vol. 54 (January 1960), pp. 229-304; vol. 55 (January 1961), pp. 223-306; vol. 56 (January 1962), pp. 268-356; vol. 57 (January 1963), pp. 190-267; vol. 58 (January 1964), pp. 241-331 vol. 59 (January 1965), pp. 203-242 and 434-502.

Talalayev, A.N. "Codification of the International Law of Treaties," *1962 Sovetskoe ezhegodnik mezhdunarodnogo prava* (1962 Soviet Yearbook of International Law), pp. 137-149.

_____. "The Termination of International Treaties in the History and Practice of the Soviet State," *1959 Sovetskii ezhegodnik mezhdunarodnogo prava* (1959 Soviet Yearbook of International Law). pp. 144-157.

Thierry, Hubert. "Avis Consultaif sur Certaines Dépenses des Nations Unies," (Advisory Opinion on Certain Expenses of the United Nations). *Annuaire Français de Droit International* (French Annual of International Law). 1962. pp. 247ff.

Timasheff, Nicholas S. "Soviet Jurisprudence Since W.W. II," *Russian Review*. vol. 11 (October 1952), pp. 233-240.

Toma, Peter A. "Soviet Attitude Toward the Acquisition of Territorial Sovereignty in the Antarctic," *American Journal of International Law*. vol. 50 (1956), pp. 611-626.

Trainin, Ilia Pavlovich. "Questions of Guerilla Warfare and The Law of War," *American Journal of International Law*. vol. 40 (1946), pp. 535ff.

Triska, Jan F. "Soviet Treaty Law: A Quantative Analysis," *Law and Contemporary Problems*. vol. 29 (Autumn 1964), pp. 896-909.

Triska, Jan F. and Slusser, Robert M. "Treaties and Other Sources of Order in International Relations: The Soviet View," *American Journal of International Law*. vol. 52 (October 1958).

_____. "Professor Krylov and Soviet Treaties," *American Journal of International Law*. vol. 51 (October 1957), pp. 766-770.

_____. "Ratification of Treaties in Soviet Theory, Practice and Policy," *British Yearbook of International Law*. vol. 34 (1958), pp. 312ff.

Tumanov, V.A. "What Is Hiding Behind the Revival of Natural Law in Contemporary Bourgeois Jurisprudence," *Sovetskoe gosudarstvo i pravo* (Soviet State and Law). no. 5 (1954), p. 88.

Tunkin, Grigorii Ivanovich. "Coexistence and International Law," *Recueil des Cours*. vol. 95 (1958-III), pp. 1-81.

_____. "Forty Years of Co-Existence and International Law," *1958 Sovetskii ezhegodnik mezhdunarodnogo prava* (1958 Soviet Yearbook of International Law). pp. 15-49.

_____. "International Law and Peace," *International Law In a Changing World*. Dobbs-Ferry: Oceana Publications, 1963. pp. 72-79.

_____. "Peaceful Coexistence and International Law," *Sovetskoe gosudarstvo i pravo* (Soviet State and Law). no. 7 (1956), pp. 3-13.

_____. "Peaceful Co-Existence or 'Intermediate Status'," *Novoe vremia* (New Times). vol. 14, no. 25 (June 1956), pp. 8-11.

_____. "Remarks on the Judicial Nature of Customary Norms of International Law," *California Law Review*. vol. 49 (August 1961), pp. 419-430.

_____. "The Role of International Law in Strengthening Peace," *United Nations Review*. vol. 8, no. 8 (August 1961).

_____. "Socialist Internationalism and International Law," *Novoe vremia* (New Times). vol. 15, nos. 10-11 (December 1957).

_____. "Some Developments in International Law Concerning Diplomatic Privileges and Immunities," *Mezhdunarodnaia zhizn'* (International Affairs). no. 12 (1957), pp. 70ff.

_____. "Soviet Union and International Law," *Mezhdunarodnaia zhizn'* (International Affairs). vol. 6, no. 11 (November 1959), pp. 52-60.

_____. "The Twenty-First Congress of the CPSU and International Law," *Sovetskoe gosudarstvo i pravo* (Soviet State and Law). no. 6 (June 1959), pp. 40-49.

_____. "The Twenty-Second Congress of the CPSU and the Task of the Soviet Science of International Law," *Soviet Law and Government*. vol. 1 (Winter 1962-1963), pp. 18-28. Reprint from *Sovetskoe gosudarstvo i pravo* (Soviet

State and Law). no. 5 (1962), pp. 3ff.

—————. "The United Nations: 1945-1965 (Problems of International Law)," *Soviet Law and Government*. vol. 4 (Spring 1966), pp. 3-13. Reprinted from *Sovetskoe gosudarstvo i pravo* (Soviet State and Law). no. 10 (1965).

Tunkin, Grigorii Ivanovich and Nechaev, B.N. "The Law of Treaties Discussed at the 15th Session of the United Nations International Law Commission," *Sovetskoe gosudarstvo i pravo* (Soviet State and Law). vol. 34, no. 2 (February 1964), pp. 84-92.

Tunkin, Grigorii Ivanovich and Romanov, V.A. "The Eleventh Session of the International Law Commission," *Sovetskoe gosudarstvo i pravo* (Soviet State and Law). no. 11 (November 1959), pp. 69-78.

—————. "Two Prospects of the International Law Commission," *Sovetskoe gosudarstvo i pravo* (Soviet State and Law). no. 12 (December 1958), pp. 66-74.

Usenko, E.T. "Basic Principles of International Law Which Governs the Co-Operation of Socialist States," *Sovetskoe gosudarstvo i pravo* (Soviet State and Law). no. 3 (March 1961), pp. 17-19.

Ushakov, N.A. "The Right of Veto in the United Nations," *1959 Sovetskii ezhegodnik mezhdunarodnogo prava* (1959 Soviet Yearbook of International Law). pp. 212-228.

Van Bogaert, E. "Coexistence et Droit International," (Coexistence and International Law). *Revue Générale de Droit International Public* (General Review of Public International Law). vol. 63 (April-June 1959), pp. 209-220.

Verdross, A. "General International Law and the United Nations," *International Affairs* (London). vol. 30 (July 1954), pp. 342-348.

Vilkov, G.Y. "International Legal Regulations of Questions of Statelessness," *1963 Sovetskii ezhegodnik mezhdunarodnogo prava* (1963 Soviet Yearbook of International Law). pp. 260-270.

Volchlov, A.F. and Poltorak, A.I. "Principles of the Nuremberg Sentence and International Law," *Sovetskoe gosudarstvo i pravo* (Soviet State and Law). no. 1 (January 1957), pp. 27-37.

Vyshenepolskii, S. "Freedom of the Seas in the Epoch of Imperialism," *Sovetskoe gosudarstvo i pravo* (Soviet State and Law). 1949. pp. 13-25.

Weinschel, H. "Doctrine of the Equality of States and Its Recent Modifications: The International Court of Justice," *American Journal of International Law*. vol. 45 (July 1951), pp. 440-442.

Wilh, K. "International Law and Global Ideological Conflict: Reflections on the Universality of International Law," *American Journal of International Law.* vol. 45 (October 1951), pp. 648-670.

Wilson, Robert R. "International Law and Some Contemporary Problems," *Proceedings of the American Society of International Law.* 52nd Year (1958).

"World Security and International Law At Mid-Century," *Proceedings of the American Society of International Law.* 44th Year (1950), pp. 2-230.

Wright, Quincy. "Corfu Channel Case," *American Journal of International Law.* vol. 43 (July 1949), pp. 491-494.

_____. "Custom As A Basis For International Law In The Post War Period," *Texas International Law Forum.* vol. 2 (Summer 1966), pp. 147-166.

_____. "International Law and Ideologies," *American Journal of International Law.* vol. 48 (October 1954), pp. 616-626.

_____. "Legal Aspects of the U-2 Incident," *American Journal of International Law.* vol. 54 (1960), pp. 836-854.

Wyzner, Eugeniusz. "Selected Problems of the United Nations Program for the Codification and Progressive Development of International Law," *Proceedings of the American Society of International Law.* 56th year (1962), pp. 90-99.

Zadorozhnyi, G.P. "International Legal Principles Relating to the Peaceful Coexistence of States," *Sovetskoe gosudarstvo i pravo* (Soviet State and Law). no. 8 (1955), pp. 89-96.

Zadorozhnyi, G.P. and Kozhevnikov, Fedor Ivanovich. "The Twenty-Second Congress of the CPSU and Some Basic Problems of the Soviet Theory of International Law," Ministerstvo vysshego i srednego spetsialnogo obrazovaniia. *Izvestiia vysshikh uchebnykh zavedenii: pravovedenie* (Ministry of Higher and Secondary Specialized Education. Bulletin of the Institute of Higher Learning: Jurisprudence). no. 10 (1962), pp. 3-26.

Zile, Zigurds L. "Soviet Contribution to International Adjudication: Professor Krylov's Jurisprudential Legacy," *American Journal of International Law.* vol. 58 (April 1964), pp. 359-388.

II. SOVIET MUNICIPAL LAW

Books

The Anti-Stalinist Campaign and International Communism. Edited by the Russian Institute, Columbia University. New York: Columbia University Press, 1956.

Archer, Peter. *Communism and the Law: A Background Book.* n.p.:Dufour, 1963.

Babb, Hugh and Hazard, John N. *Soviet Legal Philosophy.* Cambridge: Harvard University Press, 1951.

Berman, Harold J. *Justice in Russia.* Cambridge: Harvard University Press, 1950.

——————. *Justice in the USSR.* Cambridge: Harvard University Press, 1963.

——————.*Russians in Focus.* Boston: Little Brown and Company, 1953.

Blum, Jerome. *Lord and Peasant in Russia.* Princeton: Princeton University Press, 1961.

Bodenheimer, Edgar. *Jurisprudence.* New York: McGraw-Hill Book Company, 1940.

Bober, Mandell M. *Karl Marx's Interpretation of History.* Cambridge: Harvard University Press, 1948.

Denisov, Andrei I. *Soviet State Law.* Moscow: Foreign Languages Publishing House, 1960.

Documents on Catherine the Great. Edited by W.F. Reddaway. London: Cambridge University Press, 1931.

Fainsod, Merle D. *How Russia Is Ruled.* Cambridge: Harvard University Press, 1963. Revised Edition.

Feifer, George. *Justice in Moscow.* New York: Simon and Schuster, 1964.

Florinsky, Michael T. *Russia: A History and An Interpretation.* New York: MacMillan Company, 1953. vols. I and II.

Friedrich, Carl J. *The Philosophy of Law In Historical Perspective.* Chicago: Chicago University Press, 1963.

Friedrich, Carl J. and Brzezinski, Zbigniew K. *Totalitarian Dictatorship and Autocracy.* New York: Praeger, 1962.

Grzybowski, Kazimierz. *Soviet Legal Institutions.* Ann Arbor: University of Michigan Press, 1962.

Gsovski, Vladimir and Grzybowski, Kazimierz. *Government, Law and Courts in the Soviet Union and Eastern Europe*. London: Stevens and Sons Ltd., 1959. vols. I and II.

Gsovski, Vladmir. *Soviet Civil Law*. Ann Arbor: University of Michigan Press, 1948. vols. I and II.

Guins, George C. *Soviet Law and Soviet Society*. The Hague: Martinus Nijhoff, 1954.

Harcave, Sidney. *Russia: A History*. New York: J.P. Lippincott, 1959.

Hazard, John N. *Settling Disputes in Soviet Society*. New York: Columbia University Press, 1960.

_____. *The Soviet System of Government*. Chicago: University of Chicago Press, 1957.

Hazard, John N. and Shapiro, Isaac. *The Soviet Legal System*. New York: Columbia University Press, 1962.

Hazard, John N. and Weisburg, Morris L. *Cases and Readings on Soviet Law*. New York: Columbia University Press, 1950.

Hoffman, George M. *Recent Soviet Trends*. Austin: University of Texas Press, 1956.

Hsiao, Kung-Chian. *Political Pluralism: A Study in Contemporary Political Theory*. New York: Harcourt Brace and Company, 1927.

Karamzin's Memoir on Ancient and Modern Russia. Translated by Richard Pipes. Cambridge: Harvard University Press, 1959.

Karpovich, Michael. *Imperial Russia 1801-1917*. New York: Henry Holt and Company, 1932.

Kluchevsky, Vasili. *Peter the Great*. New York: Vintage, 1961.

_____. *A History of Russia*. Translated by C.J. Hogarth. New York: Russell and Russell, 1960. vols. I and II.

Konstantinovsky, Boris A. *Soviet Law in Action*. Edited by Harold Berman. Cambridge: Harvard University Press, 1953.

Kucherov, Samuel. *Courts, Lawyers and Trials Under the Last Three Tsars*. New York: Praeger, 1953.

Kulski, Wladyskaw W. *The Soviet Regime*. Syracuse: Syracuse University Press, 1959.

Lamb, Harold. *Genghis Khan: Emperor of All Men*. New York: Bantam, 1957.

_____. *The March on Muscovy*. New York: Doubleday, 1951.

Laqueur, Walter and Labedz, Leopold. *The Future of Communist Society*. New York: Praeger, 1962.

Leites, Nathan and Bernaut, Elsa. *The Ritual of Liquidation: The Case of the Moscow Trials*. Glencoe; The Free Press, 1954.

Leningrad. Universitet. IUridicheskii Fakultet. *Sorok let Sovetskogo prava* (Forty Years of Soviet Law, 1917-1957). Leningrad: Izd-vo Leningradskogo Universitet. 1958.

McClosky, Herbert and Turner, John E. *The Soviet Dictatorship*. New York: McGraw-Hill Publishing Company, 1960.

Medieval Russian Laws. Translated by George Vernadsky. New York: Columbia University Press, 1947.

Meisel, James H. and Kozera, Edward S. *Materials for the Study of the Soviet System*. Michigan: George Wahr Publishing Company, 1950.

Mendel, Arthur P. *Essential Works of Marxism*. New York: Bantam, 1961.

Meyer, Alfred G. *Leninism*. New York: Prager, 1957.

Mosse, W.E. *Alexander II and the Modernization of Russia*. London: The English University Press Ltd., 1958.

Nowak, Frank. *Medieval Slavdom and the Rise of Russia*. New York: Henry Holt and Company, 1930.

Pares, Bernard. *A History of Russia*. New York: Alfred A. Knopf, 1934.

Pushkarev, Sergei. *The Emergence of Modern Russia 1801-1917*. New York: Holt Rinehart and Winston, Inc., 1963.

Raeff, Marc. *Michael Speransky: Statesman of Imperial Russia*. The Hague: Martinus Nijhoff, 1957.

Revisionism: Essays on the History of Marxist Ideas. Edited by Leopold Labedz. New York: Praeger, 1962.

Romashkin, Petr Semenovich. (ed). *Fundamentals of Soviet Law*. Moscow: Foreign Languages Publishing House, [1960?]

Schapiro, Leonard. *The Communist Party of the Soviet Union*. New York: Random House, 1960.

Schlesinger, Rudolf. *The Soviet Legal Theory*. New York: Oxford University Press, 1945.

Scott, Derek J.R. *Russian Political Institutions*. New York: Praeger, 1961.

Soviet Society: A Book of Readings. Edited by Alex Inkeles and Kent Geiger. Boston: Houghton Miffin and Company, 1961.

The Transformation of Russian Society. Edited by Cyril E. Black. Cambridge: Harvard University Press, 1960.

The Trial of the U-2: Exclusive Authorized Account of the Proceedings of the Case of Francis Gary Powers, Heard Before the Military Division of the Supreme Court of the USSR, Moscow, August 17-19, 1960. Introduction by Harold J. Berman. Chicago: Translation World Publishers, 1960.

Utechin, S.V. *Russian Political Thought: A Concise History*. New York: Praeger, 1963.

Vernadsky, George. *A History of Russia*. New Haven: Yale University Press, 1961. 5th Revised Edition.

Vyshinskii, Andrei IAnuaryevich. *The Law of the Soviet State*. New York: MacMillan Company, 1948.

Zatsev, Yergeny and Poltorak, A. *The Soviet Bar*. Moscow: Foreign Languages Publishing House, 1959.

Articles

Barry, Donald D. "The Specialist in Soviet-Policy-Making: The Adoption of a Law," *Soviet Studies*. vol. 16 (October 1964), pp. 152-165.

Belinsky, A. "Lawyers and Soviet Society," *Problems of Communism*. vol. 14 (1965), pp. 62-71.

Berman, Harold J. "The Challenge of Soviet Law," *Harvard Law Review*. vol. 62 (1948), pp. 220-265.

_____. "The Comparison of Soviet and American Law," *Indiana Law Review*. vol. 34, no. 4 (Summer 1959), pp. 559-570.

_____. "The Devil and Soviet Russia," *The American Scholar*. vol. 27, no. 1 (Spring 1958), pp. 147-152.

_____. "Law and Social Change in the USSR," (review). *Yale Law Review*. vol. 63, no. 7 (May 1954), pp. 1044.

_____. "Law Reform in the Soviet Union," *American Slavic and Eastern European Review.* vol. 15 (1956), pp. 179ff.

_____. "Limited Rule of Law," *The Christian Science Monitor.* April 29, 1958.

_____. "Powers Case," *Nation.* vol. 191 (September 3, 1960), pp. 103-105.

_____. "Principles of Soviet Criminal Law," *Yale Law Review.* vol. 56 (1947), pp. 802-836.

_____. "Soviet Law and Government," *Modern Law Review.* vol. 21 (January 1958), pp. 19ff.

_____. "Soviet Justice and Soviet Tyranny," *Columbia Law Review.* vol. 55 (1955), pp. 795-807.

_____. "Soviet Law Reform — Dateline Moscow 1957," *Yale Law Review.* vol. 66 (1957), pp. 1191-1215.

Jurists Against a Return to Stalinist Terror," *Slavic and East European Review.* vol. 22 (1963), pp. 314-320.

Bilinsky, Andreas. "Socialist Legality and the Personality Cult," *Bulletin* (Institute for the Study of the USSR). vol. 10 (September 1963), pp. 3-16.

Bingham, A.M. "Law and Justice in the Soviet Union," *Connecticut Bar Journal.* vol. 33 (December 1959), pp. 378ff.

"Changes in the Soviet Criminal Law Procedure Since the 20th Party Congress," *Bulletin* (Institute for the Study of the USSR). vol. 3, no. 7 (June 1956), pp. 21ff.

Chkhikvadze, V. "Questions on Soviet Law," *Current Digest of the Soviet Press.* vol. 17 (September 19, 1965), pp. 7-8.

"Complicity and Presumption of Guilt in Soviet Law," *Current Digest of the Soviet Press.* November 14, 1956.

Craig, W.E. "Opportunitites for the Legal Profession," *American Bar Association Journal.* vol. 46 (December 1960), pp. 1307ff.

Dewey, Horace W. "The 1497 Sudebnik — Muscovite Russia's First National Law Code," *Readings in Russian History.* Edited by Sidney Harcave. New York: Thomas Y. Cromwell, 1962.

Dulles, A.W. "Soviet Concept of Legal Institutions," *Mercer Law Review.* vol. 7 (Spring 1956), pp. 250ff.

Evans, Joseph W. "Jacques Maritan and the Problem of Pluralism in Political Life," *Review of Politics.* vol. 22 (1960), pp. 307-323.

Fledburgge, F.J.M. "A Precarious Legality," *Problems of Communism*. July-August 1964. pp. 34-39.

Friedman, Lawrence and Zile, Zigurds L. "Soviet Legal Profession: Recent Developments in Law and Practice, Provides New View of the Practice of Law in the Soviet Union by Annotating the Most Recent Statutes Defining the Role of the Lawyer in the Soviet System," *Wisconsin Law Review*. January 1964. pp. 32-37.

Gorkin, A.F. "The USSR Judicial System," *Current Soviet Documents*. vol. 1 (June 24, 1963), pp. 3ff.

Grzybowski, Kazimierz. "Extraterritorial Effect of Soviet Criminal Law After the Reform of 1958," *Journal of Comparative Law*. vol. 8 (Autumn 1959), pp. 515ff.

Guins, George C. "Law Does Not Wither Away in the Soviet Union," *Russian Review*. vol. 9 (July 1950), pp. 187-204.

_____. "Soviet Law in the Mirror of Legal Science," *American Slavic Review*. vol. 16 (February 1957), pp. 66-73.

_____. "Soviet Law — Terra Incognita," *Russian Review*. vol. 9 (January 1950), pp. 16-29.

Hammar, Darrell P. "Russian and Roman Law," *American Slavic and Eastern European Review*. vol. 16 (February 1957), pp. 1-13.

Hampsch, G.H. "Marxist Jurisprudence in the Soviet Union, 'A Preliminary Survey'," *Notre Dame Law Review*. vol. 35 (August 1960), pp. 525ff.

Hazard, John N. "The Functioning Law," *Survey*. no. 38 (October 1961), pp. 72-80.

_____. "The Future Codification in the USSR," *Tulane Law Review*. vol. 29 (February 1955), pp. 239-248.

_____. "Has the Soviet State a New Function?" *Political Quarterly*. October-December 1963.

_____. "Laws and Men in Soviet Society," *Foreign Affairs*. vol. 36 (January 1958), pp. 267-277.

_____. "Legal Framework," *New Republic*. vol. 105 (November 17, 1941), pp. 661-663.

_____. "Socialism, Abuse of Power in Soviet Law," *Columbia Law Review*. vol. 50 (1950), pp. 448-474.

_____. "Soviet Codifiers Receive New Orders," *American Journal of Comparative Law*. vol. 6 (Autumn 1957), pp. 540-546.

_____. "Soviet Codifiers Release First Drafts," *American Journal of Comparative Law*. vol. 8 (1959), pp. 72-81.

_____. "The Trend of Law in the USSR," *Wisconsin Law Review*. no. 2 (March 1947), pp. 223-243.

Horowitz, S. "The Basis of Soviet Justice," *Challenge*. January 1957.

Kiralfy, A.K.R. "Campaign for Legality in the USSR," *International and Comparative Law Quarterly*. October 1957.

_____. "Recent Legal Changes in the USSR," *Soviet Studies*. July 1957.

Lapenna, Ivo. "Bar in the Soviet Union and Yugoslavia," *International and Comparative Law Quarterly*. vol. 12 (April 1963), pp. 631ff.

"Law and Legality in the USSR," *Problems of Communism*. vol. 14 (March 1965), pp. 2-111.

LeMay, G.H.L. "Law and Politics in Soviet Russia," *South African Law Review*. vol 71 (May 1954), pp. 137-144.

Levitsky, S.L. "Directives of the Soviet Supreme Court as a Source of Law," *Etudes Slaves et Est-Européennes* (Slavic and East European Studies). Spring 1958.

_____. "Soviet Law and the Press," *Bulletin* (Institute for the Study of the USSR). October 1956.

Lipson, Leon. "Socialist Legality: The Mountain Has Labored," *Problems of Communism*. March-April 1959.

_____. "Socialist Legality: The Road Uphill," *Russia Under Khrushchev*. Edited by Abraham Brumberg. New York: Praeger, 1962. pp. 444-470.

Lochak, P. "Justice and Judges in the Soviet Union," *Lawyer's Journal*. vol. 22. pp. 230-232.

MacKey, Maurice C. "Some Basic Considerations of Soviet Law and Socialist Legality," *Alabama Law Review*. vol. 11 (Spring 1959), pp. 254-270.

Malone, A.C. Jr. "Soviet Bar," *Cornell Law Quarterly*. vol. 46 (Winter 1961), pp. 258ff.

Malone, Reiss L. "Lawyers in the Sputnik Era," *Wyoming Law Review*. Winter 1959.

Maxwell, David F. "A Contrast in Viewpoints: Lawyers in the US and Russia," *American Bar Association Journal*. vol. 18. pp. 219ff.

Mironenko, Yuri P. "The Re-Emergence of the Death Penalty in the Soviet Union," *Soviet Affairs Analysis Service* (Institute for the Study of the USSR). Munich. no. 28 (1961-1962).

―――――. "The Role of the Military Tribunal in the Soviet Legal System," *Bulletin* (Institute for the Study of the USSR). September 1965. pp. 40-46.

"New Principles of Soviet Criminal Legislation," *Bulletin* (Institute for the Study of the USSR). vol. 6 (May 1959). pp. 47ff.

"The New Justice in the USSR," *Soviet Affairs Notes*. March 28, 1960.

"New Soviet Civil Legislation and the Problem of Private Property in a Communist State," *Soviet Affairs Analysis Service* (Institute for the Study of the USSR). Munich. no. 20 (1961-1962).

Nikeforov, Boris S. "Fundamental Principles of Soviet Criminal Law," *Modern Law Review*. vol. 23 (January 1960), pp. 31ff.

Perlov, Ilya. "Soviet Judiciary System," *USSR*. no. 12 (1963), pp. 87ff.

Radin, Max. "Moscow Trials: A Legal View," *Foreign Affairs*. vol. 16 (October 1937), pp. 64-79.

Razi, G.M. "Around the World's Legal Systems: The Soviet System," *Howard Law Review*. vol. 6 (January 1960), pp. 1ff.

―――――. "Legal Education and the Role of the Lawyer in the Soviet Union and in the Countries of Eastern Europe," *California Law Review*. vol. 48 (December 1960). pp. 776ff.

Rhyne, Charles. "The Law: Russia's Greatest Weakness," *American Bar Association Journal*. March 1959.

Rivto, Herbert. "The Dynamics of De-Stalinization," *Survey*. no. 47 (April 1963), pp. 13-23.

"Rudenko on the Problems of Strengthening Soviet Law," *Current Digest of the Soviet Press*. September 19, 1956.

Schapiro, Leonard. "Judicial Practice and Legal Reform," *Survey*. no. 29 (July-September 1959), pp. 54-61.

Schlesinger, Rudolf. "Diversity and Unity in Socialist Law of Property," *Soviet Studies*. April 1964.

_____. "Soviet Law: System and Institutions," *Science and Society*. vol. 28 (Fall 1964), pp. 453-460.

Shapiro, Isaac. "Soviet Bar — Past and Present," *Russian Review*. vol. 20 (April 1961), pp. 143-150.

Shuman, I.I. "Soviet Legality as Revealed by Soviet Jurisprudence," *Wayne Law Review*. vol. 5 (Spring 1959). pp. 209ff.

"Standards of Objective Truth in Soviet Courts," *Current Digest of the Soviet Press*. November 7, 1956.

Stason, E.B. "Law and the Administration of Justice in the Soviet Union," *Cleveland Bar Association Journal*. vol. 31 (October 1960), pp. 243ff.

Sukharev, A.IA. "Pressing Problems Facing the Soviet Legal Profession," *Soviet Review*. vol. 6, no. 2 (Summer 1965), pp. 55-64.

Taylor, Pauline B. "Soviet Courts in the Social Complex," *Russian Review*. January 1964.

Timasheff, Nicholas S. "Soviet Law," *Virginia Law Review*. vol. 38 (November 1952), pp. 871-885.

Towster, J. "Law and Government in the USSR," *Hastings Law Journal*. vol. 11 (February 1960), pp. 231ff.

Verkhovnyi sud (Bulletin of the Supreme Court of the USSR). Moskva. 1957-*seriatim*.

Yaney, George L. "Law, Society and the Domestic Regime in Russia in Historical Perspective," *American Political Science Review*. vol. 59 (June 1965), pp. 379-390.

Yurchenko, A. "The Present Soviet Interpretation of Law," *Bulletin* (Institute for the Study of the USSR). September 1962.

Yuriev, Grigorii V. "Internal Contradiction in the Soviet Penal Policy," *Analysis of Current Developments* (Institute for the Study of the USSR). Munich. no. 4 (1962-1963).

III. IDEOLOGY AND THE SOVIET UNION

Books

Bouscaren, Anthony T. *Soviet Foreign Policy: A Pattern of Persistence*. n.p.: Fordham University Press, 1962.

Brzezinski, Zbigniew K. *Ideology and Power in Soviet Politics*. New York: Praeger, 1962.

_____. *Soviet Bloc: Unity and Conflict*. New York: Praeger, 1960. Revised Edition.

Crankshaw, Edward. *The New Cold War: Moscow v. Pekin*. New York: Penguin, 1963.

Dallin, David J. *From Purge to Coexistence*. Chicago: Henry Regnery Company, 1964.

Floyd, David. *Mao Against Khrushchev*. New York: Praeger, 1963.

Gilbert, Ridney. *Competitive Coexistence*. n.p.: Bookmailer, 1956.

Hudson, G.F. *et. al. The Sino-Soviet Dispute*. New York: Praeger, 1963.

History of the Communist Party of the Soviet Union. Moscow: Foreign Languages Publishing House, [1964?].

Khrushchev, Nikita Sergeivich. *For Victory in Peaceful Coexistence With Capitalism*. New York: E.P. Dutton and Company, Inc., 1960.

_____. *On Peaceful Coexistence*. Moscow: Foreign Languages Publishing House, 1961.

_____. *World Without Arms, World Without Wars*. Moscow: Foreign Languages Publishing House, 1959. vols I and II.

Korovin, Evgenii Aleksandrovich. *Osnovnye problemy sovremennykh mezhdunarodnykh otnoshenii* (Essays on the Problems of Present-Day International Relations). Moskva: Sotsekgiz, 1959.

Kovner, Milton. *The Challenge of Coexistence*. Washington, D.C.: Public Affairs Press, 1961.

Kulski, Wladyslaw W. *Peaceful Coexistence: An Analysis of Soviet Foreign Policy*. Chicago: Henry Regnery Company, 1959.

Laqueur, Walter and Labedz, Leopold (eds). *Polycentrism*. New York: Praeger, 1959.

Lenin: Collected Works. vols 1-32 and 38. Moscow: Foreign Languages Publishing House, n.d.

Lindsay, Michael. *Is Peaceful Coexistence Possible?* East Lansing: Michigan State University Press, 1960.

Moore, Barrington Jr. *Soviet Politics — The Dilemma of Power: The Role of Ideas in Social Change*. Cambridge: Harvard University Press, 1950.

Neimeyer, Gerhart. *An Inquiry into Soviet Mentality*. New York: Praeger, 1956.

The New Soviet Society: Final Text of the Program of the CPSU. New York: New Leader Paperback, 1962.

Northrop, F. S. C. *Ideological Difference and World Order*. New Haven: Yale University Press, 1949.

Rothstein, Andrew. *Peaceful Coexistence*. Harmondsworth, England: Penguin Books, 1955.

Rubinstein, Alvin J. *The Foreign Policy of the Soviet Union*. New York: Random House, 1960.

Scott, John. *Political Warfare: A Guide to Competitive Coexistence*. New York: Day, 1955.

Strausz-Hupe, Robert *et. al. Protracted Conflict*. New York: Harper Colophon Books, 1959.

Articles

"Against Peaceful Coexistence in the Field of Ideology," *Pravda* (Truth). JPRS 18,252. Mrach 17. pp. 6-9.

Aleksandrov, K. "Sino-Soviet Differences Over War and Peaceful Coexistence," *Bulletin* (Institute for the Study of the USSR). vol. 8 (1961), pp. 41-45.

Bailey, S.D. "Precarious Coexistence," *Christian Century*. August 27, 1958.

Bell, David. "Ten Theories in Search of Reality: The Prediction of Soviet Behavior in the Social Sciences," *World Politics*. April 1958.

Bowles, Chester. "Is Communist Ideology Becoming Irrelevant?" *Foreign Affairs*. July 1962.

Brzezinski, Zbigniew K. "Communist Ideology and International Affairs," *Journal of Conflict Resolution*. vol. 4, no. 3 (September 1960), pp. 266-292.

_____. "Deviation Control: The Dynamics of Doctrinal Conflict," *American Political Science Review*. vol. 56, no. 1 (March 1962), pp. 5-22.

"Building Communism and the Study of Reactionary Theory," *Kommunist* (Communist). September 14, 1964. pp. 1-10.

Daniels, Robert V. "What Russia Means," (Contemporary Analysis) *Commentary*. October 1962.

Fifield, Russell H. "The Five Principles of Coexistence," *American Journal of International Law*, vol. 52 (July 1958). pp. 504-510.

Gerschenkron, Alexander. "The Changeability of a Dictatorship," *World Politics*. July 1962.

Gsovski, Vladimir. "Essence of a Totalitarian State of the Soviet Type," *Law Journal*. vol. 21 (July 1956). pp. 313ff.

Khrushchev, Nikita Sergeivich. "On Peaceful Coexistence," *Foreign Affairs*. vol. 38 (October 1959). pp. 1-18.

Kux, E. "Coexistence or World Revolution," *Swiss Review of World Politics*. February 1961.

Halperin, E. "Is Russia Going Titoist?" *Problems of Communism*. September-October 1956.

Labedz, Leopold, "Ideology Under Khrushchev," *Problems of Communism*. November-December 1959.

Mosley, Philip E. "The Meaning of Coexistence," *Foreign Affairs*. vol. 39 (October 1962), pp. 36-46.

Pachter, E. "The Meaning of 'Peaceful Coexistence'," *Problems of Communism*. January-February 1961.

Rogger, Hans. "Politics, Ideology and History in the USSR: The Search for Coexistence," *Soviet Studies*. vol. 16 (January 1965). pp. 253-275.

Ulam, Adam B. "Soviet Ideology and Soviet Foreign Policy," *World Politics*. January 1959.

Wetter, G.A. "The Soviet Concept of Coexistence: Are Lenin's Views Still Valid?" *Soviet Studies*. October-December 1959.

Wolfe, Bertram. "Communist Ideology and Soviet Foreign Policy," *Foreign Affairs*. October 1962.

_____. "The Durability of Despotism in the Soviet System," *Russian Re-*

view. vol. 17 (1958), pp. 83-93 and 163-175.

Zinner, Paul E. "Ideological Bases of Soviet Foreign Policy," *World Politics*. vol. 4 (July 1952). pp. 488-511.

IV. FOREIGN POLICY OF THE USSR

Books

Collier, David S. and Glaser, Kurt (eds). *Western Policy and Eastern Europe*. Chicago: Henry Regnery Company, 1956.

Dallin, David J. *Soviet Foreign Policy After Stalin*. New York: J.B. Lippincott Company, 1961.

Goodman, Elliot R. *The Soviet Design for a World State*. New York: Columbia University Press, 1960.

Griffith, William E. *The Sino-Soviet Conflict*. Cambridge: MIT Press, 1964.

Lederer, Ivo J. (ed). *Russian Foreign Policy*. New Haven: Yale University Press, 1962.

London, Kurt. *The Making of Foreign Policy: East and West*. New York: J.B. Lippincott, 1965.

Mackintosh, J.M. *Strategy and Tactics of Soviet Foreign Policy*. New York: Oxford University Press, 1963.

Warth, Robert D. *Soviet Russia in World Politics*. New York: Twayne, 1963.

Werth, Alexander. *Russia Under Khrushchev*. New York: Crest Paperback, 1962.

Zagoria, Donald S. *The Sino-Soviet Conflict 1956-1961*. New York: Antheneum, 1964.

Articles

Anisimov, O. "The New Orientation of Soviet Foreign Policy," *Russian Review*. January 1957.

Bauer, Raymond H. "Some Basic Keys to Soviet Foreign Policy," *Soviet Studies*. October 1958.

Bretscher, W. "Change and No Change in Soviet Foreign Policy," *Swiss Review of World Politics*. September 1956.

Kulski, Wladyslaw W. "Soviet Diplomatic Technique," *Russian Review*. July 1960.

Meissner, Boris. "Soviet Russia's Foreign Policy, Ideology and Power Politics," *Modern Age*. Winter 1963-1964.

Salisbury, H.E. "Characteristics of Soviet Foreign Policy," *International Journal*. Autumn 1956.

Ulam, Adam B. "Expansion and Coexistence: Counterpoints in Soviet Foreign Policy," *Problems of Communism*. September-October 1959.

INDEX

A

Academy of Sciences of the USSR (Akademii nauk SSSR), 10, 149
Aggression, 56, 86, 116, 145
Agreement as the Factor in Custom-Creation, 5, 8, 10, 13n, 14, 15, 17-18, 28-29, 32-35, 37, 38, 39, 49, 75, 79, 84, 96, 142n, 158, 160
Air Commerce Act (1926), 115
Air Law *see Usque Ad Coelum*, Principle of
Aliens, 130, 147
"All States" Doctrine, 34, 54, 163
"All States" Principle, 83-85, 106
Alvarez, A., 38n
Anglo-Egyptian Treaty (1936), 79
Anglo-Iranian Oil Company Case, Preliminary Objections (ICJ Reports, 1952), 144
Anglo-Norwegian Fisheries Case (ICJ Reports, 1951), 123, 144
Antarctica, 82, 120, 127-128
Antarctica, Treaty on (1959), 120, 128, 143n
Arbitration, 81
Arcos Raid (1927), 100n
Arctic, 128
Asylum, 105

B

Baginian, K. A., 146
Balloons, High Altitude, 115
Bandung Conference (1955) *see* Declaration of Bandung (1955)
Basadevant, Jules, 31n, 35n
Bay of Peter the Great, 124
Bays and Gulfs, 123, 123-124
Belgrade Declaration of the Non-Aligned Countries (1961), 59, 147
Belligerents, 59, 60
Bellinghausen (Russian Navigator), 127
Berlin Corridor, 117, 162
Bern Incident of 1955, 101-102
Bogdanov, O. V., 149
Bourgeois Law, 2, 8, 9, 28, 156
Boycott, 145
British Diplomatic Immunities Act (1955), 98
Brest-Litovsk, Treaty of (1918), 96
Brezhnev Doctrine, 52-53
Brierly, James L., 30, 31n, 35, 54, 83

C

Capitulations, 79
Case Concerning Rights of Nationals of the United States of America in Morocco (ICJ Reports, 1952), 79, 144

Case of the Application of the Convention of 1902 Governing the Guardianship of Infants, Netherlands v. Sweden (ICJ Reports, 1958), 74
Castérn, Eric, 148
Ceiling of Air Space, 114-116
Charter of Nuremberg Tribunal (1945) *see* Nuremberg Tribunal, Charter of (1945)
Charter of the United Nations *see* United Nations, Charter of
Cherpov, I. I., 117, 118
Chicago Air Convention (1944), 116
The Christina (1938), 55
Citizenship, 113, 129
Civil Aeronautics Act (1938), 115
Civil Wars, 146
Civilian Populations in Time of War *see* Inviolability of Civilian Populations in Time of War, Principle of
Class Law, 1, 2, 4, 8, 14, 18, 32
Clausula Rebus Sic Stantibus, Principle of, 74, 75-77, 81-82, 160, 163
Clipperton Island Arbitration, France v. Mexico (1931), 127
Codification of Customary Principles, 38, 50, 57, 62, 75, 87, 96n, 105-106, 144, 149, 159
Colonies, 146 *See also* General Assembly Resolution 1514 (XV), (1960).
Comitas Gentium see Comity
Comity, 31, 97, 98, 140
"Common Use" Principle of the High Seas *see* High Seas as *Res Communis*, Principle of
"Common Use" Principle of Outer Space *see* Outer Space as *Res Communis*, Principle of
Communist International (2d Comintern Congress) (1920), 1
Communist Party of the Soviet Union, 20th Party Congress (1956) *see* Twentieth Party Congress of the CPSU (1956)
Communist University (Moscow), 3
Compulsory Arbitration, 141, 142, 142-143, 144
"Concept of Functional Necessity", 99
Conflict of Laws, 51
Congress of Marxist Theoreticians of Law (1931), 7
Consensus Doctrine, 17-18, 157, 158 *See also* Agreement as the Factor in Custom-Creation.
"Constitutive Theory" of Recognition, 59
Consular Immunity, Principle of, 99-101

Consular Relations, Convention on (1963), 59, 100, 106, 106-107
Consular Treaty Between the United States and the USSR (1968), 101, 104
Continental Shelf, Convention on (1958), 113, 126
"Continuity" as a Factor in Custom-Creation, 14, 31, 38
Convention on Consular Relations (1963) see Consular Relations, Convention on (1963)
Convention on the Continental Shelf (1958) see Continental Shelf, Convention on (1958)
Convention on Diplomatic Intercourse and Immunities (1961) see Diplomatic Intercourse and Immunities, Convention on (1961)
Convention on Fishing and Conservation of Living Resources of the High Seas (1958) see Fishing and Conservation of Living Resources of the High Seas, Convention on (1958)
Convention on the High Seas (1958) see High Seas, Convention on (1958)
Convention on the Reduction of Stateless Persons see Reduction of Stateless Persons, Convention on
Convention on the Territorial Sea and Contiguous Zones (1958) see Territorial Sea and Contiguous Zones, Convention on (1958)
"Co-ordination of Wills," 32-33, 37
Corbett, Percy, 122
Corfu Channel Case, Merits (ICJ Reports, 1949), 124-125, 144
CPSU, 20th Party Congress (1956) see Twentieth Party Congress of the CPSU (1956)
"Crimes Against Humanity", 51-52 See also Nuremberg Tribunal, Charter of (1945).
Cruz, Alvaro, 97-98
Custom, Creation of, 13-14, 16, 17-18, 27, 29
Custom, Impact of Soviet Views on, 163-165
Czechoslovakia 1968, 52-53

D

Declaration of Bandung (1955), 49, 57, 59, 147
Declaration of the Heads of State and Government of Non-Aligned Countries (1961) see Belgrade Declaration of Non-Aligned Countries (1961)
Declaration of Lima (1938), 58
Declaration of War, 146
Declaration on Granting of Independence to Colonial Countries and Peoples (1960) see General Assembly Resolution 1514 (XV), (1960)

De Facto Recognition, 60
De Jure Recognition, 59
Denial of Justice, 147
Denisov, A. I., 13n
Derying, Antoni, 38n
De Visscher, Charles, 52
Diplomatic Dictionary (Diplomaticheskii slovar) (1950), 12
Diplomatic Immunity, Principle of, 46n, 97-99, 158, 160, 161
Diplomatic Intercourse and Immunities, Convention on (1961), 30n, 59, 99, 106
Diplomatic Law, 6, 31
Diplomatic Pouch, 104
Discovery and Occupation as a Basis for Land Acquisition, Principle of, 118-119, 127-128, 160
Draft Convention on the Law of Treaties see Law of Treaties, Draft Convention on
Drago-Porter Convention (1907), 58
Dual Nationality, 129
Durdenevskii, V. N., 123
Duress, Notion of, 77

E

Eastern Carelia Case (PCIJ Reports, 1923), 143
Eastern Europe, 76
Eastern Greenland, Legal Status of (PCIJ Reports, 1933), 127
Economic Relations, 100
Embargo, 145
Engels, Frederick, 2
Equality, Concept of, 53-54
The Esposenda, 55
Essays on International Law (Ocherki po mezhdunarodnomu pravu) (1935), 7-8
Evian Agreement (1962), 79
Exequatur, 99, 103
Extradition, 130

F

Families of Envoys, 97-98
Fauchille, P., 127
Federalism, 56,
Fisheries Case (ICJ Reports, 1951), 30
Fishing and Conservation of Living Resources of the High Seas, Convention on (1958), 113, 126
Force, Use of, 146
Foreign Policy, 47, 51-52, 74, 76, 86, 159-163
Foreign Vessels in Port, 125
"Form-Content" Formula, 1, 7, 11-12, 16-17, 46, 163
Foscanéanu, Lasar, 49
Free Communication, Principle of, 104-105
Free Zones of Upper Savoy and the District of Gex (PCIJ Reports, 1932), 36
French "Zone of Identification", 121

"Fundamental Change of Circumstances" *see Clausula Rebus Sic Stantibus*
Fundamental Principles of International Law, 38, 46, 47, 48, 73, 158

G

The Gagara (1919), 55
Galina, A., 115, 117, 119
General Assembly Resolution 110 (II), (1947), 146-147
General Assembly Resolution 1514 (XV), (1960), 56, 147
General Assembly, United Nations, Sixth (Legal) Committee *see* Sixth (Legal) Committee of the United Nations General Assembly
General Principles of International Law, 12-13, 16, 29
Geneva Convention on the Continental Shelf (1958) *see* Continental Shelf, Convention on (1958)
Geneva Convention on Fishing and Conservation of Living Resources of the High Seas (1958) *see* Fishing and Conservation of Living Resources of the High Seas, Convention on (1958)
Geneva Convention on the High Seas (1958) *see* High Seas, Convention on (1958)
Geneva Convention on the Territorial Sea and Contiguous Zones (1958) *see* Territorial Sea and Contiguous Zones, Convention on (1958)
Geneva Convention Relative to the Treatment of Prisoners of War (1949) *see* Prisoners of War, Geneva Convention Relative to the Treatment of (1949)
Geneva Protocol of 1925, 149
Genocide Convention (1949), 52, 143
Gidel, G., 125
Giradoux, Jean, 162
Gore, Albert, 48
Great Powers, Role of, 53-54
Gromyko, Andrei, 113
Gross, Leo, 142
Grotius, Hugo, 2n
Gulf of Aquba, 124
Gulfs *see* Bays and Gulfs

H

Habit as Distinguished from Custom *see* Usage as Distinguished from Custom
Hackworth, Green H., 35n
Hague Academy of International Law (Hague Academie de Droit International), 14, 29
Hague Convention (1907), 149
Hazard, John N., 6, 129
High Seas, Convention on (1958), 30, 55, 113, 121

High Seas as *Res Communis*, Principle of, 30, 46n, 86, 119, 120-122, 160
Historic Bays, 124
History of the Communist Party of the Soviet Union, 47
Holy See *see* Vatican
Honorary Consul, 100n, 102
Hot Pursuit, 121
Hudson, Manley O., 35
Hughes, Charles Evans, 49
Hungary 1956, 57
Hyde, Charles Cheney, 127

I

ICJ *see* International Court of Justice of the United Nations
Ideology, 1-18, 27, 61, 113, 156-157, 161
ILA *see* International Law Association (Brussels), Soviet Branch
ILC *see* International Law Commission of the United Nations
Impartiality, 140, 142, 144n
Importance of Customary International Law, 2, 3, 12, 27, 27n, 28-29, 37, 87, 156
Individual as a Subject of International Law, 53
Innocent Passage, Right of, 123, 124-125, 126, 164
In Situ (Diplomatic Immunity), 99
Institute of Law of the Academy of Sciences of the USSR *see* Academy of Sciences of the USSR (Akademii nauk SSSR)
Institute of Soviet Construction and Law, 7
Insurgents, 59, 60
International Association of Democratic Lawyers, Congress of (1956), 48n
International Atomic Energy Statute, 143
International Civil Aviation, Convention on, 115
International Court of Justice of the United Nations, 13, 14, 52, 74, 79, 123, 124, 143, 144
International Criminal Code, 52
International Labor Organization, Convention on, 143
International Law Association (Brussels), Soviet Branch, 47, 48, 48n, 82, 120, 141
International Law Commission of the United Nations, 12, 14, 37, 38n, 48, 48n, 62, 73, 75, 84, 87, 88, 99, 100, 106, 123, 124, 131, 147, 148, 159
International Law During the Transitional Period (Mezhdunarodnoe pravo perekhodnogo vremeni) (1924), 3
International Organizations as Subjects of International Law, 53
International Status of South-West Africa (ICJ Reports, 1950), 144
International Straits, 124
Interpretation of Peace Treaties (ICJ Re-

ports, 1950), 144
Intervention, 50, 146n
In Transitu (Diplomatic Immunity), 99
Inviolability of Civilian Populations in Time of War, Principle of, 148-149
Inviolability of Diplomatic and Consular Premises, Principle of, 101-104

J

The Jassy (1906), 55
Jessup, Philip C., 53
Jus Cogens, Principle of, 13, 85-87, 158
Jus Sanquinis, 129
Jus Soli, 129
Just Wars of National Liberation *see* Wars of National Liberation

K

Kalesnik, S., 127
Kasenkina Case (1948), 102-104
Kearney, Richard, 88
Keilin, A. D., 55
Kelsen, Hans, 2, 30, 34, 35n, 82n, 86
Khlestov, O. N., 51, 86
Khrushchev, Nikita S., 47, 118, 161
Kiritchenko, N. G., 13n
Kislov, A., 114
Komsomol Truth (Komsomsolskaya prava), 127
Konshukov, I., 105
Koretskii, Vladimir M., 12, 37, 52, 148
Korovin, Evgenii A., 1, 2n, 3-6, 7, 9, 10, 10-11, 11n, 12, 13, 13n, 14, 16-17, 51, 81, 117, 118, 119, 141, 156
Kosters, J., 38n
Kovalov, F. N., 117, 118
Kovalyov, S., 52-53
Kozhevnikov, Fedor I., 2n, 7, 10-11, 11n, 13n, 74, 140, 142, 144n, 156
Krylov, Sergei B., 14, 50, 74, 79, 114, 123, 124, 125, 142-143, 156
Kunz, Josef L., 30, 31n, 35

L

Larson, Arthur, 144n
Lauterpacht, Sir Hersch, 53
"Law as a System of Social Relationships", 2
"Law of the Transitional Period", 1, 2, 3-4
Law of Treaties, Draft Convention on, 73, 77, 77n, 87, 87-88
Lawrence, T. J., 127
Laws of Treaty-Making, 73
Laws of War, 146, 148-149
Lazarev (Russian Navigator), 127
League of Arab States (1945), 59
League of Nations, 5n, 52n, 143
League of Nations, Permanent Court of International Justice *see* Permanent Court of International Justice of the League

of Nations
Legal Education, 10
"Legal Vacuum" Principle of Outer Space *see* Outer Space as *Res Nulles*, Principle of
"Legalism", 162
Lenin, V. I., 2, 122
Levin, David B., 56, 96, 101-102
Lissitzyn, Oliver J., 98, 116
Lissovskii, Vladim I., 15
Litvinov, Maxim, 140-141
Lomankin, Y. M., 103-104
Lovett, Richard A., 103-104
Lukashuk, I. I., 77, 82
Lunkin, Pavel I., 37

M

The Maipo (1919), 55
Marriage, 97-98
Marshall Plan, 97-98
Martens, Professor, 141
Marx, Karl, 2
"Mass-Man", 113
McWhinney, Edward, 48
Meshara, V. P., 119
Middle East Crisis (1956-1958), 57
Military Bases, 52, 78
Military Operations on the High Seas, 121
Minasian, N. M., 46n
Minorities, 56
Mirbach-Garff, Count, 97
Molodtsov, S. V., 117, 119, 127
Monroe Doctrine, 49, 58
Morozov, Platon D., 58, 125, 126, 130, 146, 147
Moscow Space Policy Symposium (1959), 118
Municipal Law, Defined, 27n
Municipal Law, Importance of, 51

N

Narkomindel see People's Commissariat of Foreign Affairs
National Liberation Struggle, 82
National Self-Determination, Principle of, 28, 33, 38, 46, 46n, 55-57, 59, 60, 61-62, 158, 161-162, 163
National Sovereignty *see* State Sovereignty
Nationality, 113, 129, 163
Natural Law, 4
The Navemar (1938), 55
"Negative Actions" of States, 30
Nemo Debet Esse Judex in Propria Causa (Third Party Judgment), Principle of, 140-141, 163
NEP *see* New Economic Policy
New Economic Policy, 3, 7
Newly Emerging Nations, 35-36, 78
"New" States and "old" Customary Norms, 18, 35-36, 157, 158, 160, 161
Nikolayev, A. N., 122, 123, 124, 124n

Non-Aggression, Principle of, 33 46n, 146-148
Non-Intervention, Principle of, 13, 30, 38, 46, 46n, 57-59
Non Self-Governing Territories see Trust Territories
"Non Territory" Defined, 113
Nuclear Test Ban Treaty, 120
Nuclear Weapons, 149
Nuremberg Tribunal, Charter of (1945), 12, 51-52
Nyon Agreement (1937), 122

O

OAS see Organization of American States
OAU see Organization of African Unity
"Oneness Theory" 11, 14-15, 17
"Open Skies" Policy, 116
Opinio Juris Sive Necessitatis, 35, 38
Oppenheim, L., 35, 38n
Oral Treaty, 73
Ordering Function of Customary International Law, 159-163
Organization of African Unity, 49, 59
Organization of American States, 59, 147
Osnitskii, G. A. see Galina, A.
Outer Space as Res Communis, Principle of, 30-31, 113, 115, 117-120, 160
Outer Space as Res Nulles, Principle of, 118

P

Pacta Sunt Servanda, Principle of, 13, 46n, 73-75, 77, 80, 86, 158, 159, 160, 161, 163
Palmas Islands Case, United States v. Netherlands (PCIJ Reports, 1932), 127
Panamanian Treaty (1903), 86
Panyushkin, Soviet Ambassador, 103-104
Par In Parem Non Habet Imperium (An Equal Has No Dominion Over An Equal), 55
The Parlement Belge (1880), 55
Party Congress of the CPSU, 20th Congress (1956) see Twentieth Party Congress of the CPSU (1956)
Pashukanis, Evgenii B., 1, 7, 7-8, 8-9, 14, 27, 124, 156
PCIJ see Permanent Court of International Justice of the League of Nations
Peaceful Coexistence, 2, 4, 17, 163
Peaceful Coexistence, Principle of, 28, 33, 46, 46n, 46-50, 61-62, 118, 161
Peaceful Competition, 47
Peaceful Settlement of Disputes by Voluntary Negotiation, Arbitration and/or Adjudication, Principle of, 46n, 141-145
People's Commissariat of Foreign Affairs, 6
People's Republic of China, 84
Permanent Court of International Justice of the League of Nations, 52

Persona Non Grata, Principle of, 101
The Pesaro (1926), 55
Piracy, 122,
Polianskii, Nikolai N., 13, 13n
Policy-Oriented International Law, 8, 38, 158
See also Pragmatism.
Poltorak, A. I., 148
Populations see Status of Populations as Within the Jurisdiction of Municipal Law, Principle of
The Porto Alexandre (1920), 55
Positive Actions of States, 29-30
Poutiatin, Russian Admiral, 124
Powers, Francis Gary, 115-116, 162
Practice as an Indication of Custom, 14, 29-30, 32, 38
Pragmatism, 13, 15, 16, 17, 27, 29, 51-52, 56, 61, 74, 75, 82, 96, 98, 113, 117, 156, 160, 161
Primary Sources of International Law, 5-6, 6-7, 8, 9, 12-13, 14, 16, 18, 27, 28, 38, 87, 158
Prisoners of War, Geneva Convention Relative to the Treatment of (1949), 149
Problems of Territorial Waters in International Law (Problema territorialnykh vod v mezhdunarodnom prava) (1957), 124
Provocative Function of International Law, 159-163

Q

The Quilmark, 55

R

Ramundo, Bernard, 49
Radio Free Europe, 146
Reciprocity, 98, 99, 122n, 161
Recognition, Principle of, 59-61, 158, 160, 163
Reduction of Stateless Persons, Convention on, 113, 130
Refugees, 130
Regulation of Air Navigation, Paris Convention on (1919), 115
"Repetition" as a Factor in Custom-Creation, 31, 31-32, 38
Reprisals, 145
Republics of the USSR, 52
Reservations, 52
Res Inter Alios Gesta (State Succession), Principle of, 46, 74, 76, 76-77, 80-83, 160
Res Judicata, 142
Resolutions of the General Assembly of the United Nations, 144
Revolutionary Change, 12, 163
Right of Legation, 104
Rights and Duties of States, Draft Convention on, 148
Role of Law and the Revolutionary State

(Revolutsionaya rol prava i gosudarstva) (1921), 2

Romashkin, Petr, 120, 149

Rousseau, Charles, 30

Roxburgh, Ronald F., 38n

S

Sabinin, Andrei, 6-7, 7, 14, 156

Saint Petersburg Convention (1868), 149

Satellites, Effect on *Usque Ad Coelum* Principle, 114-115, 116

Savinskii, L. I., 148

Schooner Exchange v. McFadden (1812), 55

Schwarzenberger, Georg, 35, 38n

"Secret Treaties" *see* Tsarist Treaties

Sector Theory, 128

Self Determination, Principle of *see* National Self Determination, Principle of

Self-Help, Principle of, 145

Shurshalov, V. M., 78, 82, 86

"Single Superstructure" of Customary International Law *see* Universality of International Law

Sino-Indian Treaty (1954), 49

Sixth (Legal) Committee of the United Nations General Assembly, 48n, 50, 78, 85

Slavery, Supplementary Convention on, 143

Slusser, Robert M., 38

Socialist International Law, 3-4, 6-7, 7-8, 15, 47

Socialist Legality, 9

Soloveitchik, Samson, 146n

Sources of International Law *see* Primary Sources of International Law

Sovereign Equality of States, Principle of, 5, 10, 13, 30, 34, 36, 38, 46, 46n, 50-55, 60, 83, 85, 86, 106, 118, 162, 163

Soviet Air Code (1935), 115

Soviet Association of International Law, 49, 143

Soviet Branch of the International Law Association (Brussels) *see* International Law Association (Brussels), Soviet Branch

Soviet Geographical Society, 127

Soviet Law *see* Soviet Municipal Law

Soviet Municipal Law, 27, 51, 115, 121

Soviet Scholarship, 28

Soviet State (Sovetskoe gosudarstvo), 9

Soviet State and Law (Sovetskoe gosudarstvo i pravo), 11, 14

Soviet State and Revolutionary Law (Sovetskoe gosudarstvo i revolutsiya prava), 7

Soviet Statute on the Protection of the USSR (1927), 121

Spy Satellite, 117-118

Starushenko, Gleb B., 56, 57

State-Owned Instrumentalities, 52, 55, 122, 125, 126, 164

State Responsibility, 147, 148

State Sovereignty, 5, 36, 46, 50-52, 57, 61, 102, 113, 122-123, 131, 140, 142, 148, 158

State Succession *see* Res Inter Alios Gesta (State Succession), Principle of

Statelessness, 129

Status of Populations as Within the Jurisdiction of Municipal Law, Principle of, 128-130, 160, 163

Statute of the International Court of Justice (Article 38), 16, 32, 73, 143, 144

Straits *see* International Straits

Strict Construction of the United Nations Charter, 50n, 74, 75, 80, 85

"Struggle and Competition", 3, 15, 17, 47

"Struggle and Cooperation", 2, 11, 15, 17

Strupp, K., 33n

Stuchka, Pavel I., 2-3, 156

Subjects of International Law, Defined, 46, 52

Suez Canal *see* Anglo-Egyptian Treaty (1936)

Summa Potesta, 50

Supplementary Convention on Slavery *see* Slavery, Supplementary Convention on

Sverdlov University *see* Communist University (Moscow)

T

Talalayev, A. M., 77

Taracouzio, Timothy A., 113, 130

Territorial Sea and Contiguous Zones, Convention on (1958), 113, 123, 123n, 125

Territorial Waters as a Part of the Littoral State, Principle of, 122-127

Territorial Waters, Defined, 122

Territorial Waters, Width of, 123-124, 125, 126, 164

Third Party Judgment *see* Nemo Debet Esse Judex in Propria Causa (Third Party Judgment), Principle of

"Time" as a Factor in Custom-Creation, 30-31, 31-32, 38, 117

Trade Missions, 100

Traditional International Law *see* Western International Law

Treaty, Defined, 73

Treaty Law, 10, 27, 28, 49, 54, 57, 58, 61, 62, 75, 79, 83, 106, 120, 122n

Treaty of Dorpat (1920), 143

Treaty on Principles Governing the Activities of States in the Exploration and Use of Outer Space, Including the Moon and Other Celestial Bodies (1967), 120

Triska, Jan F., 38

Trotskii, Leon, 73

Trust Territories, 55
Tsarist Debt, 80-82
Tsyba, V., 105
Tunkin, Grigorii I., 11-12, 14-16, 17, 27, 29, 31, 32, 33, 34, 35, 37, 47, 49, 58, 77, 79, 84, 86. 99, 100, 104, 123, 124n, 125, 140, 144, 147, 156-157, 162
Twentieth Party Congress of the CPSU (1956), 47
Two-Line Formula, 11-12, 14-15, 16-17

U

U-2 Flights, 115, 162
Unequal Treaties, Principle of, 28, 74, 76, 76-77, 77-80, 82, 85, 86, 163
UNESCO Conferences, 48n
UNESCO Convention, 143
United Nations Charter, 12, 29, 36-38, 49-50, 54, 57. 58-59, 62, 75, 79, 85, 86-87, 143, 144, 145, 147, 148, 149
United Nations Convention on Consular Relations (1963) see Consular Relations, Convention on (1963)
United Nations Convention on the Continental Shelf (1958) see Continental Shelf, Convention on (1958)
United Nations Convention on Diplomatic Intercourse and Immunities (1961) see Diplomatic Intercourse and Immunities, Convention on (1961)
United Nations Convention on Fishing and Conservation of Living Resources of the High Seas (1958) see Fishing and Conservation of Living Resources of the High Seas, Convention on (1958)
United Nations Convention on the High Seas (1958) see High Seas, Convention on (1958)
United Nations Convention on the Reduction of Stateless Persons see Reduction of Stateless Persons, Convention on
United Nations Convention on Territorial Sea and Contiguous Zones (1958) see Territorial Sea and Contiguous Zones, Convention on (1958)
United Nations Draft Convention on the Law of Treaties see Law of Treaties, Draft Convention on
United Nations Draft Convention on the Rights and Duties of States see Rights and Duties of States, Draft Convention on
United Nations Educational, Scientific and Cultural Organization Conferences see UNESCO Conferences
United Nations General Assembly Resolution 1514 (XV) (1960) see General Assembly Resolution 1514 (XV) (1960)
United Nations General Assembly, Sixth (Legal) Committee see Sixth (Legal)

Committee of the United Nations General Assembly
United Nations Genocide Convention (1949) see Genocide Convention of the United Nations (1949)
United Nations International Court of Justice see International Court of Justice of the United Nations
United Nations International Law Commission see International Law Commission of the United Nations
United Nations Special Committee on Principles of International Law Concerning Friendly Relations and Cooperation Among States, Mexico City (1964), 51, 58
United States Information Agency (USIA), 146
United States v. Coplon and Gubitchev (1949), 97
Universality of International Law, 4, 7-8, 10, 11, 15. 17, 33-34, 35-36, 39, 47, 49, 54, 56, 58, 62, 79, 83, 84, 85, 86, 96, 100, 116, 128, 149
University of Moscow, 7
"Unwritten Law", Custom as, 28-29, 39, 106, 157
Usage as Distinguished from Custom, 31, 35
Ushakov, N. A., 53
Usque ad Coelum, Principle of, 114-117, 158, 160, 162

V

Vatican, 52n
Vendross, Alfred, 31n, 35, 35n, 86
Veto (United Nations), 54
Vienna Convention on Consular Relations (1963) see Consular Relations, Convention on (1963)
Vienna Convention on Diplomatic Intercourse and Immunities (1961) see Diplomatic Intercourse and Immunities, Convention on (1961)
Vietnam, 146. 148
Vyshinskii, Andrei Ia., 2, 8-10, 11, 156

W

Waiver of Diplomatic Immunity, 99
"War Propaganda", 146
Wars of National Liberation, 146, 148
Warsaw Treaty (1955), 59
Western International Law, 5, 17,: 28, 58
Withering Away of Law, 8, 9, 61
Withering Away of the State, 113
Wolfke, Carol, 27n, 30, 32
World Health Organization Convention, 143
World Meterological Organization Convention, 143

253

Wright, Quincy, 38

Z

Zadorozhnyi, G. Y., 115, 117, 119
Zhukov, G., 117, 120
Zile, Zigurds, 123
Zorin, V., 120